Visit us at

www.syngress.com

Syngress is committed to publishing high-quality books for IT Professionals and delivering those books in media and formats that fit the demands of our customers. We are also committed to extending the utility of the book you purchase via additional materials available from our Web site.

SOLUTIONS WEB SITE

To register your book, visit www.syngress.com/solutions. Once registered, you can access our solutions@syngress.com Web pages. There you may find an assortment of valueadded features such as free e-books related to the topic of this book, URLs of related Web sites, FAQs from the book, corrections, and any updates from the author(s).

ULTIMATE CDs

Our Ultimate CD product line offers our readers budget-conscious compilations of some of our best-selling backlist titles in Adobe PDF form. These CDs are the perfect way to extend your reference library on key topics pertaining to your area of expertise, including Cisco Engineering, Microsoft Windows System Administration, CyberCrime Investigation, Open Source Security, and Firewall Configuration, to name a few.

DOWNLOADABLE E-BOOKS

For readers who can't wait for hard copy, we offer most of our titles in downloadable Adobe PDF form. These e-books are often available weeks before hard copies, and are priced affordably.

SYNGRESS OUTLET

Our outlet store at syngress.com features overstocked, out-of-print, or slightly hurt books at significant savings.

SITE LICENSING

Syngress has a well-established program for site licensing our e-books onto servers in corporations, educational institutions, and large organizations. Contact us at sales@syngress.com for more information.

CUSTOM PUBLISHING

Many organizations welcome the ability to combine parts of multiple Syngress books, as well as their own content, into a single volume for their own internal use. Contact us at sales@syngress.com for more information.

SYNGRESS®

Microsoft Forefront Security Administration Guide

Jesse Varsalone Technical Editor

Ed Collins
Adam Gent
Chris Hughes
Jan Kanclirz
Mohan Krishnamurthy
Daniel Nerenberg

Matthew Shepherd
Arno Theron
Robert Valentine
Gene Whitley
James Yip

KEY	SERIAL NUMBER
001	HJIRTCV764
002	PO9873D5FG
003	829KM8NJH2
004	BPOQ48722D
005	CVPLQ6WQ23
006	VBP965T5T5
007	HJJJ863WD3E
008	2987GVTWMK
009	629MP5SDJT
010	IMWQ295T6T

PUBLISHED BY
Syngress Publishing, Inc.
Elsevier, Inc.
30 Corporate Drive
Burlington, MA 01803

Microsoft Forefront Security Administration Guide

Printed and bound in the United Kingdom
Transferred to Digital Printing, 2010

ISBN 13: 978-1-59749-244-7

Publisher: Amorette Pedersen   Page Layout and Art: SPI
Acquisitions Editor: Andrew Williams   Copy Editors: Judy Eby, Michelle Lewis, and Adrienne Rebello,
Technical Editor: Jesse Varsalone   Indexer: Michael Ferreira
Project Manager: Gary Byrne   Cover Designer: Michael Kavish

For information on rights, translations, and bulk sales, contact Matt Pedersen, Commercial Sales Director and Rights, at Syngress Publishing; email m.pedersen@elsevier.com.

Technical Editor

Jesse Varsalone (A+, Linux+, Net+, iNet+, Security+, Server+, CTT+, CIW Professional, CWNA, CWSP, MCT, MCSA, MSCE 2000/2003, MCSA/MCSE Security, MCDBA, MCSD, CNA, CCNA, MCDST, Oracle 8i/9i DBA, Certified Ethical Hacker) is a computer forensic senior professional at CSC. For four years, he served as the director of the MCSE and Network Security Program at the Computer Career Institute at Johns Hopkins University. For the 2006 academic year, he served as an assistant professor of computer information systems at Villa Julie College in Baltimore, MD. He taught courses in networking, Active Directory, Exchange, Cisco, and forensics.

Jesse holds a bachelor's degree from George Mason University and a master's degree from the University of South Florida. Jesse was a contributing author for *The Official CHFI Study Guide (Exam 312-49)* and *Penetration Tester's Open Source Toolkit, Second Edition*. He runs several Web sites, including mcsecoach.com, which is dedicated to helping people obtain their MCSE certifications. He currently lives in Columbia, MD, with his wife, Kim, and son, Mason.

Contributing Authors

Edward Collins (CISSP, CEH, Security+, MCSE:Security, MCT) is a senior security analyst for CIAN, Inc., where he is responsible for conducting penetration tests, threat analysis, and security audits. CIAN (www.ciancenter. com) provides commercial businesses and government agencies with all aspects of information security management, including access control, penetration testing, audit procedures, incident response handling, intrusion detection, and risk management. Edward is also a training consultant, specializing in MCSE and Security+ certifications. Edward's background includes positions as information technology manager at Aurora Flight Sciences and senior information technology consultant at Titan Corporation.

Adam Gent (MCSE: Messaging & Security, MCTS: LCS, Security+) is a technical consultant with Datapulse Ltd., a Nortel Developer Partner specializing in attendant consoles, call-billing applications, and value-add applications for Office Communications Server (OCS). Adam works with the company's Product Group to architect and manage products that relate to OCS. He also works with customers consulting on the deployment of OCS within enterprises.

Adam holds a bachelor's degree in computer science from Cardiff University and is a member of the British Computer Society.

Chris Hughes (MCSE 2003 Messaging/Security, MCDBA, MCT, Security+, CISSP, ITIL Service Foundations) is a systems architect at the University of Florida (UF), where he has worked for the past 11 years. He currently works in the College of Medicine, supporting and implementing its budgeting and business intelligence systems with revenue in excess of $500 million.

Chris has a wide variety of experience with nearly the entire Microsoft product portfolio, from performing Active Directory migrations for the 60+ statewide sites at UF's Institute of Food and Agricultural Sciences to supporting the infrastructure behind one of the first Internet MBA programs at UF's Warrington College of Business. He has a special interest in distributed administration, infrastructure optimization, and IT governance with an emphasis on their implementation in an academic environment.

Chris would like to thank his wife, Erica, for her love, patience, and encouragement.

Jan Kanclirz Jr. (CCIE #12136 - Security, CCSP, CCNP, CCIP, CCNA, CCDA, INFOSEC Professional, Cisco WLAN Support/Design Specialist) is currently a senior network consulting architect at MSN Communications out of Colorado.

Jan specializes in multivendor designs and post-sale implementations for several technologies such as VPNs, IDS/IPS, LAN/WAN, firewalls, client security, content networking, and wireless. In addition to network design and engineering, Jan's background includes extensive experience with open source applications and operating systems such as Linux and Windows. Jan has contributed to the following Syngress book titles either as a technical editor or author: *Managing and Securing Cisco SWAN*, *Practical VoIP Security*, *How to Cheat at Securing a Wireless Network*, *Microsoft Vista for IT Security Professionals*, and *How to Cheat at Microsoft Vista Administration*.

In addition to his full-time position at MSN Communications, Jan runs a security portal, www.MakeSecure.com, where he dedicates his time to security awareness and consulting. Jan lives in Colorado, where he enjoys outdoor adventures such as hiking Colorado's 14ner peaks.

Mohan Krishnamurthy Madwachar (MCSE, CCSA) is the GM, Network Security, at Almoayed Group, Bahrain. Mohan is a key contributor to Almoayed Group's Projects Division and plays an important role in the organization's network security initiatives. Mohan has a strong networking, security, and training background. His tenure with companies such as Schlumberger Omnes and Secure Network Solutions India adds to his experience and expertise in implementing large and complex network and security projects.

Mohan holds leading IT industry-standard and vendor certifications in systems, networking, and security. He is a member of the IEEE and PMI.

Mohan would like to dedicate his contributions to this book to his friends: Krishnan, Rajmohan, Sankaranarayanan, Vinayagasundaram, Rajagopalan, N.K. Mehta, and Ramesh.

Mohan has coauthored four books published by Syngress: *Designing & Building Enterprise DMZs* (ISBN: 1597491004), *Configuring Juniper Networks NetScreen & SSG Firewalls* (ISBN: 1597491187), *How to Cheat at Securing Linux* (ISBN: 1597492078), and *How to Cheat at Administering Office Communications Server* (ISBN: 1597492126). He also writes in newspaper columns on various subjects and has contributed to leading content companies as a technical writer and a subject matter expert.

Daniel Nerenberg (MCT, MCSE, MCITP, MCTS) is an IT strategy adviser with InfraOp. He delivers training and consulting for companies across North America. He specializes in Microsoft infrastructure technologies, with a particular focus on deploying secure environments.

Daniel is a founding member and current president of the Montreal IT pro user group. He is also a Microsoft MVP and an active member of the Quebec Federation of IT professionals (FiQ). He lives in Montreal, Quebec, with his wife, Emily.

Matt Shepherd (CISSP, MCSE, MCDBA, GCFW, CEH) is a consultant in the Security and Privacy Division at Project Performance Corporation of McLean, VA. Matt uses his experience as a network administrator, IT manager, and security architect to deliver high-quality solutions for Project Performance Corporation's clients in the public and private sector. Matt holds bachelor's degrees from St. Mary's College of Maryland, and he is currently working on his master's of science in information assurance.

Matt would like to thank his wife, Leena, for her wonderful support during this project and throughout their relationship. He thanks his family for a lifetime of love and support and Olive for making every day special.

Arno Theron (MCSA, MCSE, MCITP, MCTS, and MCT) is an independent information security professional with seven years of network/server administration experience and six years of IT training experience as a Microsoft Certified Trainer. He is dedicated to improving training policy and implementation with high-quality technical information. Arno's current interests are focused on SharePoint, Windows Mobile, and ITIL.

Robert Valentine has had a career of more than 20 years in the IT and engineering simulation industry. For most of his career, he has been working as a senior systems engineer. He currently is an IT manager and consults as a trainer.

Over the years, Robert's work has varied with implementing corporate standards for software and hardware, along with coordinating and implementing large corporate deployments while setting corporate migration standards for both client- and server-based platforms for small to enterprise-scaled businesses.

Robert holds numerous IT industry certifications, including MCSE, MCSA, MCTS, MCITP, MCT, and Comptia A+. He is also a Dell Certified Systems Engineer and holds two university engineering degrees.

Robert has also coauthored multiple engineering papers that have been published within the engineering community, and he has successfully coauthored multiple information technology books.

Gene Whitley (MBA, MCSE, MCSA) is the president of SiGR Solutions (www.sigrsolutions.com), a systems integrator and value-added reseller in Charlotte, NC. He entered into the systems integration and value-added reseller industry in 1995, and in 2005, he started his own company, SiGR Solutions, which provides services and product procurement for businesses of all sizes, including Fortune 1000 companies.

Gene started his IT career in 1992 with Microsoft, earning his MCP in 1993 and MCSE in 1994. He has been the lead consultant and project manager on numerous Active Directory and Exchange migration projects for companies throughout the U.S. When not working, he spends his time with his wife and best friend, Samantha. Gene holds an MBA from Winthrop University and a BSBA in management information systems from the University of North Carolina at Charlotte.

James Yip (MCT, MCITP, MCPD, MCSE, MCDBA, MCSD, MSF Practitioner, OCP DBA) is a consultant for the Asia region of PerTrac Financial Solutions, a global software vendor that produces software for investment professionals. PerTrac Financial Solutions is headquartered in New York and has offices worldwide. James is stationed in Hong Kong and is responsible for helping customers install and troubleshoot issues related to the company's software, which is based on Microsoft technologies such as .NET, Microsoft Exchange Server, and SQL Server.

James is also working as a managing consultant at Eventus Limited, a leading system integration solution and consulting services provider for the Asia region. He is involved as an architect or project manager for various technologies, consulting studies, and implementation projects. He also is working as a part-time training consultant for Microsoft technologies at Kenfil Hong Kong Limited, a leading Microsoft Certified Learning Solution Provider in Hong Kong. In this role, he provides official Microsoft training solutions to corporate customers in the region.

Contents

Chapter 1

Introduction to Microsoft Forefront Security Suite

Solutions in this chapter:

- Components of the Microsoft Forefront Security Suite

- Benefits of Using the Microsoft Forefront Suite

☑ Solutions Fast Track

☑ Frequently Asked Questions

Introduction

Forefront is a comprehensive suite of security products that will provide companies with multiple layers of defense against threats. Computer and Network Security is a paramount issue for companies in the global marketplace. Businesses can no longer afford for their systems to go down because of viruses, malware, bugs, trojans, or other attacks.

In the past, companies often underestimated the importance of Computer and Network Security. Companies often failed to allocate adequate financial resources toward implementing and maintaining security in the workplace. There are a growing number of companies now using the Internet as part of their day-to-day operations, and there are new federal laws mandating the implementation of adequate network security practices.

Using the Forefront Security Suite from Microsoft makes sense for many companies. A large percentage of these companies already have Microsoft Infrastructures in place, including Domain Controllers, Exchange Servers, and Vista and XP workstations. The Forefront Security Suite will integrate well with existing Microsoft products and infrastructures. Now, computer and network security are top priorities for many companies, and no longer an afterthought. Microsoft Forefront will help companies be at the forefront of dealing with network- and computer-related security threats.

Components of the Microsoft Forefront Security Suite

Forefront Security Suite is developed from multiple components that operate together in an orchestrated way to protect and provide overall end-to-end security for IT environments. Forefront components easily integrate with each other as well as with third-party solutions enabling depth defense, simplified management, deployment, and security analysis.

Forefront Security Suite consists of several components, which are separated into three main categories: Client Security, Server Security, and Edge Security. Client Security includes end-user PCs running Microsoft the Business, Enterprise, or Ultimate Editions of Vista, XP Professional, and 2000 Professional. Server Security components include: Security for Exchange Server, Security for SharePoint Server, and Server Security Management Console. Edge Security includes Microsoft ISA Server and Intelligent Application Gateway. Table 1.1 reviews current components and their categories.

Table 1.1 Forefront Client, Server, and Edge Components

Component	Category
Client Security	Microsoft Client Security—Microsoft 2000, Windows XP, Windows Server 2003, Windows Vista—32- and 64-bit OS
Server Security	Security for Exchange Server, Security for SharePoint, Security Management Console
Edge Security	Internet Security and Acceleration Server (ISA), Intelligent Application Gateway (IAG)

A picture tells a thousand words—Figure 1.1 displays the correlation between the three categories for better understanding.

Figure 1.1 The Correlation between Client, Server, and Edge Security

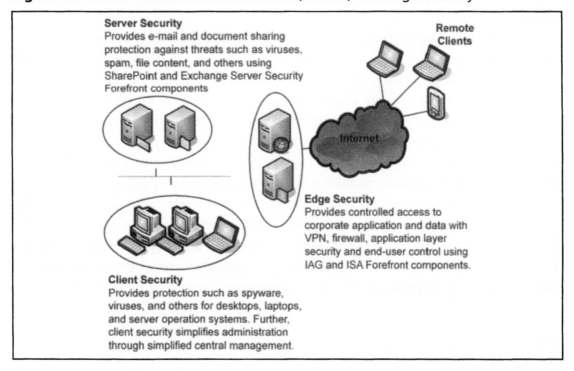

NOTE

For those of you familiar with Antigen products from Microsoft, these products have been rebranded under the new Forefront Security product line. Forefront Security for Exchange Server (formerly Microsoft Antigen for Exchange and Microsoft Antigen for SMTP Gateways), Forefront Security for SharePoint (formerly Antigen for SharePoint), and Forefront Server Security Management Console (formerly Antigen Enterprise Manager) all have been rebranded. Antigen is still used for Instant Messaging security, but it is expected to be rebranded in the near future.

Forefront Security for Clients

Microsoft Forefront for clients enables security for your desktop, laptop, and server operation systems within your environment. It is supported on Windows 2000 Professional and Server, Windows XP Professional, Windows Server 2003, and Windows Vista systems for both 32-bit and 64-bit system environments. Forefront Security for clients helps guard clients against threats such as spyware, rootkits, viruses, worms, and Trojan horses.

Forefront Security for clients includes several components such as the management server, reporting and alerting servers, and the actual client that is installed on the PC. The management server runs on a central console and all clients can be controlled via this central console. From the central console you can select preconfigured client settings or change specific client settings to best fit your environment as a whole. To simplify the environment and distribution of client policy settings from the management server, Forefront security for clients can use Active Directory Group Policy to propagate policies to clients. The reporting and alerting server accepts alerts from events that happen on the client. The alerting server will then store the alert and alarm you if needed, depending on the severity of the alert. Alerts will be generated by events such as a malware outbreak or a failure to remove a threat. Further, the reporting server has the ability to generate overall or specific reports; these reports can be pulled from your management central console server.

TIP

Forefront Client Security uses database and reporting systems from Microsoft SQL Server, which is included in the purchase of Forefront Client Security. (Customers also have the option of purchasing Forefront Client Security without SQL Server if they have an existing installation.)

Malware definitions and updates for clients can be updated either directly from the Microsoft Update Web site or from your Microsoft Windows Server Update Services (WSUS). WSUS has many benefits; for one, it saves your Internet bandwidth because it has to download updates only once from the Internet and then locally distribute to clients. WSUS enables you to auto-approve the latest updates and signatures or first test and then approve the updates. Figure 1.2 shows how the Forefront security components for clients work together.

Figure 1.2 Forefront Security for Clients

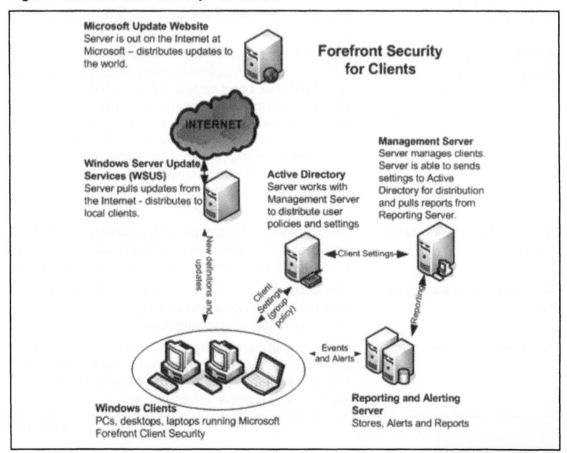

Client Security Features

Forefront Security for clients introduces many new features and benefits. Some of the core features include the integrated anti–virus and anti–spyware that work in real time or on scheduled times to protect individuals from new threats. Filter Manager, which is part of the client security feature, is able to run virus and malware scans before a file is executed, thus giving better protection capability against threats. According to the Microsoft Web site, the Forefront client suite contains the features displayed in Table 1.2. For further features and a detailed updated description visit www.microsoft.com/forefront/clientsecurity/prodinfo/features.mspx.

Table 1.2 Client Features (from Microsoft)

Feature	Description
Integrated anti-virus and anti-spyware engine	Single engine enhances client machines performance and detection capabilities by minimizing end user disruptions.
Real-time protection with the Windows Filter Manager	By using "mini-filter" technology with the Windows Filter Manager, Forefront Client Security is able to scan both virus and spyware files before they run, thus providing better security against spyware and blended threats (for example, spyware that gets on a PC through backdoor Trojans or other means). The other benefit to using the Windows Filter Manager is that end user disruption (system slow-downs) is minimized during real-time scans for both viruses and spyware.
Scheduled and on-demand scans	Quickly scan in-memory processes, targeted directories, and common malware extensibility points to ensure that the client machine is malware-free at all times.
Malware removal and system recovery	The Microsoft anti-malware engine removes malware and runs cleaning scripts to help ensure that the machine is still in a usable state.
Archives and packers scans	Archives and packers are a common way for malware authors to try to hide from anti-malware technologies, but the engine is able to look inside archives and packers and remove infected files.

Continued

Table 1.2 Continued. Client Features (from Microsoft)

Feature	Description
Advanced protection mechanisms	The engine includes advanced protection mechanisms to find user-mode rootkits, polymorphic viruses based on behavior analysis, tunneling signatures, and heuristic detection mechanisms that find new malware and variants.
Compatible with Windows Security Center and Vista Network Access Protection (NAP)	Forefront Client Security provides customers with the ability to see whether Forefront Client Security is running and up to date. IT administrators are able to configure Network Access Protection (NAP) on Windows Server 2008 so that Forefront Client Security-managed machines attempting to connect to the network are checked to ensure that the security agent is up to date and actively protecting clients. If the client machine does not have the Forefront Client Security agent or it is not up to date, the user is not allowed to connect to the network and gets notified within Windows Security Center. If the user installs the security agent for Forefront Client Security with updated signatures, they can then connect to the network.
Central Management System	With one console for simplified client security administration, Microsoft Forefront Client Security saves time and reduces complexity.
Single policy to manage client protection settings	Forefront Client Security helps increase your efficiency through a single policy that configures the anti-spyware, anti-virus, and state assessment technologies for one or more protected computers. New policies are created with preconfigured settings that can be easily tailored to the needs of your environment. Policies also include alert level settings that can be easily configured to specify the type and volume of alerts and events generated by different groups of protected machines.
Integration with Active Directory for policy deployment	Integrating with familiar Microsoft infrastructure saves administrative time and reduced "learning curve." Target policy based on Active Directory organizational units (OUs) and security groups.

Continued

Table 1.2 Continued. Client Features (from Microsoft)

Feature	Description
Integration with WSUS/MU for client deployment	Installing client agents throughout the organization can be a time consuming process for administrators. Deploying client agents using Microsoft Windows Server Update Services (WSUS) reduces administrative workload as these agents get installed automatically through WSUS sync. Administrators do not require additional software or technology, but can leverage their WSUS distribution infrastructure that provides deployment, status, and reporting. Furthermore, as this is an administrative controlled policy, even rogue machines (that is, machines that have removed client agents accidentally or intentionally) receive the client agent automatically when they sync with the WSUS server.
Signature updates for roaming users	Forefront Client Security provides a failover system for mobile users that allows them to connect to Microsoft Update (MU) to download the latest definition updates if they cannot get access to the corporate network. The administrator will have the ability to centrally manage the opt-in process for managed clients using the Forefront Client Security policy.
Security state assessment checks	The security state assessment (SSA) checks to examine data from the registry, the file system, WMI, IIS metabase, SQL, and more. Those checks allow a security administrator to detect common vulnerabilities in their environment as well as configuration issues that increase their exposure. These checks are a set of risk criteria defining industry best practices and known vulnerabilities. The reporting functionality that includes the security state assessment capabilities in Forefront Client Security enables customers to measure their security risk profile based on security best practices. As a result, customers can focus critical IT resources on the right security issues, and spend less time trying to find and then analyze information from disparate sources.

Continued

Table 1.2 Continued. Client Features (from Microsoft)

Feature	Description
Reports that can be drilled down into for investigation	Expanding the Security Issue tab in the Alerts Summary report, and the top alert underneath, allows the analyst to view the list of computers that were repeatedly infected with malware. After identifying the extent of the infection, reported through the total number of machines infected with each type of malware, the analyst can drill into an infected computer to further explore its detailed security status.
Customized alerts based on incidents and assets	Following receiving an e-mail/page message about alerts being present in the enterprise, the security analyst logs into the corpnet and opens the Forefront Client Security Summary report. As the top alert shows a number of computers infected with a malware, the analyst decides to start investigating this problem. The analyst follows the Alerts Summary link to get more information on this alert.
Flood protection	Forefront Client Security is designed to prevent machines from generating alerts when it hits the threshold of 5,000 alerts within a specific time, thus preventing the Microsoft Operations Management server from getting flooded. The client machine will still be protected from new malware through FCS real-time scans. This preventative measure ensures that during virus outbreaks administrators do not get data dumped taking up valuable bandwidth.

In the next three chapters, we will go into details of all these features and how to use and configure them to best protect your environment and your policy needs.

In order for you to install Forefront SP1 for Exchange Server your computer must meet these minimum requirements:

- Your operating system must be either Windows Server 2003 x64 or Longhorn or Windows Small Business Server 2003.

- You must have at least 1 gigabyte (GB) of available memory.

- You must have at least 550MB of available disk space.

- Your Intel processor must be 1 GHz or higher.

Forefront Security for Exchange Server

Forefront Security for Exchange Server helps you protect your e-mail system. It is a single solution that integrates multiple scan engines from security industry leading applications to combat viruses, spam, worms, and inappropriate content in your e-mail. Forefront Security for Exchange can run up to five anti-virus scan engines in different combinations. The included anti-virus engine scans are AhnLab, Authentium, CA, Kaspersky Labs, Norman Data Defense, Microsoft, Sophos, and VirusBuster. All these security engines are automatically patched and updated with latest signatures and policies.

Service Pack One (SP1) for Forefront Security Exchange Server adds several new features. Some new features in the new upgrade include:

- Exchange Server 2007 support with SP1

- Windows 2008 support

- IPv6 support

- New localized content filtering

- New scanning and blocking options for compression ZIP and RAR files

- New health monitoring logs and alerts

NOTE

Normal Scanning Engines do not look within compressed files for viruses. Scanning ZIP and RAR files, two of the most commonly used types of compression, will help keep viruses from entering the network. However, there are other compression utilities that can be used on files, such as Winace. Forefront Security for Exchange will not detect attachments in these types of files, so be aware of this issue.

Aside from anti-virus engines, Forefront for Exchange Server offers anti-spam features that will help you combat spam e-mails. The anti-spam features include IP block list of offending spammers out on the Internet, and content filtering updates that detect phishing Web site spam, and others.

A phishing attack is when an attacker tries to acquire sensitive information from users such as usernames and passwords by posing as a trustworthy entity. For example, you will receive a web link via e-mail from your bank asking you to verify your credentials. Although this e-mail link and the Web site look just like your real bank, it is a fake Web site set up by the attacker to look just like the real Web site in order to capture your credentials. Microsoft captures these type of phishing e-mails from its servers that it has deployed on the Internet and then adds them to the content filtering policy that is distributed to you and your Forefront for Exchange Server either automatically or manually. Forefront for Exchange server will compare each of your e-mails against its content filtering policy to detect and delete any phishing e-mails.

IP Block list is a list of IP addresses that are detected and known for sending spam e-mail on the Internet. IP Block list is part of the connection filtering where e-mail is inspected based on the IP address of the server sending the e-mail to your Exchange Server. After the IP inspection, e-mail is either passed on or detected and deleted. IP Block list can be automatically or manually downloaded from Microsoft Update server or Web site as it is part of your Forefront Security for Exchange Server. To manage it all, Microsoft offers you Forefront Server Security Management Console, which is capable of managing the Exchange Server and all other Forefront products with central configurations, updates reporting, and other security settings. According to the Microsoft Web site, the Forefront Security for Exchange Server suite contains the features displayed in Table 1.3. For further updates and new features visit the feature list at www.microsoft.com/forefront/serversecurity/exchange/features.mspx.

TIP

Microsoft allows you to freely download and try all the Forefront security products including the Forefront Security for Exchange Server. You have up to 120 days to evaluate the application for free. Visit http://technet.microsoft.com/en-us/bb738109.aspx to evaluate Forefront for Exchange Server.

Table 1.3 Features for Forefront Security for Exchange Server

Feature	Description
Multiple anti-virus engines for advanced protection	Forefront Security for Exchange Server includes industry-leading anti-virus engines from global security firms such as Kaspersky Labs, CA, and Sophos. Businesses can run up to five scan engines at once, and in different combinations across the server system. This provides rapid response to new threats regardless of where the threat originates. Forefront Security for Exchange Server automatically downloads the latest signatures and selects the optimal combination of engines to use, ensuring a high level of protection, and reducing the window of exposure to any given threat. Diversity of anti-virus engines across messaging servers and client devices protects against a single point of failure in the IT environment.
Premium spam protection	Forefront Security for Exchange Server customers receive Premium Anti-spam Services. Built upon the base level of anti-spam protection within Exchange Server 2007, Premium Anti-spam Services adds Exchange Server 2007 IP reputation filter—an IP Block list that is offered exclusively to Exchange Server 2007 customers. Premium Spam Protection also includes automated updates for this filter. Automated content filtering updates for Microsoft Smartscreen spam heuristics, phishing Web sites, and other Intelligent Message Filter (IMF) updates. Targeted spam signature data and automatic updates to identify the latest spam campaigns. These capabilities help ensure organizations have the most up-to-date protection against the latest spam attacks.
Fail-safe protection	Forefront Security for Exchange Server incorporates a multiple engine manager that ensures if one engine goes offline to update or even fails, other engines continue to protect your messaging environment without delaying mail delivery.

Continued

Table 1.3 Continued. Features for Forefront Security for Exchange Server

Feature	Description
Layered protection	Forefront Security for Exchange Server provides protection at multiple checkpoints in the messaging infrastructure, including Exchange Server 2007 Edge, Hub, and Mailbox servers, helping to stop viruses, worms, and spam before they impact the network or user productivity.
Protection against new and hidden threats	Forefront Security for Exchange Server includes heuristics technologies that detect malicious code based on behavioral characteristics. It also has configurable file filtering rules that help customers eliminate file types known for carrying viruses (for example, .exe).
Multi-vendor response to new threats	The critical hours between discovering a new threat in the wild and delivering a signature to catch it leave a business highly vulnerable to attack. Dependence upon a single-engine solution only increases this risk. One security vendor may be first to deliver a signature for one threat, but last to deliver the signature for the next one, giving single-engine solutions fluctuating levels of effectiveness. With the multiple-engine solution of Forefront Security for Exchange Server, multiple vendors are responding to a new virus at once, increasing the odds for a quick response and lowering a business' overall risk of exposure to each new threat, regardless of its origin around the world. Automatic downloads help ensure that the first valid solution to the attack gets loaded to the engine set of Forefront Security for Exchange Server.
Performance optimization and control	Forefront Security for Exchange Server scans messages and attachments using in-memory scanning, significantly improving performance over more traditional techniques such as spooling to disk. Its multithreaded scanning increases mail throughput by enabling the software to analyze multiple messages simultaneously. With performance settings,

Continued

Table 1.3 Continued. Features for Forefront Security for Exchange Server

Feature	Description
	IT administrators can balance the wanted level of security against the level of server performance required to meet the changing needs of their environment.
Improved e-mail Store scanning efficiency	Forefront Security for Exchange Server uses the antivirus transport stamp in Exchange Server 2007 to ensure that, if a message is scanned once at an Exchange Server 2007 Edge or Hub server, it does not need to be scanned again later in the pipeline. The program's incremental background scanning provides an efficient way to scan the Store for messages that are the most likely to carry the latest threats (such as e-mail that's a few hours or days old), without also repeatedly scanning the entire Store. These features enable the IT administrator to conserve valuable messaging server resources.
Increased uptime	Unlike single-engine solutions, Forefront Security for Exchange Server has the ability to continue scanning e-mail with all available engines, even during engine or signature updates. If an update is available, each engine is taken offline independently while the other engines continue to scan e-mail messages. Forefront Security for Exchange Server also ensures that if an engine or signature update fails, it automatically comes back online with the last known good engine and signatures. These capabilities prevent message queuing and delay on the Exchange server, and help to ensure uninterrupted mail flow.
Efficient threat removal	Forefront Security for Exchange Server prevents spam and worm traffic from ever reaching mailboxes, reducing workload on the mail server and preserving disk space for business-critical information. Forefront Security for Exchange Server's WormPurge feature automatically purges messages that match known worm signatures to reduce unnecessary mail traffic, free up storage, and improve mail server performance.

Continued

Table 1.3 Continued. Features for Forefront Security for Exchange Server

Feature	Description
	Removing these messages avoids user confusion and reduces unwarranted calls to the helpdesk.
Effective mail cluster support	Forefront Security for Exchange Server supports Cluster configurations including Exchange Server 2007 Continuous Cluster Replication (CCR). This helps ensure that both active and passive nodes have the most up-to-date configuration information and signatures, so messaging traffic can remain secure even if individual mail servers fail.
Exchange Server 2007 integration	Use of Exchange transport agents and Virus Scanning API (VSAPI) helps provide tight compatibility and stability with Exchange Server 2007 servers. Forefront Security for Exchange Server utilizes the transport agents and virus scanning API technologies of Exchange Server 2007, ensuring close integration.
Forefront server security administration	The built-in management console enables administrators to fully configure Forefront Security for Exchange Server, either locally or remotely.
Centralized Web-based control	Forefront Security for Exchange Server works with the Microsoft Forefront Server Security Server Management Console, which provides central configuration, deployment, and updating for all Forefront server security products in enterprise environments that have multiple Exchange servers. This enables IT administrators to easily manage servers remotely, generate comprehensive reports, and receive outbreak alerts from across the infrastructure.
One-stop automated updates	Through its Rapid Update Process, Microsoft monitors all scan-engine vendor Web sites for updates and downloads, and validates new engine versions and signatures as they become available; then it posts them online for Forefront Security for Exchange Server to automatically download and install. No IT involvement is needed to keep all the

Continued

Table 1.3 Continued. Features for Forefront Security for Exchange Server

Feature	Description
	engines and signatures up to date. For environments that have multiple Exchange servers, Forefront Server Security Management Console automatically distributes the signature and engine updates to all Forefront Security for Exchange Server deployments within the environment.
Migration protection	Customers who purchase Forefront Security for Exchange Server to help protect Microsoft Exchange Server 2007 will also be licensed to use the Microsoft Antigen for Exchange, Microsoft Antigen for SMTP Gateways, and Antigen Spam Manager to help protect their Microsoft Exchange Server 2003 and Microsoft Exchange 2000 Server environments. This helps ensure that the entire messaging environment is protected during migration to Exchange Server 2007.
Localization	Forefront Security for Exchange Server is now localized into 11 languages, making it easier for administrators to manage their messaging server security in the language of their region. Manage Exchange Server security in the regional language of choice by obtaining Forefront Security for Exchange Server in one of these 11 languages: English, German, French, Japanese, Italian, Spanish, Korean, Chinese (Simplified), Chinese (Traditional), Portuguese (Brazil), and Russian.
Integrated monitoring	A management pack for Microsoft Operations Manager enables the IT administrator to monitor the health of Forefront Security for Exchange Server as part of corporate operational management practices.

In order for you to install Forefront SP1 for Exchange Server your computer must meet these minimum requirements:

- 32- or 64-bit architecture based computer including Intel Xeon or Intel Pentium processor with support of EM64T technology or AMD Opteron or AMD Athlon 64 processor, which supports the AMD64 platform

- 1GB of available memory (2GB is recommended for better performance)

- 550MB of available disk space

- Microsoft Windows Server 2003 or 2008 operating system

- Microsoft Exchange Server 2007

Refer to Chapter 5 for details on how to configure your Forefront for Exchange Server security and detail security settings.

Forefront Security for SharePoint Server

Forefront Security for SharePoint protects stored documents on the SharePoint Server that are shared by multiple client hosts. Just like Forefront for Exchange Server, SharePoint builds on multiple scanning engines that scan documents on the server for any malicious code, virus, or confidential or inappropriate content contained within the document. Files and documents are scanned as they are stored or uploaded to the SharePoint server for any viruses and the like.

NOTE

Service Pack One (SP1) for Forefront Security SharePoint Server adds several new features. In addition to many new bug fixes and updates to the code, some new features in the new upgrade enable users to upload file and scan files up to 2MB in size, detect non-ASCII keywords, and select a new consolidated CA engine.

According to the Microsoft Web site, the Forefront Security for SharePoint Server suite contains the features displayed in Table 1.4. For a complete list of new updates to the feature set you can visit the www.microsoft.com/forefront/serversecurity/sharepoint/features.mspx feature link.

Table 1.4 Features for Forefront Security for SharePoint

Feature	Description
Multiple anti-virus engines for comprehensive protection	Forefront Security for SharePoint includes industry-leading anti-virus engines from global security firms such as Kaspersky Labs, CA, and Sophos. Forefront Security for SharePoint maximizes threat protection by enabling IT to run up to five scan engines at once from industry-leading anti-virus labs around the world. All documents are scanned as they are uploaded to, and retrieved from, SharePoint libraries. This provides rapid response to new threats, regardless of where the threat originates. Forefront Security for SharePoint automatically downloads the latest signatures and selects the optimal combination of engines to use, ensuring a high level of protection and reducing the window of exposure to any given threat. Diversity of anti-virus engines across messaging servers and client devices protects against a single point of failure in the IT environment.
Protection against inappropriate content	Forefront for SharePoint scans for administrator-defined keywords within most Microsoft Office documents—including Open XML documents and IRM-protected documents—helping to enforce compliance with corporate policy for language usage and confidentiality. On-the-fly encryption and decryption allows IRM-protected documents to be checked for malware and unwanted text while retaining security settings applied by information rights management (IRM). Forefront Security for SharePoint can also unpack and selectively repack compressed files, such as .zip, after removing an infected or unwanted item.
Document filtering	Forefront for SharePoint has configurable file filtering rules that help customers eliminate file types known for carrying viruses (for example, .exe) or opening organizations to legal exposure (for example, .mp3).

Continued

Table 1.4 Continued. Features for Forefront Security for SharePoint

Feature	Description
Protection against new and hidden threats	Forefront Security for SharePoint includes heuristics technologies that detect malicious code based on behavioral characteristics. It also has configurable file filtering rules that help customers eliminate file types that are known for carrying viruses (for example, .exe), and can identify threatening documents even if the file extension has been changed.
Multivendor response to new threats	The critical hours between the discovery of a new threat in the wild and the delivery of a signature to catch it leave a business highly vulnerable to attack. Dependence upon a single-engine solution only increases this risk. One security vendor may be first to deliver a signature for one threat, but last to deliver the signature for the next one, giving single-engine solutions fluctuating levels of effectiveness. With the multiple-engine solution of Forefront Security for SharePoint, multiple vendors are responding to a new virus at once, increasing the odds for a quick response, and lowering a business' overall risk of exposure to each new threat, regardless of its origin around the world. Automatic downloads help ensure that the first valid solution to the attack gets loaded to the engine set of Forefront Security for SharePoint.
Performance optimization and control	With features like in-memory scanning, multithreaded scanning, performance control settings, and the ability to track a document's scan status to avoid redundant scanning, businesses can gain the benefits of multiple-engine scanning while making smart use of available processing time and server capability. Forefront Security for SharePoint scans documents during upload and download, using in-memory scanning, significantly improving performance over more traditional techniques (such as spooling to disk). Its multithreaded scanning increases mail throughput by enabling the software

Continued

Table 1.4 Continued. Features for Forefront Security for SharePoint

Feature	Description
	to analyze multiple documents simultaneously. With performance settings, IT administrators can balance their wanted level of security against the required level of server performance to meet the changing needs of their environment.
SharePoint VSAPI integration	Microsoft Virus Scanning API 1.4 performs real-time scanning to help ensure that documents are safe before they are saved to, or retrieved from, the SQL document library. Forefront Security for SharePoint also offers manual and scheduled scanning options.
Out-of-Policy file blocking	Forefront for SharePoint helps prevent unwanted or out-of-policy file types from consuming valuable disk space.
Performance control settings	Leverage how many engines are used for a given scan job for greater flexibility and control over security and server performance. Choose from performance control settings like "Maximum Certainty," which scans with all available engines, and "Neutral," which scans with approximately 50 percent of available engines.
Forefront server security administration	The built-in management console enables administrators to fully configure Forefront Security for SharePoint, locally or remotely.

TIP

Microsoft offers a free virtual lab for you to log into and try Forefront Security for SharePoint and other Forefront-related products via remote. This is great way to test the product without having to install it yourself. Microsoft offers a 90-minute interval for its virtual lab with additional intervals after your session expires. For further information and to sign up for these free virtual labs visit http://technet.microsoft.com/en-us/bb499665.aspx.

In order for you to install Forefront for SharePoint your computer must meet these minimum requirements:

- Dual processor with 2.5 GHz clock speed

- Microsoft Server 2003 (standard, enterprise, web edition, or datacenter) with SP1

- 1GB of available memory (2GB is recommended for better performance)

- Microsoft Office SharePoint Server 2007 or Microsoft Windows SharePoint Services v3

Refer to Chapter 6, which covers all these features and how to configure and manage them in detail.

NOTE

Forefront Security for Exchange Server is International Computer Security Association (ICSAlabs) certified. Forefront Security for Exchange Server is the first server antivirus product for Exchange Server 2007 to be ICSA Lab certified.

ISA Server 2006

The Internet Security and Acceleration (ISA) Server 2006 is part of the Forefront security for your edge environment. ISA Server is used mainly for firewalling your network environment from outside as well as inside originating threats. ISA Server also provides secure communication through the use of virtual private network (VPN) services. ISA Server uses hybrid proxy-firewall and deep content inspection with security policies to filter unwanted and malicious traffic from entering your organization at the edge of your network (see Figure 1.3). ISA Server is capable of building a VPN between your remote branch offices to ensure privacy and encryption (see Figure 1.4). Although the ISA Server is designed to protect your environment from external threats, you can install ISA Server to protect individual internal segments from within your environment from malicious employees (see Figure 1.5).

Figure 1.3 Filtering Unwanted Traffic with ISA

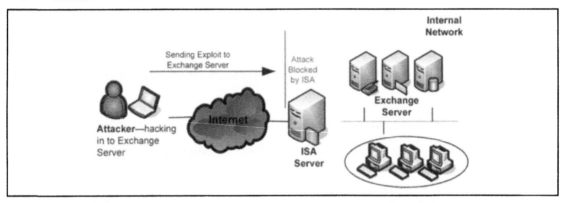

Figure 1.4 VPN between a Corporate Site and Its Branch Office
Using ISA Servers

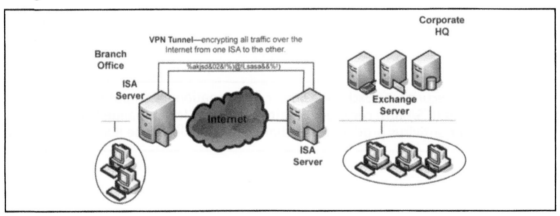

Figure 1.5 Protecting the Internal Segment from Malicious Employees
Using ISA Server

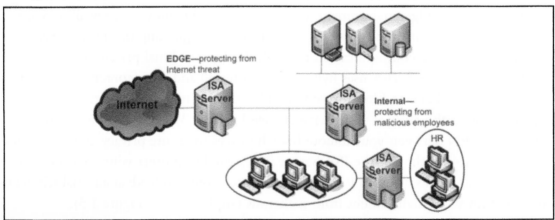

ISA Server comes in two flavors, the Standard Edition and the Enterprise Edition. The biggest difference between these two flavors is that Enterprise Edition offers greater scalability. Table 1.5 compares the two ISA flavors and differences.

Table 1.5 ISA Server Standard vs. Enterprise Edition

Feature	Standard Edition	Enterprise Edition
Networks	Unlimited	Unlimited and adds enterprise networks
Scaling up	Up to 4 CPUs and 2 GIG RAM Server	Unlimited
Scaling out	Single server	Up to 32 nodes using Network Load Balancing (NLB) feature
Caching	Single server	Unlimited using Cache Array Routing Protocol
Network Load Balancing (NLB)	Not supported	Supported
Policies	Local	Capable of using Active Directory Application Mode (ADAM)
Branch Office Support	Manual policy push policies	Enterprise level and array level
Monitoring and Alerting	Single server console	Multiserver console

In order for you to install ISA Server 2006, both Standard and Enterprise, your computer must meet these minimum requirements:

- CPU speed of 733MHz Pentium III and higher

- 512MB of RAM (1GIG is recommended)

- NTFS local partition with 150MB of free space (additional space required with for web cache)

- Microsoft Windows Server 2003 32-bit with SP1 or Microsoft Windows Server 2003 32-bit R2

TIP

You can purchase ISA Server 2006 as a hardware appliance that is already hardened, configured, and runs on a compatible server. For more information on ISA Server 2006 and IAG 2007 hardware solutions visit Microsoft at www. microsoft.com/isaserver/hardware/default.mspx.

We will cover the steps on how to configure ISA Server and its VPN, firewalling, and proxy services in Chapters 11, 12, and 13.

Intelligent Application Gateway (IAG) 2007

The Intelligent Application Gateway (IAG) from Microsoft provides a comprehensive secure remote solution via Secure Socket Layer (SSL) as a Virtual Private Network (VPN) solution that allows you to perform web application firewalling, access control, authorization, and content inspection for a number of known applications. The IAG SSL VPN provides a flexible connectivity for broad range of remote devices. One of the biggest advantages of SSL VPN versus IPSec VPN is that your remote connecting hosts do not require any installation of VPN client software in order to securely connect via remote. SSL technology is already built into applications such as your web browser, thus providing easy and secure connectivity access right out of the box. IAG and its application layer awareness provides a comprehensive secure remote solution that fills in gaps offered by ISA Server. Combining the ISA and IAG solutions together brings great benefits and complete security service offerings.

IAG provides a very granular application control. Unlike with ISA where you have the ability to restrict users to connect to a specific port or IP address, IAG can go deeper and restrict commands within a specific application. IAG helps application security by inspecting multiple application layer protocols such as HTTP for known applications to ensure proper user input, thus detecting and mitigating threats such as scripting attacks.

IAG 2007's Host Integrity Checker has the ability to verify that your client is running proper security tools prior to granting access to your network. The Host Checker looks for tools such as anti-malware, anti-spyware, anti-virus, firewalls, and other software to ensure proper client's health status before granting access. IAG's Host Checker assures only healthy clients are allowed to connect to your network.

NOTE

For complete list of supported anti-virus, anti-spyware, and firewalls by the IAG Host Checker visit these Microsoft sites:

Anti-virus:
www.microsoft.com/TechNet/forefront/edgesecurity/IAG/TechRef/eef0ba63-ef71-42bc-b0d3-abf587729152.mspx?mfr=true

Anti-spyware:
www.microsoft.com/TechNet/forefront/edgesecurity/IAG/TechRef/2d136057-1818-41f3-9958-005a06ff42e1.mspx?mfr=true

Personal firewall:
www.microsoft.com/TechNet/forefront/edgesecurity/IAG/TechRef/48fd22bb-8438-4f0f-bccc-1b7d911553e3.mspx?mfr=true

TIP

Microsoft acquired IAG from Whale Communications, where it was originally named the eGap Appliance. Existing customers with current service and support contracts that are running the older version Whale Communications eGap appliances will be provided with a migration path solution to the new IAG server. If you do not have maintenance agreements you will need to purchase new appliances and CALs.

According to the Microsoft Web site, the Forefront Security for Exchange Server suite contains the features displayed in Table 1.6.

Table 1.6 Key IAG Features

Feature	Description
Users	Supports large numbers of users on a single gateway.
High availability	Scales linearly with up to 64 high-availability node configurations.

Continued

Table 1.6 Continued. Key IAG Features

Feature	Description
Flexibility	Delivers out-of-the-box software configurations for widely-deployed enterprise applications, as well as customization capabilities including authentication, authorization and endpoint compliance profiles, and context-sensitive Web portals. Supports positive-logic rule sets and URL filter customization, and has the ability to develop rule sets for customized or proprietary applications.
SSL VPN portal	A secure socket layer (SSL) virtual private network (VPN) portal enables a convenient single access point for applications, yet supports multiple access points with distinct policy parameters such as partner extranets and employee portals on a single gateway.
Logging and reporting	Supports monitoring, logging, and reporting for integrated management and accounting (system, user security, and session views): Event Monitor provides comprehensive event monitoring by user, application, and time period. Integrated Event Logger that records system usage and user activities, and sends alerts about security events to an administration console. Integrated Event Query tool with preconfigured query templates and full reporting capabilities.
Comprehensive policy framework	Out-of-the-box application access settings and endpoint policy configurations designed to ensure minimal integration overhead and low ongoing management costs. Supports Intelligent Application Optimizer Toolkit for defining positive-logic rule sets, URL filters to supplement Optimizer settings and to develop policies for customized or proprietary applications. Supports Intelligent Application templates that provide a framework to build an Application Optimizer for both generic Web applications and

Continued

Table 1.6 Continued. Key IAG Features

Feature	Description
	complex enterprise applications incorporating components, Web parts, and objects.
Endpoint compliance checks	Endpoint policy allows administrators to define compliance checks according to out-of-the-box variables including presence of security software and IAG-specific components such as Attachment Wiper. Supports complex endpoint policy rules with customizable compliance checks using Boolean operations.
End user experience	Delivers a highly-customizable SSL VPN portal and login pages to enable easy set up and low administrative overhead. Supports comprehensive portal and login page customization to replicate existing intranet. Does not require conformance to a vendor portal template.
Integrated certificate authority management	Provides a built-in certificate authority in the event the administrator chooses not to use an external certificate authority. Enables administrators to grant a user a trusted endpoint certificate for a specific machine on request.

Benefits of Using the Microsoft Forefront Suite

Running a Microsoft Forefront Suite within your environment brings many different benefits. Three of the main benefits for Forefront security include comprehensiveness, integration, and simplifying your deployment.

Forefront comprehensiveness includes protection all the way from your client and server to the edge of your Internet gateways. Forefront for clients is capable of providing up-to-date anti-malware protection ensuring your workstations are protected against worms, viruses, and rootkits. Forefront for Servers is capable of providing services such as application filtering, VPN, and firewalling using the ISA 2006 Server.

Forefront is capable of securing your e-mail services and providing secure distribution of documents using the Forefront for Exchange and SharePoint Servers. Forefront comprehensives provide overall security for clients all the way to the edge of your environment.

Forefront integration allows for synergy between its security products and your existing Microsoft products. Forefront integrates with services such as Active Directory (AD) Group Policy, and Windows Server Updates Services (WSUS) to work side by side with its security product line. Integration with existing Microsoft technology reduces costs, training, finding new knowledge and freeing up time and resources. Further, Forefront benefits and its supports for open standards such as IPSec VPNs on ISA Server allow for interconnectivity between a third party and its solutions.

Forefront simplifies its operations by providing a central view for all your deployed Forefront products. Central reporting and log server allows you to query and view your security threat from a single solution. Further, Forefront simplifies manageability of your deployed products with a central management console.

Although there are many benefits of Forefront, it is mainly a Microsoft product supporting only Microsoft operation systems. If you are running a mixed environment that perhaps includes an operating systems such as Linux, you will have to purchase different management and monitoring applications.

Solutions Fast Track

Components of the Microsoft Forefront Security Suite

- ☑ Forefront Security includes components for securing your clients, securing your servers and components that provide edge security by firewalling and VPN connectivity.

- ☑ Forefront edge security components include the ISA Server and IAG Server that provide servers such as IPSec/SSL VPN and mitigation of outside threats by the use of firewalling and application inspection.

- ☑ Forefront server components include security for Exchange Server and SharePoint Server. Forefront for Exchange Server provides security against threats such as viruses, worms, and spam. Forefront for SharePoint Server provides security for documents by scanning them for viruses and company confidential content before they are allowed to be distributed.

- ☑ Forefront client security component includes unified malware protection for desktops, laptops, and servers running Microsoft operation systems.

Benefits of Using the Microsoft Forefront Suite

- ☑ Three of the main benefits for Forefront security include comprehensiveness, integration, and simplifying your deployment.

- ☑ Forefront comprehensiveness includes protection all the way from your client and server to the edge of your Internet gateways. Some of the security provided include VPN, firewall, anti-malware, spam, security patches, and management.

- ☑ Forefront integration allows for synergy between its security products and your existing Microsoft products by working side by side with Microsoft products such as Active Directory, Group Policy, and Microsoft Update Services.

- ☑ Forefront simplifies its operations by providing a central view for all your deployed Forefront products using central reporting and management services.

Frequently Asked Questions

Q: On Forefront client security, do I need to separate my third-party anti-virus solution if I'm using client security?

A: No, Forefront for client does continuous, scheduled, or on-demand manual scans for viruses and malware.

Q: How do I update my Forefront client with new definitions for my malware scanners?

A: You can either update your definitions manually or automatically from Microsoft update server on the Internet, you can update your definitions via Windows Server Update Services (WSUS), or you can continue to use your third-party solution to distribute updates to your clients.

Q: What anti-virus engines are included in Forefront SharePoint and Exchange Servers?

A: Anti-virus applications included are AhnLab, Authentium, CA, Kaspersky Labs, Norman Data Defense, Microsoft, Sophos, and VirusBuster.

Q: Can I run Forefront Security for Exchange Server 2003 or Exchange Server 2000 SP1?

A: No, Forefront Security will run on Exchange Server 2007 or 2007 with SP1. However, if you purchase the license, Microsoft will provide a downgraded older version of Antigen for Exchange that you can install.

Q: What is one of the biggest differences between the Standard and Enterprise versions of ISA 2007 Server?

A: One of the biggest differences between the two versions is scalability. The enterprise version scales up to 32 nodes using the Network Load Balancing (NLB) technology versus a single server only with the standard solution.

Q: Can I create a secure tunnel between a Cisco VPN device and ISA Server in order to encrypt communication over the Internet?

A: Yes, you can. ISA Server uses standard IPSec protocol features allowing third-party devices such as Cisco VPN to interconnect.

Chapter 2

Forefront Security for Microsoft Windows Clients

Solutions in this chapter:

- **How to Use Microsoft Forefront Client Security**

- **Troubleshooting Microsoft Forefront Client Security**

☑ **Summary**

☑ **Solutions Fast Track**

☑ **Frequently Asked Questions**

Introduction

Microsoft is a recent player in the anti-virus and anti-spyware market. For this reason, customers have looked to other companies in the past for anti-virus and anti-spyware solutions. Companies such as Norton and McAfee have dominated the anti-virus market for years. Software like Spy-Ware Search and Destroy and Ad-Aware from Lavasoft are some of the most popular anti-spyware products. Some of these products have suited home users well, but companies needed a more comprehensive solution to combat the virus, malware, and spyware problems they face on a daily basis.

The Microsoft Forefront line of products is that comprehensive suite that many companies need to implement a level of protection necessary to deal with today's threats. There have been a number of cases in past years where malware, worms, or viruses have bought businesses and agencies to a complete standstill. For example, in 2003, Maryland's Motor Vehicle Administration was shut down due to the blaster worm. Examples of agency shutdowns like this are quite common, and as more agencies grow to depend on computers, the likelihood of additional incidents continues to grow. Companies and agencies can no longer afford to be lax on security; they need a comprehensive solution that will help to ensure their systems will stay up and running.

Microsoft has not always been at the forefront of security-related issues. In the past, their operating systems have been known to have bugs and flaws that led to wide-scale security problems for companies and agencies. Starting with the release of Server 2003, Microsoft began using the idea of "trustworthy" computing. The idea of trustworthy computing basically meant that consumers should have a reasonable expectation of security out of the box. In a nutshell, this meant that Microsoft would no longer start unnecessary services or install optional components by default on their operating system. Microsoft Sever 2003 had a much better reputation for security compared to previous Microsoft products, and this has helped to sway opinions that Microsoft was a company unconcerned with security. And with the release of Vista, Microsoft has shown the public that the security of their operating systems is a very high priority.

Microsoft Forefront Client Security will help companies and agencies in the fight to keep their computers free of spyware, malware, and viruses. In order for the product to work effectively, companies need to implement procedures so that definitions are kept up to date. With the release of their Client Security offering, Microsoft provides the mechanisms for the security of clients. However, administrators need to have a good grasp on the Forefront line of products in order to utilize and deploy the product effectively.

Although knowing the Forefront product inside and out will certainly will benefit the network administrator, it is not enough. Written company policies should be in place to ensure that workers remain compliant and vigilant in the fight against computer threats. Finally, user education is also an important component of a company's fight against various computer threats. Software security product solutions will be effective only if users know how to utilize them properly. A security professional should learn the product well and be able to explain to employees the reasons that these security measures are in place.

How to Use Microsoft Forefront Client Security

Microsoft Forefront Client Security (FCS) provides unified malware protection for desktops, laptops, and servers. It provides simple administration through central management while providing critical visibility and reporting capabilities. Table 2.1 lists each feature within services provided earlier. FCS simplifies security management by using a single policy that configures anti-virus, anti-spyware, and state assessment technologies for all computers within a network. FCS consists of a security agent that is installed on desktops, laptops, and server operating systems. It provides real-time protection and scheduled scanning against threats such as spyware, viruses, and rootkits. FCS also consists of a central management server that allows administrators to easily manage and update preconfigured or customized malware protection agents. Administrators are also able to generate reports and alerts about the security status of their environment. FCS is able to protect Windows 2000, Windows XP, Windows Server 2003, and Windows Vista. It works with both 32-bit and 64-bit environments.

Table 2.1 FCS Client Security Features

Services	Features
Unified Protection	■ Integrated antivirus and antispyware engine
	■ Real-time protection with the Windows Filter Manager and mini-filter technology
	■ Scheduled and on-demand scans
	■ Malware removal and system recovery
	■ Archive and packers scans

Continued

Table 2.1 Continued. FCS Client Security Features

Services	Features
	■ Advanced protection mechanisms
	■ Compatibility with Network Access Protection (Windows Server 2008)
Simplified Administration	■ Central Management System
	■ Single policy to manage client protection settings
	■ Integration with Active Directory
	■ Integration with Microsoft Windows Server Update Services (WSUS)
	■ Signature updates for roaming users
Critical Visibility and Control	■ Security state assessment checks
	■ Reports that can be drilled down for investigation
	■ Customized alerts based on incidents and assets
	■ Flood protection

Configuring and Installing

Before we begin installing Forefront Client Security (FCS), we need to know exactly what we will be installing. We must understand the roles that are required in a successful FCS deployment and what the hardware and software requirements are. FCS isn't just client software; as we mentioned earlier it provides simple administration through central management. Hence a server or servers, depending on your environment, is required.

An FCS server consists of four roles, each which can reside on a single physical box or on separate systems depending on your environment and requirements. Those roles are management server, collection server, reporting server, and distribution server. An explanation of each role is shown later in this chapter. During installation FCS installs its own Microsoft Operations Manager (MOM) server, which it leverages for client alerts and event management.

FCS can be implemented in numerous topologies. It can hold all roles on a single system or expand out to six servers depending on the environment. Most small- to medium-sized companies will implement one to three servers, with three servers supporting up to 5000 users. Figures 2.1, 2.2, and 2.3 shows what a one-, two-, and three-server implementation looks like. Larger installations can include four, five, or six servers and can manage well over 10,000 managed systems. Table 2.2 lists the hardware and software requirements for an FCS implementation as provided by Microsoft.

As we mentioned earlier, most companies will implement one to three servers. Figure 2.1 shows all roles and databases residing on a single physical computer.

Figure 2.1 Single-Server Topology

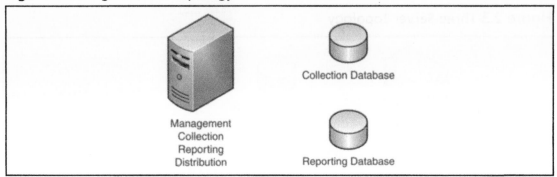

An administrator may require a two-server implementation if they already have a WSUS server in their environment, but the current server cannot support all FCS roles. Figure 2.2 shows a typical two-server implementation.

Figure 2.2 Two-Server Topology

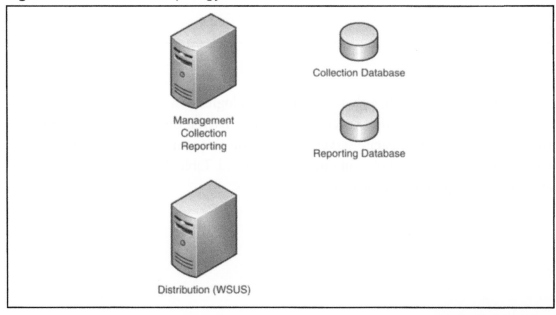

A three-server topology usually appears when the reporting database is used heavily and the load from it significantly slows down the primary FCS system running the Management, Collection, and Reporting roles. Although we are not moving the Reporting role from the primary server we are moving the database to a dedicated or existing SQL Server 2005 system in an effort to improve performance. Figure 2.3 shows a three-server implementation.

Figure 2.3 Three-Server Topology

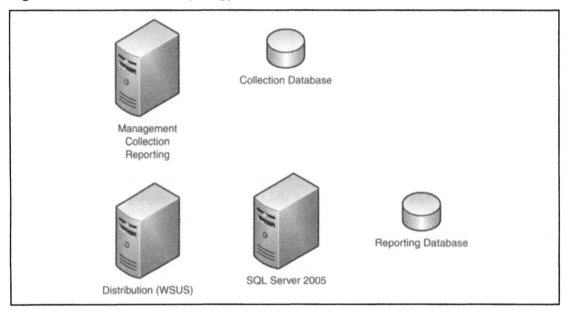

As we mentioned earlier, there are other topologies that expand to six servers in an attempt to improve performance. This includes having the individual server roles running on their own separate servers. Once again this would benefit mostly large enterprises managing 10,000 computers and beyond. Table 2.2 lists FCS hardware and software requirements for various server roles.

Table 2.2 FCS Hardware and Software Requirements

Server Role	Processor and Memory	Operating System	Software	Hard Disk
Management Server	1 GHz or faster with at least 1 GB RAM	Windows Server 2003 Standard or Enterprise with Service Pack 1 or Windows Server 2003 R2. No x64 editions	.NET Framework 2.0 GPMC with SP1 IIS 6.0 or greater ASP.NET Microsoft FrontPage Server Extensions MMC 3.0	512 MB or more
Collection Server without database	1 GHz or faster with at least 512 MB RAM	Windows Server 2003 Standard or Enterprise with Service Pack 1 or Windows Server 2003 R2. No x64 editions	.NET Framework 2.0	1 GB or more
Collection Server with database or SQL Server with just the collection database	Dual 2 GHz or faster with at least 2 GB RAM	Windows Server 2003 Standard or Enterprise with Service Pack 1 or Windows Server 2003 R2. No x64 editions	SQL Server 2005 with SP1 Standard or Enterprise	30 GB or more
Reporting Server without database	1 GHz or faster with at least 512 MB RAM	Windows Server 2003 Standard or Enterprise with Service Pack 1 or Windows Server 2003 R2. No x64 editions	IIS 6.0 or later, ASP.NET, and FrontPage Server Extensions	512 MB or more
Reporting Server with database or SQL Server with just reporting database	Dual 2 GHz or faster with 2 GB RAM or more	Windows Server 2003 Standard or Enterprise with Service Pack 1 or Windows Server 2003 R2. No x64 editions	SQL Server 2005 with SP1 Standard or Enterprise (with Reporting Services)	75 GB or more

Continued

Table 2.2 Continued. FCS Hardware and Software Requirements

Server Role	Processor and Memory	Operating System	Software	Hard Disk
Distribution Server	WSUS guidelines found at http://go.microsoft.com/fwlink/?LinkId=77980	Windows Server 2003 Standard or Enterprise with Service Pack 1 or Windows Server 2003 R2. No x64 editions	IIS 6.0 and ASP.NET .NET Framework 2.0 with SP1	See WSUS guidelines
Combined: Management, Collection, and Reporting Server	Dual 2.85 GHz or faster with 4 GB RAM or more	Windows Server 2003 Standard or Enterprise with Service Pack 1 or Windows Server 2003 R2. No x64 editions	SQL Server 2005 with SP1 Standard or Enterprise (with Reporting Services) .NET Framework 2.0 GPMC with SP1 IIS 6.0 or wlater, ASP.NET, and FrontPage Server Extensions MMC 3.0	100 GB or more
Combined: Collection Database and Reporting Database server	Dual 2.85 GHz or faster with 4 GB RAM or more	Windows Server 2003 Standard or Enterprise with Service Pack 1 or Windows Server 2003 R2. No x64 editions	SQL Server 2005 with SP1 Standard or Enterprise (with Reporting Services)	100 GB or more
Combined: Single Server with all roles including distribution	Dual 2.85 GHz or faster with 4 GB RAM or more	Windows Server 2003 Standard or Enterprise with Service Pack 1 or Windows Server 2003 R2. No x64 editions	SQL Server 2005 with SP1 Standard or Enterprise (with Reporting Services) . NET Framework 2.0 GPMC with SP1 IIS 6.0 or later, ASP.NET, and Front-Page Server Extensions MMC 3.0 WSUS 2.0 with SP1 or higher	100 GB or more

Continued

Table 2.2 Continued. FCS Hardware and Software Requirements

Server Role	Processor and Memory	Operating System	Software	Hard Disk
Client Computer	500 MHz or faster with 256 MB RAM or more	Windows 2000 with SP4 and Update Rollup 1 and GDI+ installed Windows XP with SP2 and waith filter manager rollup package Windows Server 2003 with SP1 Windows Server 2003 R2 Windows Vista Business Windows Vista Enterprise Windows Vista Ultimate X64 editions are supported for clients TabletPC version of Windows is NOT supported	Windows Update Agent 2.0 Windows installer 3.1	350 MB or more

Management Server

The Management Server role is used to manage Forefront Client Security, and includes the FCS console and the MOM console. You use the FCS console to examine the Dashboard, which reveals information such as detecting malware, vulnerabilities, out-of-date policies, and alerts. It also allows administrators to create policies such as malware scanning, security state assessments, and whether virus protection and spyware protection are enabled, to name a few.

Collection Server

The Collection Server role requires the use of Microsoft SQL Server 2005 Standard or Enterprise, depending upon the number of managed systems you plan to support. It is in charge of event and heartbeat data. The database can reside on the Collection Server itself or sit on a separate SQL Server 2005 system.

Reporting Server

This server role also requires SQL Server 2005. If it resides on the same box as the Collection Server's database, then only one copy of SQL Server 2005 is required. This role also requires SQL Server Reporting Service 2005, which enables administrators to run preset or customized reports. The reporting server acts as an archive of data that is no longer stored on the Collection Server.

Distribution Server

This is the server role that delivers anti-malware definitions to clients. This is typically a WSUS server but can be an SMS system as well.

Installing FCS Server Software

Now that we are familiar with the server roles, software and hardware requirements, clients that are supported, and the different topologies available we can focus on installing Forefront Client Security. For our example we will be using a single-server topology, meaning that all roles and databases will reside on one box. At this point we have following installed on our server:

- Windows Server 2003 Standard R2 with SP2
- SQL Server 2005 Standard with SP2 and Reporting Services (also Integration Services and Workstation components)
- .NET Framework 2.0

- Internet Information Services 6.0

- ASP.NET

- FrontPage Server Extensions

- GPMC SP1

- WSUS 3.0

MMC 3.0 already comes with the R2 release of Windows Server 2003, so we don't have to download it. FCS requires the use of four service accounts, and you can use a single domain user account to fill all four roles. Table 2.3 lists the service accounts used in FCS.

Table 2.3 Service Accounts Used in FCS

Account	Type	Description
Data Access Server (DAS)	Domain user, but if also used on the collection server it needs to have local administrator rights	The Collection Server uses the DAS account to access the colletion database.
Reporting Account	Domain user	Used on the Reporting Server to access both the reporting and collection databases.
Action Account	Domain user and local administrator on the Collection Server	This account must be a local administrator on the Collection Server. The Collection Server uses this account to run server side scripts and security state assessment scans. The action account MUST be a domain user account.
Domain Transformation Services (DTS)	Domain user	Used by the reporting server to run a DTS job that transfers data from the collection database to the reporting database.

As you see, it really makes things a lot simpler if we just use one domain-based account that meets the security requirements of each role. Once we've verified that our prerequisites are met we can now install Forefront Client Security on the server. Follow these steps to install FCS:

1. With an account that has local administrator privileges, logon to the server that will run FCS.

2. Insert the Microsoft Forefront Client Security DVD in the DVD-ROM drive.

3. On the FCS Startup screen, choose **Run the Setup wizard** as shown in Figure 2.4.

Figure 2.4 FCS Startup Screen

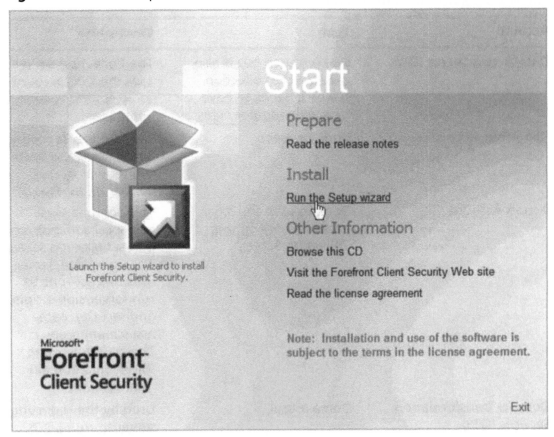

4. At the **Before You Begin** screen, verify that your name and organization are correct, and then click **Next**.

5. At the **License Agreement** screen, you'll be asked to select **I accept the terms in the license agreement**. If you agree to them, just put a check mark in the appropriate box and click **Next**.

6. Now you'll come to the **Component Installation** screen. For our scenario, a single-server, **Select** each component as shown in Figure 2.5, then click **Next**.

Figure 2.5 Component Installation Screen

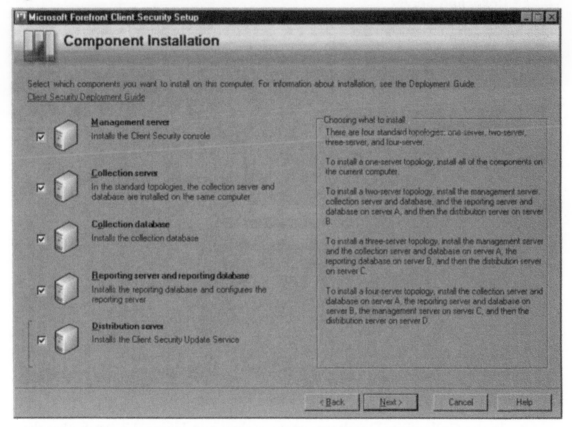

7. At the **Collection Server** screen shown in Figure 2.6, enter the server's computer name in the **Collection server** box (done by default). In the **Management group name** box, enter the name of the group name or accept the default, ForefrontClientSecurity. Make sure you record the Management group name because you will need it when configuring Client Security. In the **DAS account** box, enter the username and password for the DAS account created during the prerequisites. In our example, we actually

created a username DAS. We recommend that you use a name less conspicuous, but for our example, we chose something easy to remember. Remember that the account is a domain user, and then click **Next**.

Figure 2.6 Collection Server Screen

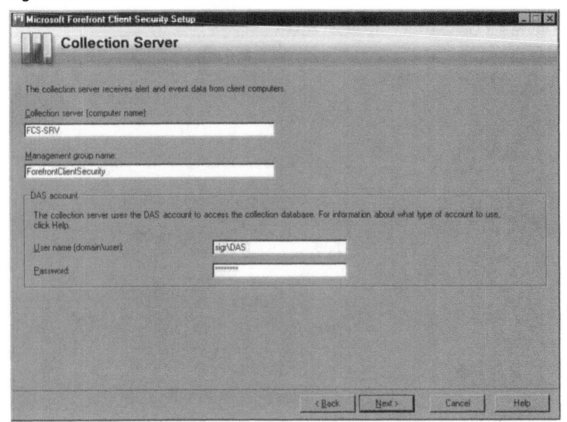

8. In the **Collection Database** screen as shown in Figure 2.7, verify that the Collection database will be stored on the current server and then accept the default size of the database or modify it. Note: If you select a size for the database that exceeds the amount of drive space available, the setup will fail.

In the **Report account** portion you can use either the DAS account you created earlier or another domain user account at your discretion. In our example, you see that we are continuing to use the DAS account. Now click **Next**.

Figure 2.7 Collection Database Screen

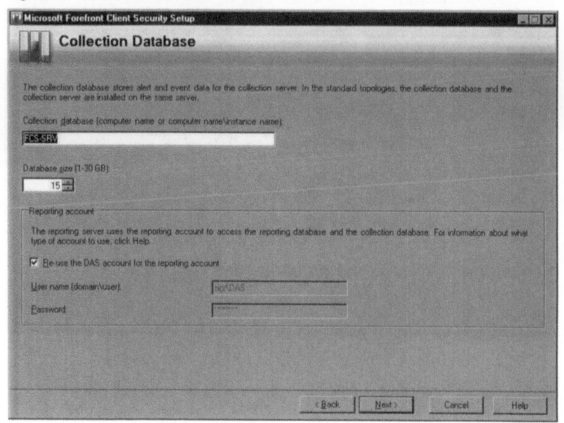

9. At the **Reporting database** screen shown in Figure 2.8, verify that the **Reporting database** is the current server and that the database size is appropriate for your expected amount of reporting. In the **DTS account** section either reuse the DAS account for the DTS account or use a different domain user account. Click **Next**.

Figure 2.8 Reporting Database Screen

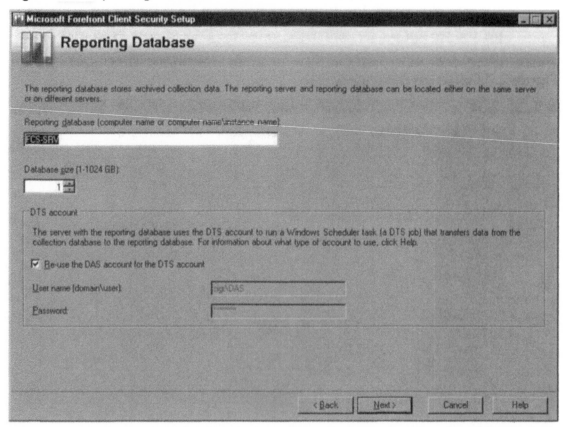

10. On the **Reporting Server** screen shown in Figure 2.9, verify that the **Reporting server** is correct. In the **URLs for reports** section, verify that the **URL for Report Server** and the **URL for Report Manager** boxes are correct. They should be the ones you specified when setting up SQL Server Reporting Services. If you used the default values (http://<servername>/

ReportServer and http://<servername>/Reports), click **Next**. If they are not the default values, enter the correct URLs, then click **Next**.

Figure 2.9 Reporting Server Screen

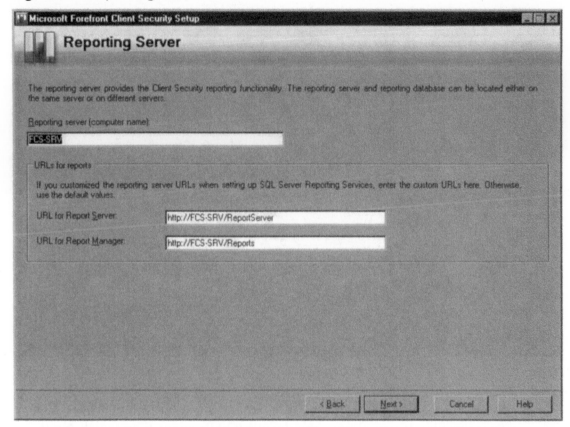

11. In the **Action Account** screen shown in Figure 2.10, either use the DAS account you've used earlier or enter a new domain user account, then click **Next**.

Figure 2.10 Action Account Screen

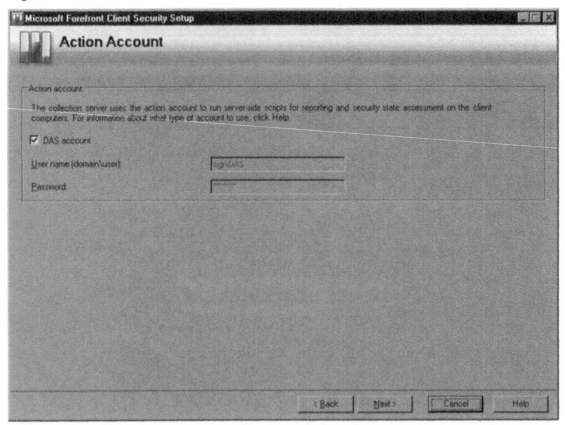

12. Now you need to specify the location where you want to install the Client Security files. If you choose the default (C:\Program Files), click **Next**. Otherwise, enter a location where you would like these files (see Figure 2.11).

Figure 2.11 Client Security Files Location

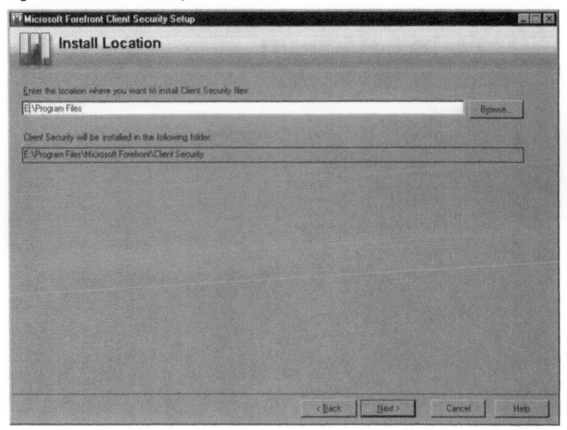

13. Next is the **Verifying Settings and Requirements** screen as shown in
     Figure 2.12. **Forefront Client Security setup** will verify that you meet
     the system requirements. If you receive an error, you will not be able to
     install FCS until the error(s) is resolved. If you receive a warning, you have
     the option of taking the suggestion from FCS or not, but you can continue
     the installation. In our example, we are given a warning that having two or
     more processors is recommended. For now, we will continue. After the
     verification is complete, click **Next**.

Figure 2.12 Verifying Settings and Requirements

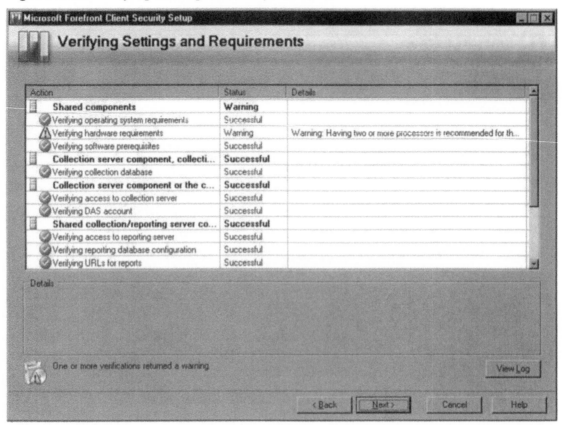

14. The **Completing Setup** screen is shown in Figure 2.13. FCS will complete the setup and provide you a status of each item being installed. Once it's finished, click **Close**.

Figure 2.13 Completing Setup

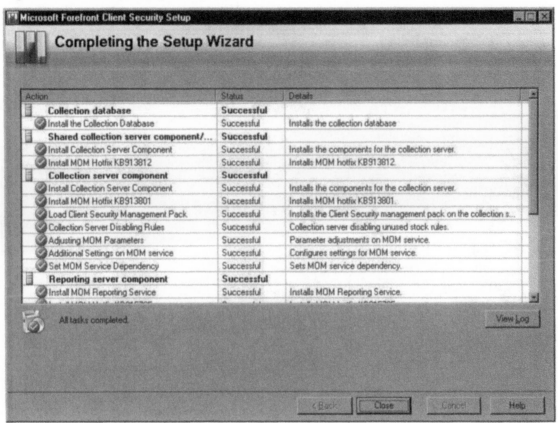

Once the installation is complete, you'll notice two new programs: Forefront Client Security, which is the actual client piece that can be seen on the system tray in the bottom-right corner and the Forefront Client Security Console, which is used as the primary interface for managing FCS.

Forefront Client Security Console

To get to the FCS Console, click **Start | All Programs | Microsoft Forefront | Client Security | Microsoft Forefront Client Security Console**. When you run the FCS Console for the first time, you will run through a wizard that will take you through the rest of the configuration.

1. At the **Before You Begin** screen shown in Figure 2.14, click **Next**.

Figure 2.14 Before You Begin Screen

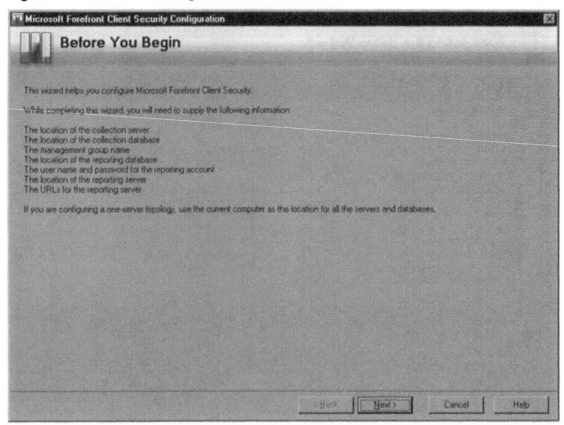

2. At the **Collection Server and Database** screen, shown in Figure 2.15, verify that the correct Collection server, Collection database, and Management group name are shown. Click **Next**.

Figure 2.15 Collection Server and Database

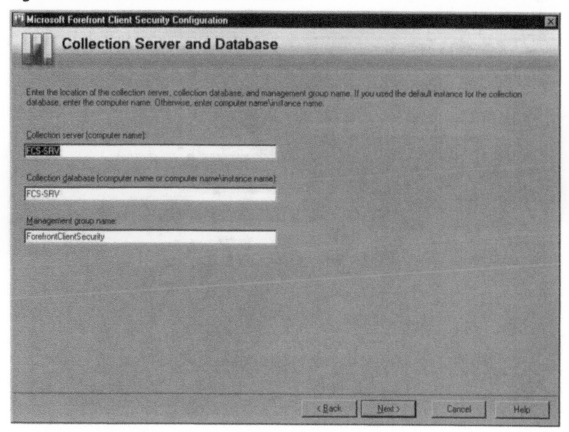

3. On the **Reporting Database** screen seen in Figure 2.16, verify the computer name is correct in the **Reporting database** box, and then enter the username and password used for reporting. This should be the domain user account you created earlier.

Figure 2.16 Reporting Database

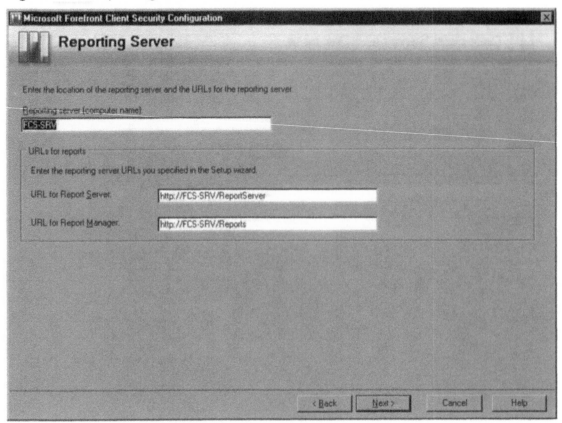

4. In the **Reporting Server** screen, verify the correct computer name is entered for the **Reporting server** and that the URLs for both the **Report Server** and the **Report Manager** are correct. Once you've confirmed this, click **Next**. Figure 2.17 has the information entered for our scenario.

Figure 2.17 Reporting Server

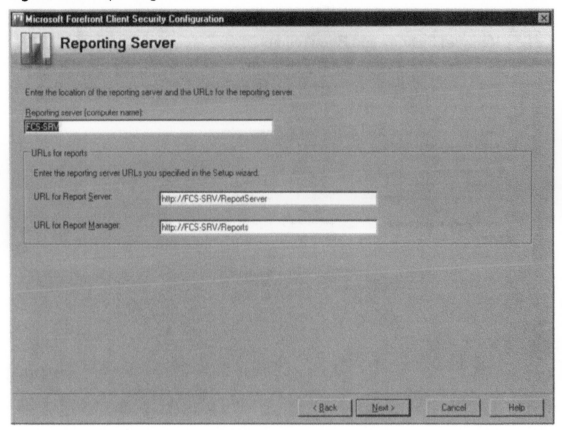

5. Next you'll come to the **Verifying Settings and Requirements**, which setup will do. If everything is successful as you see in Figure 2.18, click **Next**. Otherwise, examine the details of any failures and troubleshoot from there.

Figure 2.18 Verifying Settings and Requirements

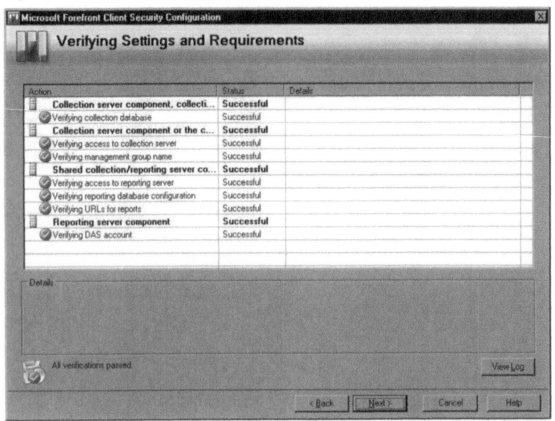

6. Next you'll come to the **Completing the Configuration Wizard** shown in Figure 2.19, where setup will complete the tasks listed in the **Action** column. After all tasks have completed successfully, click **Close**.

Figure 2.19 Completing the Configuration Wizard

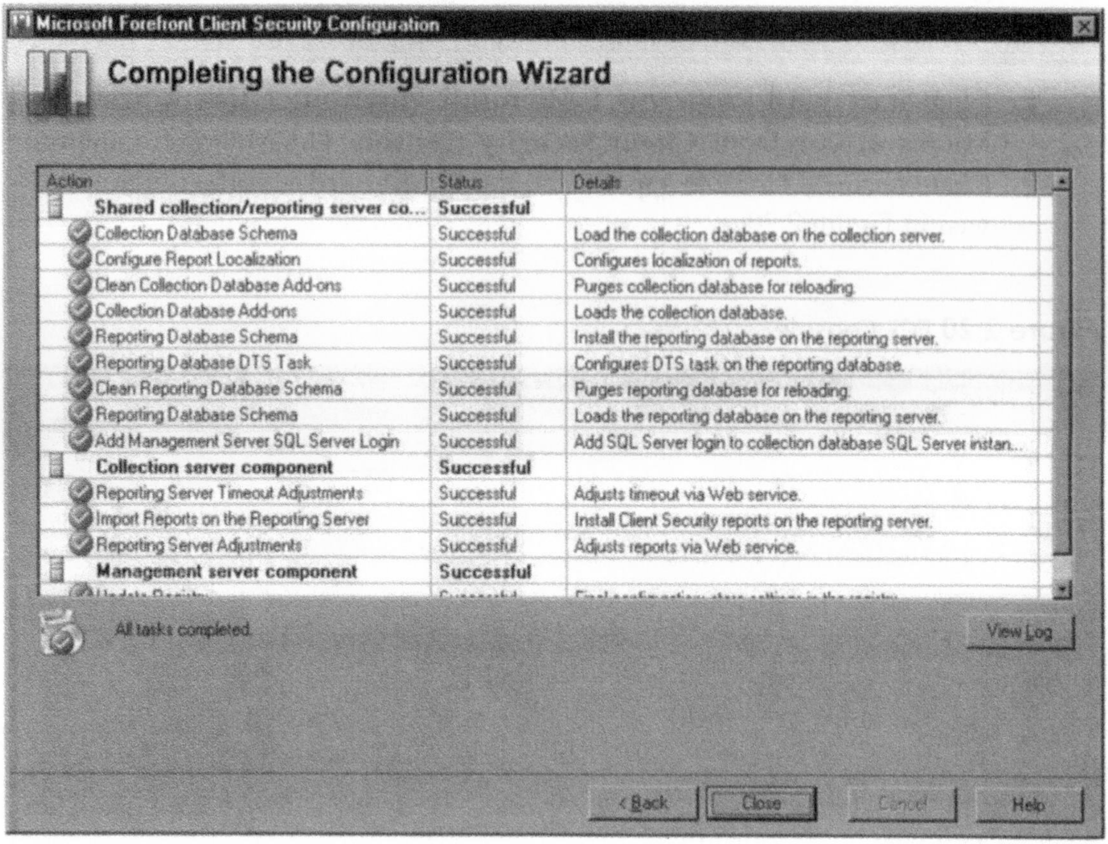

Creating and Deploying Policies

In deploying the Client Security to client systems (XP, Vista, Windows 2000, Windows Server 2003), we need to create and deploy a policy to those systems. Policies are where we decide centrally what the scan schedules and configuration will be. Once the client system has a policy, the computer will download the client software from the distribution server. After deployment, the client systems need to be approved in MOM before they are able to report data. Typically this happens within an hour.

Creating a Policy

Here are the steps required for creating and deploying policies in FCS.

1. Click **Start | All Programs | Microsoft Forefront | Client Security | Microsoft Forefront Client Security Console**. The Microsoft Forefront Client Security Console appears and the **Dashboard** is at the forefront as seen in Figure 2.20.

Figure 2.20 FCS Console

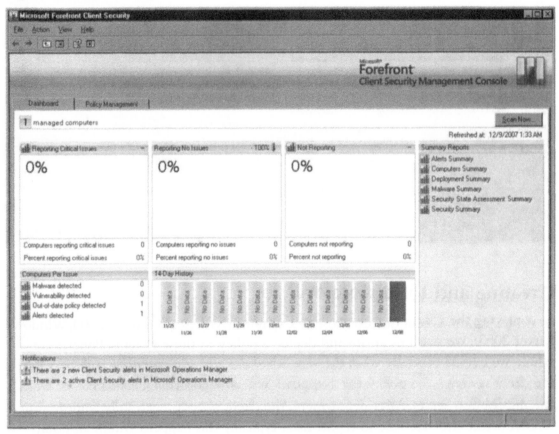

2. Now we need to create a policy. In the FCS Console, click the **Policy Management** tab, then click **New**. On the **General** Tab, enter a **Name** and any **Comments** you like about the policy. In our example, we are calling this policy **Client Settings**.

3. Now go to the **Protection** tab, where you will select what protection you want on. You can turn **Virus protection** and **Spyware protection** On or Off. You can choose to **Use real-time protection**, which scans programs and services when they are accessed. You can schedule to **Run a scan** at a certain day, everyday, and an exact time. You can choose the type of scan such as a **Full scan**, or a **Quick scan**. You can also choose to run a **Quick scan** at certain hourly intervals. **Security state assessment scans** can also be set or not. For our scenario, we've decided on all the defaults plus to **Run a Quick Scan** every four hours as you see in Figure 2.21.

Figure 2.21 New Policy Protection Settings

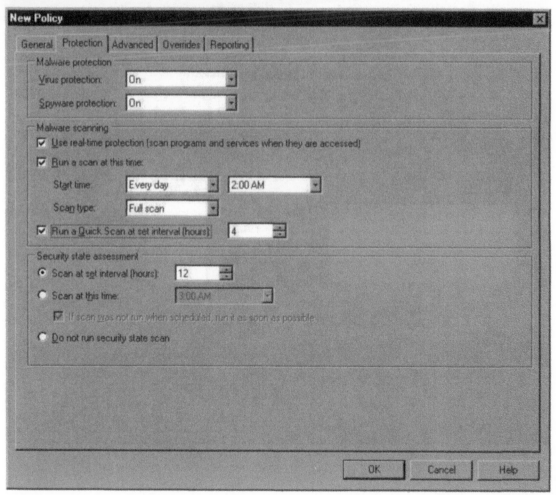

4. Once finished, click the **Advanced** tab; the options seen in Figure 2.22 appear. Here we have kept the defaults for **Check for updates before starting a scan**, **Check for updates at set interval (hours) 6**, **Scan archive files**, and **Use heuristics to detect suspicious files**. We have modified the Client options to **Users can view all Client Security agents settings and messages** and **Only administrators can change Client Security agent settings**. The **Overrides** tab allows you to change responses to specific malware threats that may be default.

Figure 2.22 New Policy Advanced Settings

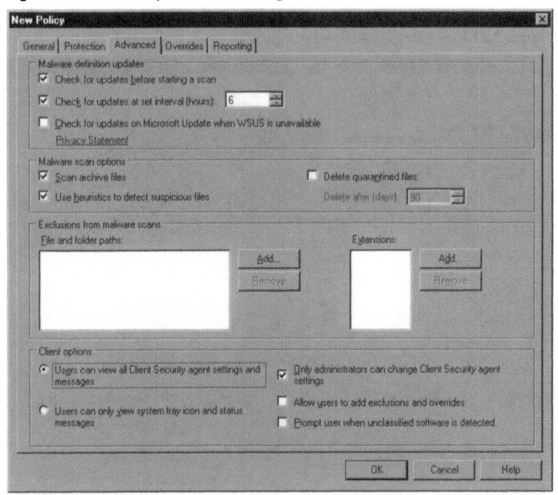

5. Although we are not changing anything in the **Reporting** tab, Figure 2.23 shows all the options available, including the ability to specify **Alert levels**, **Logging**, and **SpyNet** settings. SpyNet will be covered later in this chapter. Now click **OK**.

Figure 2.23 Reporting Tab

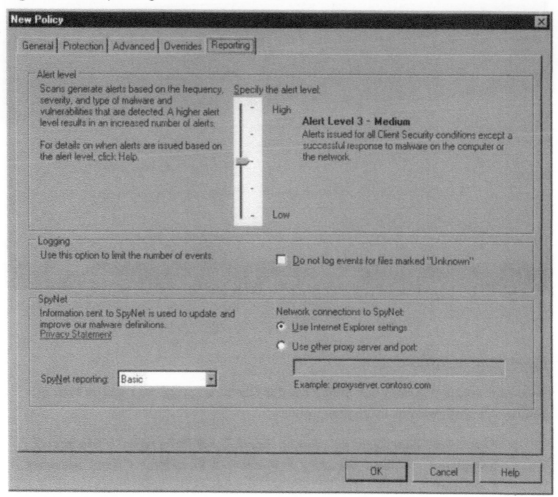

Once completed you will see the new policy listed in FCS as shown in Figure 2.24.

Figure 2.24 New Policy Listed in FCS

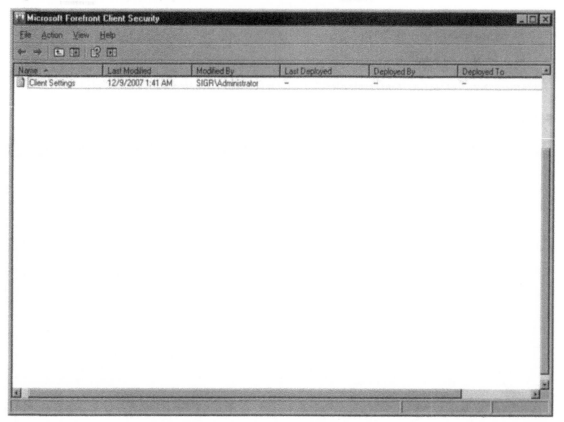

Deploying a Policy

Now that we have created our policy for the Client Security, we need to turn our attention to deploying it. To deploy a policy:

1. Open the Client Security console (**Start | All Programs | Microsoft Forefront | Client Security | Microsoft Forefront Client Security Console**).

2. Go to the **Policy Management** and click on the policy you want to deploy. In our case, we are deploying the policy called **Client Settings**. Click **Deploy** as shown in Figure 2.25.

Figure 2.25 Deploy Policy

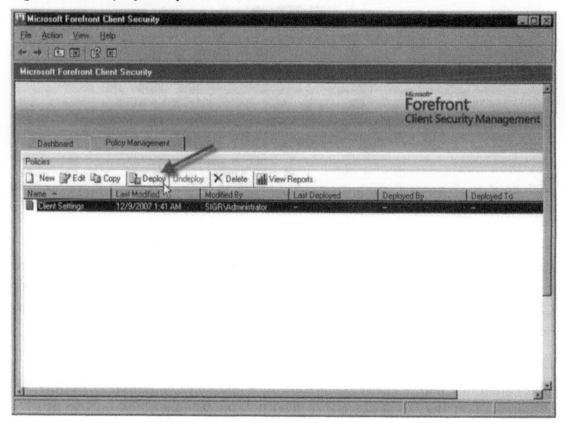

3. At the **Deploy** dialog box, you have the option of selecting where you want to deploy your target or targets. In our example, we will be deploying to an OU. As you see, not only can you deploy to an OU but you can also deploy to AD security groups, GPOs, and .reg files. Figure 2.26 shows that we are deploying to the **Workstations** OU in our Active Directory deployment.

Figure 2.26 Selecting Deployment Target(s)

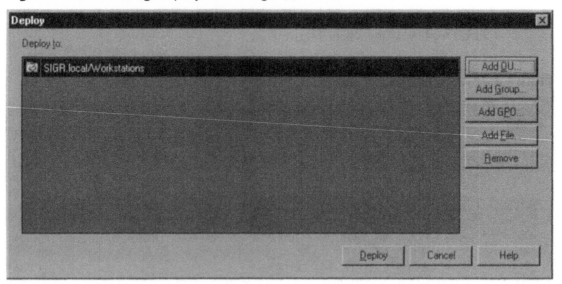

If you return to the Client Security console, you will see that information such as **Last Modified**, **Modified By**, **Last Deployed**, **Deployed By**, and **Deployed To** are now populated with the correct information. So now that we have Microsoft Forefront Client Security installed on our server and we have created and deployed our settings policy, we now need to install the client software on the client computers.

Installing Client Software Agent

The Forefront Client security agent runs on Windows Vista, Windows XP SP2, Windows 2000 SP4, Windows Server 2003 R2, and Windows Server 2003 SP1. Before installing the agent software, verify that your client is up to date on all critical updates. If there are any other anti-virus and anti-spyware software currently installed on the client system, uninstall them. In Windows Vista, be sure to disable Defender's service. For Windows 2000 SP4 clients, be sure to install the Windows Update Agent 2.0 and the Windows Installer 3.1. Installation of the client agent can be done via a logon script, automated installation via SMS, or manually. We will walk through doing it manually. To install the client agent manually:

1. Insert the Forefront Client Security DVD in the DVD-ROM drive of the client system.

2. On the DVD, copy the **CLIENT** directory somewhere on the client workstation.

3. After the **CLIENT** directory has been copied, click **Start | Run**.

4. In the **Run** dialog box, point to the **CLIENT** directory you just copied and run the **ClientSetup.exe** command. For our example, we copied the **CLIENT** directory from the C root. After that we ran the command **ClientSetup.exe /MS FCS-SRV.sigr.local /CG ForefrontClientSecurity**. The **/MS** parameter specifies the name of the FCS Server, and the **/CG** parameter specifies the name of the configuration group that you created during the FCS install. The switches for **ClientSetup.exe** are listed in Table 2.4.

Table 2.4 ClientSetup.exe Switches

/CG <ManagementGroupName>	Specify the MOM management group name. Default is ForefrontClientSecurity.
/MS <ManagementServerName>	The fully qualified domain name of the Management server. Ex: srv1.test.com.
/I	Specify a folder to install the client in besides the default.
/NOMOM	Tell **ClientSetup.exe** not to install the MOM agent. Used on a separate Collection Server.

A command window will come up with a flashing cursor in the upper left corner. After the install, the command window disappears and the Forefront agent can be seen in the lower right corner of the system tray as seen in Figure 2.27. Now that the Forefront Client Security agent is installed let's get acquainted with it.

Figure 2.27 Forefront Client Security Agent in System Tray

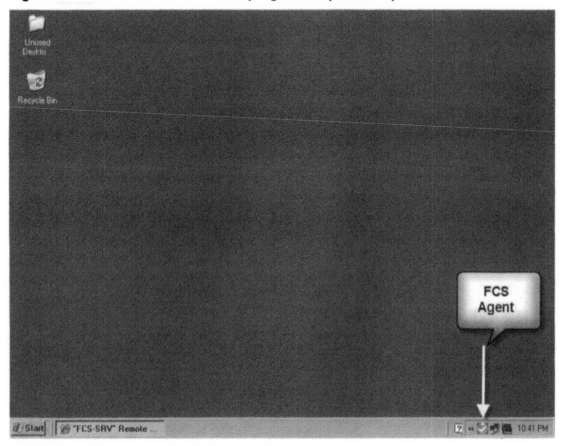

> **NOTE**
>
> After the installation you may receive Error found: Code 0x80240016. This typically happens if the system was ready for a reboot before you installed the agent. Just reboot the system and the Forefront Client Security agent should function normally and change its color from yellow to green.

Home

By opening the FCS agent, which can be done by clicking the green icon with the check mark in it on the system tray or by clicking **Start | All Programs | Microsoft Forefront | Forefront Client Security**, we see an interface very similar to that of

Defender. We have in the upper portion of the utility options for **Home, Scan, History, Tools**, and **Help** (which is displayed as a question mark inside a blue circle) FCS client on machine. Show this tab.

The Home screen provides us with information about any malware that was detected and the status of the agent in the bottom half of the screen. The Status area informs us of our **Last scan**, **Scan schedule**, **Real-time protection**, and current **Antivirus** and **Antispyware definitions**, as seen in Figure 2.28.

Figure 2.28 Home Screen in FCS Agent

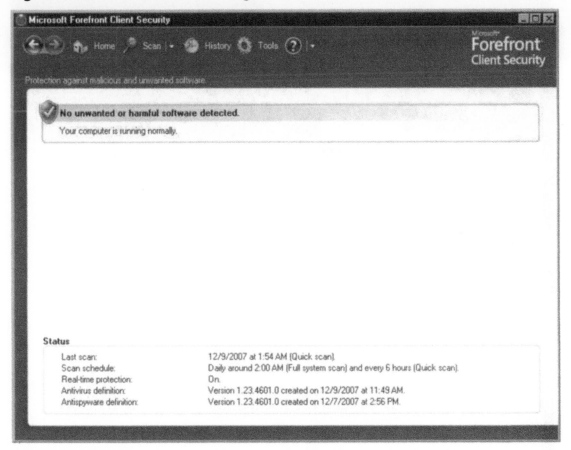

Checking for Updates

To the right of the help icon (blue button with the white question mark) is a down-arrow button. Clicking the down-arrow button provides you with an option to manually **Check for Updates**, if you would like to be even more proactive. If no new definitions are not found, the FCS agent will display a message reading **No new definitions or updates are available**. If there are updates, the FCS agent will download them and update the information on the **Home** screen.

Scan

The **Scan** button kicks off a scan of the computer. By default it will kick off a **Full Scan** of the system, but if you click the down-arrow button on the right side of the **Scan** option you can choose from a **Quick Scan**, **Full Scan**, and a **Custom Scan**, as shown in Figure 2.29.

Figure 2.29 Scanning Options

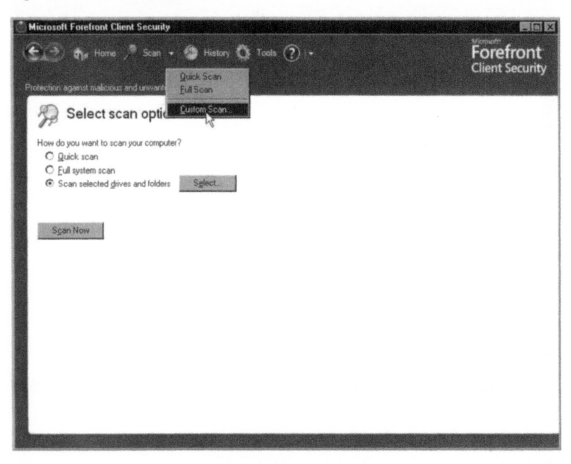

Quick Scan

A quick scan checks the most likely places on your system where malware may exist, plus it scans all running programs. To run a quick scan from the FCS agent, just click the down-arrow button beside the **Scan** button as seen in Figure 2.29 and choose **Quick Scan** or choose **Custom Scan** and select it from the list.

Full Scan

A full scan checks all files on the hard disk, and currently running programs. Conducting a full scan will effect performance, hence it might best to schedule it when you are not using the system (e.g., during the night; we will cover this under the **Tools** option of the FCS agent). Figure 2.30 shows a full scan running on a system.

Figure 2.30 Full Scan with FCS Agent

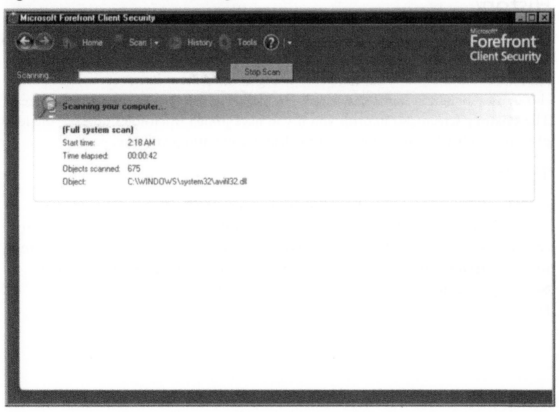

Custom Scan

If you select **Custom Scan**, you can choose your scanning options. With **Custom Scan**, you select **Scan selected drives and folders**, you can choose which drives you want to scan, which directories you would like to scan, and which directories you would prefer not to scan. Once you have made your decision, back at the **Select scan options** screen, click **Scan Now** and your custom scan will begin.

FCS Kernel Mode Minifilter

Minifilter technology in Forefront Client Security is what allows the FCS agent to perform real-time scanning via the Windows Filter Manager. This enables the scanning of files and programs before they even run. A huge benefit to this is that disruption to the user is done so at a minimum.

History

History in the FCS agent displays any actions that have been applied to malware and any other potentially unwanted software that has been detected. Here you can review and monitor items you've permitted by going to the **Allow items** section. You can also remove or restore items that have been placed in the **Quarantined items** area. The **History** screen also informs you if you have joined Microsoft's SpyNet, the level of your membership, and allows you to change any settings you like.

Tools

Possibly the busiest screen in the FCS client agent, the **Tools** option is made up of two sections. The **Settings** section and the **Tools** section. The **Settings** section consists of **Options** and **Microsoft SpyNet**, the **Tools** section consists of **Quarantined items**, **Software Explorer**, **Allowed items**, and **Microsoft Forefront Client Security website**. Figure 2.31 shows the **Tools** option screen within the FCS agent.

Figure 2.31 Tools Section of FCS Agent

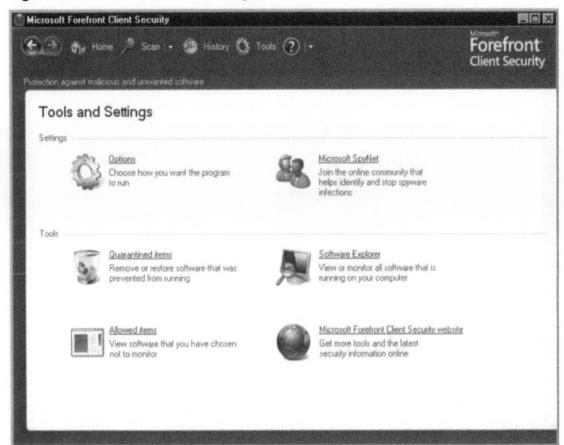

Options

Options allows you to choose how you want the FCS agent to run. Figure 2.32 shows the options available within the **Options** category. Under **Options** within **Tools,** you are able to schedule scanning on the system. You can choose how often you want to scan, the time for it to take place, and the type. You can set an interval (in hours) if you like for running a quick scan. The option of checking for updated definitions before scanning is available. Within the **Options** area, you can set what's referred to as **Default actions**. Here you can decide what to do when a certain level of alert item happens. Alert items come in **Severe**, **High**, **Medium**, and **Low**.

Figure 2.32 Options Screen

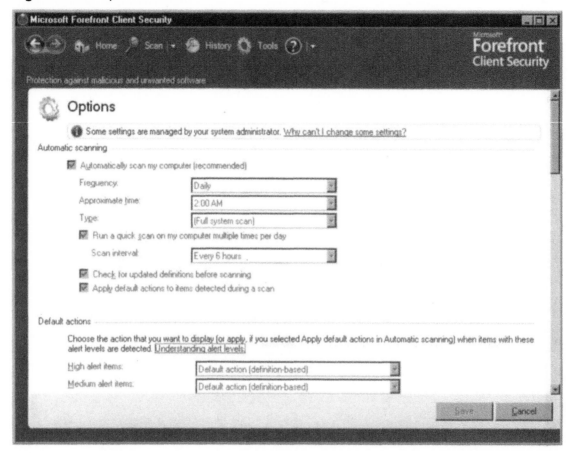

As you've probably noticed, all of our settings are grayed out. The reason is because we created a centrally managed policy that configured these settings earlier.

Microsoft SpyNet

Also in the settings section of **Tools and Settings** under the **Tools** tab in FCS client are the **Microsoft SpyNet** settings. Microsoft SpyNet is the online community network of Windows Defender and Forefront Client Security users and administrators that helps determine what software should be investigated as potential spyware. This community can help administrators see how others are responding to software that has not yet been classified for risk. Ratings from the SpyNet community are one of the factors used by Microsoft in determining which software to investigate as potential risks.

Software Explorer

Under the **Tools** section below the **Settings** section of the **Tools** tab is **Software Explorer**, which allows users to change how a program runs on their PCs. This typically is used when you are sure that you have identified a specific program causing a problem. **Software Explorer** categorizes programs in the following way: **Startup Programs**, **Currently Running Programs**, **Network Connected Programs**, and **Winsock Service Providers**. **Software Explorer** provides a great deal of information about programs on the system. It even groups them by manufacturer. For instance, all Microsoft programs will be listed under their name, even the Google Toolbar Notifier is listed—of course, under Google. Programs also are classified by **Software Explorer** as shown in Figure 2.33.

Figure 2.33 Software Explorer

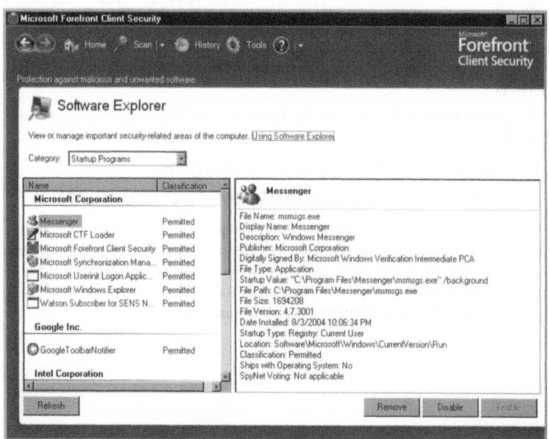

Quarantined Items

Quarantined items are found under the **Tools** section below the **Settings** section of the **Tools** tab. This is software that was found risky or unwanted that the user has decided not to remove, or has allowed to remain when originally notified. A user may find it beneficial at first to quarantine a program before having the FCS agent remove it. If the user quarantines a program, the FCS agent moves that program to another location and prevents it from running. If the user restores the program it is moved back to its original location and allowed to run. If the user chooses to remove the program then it is permanently deleted.

Microsoft Forefront Security Client Web Site

This option is also found under the **Tools** section below the **Settings** section of the **Tools** tab. By clicking this option, Internet Explorer opens and goes to the Microsoft Forefront Client Security Web site. Here you can find up-to-date helpful information like white papers, web casts, virtual labs, downloads, and a technical library. This site is very useful for administrators and users wanting to become more knowledgeable about Microsoft Forefront Client Security.

Help

The Help function is shown beside the **Tools** tab at the top of the FCS agent as a blue dot with a white question mark, and provides access to FCS agent help file.

Checking for Client Version, Engine Version, Antivirus and Antispyware Definitions

By clicking the down-arrow key beside the **Help** button, you can select **About Microsoft Forefront Client Security** and view information about what client and engine version you are running, and you can see the definition versions for the antivirus and antispyware functions. Figure 2.34 shows the system information found in the **About Microsoft Forefront Client Security** box.

Figure 2.34 About Microsoft Forefront Client Security

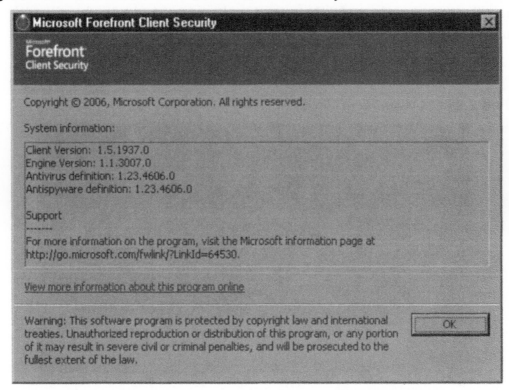

Forefront Client Security Agent in Action

So far we have gone through what Forefront provides; how to prepare for the installation, performing the installation, creating and deploying policies, installing the client security agent; and walked through the options available in the FCS agent. Now let's watch FCS in action. In our test scenario, we have attempted to download a file that will act as a test virus. The file is known as EICAR, a well-known test file that can be downloaded from numerous sites on the Internet such as www.eicar.org/

anti_virus_test_file.htm. As soon as we began to download EICAR, the Forefront Client Security agent immediately warned us that a virus had been found, which you see in Figure 2.35.

Figure 2.35 FCS Warning of Virus

If we click **Smart Clean**, the FCS agent will remove the virus. If you choose to find out more information about the virus, we can select **Review** and the **Home** screen from the agent will appear with the **Apply actions to detected items** screen, while providing information about the virus as shown in Figure 2.36.

Figure 2.36 Applying Actions to Deleted Items

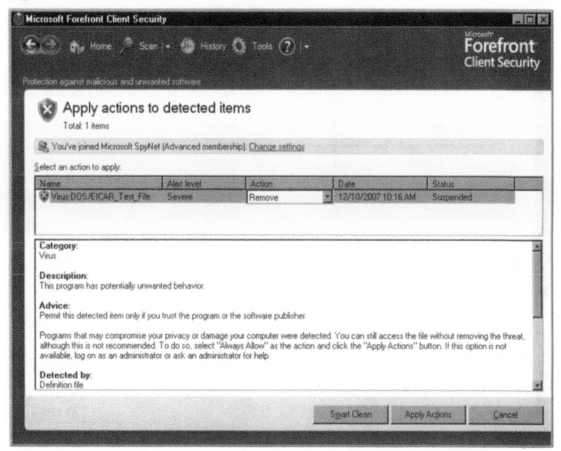

By default, for severe alert levels the action is to remove the virus. If we wanted we could select **Quarantine** or **Always allow** instead. Since this is a severe alert level we're going to take the FCS agent's default action and remove this virus. Remember we can remove the virus by selecting **Smart Clean**, or in this case we can remove it by selecting **Apply Actions**.

Once the virus is removed, the **Home** screen will inform us that the computer is running normally again. If we went to the **History** tab, we would see that we successfully removed the EICAR virus as shown in Figure 2.37.

Figure 2.37 FCS Agent's History

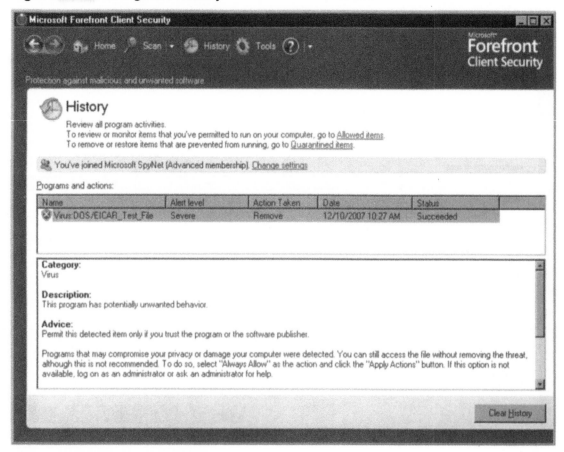

Troubleshooting Microsoft Forefront Client Security

So how do we tell when FCS is running correctly and if it is not? Where do we begin to troubleshoot if it isn't?

Like any product that runs on Windows, we need to verify functionality, verify all corresponding services are running as expected, watch for any alerts, but most importantly we need to start in Event Viewer and research any errors associated with FCS. As we've already learned, FCS makes use of quite a few number of products (SQL Server, WSUS, MOM, IIS, etc.). It's impossible to cover all issues that can arise with FCS. What we can do though, is walk you through some areas to look at when problems do arise. In this situation what we're doing is making sure that updates are being received by the client and walking through the places to look to verify that they are.

Definition Updates Folder

One of the most common issues we mentioned comes in the form of clients not receiving updated definitions. Although this mostly entails WSUS, it helps to know where clients download their updated definitions. Definition updates download to the **Definition Updates Folder**, which by default is located in the **C:\Documents and Settings\All Users\Application Data\Microsoft\Microsoft Forefront\Client Security\Client\Antimalware** directory on systems other than Windows Vista. In Windows Vista the **Definition Updates Folder** is located in the **C:\ProgramData\Microsoft\Microsoft Forefront\Client Security\Client\Antimalware**. Within the **Definition Updates** folder are four subdirectories. One folder's name is an actual GUID, which will differ from machine to machine. The other folders are **Backup**, **Default**, and **Updates**. The updates are downloaded in the **Updates** directory just until they are installed, then those updated files will no longer appear in this directory. They will appear in the folder that has a GUID as the name.

NOTE

Keep in mind that in Windows Vista the C:\Users folder replaces the C:\Documents and Settings folder from previous versions of Windows in holding each user's profile.

GUID

The subdirectory with the GUID holds the definition updates that are in use. The files are base and delta definition files. The files you will see in this folder are:

- **Mpengine.dll:** Malware scanning engine
- **Mpasbase.vdm:** Anti-spyware base definition file
- **Mpasdlta.vdm:** Anti-spyware delta definition file
- **Mpavbase.vdm:** Anti-virus base definition file
- **Mpavdlta.vdm:** Anti-virus delta definition file

Definitions that are currently loaded reside here.

Backup Folder

The backup folder holds a previous version of the files that were stored in the GUID directory and are used in case a rollback is necessary. If any of the base of delta files doesn't install correctly then FCS is able to perform a rollback, pulling the previous version from the backup folder, bringing it to its previous stable state.

Event Viewer, System Log

Since the days of NT, the first place to look for problems is Event Viewer. For FCS, events are logged in the System Log, which regardless of the client OS the path to Event Viewer should be about the same. For Windows Vista for example, you can click the **Start button | Control Panel | Administrative Tools** and click **Event Viewer**; the path is the same in Windows XP. Once Event Viewer is open, just click the icon to the left of where it says **System**. Here you can search any issues that may arise in FCS, plus you can verify that updates are being received, as you see in Figures 2.38 and 2.39 for Windows XP, and in Figures 2.40 and 2.41 for Windows Vista, by looking for Event 19s.

NOTE

Event Viewer in Windows Vista presents a newer interface with more event logs and better detailed events. It provides a summary of Administrative events such as how many errors have been received in the last hour, 24 hours, 7 days, and total to name a few. You can also examine errors or events in more detail and in different views such as an XML view or a "Friendly" view. The first place to troubleshoot problems has improved dramatically in Windows Vista.

Figure 2.38 System Log in Event Viewer in Windows XP

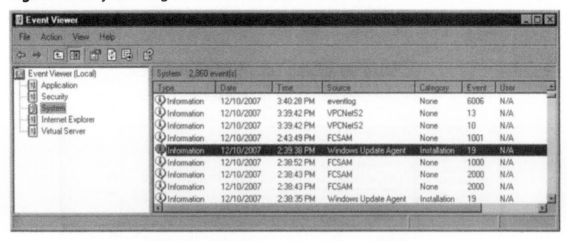

Figure 2.39 Verifying Definition Updates in Windows XP

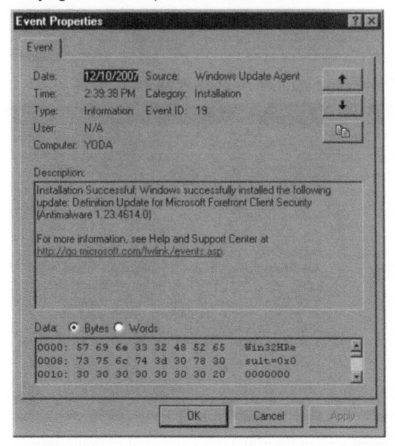

Figure 2.40 System Event Log in Windows Vista

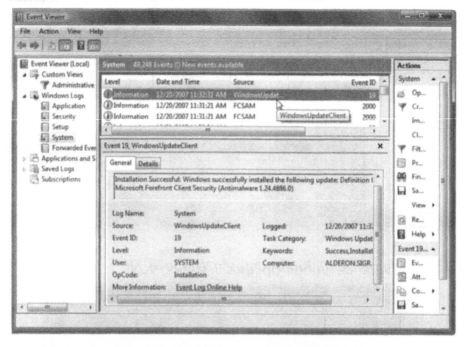

Figure 2.41 Verifying Definitions Update in Windows Vista

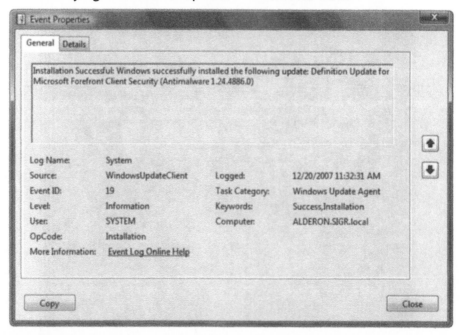

Depending on your situation and issues you need to troubleshoot, starting in Event Viewer and working your way down is usually the best way to go.

Summary

Microsoft Forefront Client Security (FCS) provides unified malware protection for desktops, laptops, and servers. It is a central management solution providing critical visibility and reporting capabilities to administrators. FCS includes server roles and components, plus client agents. There are four server roles in an FCS solution. They include a management server, a collection server, a reporting server, and a distribution server. FCS supports topologies of one to six servers in any given solution.

There are software prerequisites that are required in any FCS solution. Software and services such as SQL Server 2005 with SP1, SQL Server Reporting Services, IIS 6.0 or later, WSUS (if it is the distribution server), ASP.NET, and Windows Server 2003 SP1 or R2 to name a few. The client agent runs on Windows 2000, Windows XP, Windows Server 2003, Windows Vista, and x64 bit clients.

Policies can be deployed with settings for scheduled scanning, quick scan intervals, client options, alert level settings, and even SpyNet reporting participation. Policies can be deployed to OUs, Active Directory security groups, GPOs, and even .reg files.

The client software agent can be installed via scripting, automated installation tools, or manually. The agent has the same look and feel of Defender. With the appropriate rights a user can check for updates, conduct local scans, examine any actions that have been applied via the History button, and even view quarantined items. Troubleshooting in FCS typically begins by examining what functionality is working and what is missing, then examining the system log in Event Viewer and if necessary verifying all services are running as expected.

FCS is more than a product; it is a solution that takes advantage of the products and infrastructure that Microsoft has been perfecting for years.

Solutions Fast Track

How to Use Microsoft Forefront Client Security

- ☑ Microsoft Forefront Client Security (FCS) provides centralized unified malware protection for desktops, laptops, and servers.

- ☑ FCS consists of Unified Protection, Simplified Administration, and Critical Visibility and Control.

- ☑ FCS protects Windows 2000, Windows XP, Windows Server 2003, and Windows Vista. X64 bit is supported for the client agent.

- ☑ FCS supports one to six server topologies.

☑ Four server roles in FCS: Management Server, Collection Server, Reporting Server, and Distribution Server.

☑ FCS leverages technologies from Microsoft Operations Manager (MOM) and WSUS or SMS.

☑ Requirements for FCS are Windows Server 2003 SP2 (R2 also supported), SQL Server 2005 SP2 (Standard or Enterprise), SQL Server Reporting Services, .NET 2.0 Framework, IIS 6.0 or above, ASP.NET, FrontPage Server Extensions, GMPC SP1, WSUS, or SMS.

☑ Administrators can centrally deploy policies using Microsoft Forefront Security Console.

☑ Policies can be deployed to OUs, Active Directory Security Groups, GPOs, and .reg files.

☑ FCS Kernel Mode Minifilter performs real-time scanning of files and programs before they ever run.

Troubleshooting Microsoft Forefront Client Security

☑ Verifying FCS functionality by examining the services that are running are correct, reading logs, and viewing alerts are additional ways of checking the health of FCS.

☑ Definition Updates are held in the GUID named folder under the Definition Update folder on each client.

☑ The system log in Event Viewer is the best place to start when troubleshooting issues with FCS.

Frequently Asked Questions

Q: What is the main difference between Forefront Client Security and Defender?

A: With Forefront Client Security, administrators can centrally manage Microsoft's anti-malware solution, with options like policy deployment, managing scanning, implementing updates, and so on. With Defender, each workstation was an island and administrators had no control if users were downloading updated definition files, whether they were running scans on their systems or not.

Q: How many server roles are there in FCS?

A: There are four server roles: Distribution, Collection, Reporting, and Management.

Q: Can I use any third-party anti-virus or anti-spyware programs while using the FCS agent?

A: No. The FCS agent will not install if it detects other anti-virus or anti-spyware programs running.

Q: What is Microsoft SpyNet?

A: An online community network of FCS users and administrators that work together to help determine and identify potential spyware threats.

Q: How many servers are required for FCS?

A: That depends on your situation, such as number of client systems to be managed, hardware and software budget, existing infrastructure, and so on. FCS supports topologies of one server to as many as six.

Q: What is minifilter technology?

A: It allows the FCS agent to perform real-time scanning of programs before they even run with minimal user impact.

Q: What methods can I use to install the FCS agent?

A: You can install the agent via logon scripts, automated installation (e.g., SMS), or even manually/sneaker net.

Q: Where do you go to deploy policies?

A: FCS policies can be deployed using the Forefront Client Security Console under the Policy Management tab.

Chapter 3

Deploying Windows Server Update Services to Forefront Clients

Solutions in this chapter:

- **Using Windows Software Update Services**
- **Navigating the WSUS Console**
- **Troubleshooting WSUS**

☑ **Summary**

☑ **Solutions Fast Track**

☑ **Frequently Asked Questions**

Introduction

With the number of security threats increasing, consumers want to ensure that their computers have the latest updates, hotfixes, and patches. Consumers go to the Microsoft Windows Update Site to download the latest patches. In a corporate environment, it does not make much sense to visit every workstation and download the latest Windows Update; it would be more beneficial to download those updates to one or more centrally located servers, then deploy the updates to the clients (and servers) within the enterprise.

Microsoft originally released Software Update Services, or SUS, to allow network administrators to centrally deploy the latest Windows Updates. Software Update Services was managed from a web interface and allowed the administrator to approve or deny updates for the computers in the enterprise. Windows Software Update Services, or WSUS, replaced the discontinued Software Update Services with more features and options for the network administrator. Before SUS and WSUS, either end-users downloaded their own updates or administrators visited each machine and loaded the updates. If users failed to download updates, their systems could wind up being vulnerable and bring down the network. There was also a possibility that a user could download a patch that caused the computer's operating system to crash.

Microsoft Windows Software Update Services allows for the central deployment of updates, hotfixes, and patches. One of the importance benefits of using WSUS is that updates will only be deployed if they are authorized by the WSUS console operator. Microsoft Windows Software Update Services has advanced features like reporting, and allowing the grouping of computers. These features will make the life of a network administrator a lot easier. In order to counteract threats from bugs and vulnerabilities, network administrators need to constantly update the family of Windows operating systems. When properly utilized, Microsoft Windows Software Update Services will deploy the latest updates efficiently to help prevent computer vulnerabilities in an enterprise environment.

Using Windows Software Update Services

Microsoft Windows Software Update Services provides a robust, easy to deploy, and easy to manage patch/update management system. Although there are third party products that accomplish the same thing, WSUS provides one advantage that none of its competitors provide—it's free! Realizing the importance of customers consistently updating their systems, Microsoft provides this solution for absolutely no cost to the consumer. Administrators are able to download WSUS directly from Microsoft's Web page and begin installing immediately.

Before installing, you need to do two things: choose a WSUS topology and verify that your configuration meets the system requirements. In the next few sections we'll examine both of those, walk through the configuration and installation of WSUS 3.0, cover client requirements, demonstrate how to configure Group Policies, and see why TCP port 8530 is so important.

WSUS 3.0 Deployment Topologies

In deploying WSUS 3.0, you have the option to create different topologies depending on your environment. The most basic of deployment topologies is the single-server implementation. Here WSUS 3.0 runs on a single-server that downloads updates directly from the Microsoft Update site and then distributes them to servers, desktops, and laptops throughout the internal network. A diagram of a single-server topology is shown in Figure 3.1.

Figure 3.1 Single-Server Topology

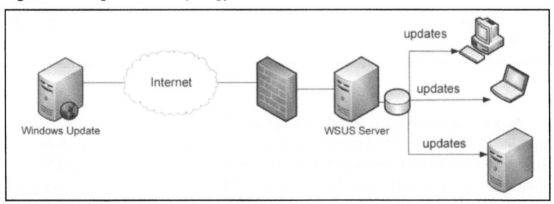

In the single-server topology, the WSUS server synchronizes with the Windows Update site on the Web. During synchronization, WSUS determines if any new updates have been made available since it last performed synchronization. During the initial synchronization, the download can take an hour or longer, depending on the bandwidth of your organization. Regardless of the bandwidth, any additional synchronizations should be significantly shorter than the initial one.

So what if you have a large organization but you don't want to overload a single-server, or your network covers multiple geographic locations? Server hierarchies probably make the most sense. In a server hierarchy setup, one server acts as the primary upstream server directly synchronizing with the Windows Update site. Downstream servers on the network then perform the same synchronization but with the upstream WSUS server and not the Windows Update site. A very simple diagram of a WSUS server hierarchy is shown in Figure 3.2.

Figure 3.2 Server Hierarchy Topology

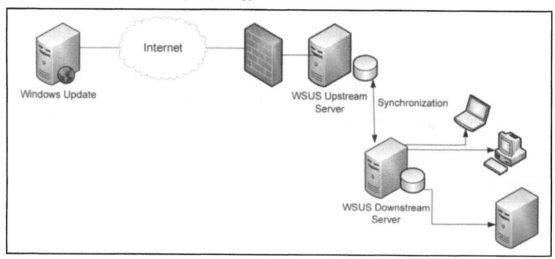

Another topology option involves failover capabilities. By using network load balancing servers, administrators can provide more reliability while also improving performance. It starts by setting a back-end SQL Server 2005 cluster, then installing multiple WSUS front-end systems with Network Load Balancing (NLB). Figure 3.3 is a simple example of such a topology.

Figure 3.3 NLB Failover for WSUS

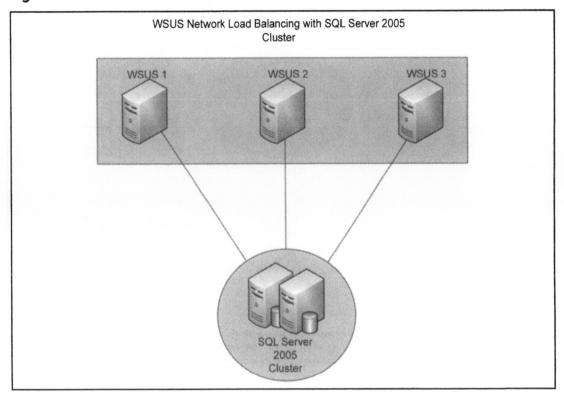

Laptops can be difficult to keep up to date on the newest patches and updates. These computers travel with their users (typically sales reps) from office to office and site to site. The roaming clients' topology takes this into consideration. The roaming client topology allows the traveling laptop to pull its updates from the closest WSUS server, thereby reducing the chances of update traffic going across WAN lines. This topology is set up by entering (A) records in DNS for the WSUS servers but doing so with the same host name and different IP addresses. Once an administrator has done that, they set up *netmask ordering* and *round robin* on the DNS server. *Netmask ordering* restricts the name resolution to computers in the same subnet; if there is a location without a WSUS server, *round robin* will rotate through the list of available hosts on other subnets. Figure 3.4 shows a simple diagram of a roaming client topology.

Figure 3.4 Roaming Client Topology

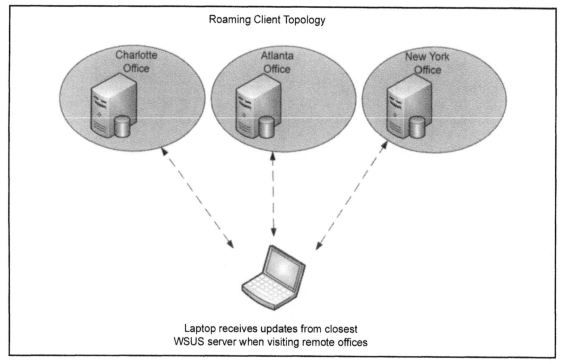

As you see, there are many different setup options with WSUS that work in various network environments. This provides administrators with the flexibility they need to design and implement WSUS. Once the topology has been decided, we then need to install a WSUS server.

Configuring and Installing WSUS

As mentioned above, before installing WSUS 3.0, choose the deployment topology. Once that's decided, verify that your system meets the minimum requirements. In the example, we will be setting up a single WSUS 3.0 server topology. Although Windows Server 2008 supports WSUS, in our example we will be installing WSUS 3.0 on Windows Server 2003. Just like any other product, certain system requirements must be met. These are shown in Tables 3.1 and 3.2.

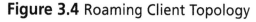

Table 3.1 WSUS Requirements on Windows Server 2003

Server Operating System	System Requirements
Windows Server 2003 Service Pack 1 or higher	Internet Information Services (IIS) 6.0
	Any updates for Background Intelligent Transfer Services (BITS) 2.0 and WinHTTP 5.1
	.NET Framework 2.0 Redistributable Package
	Report Viewer Redistributable 2005
	Microsoft Management Console (MMC) 3.0
	SQL Server 2005 Service Pack 1 (optional)
	1GB (minimum) of free space on the system partition
	2GB (minimum) of free space to store the database files
	20GB (minimum) of free space on the volume that will store the content

NOTE

WSUS 3.0 cannot be installed on compressed drives, nor is it supported on systems running as Terminal Servers.

Table 3.2 WSUS Requirements on Windows Server 2008

Server Operating System	System Requirements
Windows Server 2008	IIS 7 (enable Windows Authentication, Static Content, ASP.NET, 6.0 Management Compatibility, IIS Metabase Compatibility)
	Microsoft Report Viewer
	SQL Server 2005 Service Pack 1
	1GB (minimum) of free space on the system partition
	2GB (minimum) of free space on which the database files will be stored

---

NOTE

In Windows Server 2008, after installing IIS 7 the administrator must configure the *applicationhost.config* file. This configuration file is found in the **%windir% \system32\inetsrv** folder. In the *applicationhost.config* file, go to the **<system. webServer> <modules>** tag and remove **<add name="CustomErrorModule">** if it is present and replace it with **<remove name="CustomErrorModule">** then save the file.

Installation of WSUS 3.0 can be performed interactively by the administrator or done so in quiet mode. We will briefly cover quiet mode and unattended installations.

Quiet and Unattended Installations

Administrators have the option to install WSUS 3.0 interactively or in an automated manner. To do this an administrator will issue a command called *WSUSSetup.exe* with switches that meet their requirements. The setup command line parameters are shown in Table 3.3 and the command line properties for WSUS 3.0 are shown in Table 3.4.

Table 3.3 WSUS Setup Command-Line Parameters

Switch	Description
/q	Silent installation
/u	Uninstall WSUS
/p	Perform a prerequisite check only
/h or /?	Help
/g	Perform upgrade over WSUS 2.0. This is only valid when used with /q

Table 3.4 WSUS Setup Command Properties

Property	Description
CONTENT_LOCAL	0=content hosted locally
	1=host on Microsoft Update
CONTENT_DIR	Path to the content directory
WYUKON_DATA_DIR	Path to the Windows Internal Database data directory
SQLINSTANCE_NAME	The name of the SQL Server Instance. Format is *<servername>\SQLInstanceName*. NOTE: If database instance resides on local machine then the *<servername>* should be *%computername%*.
DEFAULT_WEBSITE	0=port 8530
	1=port 80
PREREQ_CHECK_LOG	Path and file name for log file
CONSOLE_INSTALL	0=install the WSUS server
	1=install console only
ENABLE_INVENTORY	0=do not install inventory features
	1=install inventory features
DELETE_DATABASE	0=retain database
	1=remove database
DELETE_CONTENT	0=retain content files
	1=remove content files
DELETE_LOGS	0=retain log files
	1=remove log files (used in conjunction with /u)
CREATE_DATABASE	0=use current database
	1=create database
PROGRESS_WINDOW_HANDLE	Windows handle returns MSI progress messages
MU_ROLLUP	0=do not join
	1=join Microsoft Update Improvement
FRONTEND_SETUP	0=write content location to the database (used with Network Load Balancing)
	1=do not write content location to the database

Configuring & Implementing...

An Example of WSUSSetup.exe

Here is an example of using the *WSUSSetup.exe* command to install WSUS 3.0 in quiet mode using port 80:

```
WSUSSetup.exe /q DEFAULT_WEBSITE=1.
```

WSUS 3.0 Interactive Setup

Many administrators will select the interactive setup for WSUS 3.0. To install the software you must first download it. WSUS 3.0 can be downloaded from http://go.microsoft.com/fwlink/?LinkId=89379. If you are installing on an x64 system you must download WSUS3Setupx64.exe, 32-bit systems use WSUS3Setupx86.exe. The following steps install WSUS 3.0.

1. Go to the directory where you saved **WSUS3Setupx86.exe** (or **WSUS3-Setupx64.exe**) and double-click it to start the installation.

2. At the **Open File** box choose **Run**.

3. Setup will extract the files required for installation. If there are any prerequisites that were not met, the setup program will inform you of them and you will need to install the missing software before setup will continue.

4. If the prerequisites are met, you will then come to the **Welcome** screen seen in Figure 3.5. Here you can click **Next**.

Figure 3.5 WSUS Setup Welcome Screen

5. Now you must select the type of installation you want to perform. You have two choices, as shown in Figure 3.6. You can select a **Full server installation including Administration Console** (which is what we will select in our example) or you can choose to install the **Administration Console only** if you want to install the console on a remote administration machine.

Figure 3.6 Installation Mode Selection

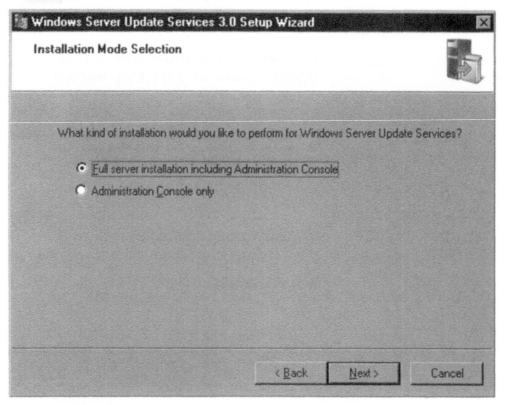

6. Now accept the terms of the license agreement and click **Next**.

7. The next step is to select the drive and directory where we will store the updates so that the client systems can download them quickly. In our example, our F drive has more free space than any other volume so we are selecting it and choosing the default directory of WSUS (Figure 3.7). Once you choose the location, click **Next**.

Figure 3.7 Selecting Update Source

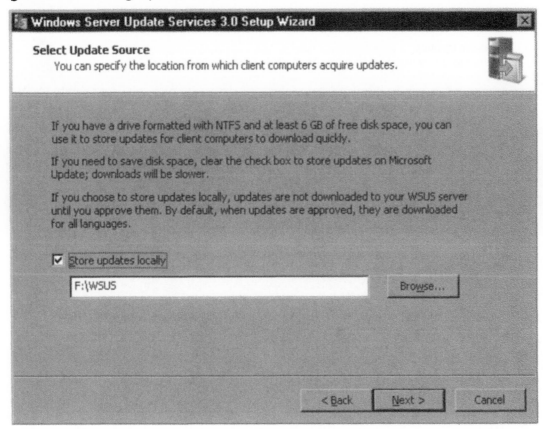

8. Now we come to the **Database Options** screen. Here, choose where to store the database file. As you see in Figure 3.8, we can choose to **Install Windows Internal Database on this computer**, which is the option chosen in the example, or **Use an existing database server on this computer**, or select **Using an existing database server on a remote computer**. Once you've chosen your location, click on **Next**.

Figure 3.8 Database Options

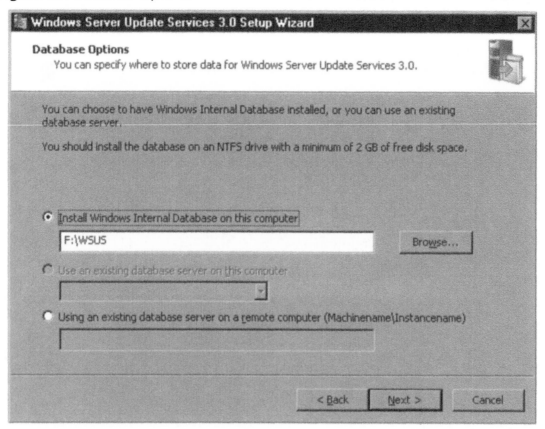

9. Next we have to select the Web site preference. In the example, we chose **Use the existing IIS Default Web site** (Figure 3.9); you can also choose to **Create a Windows Server Update Services 3.0 Web site**. If you decide to create a WSUS Web site, your client systems will need to access the update server using TCP 8530 instead of TCP 80. Once you've made your selection click **Next** to continue.

Figure 3.9 Web Site Preference

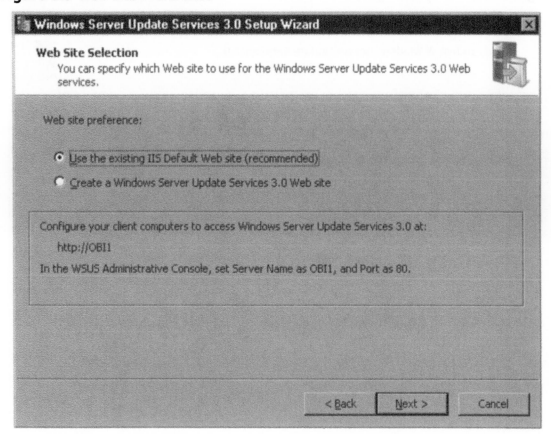

10. Now the WSUS installation program will verify the selections we've made (Figure 3.10). If any of the configuration options are incorrect then you can choose the Back button and keep selecting it until you get to the screen you need to correct. If everything is fine, just click Next and setup will install WSUS 3.0.

Figure 3.10 Verify Configuration Selections

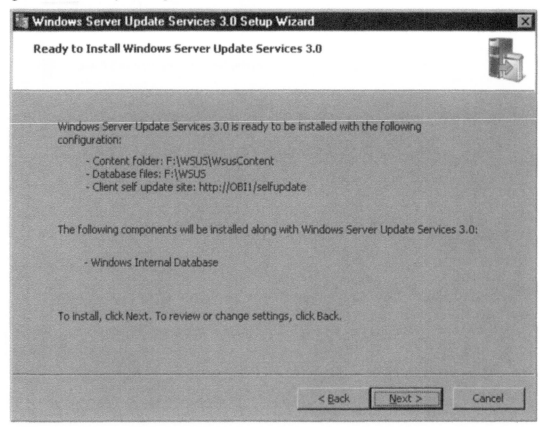

11. Once the program is finished installing, you will see a screen indicating that the WSUS setup is complete, as seen in Figure 3.11. Now just click **Finish** and you're done with the installation.

Figure 3.11 WSUS Installation Completed

After WSUS is installed you must configure it. Once the installation is done, WSUS immediately starts the Configuration Wizard. This will allow you to select options like an upstream server, proxy server, any languages supported on your network, products you want to support updates for, and more. Let's quickly run through the wizard for our setup.

NOTE

If you decide not to run through the configuration wizard immediately after the installation you can choose to run it later by launching the **WSUS Administrator** tool and going to **Options**.

First is the **Before You Begin** screen shown below in Figure 3.12. It will ask you if the server firewall is configured correctly, if the server can connect to the upstream server, which in our case will be the Microsoft Update site, and if you have user credentials for a proxy server if one is installed.

Figure 3.12 WSUS Configuration Wizard

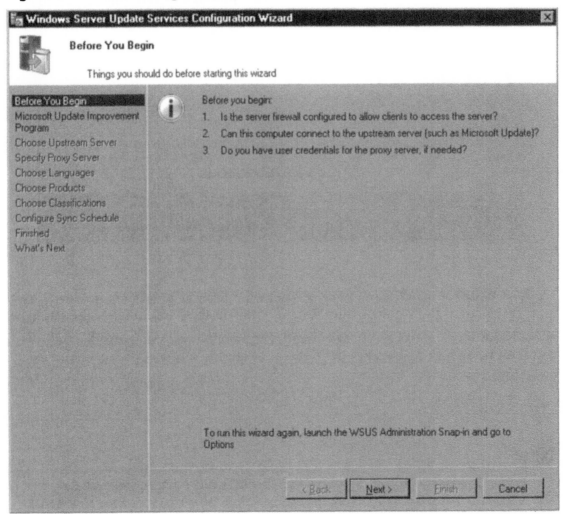

Now you have the option to **Join the Microsoft Update Improvement Program** (Figure 3.13). This program uses your WSUS server to upload information to Microsoft in an effort to improve the quality and reliability of updates. We will allow the default which is **Yes, I would like to join the Microsoft Update Improvement Program**. If you decide not to, just remove the check mark and select **Next**.

Figure 3.13 Microsoft Update Improvement Program

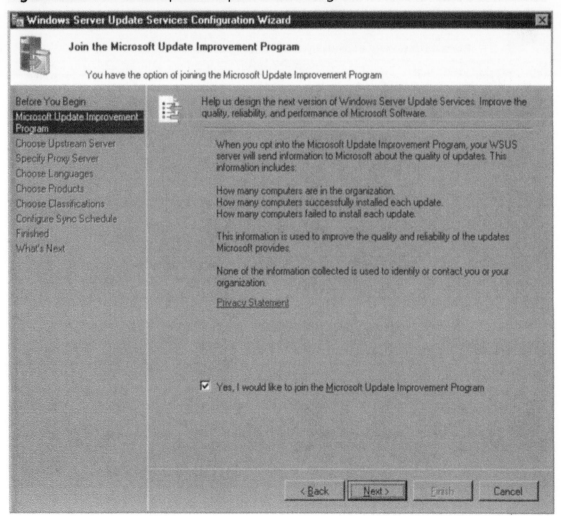

Now we choose our upstream server, demonstrated in Figure 3.14. For our example, this will be the Microsoft Update site. For some with hierarchical WSUS topologies, your upstream server will be another WSUS system on your network. Once you've selected your upstream server, click **Next**.

Figure 3.14 Choosing an Upstream Server

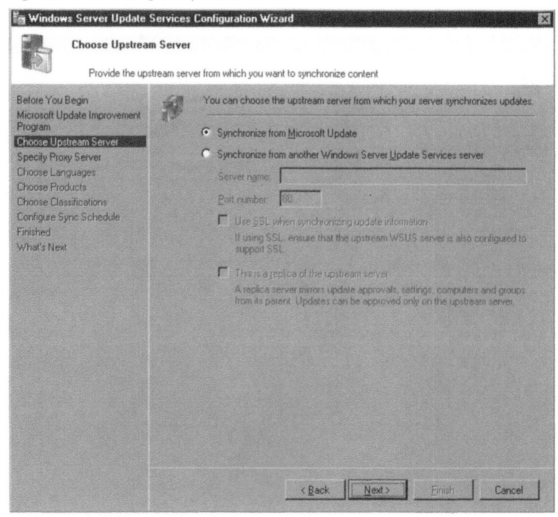

If you have a proxy server, then in Figure 3.15 in the **Specify Proxy Server** screen you must provide the server name, port number, and the user credentials so that the WSUS server can receive updates. Remember if the user account that the WSUS server uses to get through the proxy changes, if either the password or the actual account is renamed, you must type the new account and changed password in the *Proxy Server* settings for WSUS or synchronization with Microsoft Update will fail. If you do not have a proxy server then just click **Next**.

Figure 3.15 Specify Proxy Server

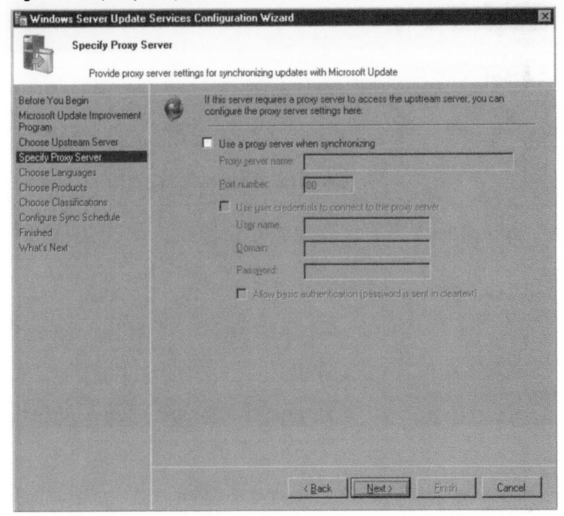

Now we must connect to the upstream server, as you see in Figure 3.16. At this point, just click **Start Connecting**.

Figure 3.16 Connect to Upstream Server

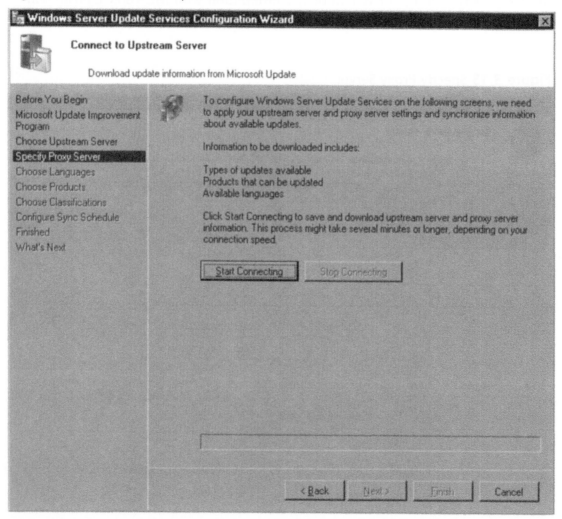

After the update information is downloaded, click **Next**.

Now choose the language(s) of the updates you need to support. You can choose to download updates in all languages, including any additional languages that Microsoft later supports, or you can select which language(s) you need to download updates for. As you see in Figure 3.17, we have chosen just to download updates in English.

NOTE

It is highly suggested that you not download updates in all languages. This takes up a tremendous amount of bandwidth and drive space. Choose only the languages that your environment uses.

Figure 3.17 Select Language(s) of Updates to Download

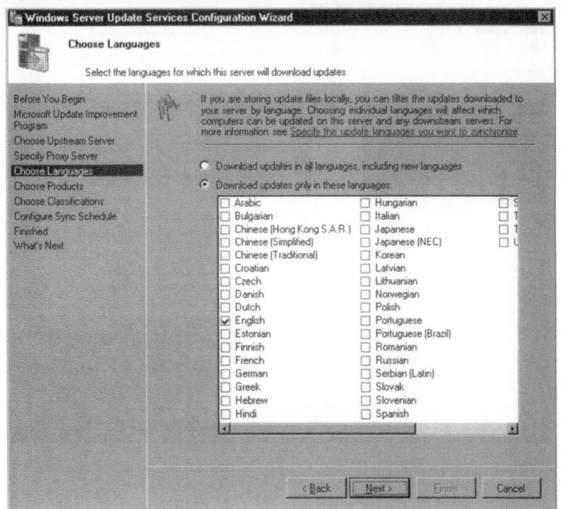

Now, choose the Microsoft products for which you want updates. You can select **All Products**, as in Figure 3.18, or individually select certain products. For our example, we have selected to download updates for: Exchange Server 2003, Forefront Client Security, all Office suites, and all Windows operating systems. Once your product(s) are selected, click **Next** to continue.

Figure 3.18 Select Product(s) to Update

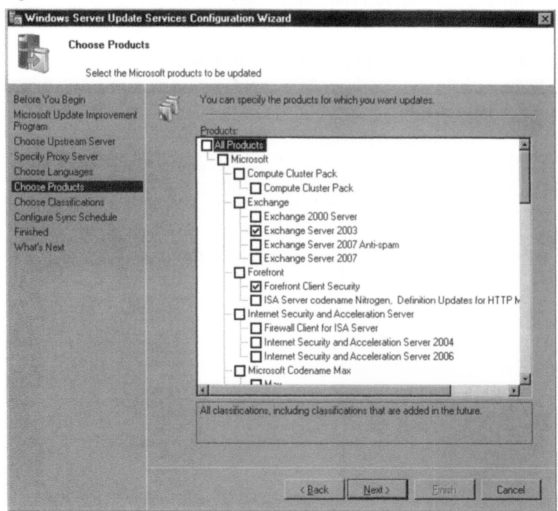

Classification selection is next, as seen in Figure 3.19. Here you can choose what type of updates you want downloaded to the WSUS server. For our example, we have chosen **Critical Updates**, **Definition Updates**, **Security Updates**, **Service Packs**, and **Updates**. Once you've made your selections, click **Next**.

Figure 3.19 Select Update Classification(s)

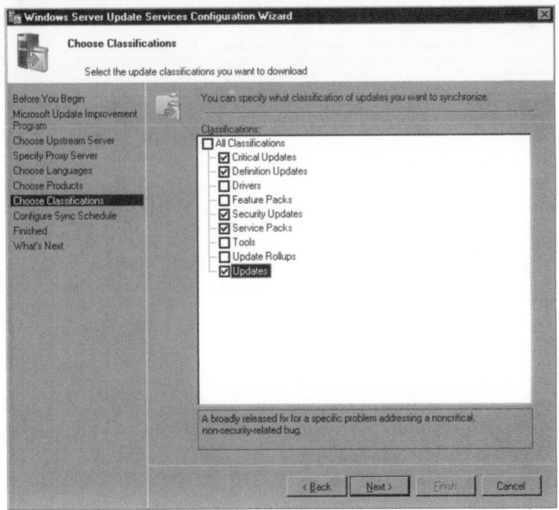

Now you must set a synchronization schedule. You can either **Synchronize manually** or **Synchronize automatically**, thereby choosing an exact time for synchronization. We've chosen to synchronize at midnight and only synchronize once per day, as you see in Figure 3.20. After selecting your synchronization strategy, choose **Next**.

Figure 3.20 Set Synchronization

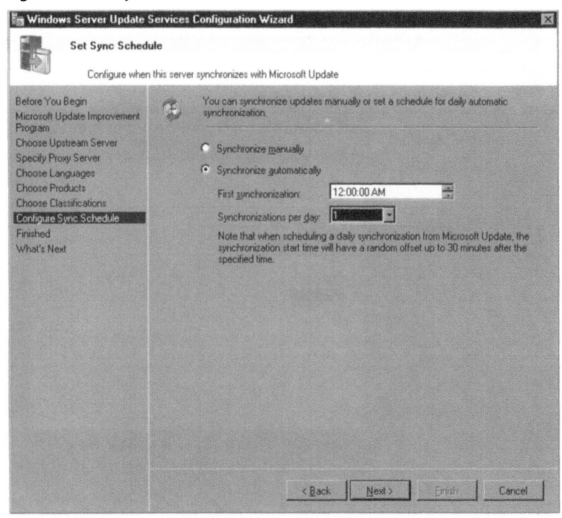

At the **Finished** screen, you can **Launch the Windows Server Update Services Administration Console** and/or **Begin initial synchronization**. Looking at Figure 3.21, you see we are choosing to do both. After your selection(s), click **Next**.

Figure 3.21 Configuration Wizard Completion Screen

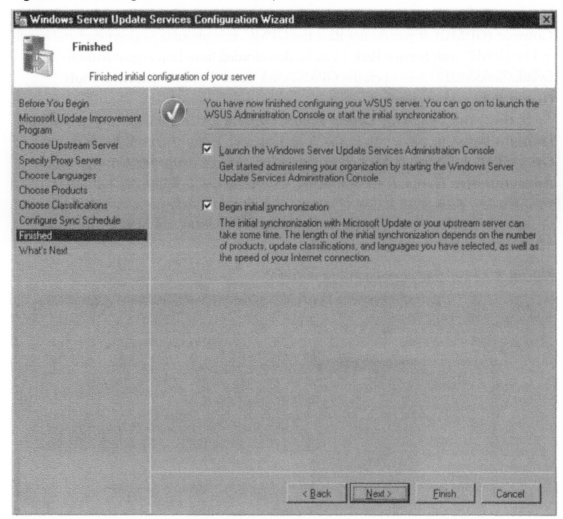

Now you come to a **What's Next** screen where you are provided suggestions such as: **Using SSL with WSUS**, **Creating computer groups**, **Assigning computers to groups using Group Policies**, and **Configuring auto-approval rules**. For our example, we will just select **Finish**.

Configuring Group Policy for WSUS Updates

After WSUS 3.0 is setup and fully configured, we need to tell the client systems that they need to download updates from our WSUS server. The easiest way to do that is via Group Policy. In our example, we will have all systems in the domain get their updates from our newly created WSUS server, whose name is OBI1. To do this we will modify the **Default Domain Policy**. On the domain controller, open up the **Group Policy Management Console (GPMC)**. If you do not have the GPMC, it is advisable to download and install it. The GPMC with Service Pack 1 can be downloaded from http://go.microsoft.com/fwlink/?linkid=21813. To open the GPMC, click **Start | Administrative Tools | Group Policy Management**.

In the GPMC, go to the **Group Policy Objects** folder and highlight the **Default Domain Policy** as you see in Figure 3.22. Left-click it and choose **Edit**. Now the **Group Policy Object Editor** should come up. Go to **Computer Configuration | Administrative Templates | Windows Components | Windows Update**. On the right window pane there is a list of settings that are most likely not configured. We want to configure two of them: **Configure Automatic Updates** and **Specify intranet Microsoft update service location**.

Figure 3.22 Default Domain Policy in GPMC

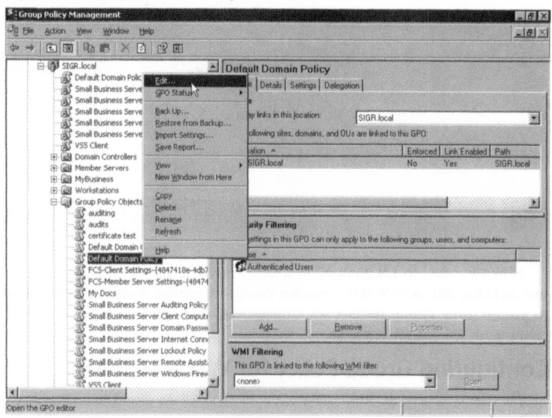

To configure the automatic updates, double-click the **Configure Automatic Updates** setting. For our example we will enable the setting and configure the automatic updating for **3-Auto download and notify for install** as you see in Figure 3.23. After configuring the setting, click **OK**. You will then come back to the **Group Policy Object Editor** but should see the **Configure Automatic Updates** setting on the right side set to **Enabled**.

Figure 3.23 Configure Automatic Updates Properties

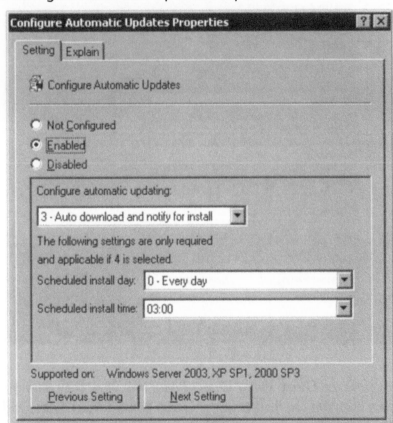

Now we need to actually tell the client systems where to get their updates by configuring the **Specify intranet Microsoft update service location** setting. On the right side of the screen, double-click on the setting **Specify intranet Microsoft update service location** and select **Enabled**. In the area for **Set the intranet update service for detecting updates**, we type in the URL for the WSUS server on our network. In this case it is http://obi1 as you see in Figure 3.24. Type the same thing for the **Set the intranet statistics server** setting.

Figure 3.24 Specify Intranet Microsoft Update Service Location Properties

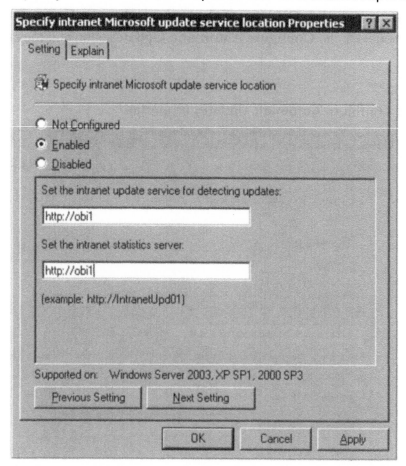

Once configured, the Group Policy Object Editor will show both settings configured as you see in Figure 3.25. You can then close the Group Policy Object Editor and the GPMC. The Default Domain Policy has been modified to provide the WSUS information.

Figure 3.25 GPO Editor After Configuration

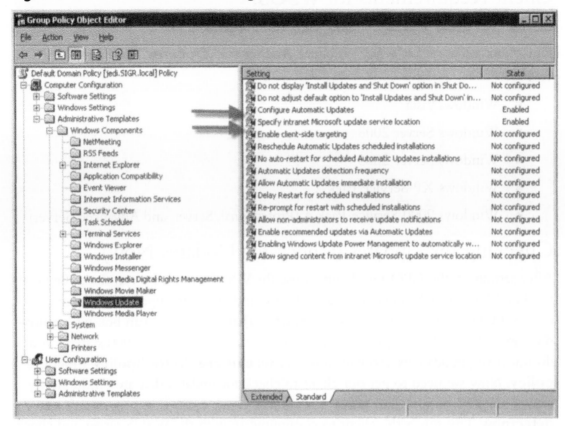

TCP Port 8530

During the installation of WSUS, you had the choice of using the default Web site which uses port 80. This is recommended by Microsoft as long as there are no other websites on the server listening on port 80. If there are, Microsoft allows you to choose **Create a Windows Server Update Services 3.0 Web Site** as you saw back in Figure 3.9. This then informs you that client systems must now use TCP 8530 to access the update server. For instance, in our example, if we had chosen to create a Web site our WSUS server would be accessed by clients with http://obi1:8530. If this had been the case then we would need to make sure that the individual firewalls on the clients (Windows XP, Windows Server 2003, and Windows Vista) allowed TCP 8530.

Client Requirements for WSUS: 2000 Service Pack 3, XP Service Pack 1

The client software for WSUS is called **Automatic Updates**. The clients supported are:

- Windows Vista

- Windows Server 2008

- Windows Server 2003

- Windows XP Service Pack 2

- Windows 2000 Service Pack 4 (Professional, Server, and Advanced Server)

Checking for Updates (Check for Updates Now)

After setting up the GPO for clients to use the WSUS server, we can force the newly modified GPO to take effect on our system(s) and check for updates. To force the changed GPO to take effect just click **Start | Run** and in the run box type **gpupdate.exe /force**. If prompted, restart your system. On Windows 2000 systems you do not have gpupdate.exe, so you must run **secedit.exe /refreshpolicy machine_policy**. Now we need to get our client to check for updates that are on the newly installed WSUS server. Click **Start | Run** and in the run box type **wuauclt.exe /detectnow**. This forces the client to communicate with the WSUS server and check for updates. To verify you are communicating with and searching for updates from the WSUS server look for the *WindowsUpdate.txt* file found in the *C:\Windows* directory. Some lines to look for in this file are:

- Under the Agent: Refreshing global settings cache
  - *WSUS server:* Error! Hyperlink reference not valid.> *(Changed)*
  - *WSUS status server:* Error! Hyperlink reference not valid.> *(Changed)*
- Under the AU: Policy changed processed section
  - *WSUS server:* Error! Hyperlink reference not valid.>
- Additional lines to watch for include:
  - *Server URL* = Error! Hyperlink reference not valid.

After confirming any of the above lines in the WindowsUpdate.txt, you are communicating successfully to the WSUS server.

Navigating the WSUS Console

In previous versions of WSUS (SUS included), servers were managed via the administrative console, which was Web-based. Although effective, moving to the MMC interface has provided administrators with a more friendly and powerful console. The new console uses MMC 3.0. To open the new console from the WSUS server, click **Start | Administrative Tools | Microsoft Windows Server Update Services 3.0** and you should see the **Update Services** console come up, similar to the one seen in Figure 3.26. The Update Services tool consists of three primary panes: *Console Tree*, *Details Pane*, and an *Action Pane*. When an administrator selects a different area of the Console Tree, the Details Pane and Action Pane change to show the pertinent information and available actions of the selection.

Figure 3.26 Update Services Console

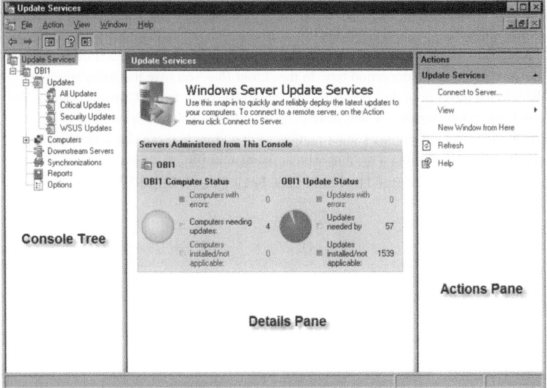

Update Services

As you see in Figure 3.26, the top level of the WSUS administrative console is *Update Services*. In the Update Services Details Pane, you are provided *Computer Status* and *Update Status*. The Computer Status area provides you with information about the clients that the WSUS server serves. Administrators can see how many computers need updates, if any have experienced errors while installing updates, and those where updates have been installed and are no longer applicable. In the Update Services Actions Pane, administrators are given the option to connect to another WSUS server by selecting **Connect to Server**.

Server Node

The node below *Update Services* is the actual WSUS server itself, as seen in Figure 3.27. In our case, it's OBI1. Under this selection, the Details Pane provides the administrator with a To Do list. This list informs the administrator of how many security updates, critical updates, and new products, along with their classifications, are waiting to be approved or have been added. Administrators are also provided an overview with the same information seen in the Update Services Details Pane along with the Synchronization Status, Download Status, Server Statistics, and Connection type. In the *Actions Pane*, you have the ability to remove the selected server from the console by clicking on **Remove from Console**. You can also search for specific updates by title, description, Knowledge Base article number, or the Microsoft Security Response Center number of all updates. You can also search for specific computers by their names if need be. Also in the Actions Pane is the ability to import updates to the WSUS server. This can be done by clicking on **Import Updates** in the Actions Pane.

Figure 3.27 Update Services: WSUS Server Details and Actions Panes

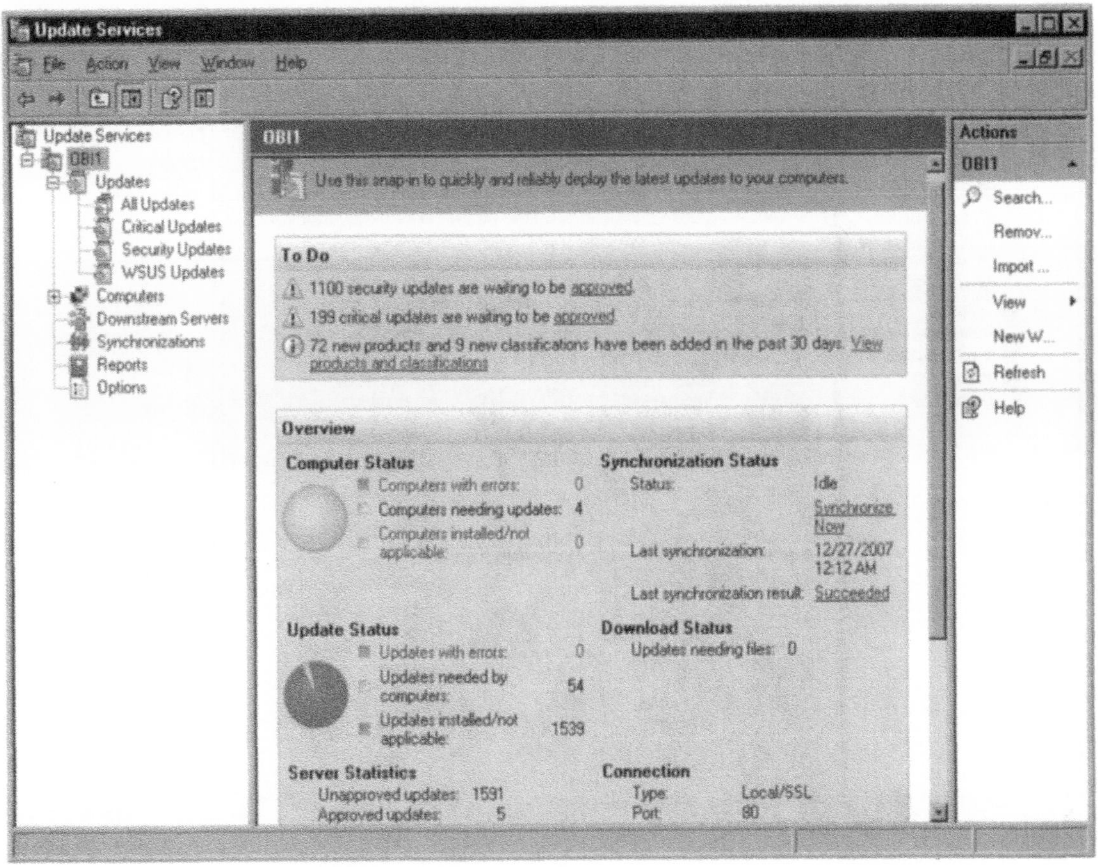

Updates

The Updates node in the Console Tree provides more information about the updates on the WSUS server. It breaks them down into four categories: **All Updates, Critical Updates, Security Updates, and WSUS Updates** (Figure 3.28). The Actions Pane allows administrators the same **Search** option previously mentioned, along with the same **Import Updates** option. It does allow some customization for the administrator in that they can click on **New Update View** and choose the properties they want to include in the view, the specifics of that property, and even a name for the customized view. For instance, if we wanted to view the updates required for all Windows Vista and XP systems we could create a custom view.

Figure 3.28 Updates Console

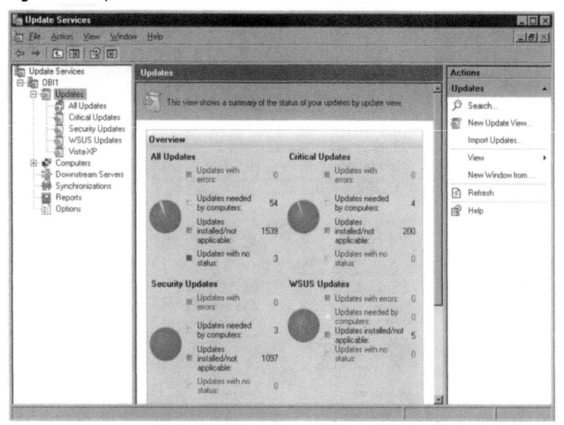

Updates Subnodes

The subnodes for the Updates folder include: **All Updates, Critical Updates, Security Updates, WSUS Updates,** and any custom views the administrator may have added. The subnodes have the same options. In the Details Pane, administrators can view a list of **Approved, Unapproved, Declined,** and **Any Except Declined**. To the right, you can view the Status of the updates, such as *Failed or Needed, Installed/ Not Applicable* or *No Status*. In Figure 3.29, we see a list of some of the updates that are currently *Unapproved* with a status of *Failed or Needed*. Below this you will see the list of the updates that meet these criteria. By highlighting an update you get information such as the *Title* of the update, its *Classification,* the *Installed/Not Applicable* percentage, and whether that update is approved or not. Below this information, you are provided data such as *Computers needing this update*, the *KB article number(s)*, a description of the update, and additional details about it.

Figure 3.29 All Updates Details Pane

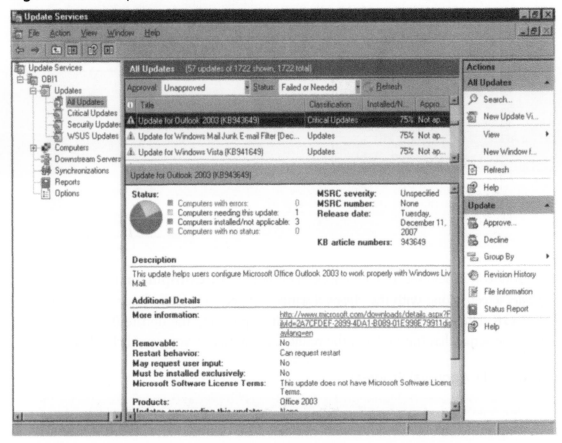

Approve

To approve an update in WSUS 3.0, highlight the update in the Details Pane, and choose **Approve** in the Actions Pane. In our example, we will choose to approve the update you see in the Details Pane from Figure 3.29, which is titled *Update for Outlook 2003 (KB943649)*. Once we click **Approve** in the Actions Pane, we see the *Approve Updates* screen, which allows us to choose the computer group we want to approve the update for. Since we don't currently have any computer groups created, for this instance we will approve the update for **All Computers**. To do this click on the down-arrow button to the left of **All Computers** in the **Computer Group** column and choose **Approved for Install**. You can see this in Figure 3.30.

Figure 3.30 Approve Update to Install

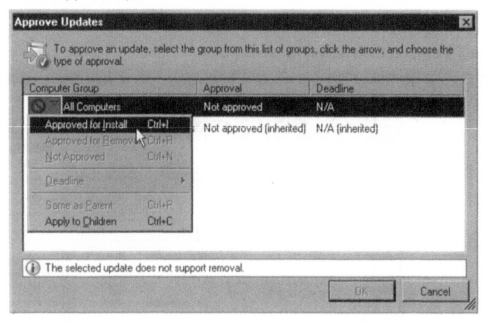

Now you should see a green check mark beside **All Computers** in the *Approve Updates* screen, along with the *Approval* status changed to **Install**. Once you see this, just select **OK**. The Approval Progress is shown after approving the update (Figure 3.31). Once the action has finished and the result reads as *Success*, you can click **Close**.

Figure 3.31 Approval Progress

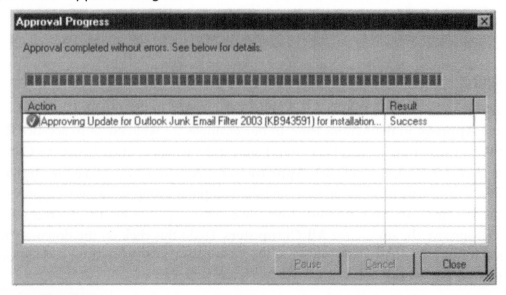

After the approval has been completed you can go back to the Details Pane in the WSUS Update Services MMC and change the *Approval* status to **Approved.** You should then see the newly approved update, as in Figure 3.32. You will probably need to hit the **Refresh** button in the upper right of the Details Pane.

Figure 3.32 Verifying Update Approval

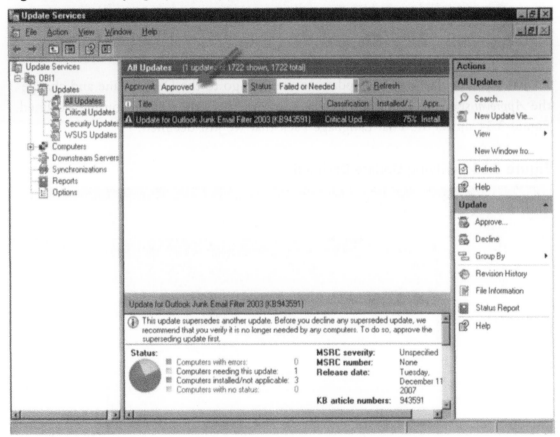

Decline

Declining an update is just as easy as approving one. To decline an update, just highlight the update you wish to decline in the Details Pane and choose **Decline** from the Actions Pane. For our example, we will decline an update titled *Thai Language Pack.* When you decline an update, after clicking the **Decline** button you come to a warning message asking you if you're sure you want to decline the update (Figure 3.33). To decline, just click **Yes.**

Figure 3.33 Declining an Update

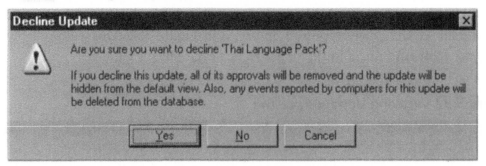

After you've declined the update, to confirm go to the Details Pane and change the *Approval* status to **Declined**, where you should see the update you just declined. Figure 3.34 shows the Thai Language Pack that we just declined.

Figure 3.34 Verifying Update Declined

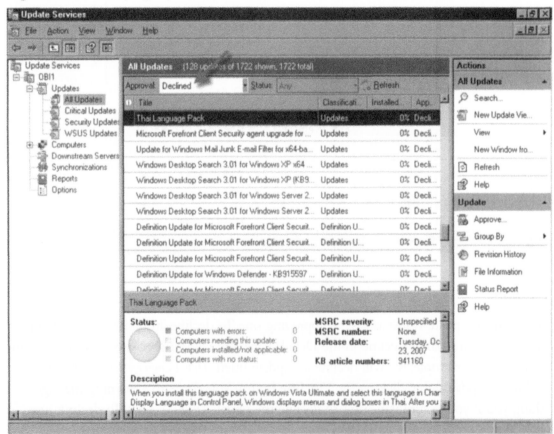

Change an Approval or Decline

Sometimes you may need to change an update's status from approved to declined or vice versa. To change an update from approval to decline, just change the *Approval* status to **Approved**, find and highlight the update whose status you want to change and click **Decline** in the Actions Pane. To change an update from decline to approval, you would do the same thing but change the *Approval* status to **Declined** to find the update, and then in the Actions Pane choose **Approve**.

Revision History

Sometimes there are revisions made to updates, whether it is metadata changes, a new update description or title, or even actual changes to the update files themselves. By highlighting a particular update in the Details Pane, you can then go to the Actions Pane and select **Revision History** to view any changes that have occurred with that particular update.

Reports

Reports from WSUS 3.0 allow administrators to monitor updates, computers, and synchronization results for computers and additional WSUS servers that are managed via your particular WSUS server. With the integration of Microsoft Report Viewer 2005, report performance has increased dramatically over WSUS 2.0. WSUS 3.0 ships with many preconfigured reports that are accessible via the *Reports* node in the Console Tree as you see in Figure 3.35. Reports are broken down into three categories: *Update Reports*, *Computer Reports*, and *Synchronization Reports*.

Figure 3.35 Reports Via Update Services

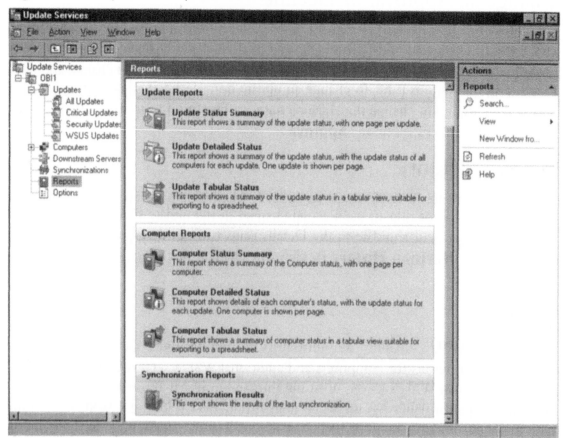

Update Reports

Update reports are available in three formats, depending on an administrator's need: *Update Status Summary*, *Update Detailed Status*, and *Update Tabular Status*. Update Status Summary provides a detailed summary on each update that is specified in the report criteria. While an Update Detailed Status report provides information about the status of all computers for each update, an Update Tabular Status report provides update status for multiple updates. The data is presented in a tabular format. For our example, we will walk through creating an Update Status Summary for critical updates for Exchange Server 2003 that has a status of *Needed, Failed*.

To do this we click on the **Reports** node in the Console Tree pane, then go to the **Details Pane** and select **Update Status Summary** under the Update Reports category. In the Updates Report screen our *New report type* will be **Summary Report**, while the *Include updates in these classifications* will be set for just **Critical Updates**. For the *Include updates for these products* criteria, we will choose **Windows Vista**. Since we don't have any groups configured in our example, we will leave this as default, which is **Any computer group**. Next we will choose **Needed, Failed** for *Include updates that have a status of*. Finally we will leave the *Include status from replica downstream servers* to their default, which is **All replica downstream servers**. Now that our report criteria have been selected, as you see in Figure 3.36, we can run our report.

Figure 3.36 Report Criteria for Update Status Summary

To run the report, just select **Run Report** from the menu at the top. After the report has run, you should see any updates that have a status of *Needed, Failed*. Figure 3.37 shows one of three pages that our report has produced.

Figure 3.37 Update Status Summary Report

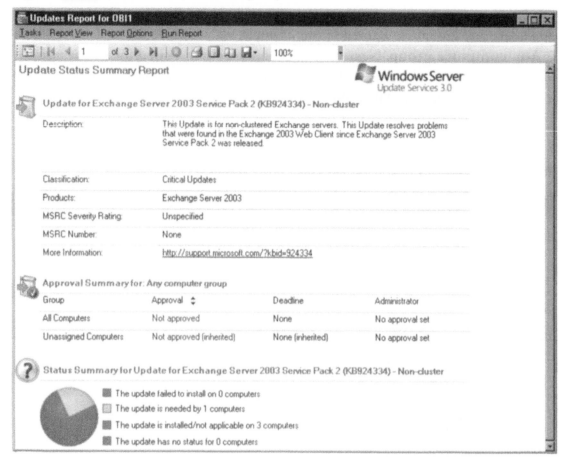

If we decided that we wanted more details about our updates, we could run a *Detailed Report* on the same criteria. The results of that report are shown in Figure 3.38; there doesn't seem to be a difference between the two on first look.

Figure 3.38 Detailed Status Report Page One

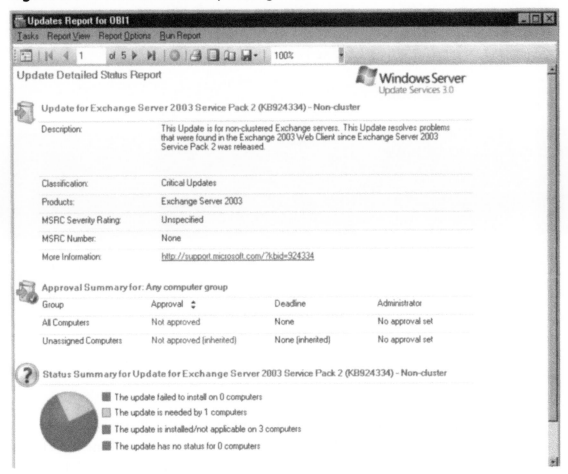

Notice that the number of pages has increased from three to five. Looking at the next page, we will see which computer needs the *Update for Exchange Server 2003 SP2 (KB924334)-Non-cluster*. Looking at Figure 3.39, you see that the computer requiring this update is *jedi.sigr.local*.

Figure 3.39 Update Detailed Status Report Page Two

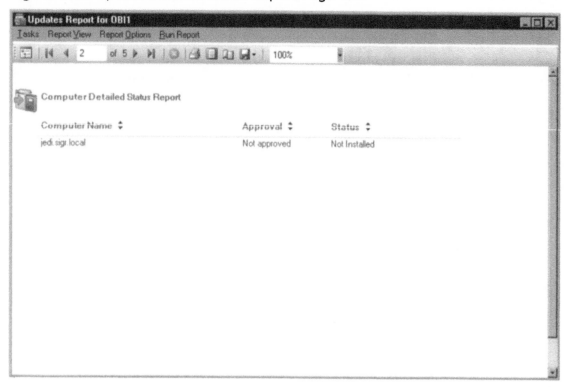

What if we just want a summary of the report but in a friendlier view—say in a tabular layout? Just select **Update Tabular Status** within the Details Pane and choose the same criteria and your report should look something similar to Figure 3.40.

Figure 3.40 Update Tabular Status Report

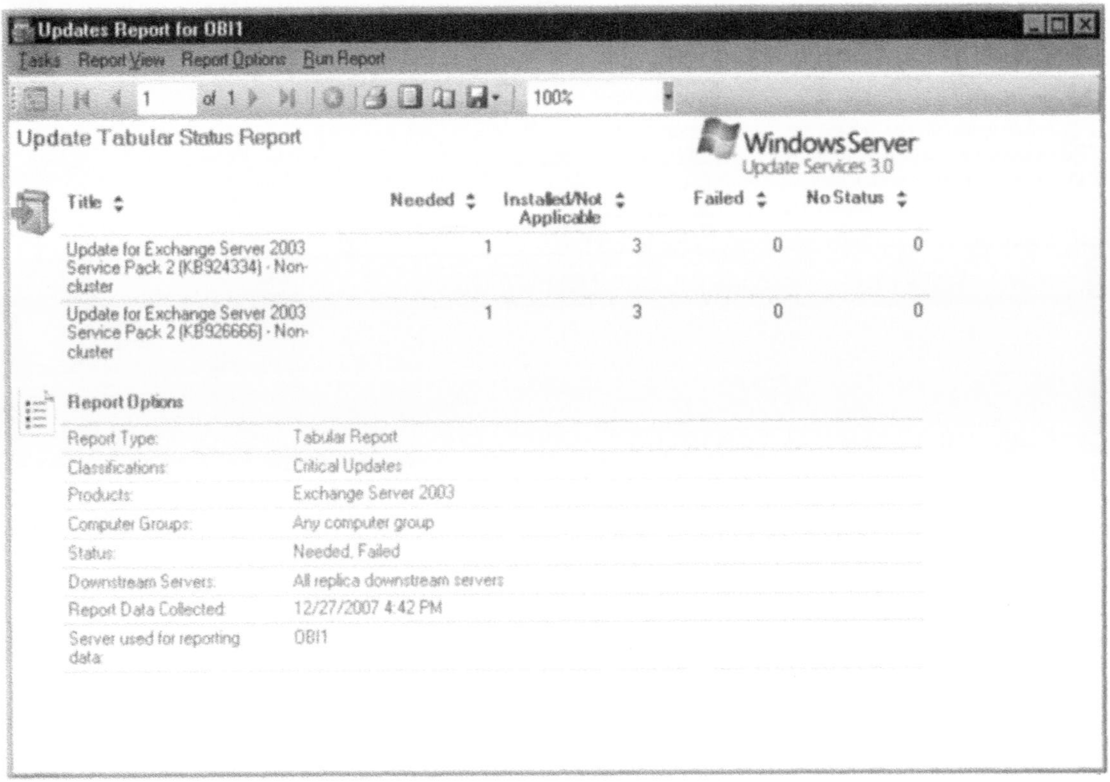

Computer Reports

Computer reports consist of *Computer Status Summary*, *Computer Detailed Status*, and *Computer Tabular Status*. The Computer Status Summary provides a detailed summary of each computer, including computer group information and update installation status. Computer Detailed Status shows a summary of computer status, with the status for each update. Computer Tabular Status provides computer status for multiple computers; this report is shown in a tabular manner. In our example here, we are going to run a Computer Status Summary report for critical updates on systems running Microsoft Office 2003 and 2007 and have either a *Needed* or *Failed* status.

To do this, just click **Reports** in the Console Pane and go to the **Computer Reports** area. Click on **Computer Status Summary** and you are shown a similar screen that you saw when creating update reports earlier. Figure 3.41 shows our report criteria for our Computers Status Summary report.

Figure 3.41 Report Criteria for Computers Status Summary

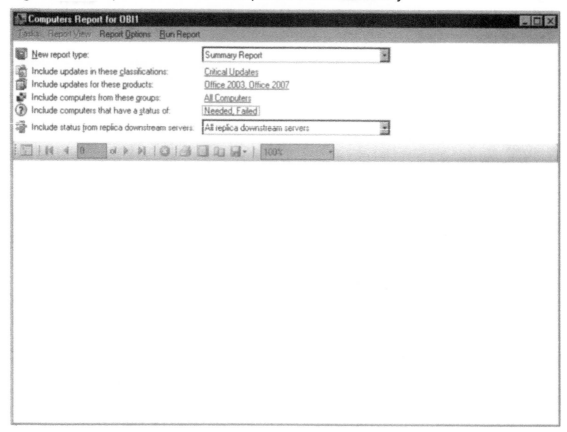

Once you've established your criteria you can click on **Run Report** in the menu at the top. Once the report generation has completed, you will see the *Computer Status Summary Report* as seen in Figure 3.42. Here we are provided information with the name of the system(s) that fall into our criteria and additional information such as: **Operating System, Service Pack, Language, IP Address,** and their **Last Status Reported** date and time.

Figure 3.42 Computers Status Summary Report

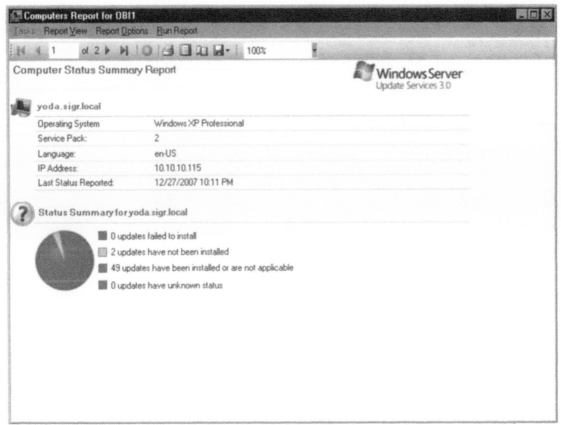

If you decided you wanted a more detailed report, one in which you were provided the actual updates that were missing on this system, you could then choose the **Computer Detailed Status** report. If you needed the summary report to present in a tabular format, you would choose to run the **Computer Tabular Status** report.

Synchronization Reports

Synchronization Results show the results of a WSUS's last synchronization or any synchronization for a given period of time. For our example, we will run a **Synchronization Report** for the dates of December 25 to December 27. To do this, click on **Reports** in the Console Pane and go down to the Synchronization Reports area in the Details Pane. Once here, click on **Synchronization Results** and a screen for the synchronization report for that WSUS server will appear. As you see in Figure 3.43, we have clicked on the radio button beside **Between these dates** and have put a start date of December 26 and an end date of December 27. After this you can go ahead and click on **Run Report** just as you've done with the previous reports.

Figure 3.43 Synchronization Report Criteria

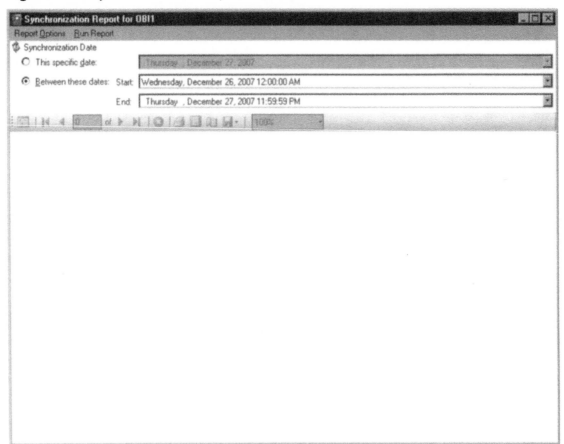

In Figures 3.44 and 3.45, you see our results. You are provided the date and time the synchronizations took place, how many new updates were downloaded, and how many updates had expired. Further down in the report (Figure 3.45), you see a list of the actual new updates and a list of the ones that have expired. As we've shown throughout this chapter, one of the biggest changes to WSUS 3.0 is the use of the Microsoft Report Viewer 2005 and it is possibly the most important, next to the ability to deliver updates to clients.

Figure 3.44 Synchronization Report Results Part 1

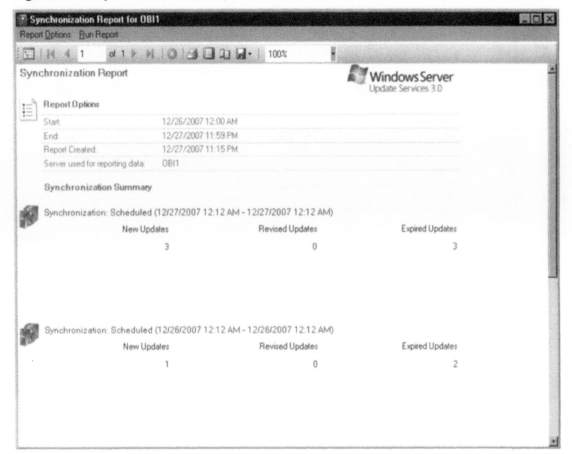

Figure 3.45 Synchronization Report Results Part 2

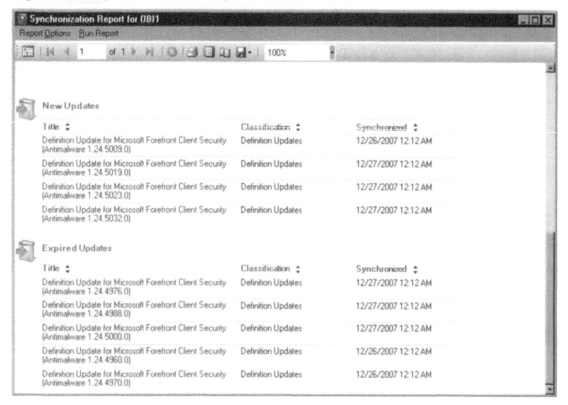

Computers

To manage computers in WSUS 3.0, you must go to the **Computers** node in the Console Tree. Here you will find any computer groups you've set up plus the default group *Unassigned Computers*. Selecting any computer groups in the **Computers** node will display those computers in the Details Pane. If you select a computer from a group, you will see its properties, which will include general details about that system and the status of updates for it. Figure 3.46 shows the details of a computer named Alderon from our test network. You can see that this system runs Windows Vista Ultimate Edition, and you can view its IP address, computer make and model, the processor type, and even the BIOS version. In the status area you see a breakdown of the updates it needs and those that are already installed.

Figure 3.46 Computer Properties

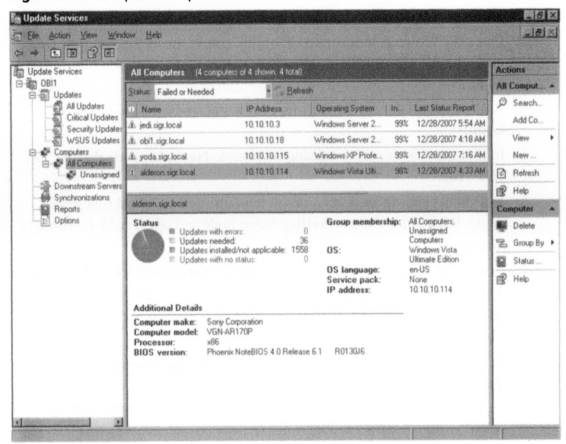

Computer Groups

1. Since WSUS 2.0, administrators have been able to organize their management of updates by targeting specific computers using computer groups. This way an administrator can ensure that specific computers get the right updates and at the most convenient times. We will walk through creating a computer group for our computers that reside in the Marketing Department. What you will notice is something new in WSUS 3.0—nested groups. We will create two nested groups under the Marketing Department. One subgroup will be for Windows XP systems and another for Windows Vista systems.1. Go to the WSUS server or a system with the WSUS Administrative Console.

2. Click **Start | Administrative Tools | Microsoft Windows Server Update Services 3.0**.

3. Once the WSUS Administrative Console comes up, in the Console Tree, go to the **All Computers** node which resides underneath the **Computers** node.

4. Right-click on the **All Computers** node and select **Add Computer Group**

5. In the *Add Computer Group* dialog box beside **Name** type **Marketing** and click **Add**.

6. You should see the Marketing group beneath the *Unassigned Computers* group. Right-click the **Marketing** group node and select **Add Computer Group**.

7. In the *Add Computer Group* dialog box beside **Name** type **Vista Computers**. This will add a sub-group or node underneath the computer group *Marketing*.

8. Back in the Console Tree right-click the **Marketing** group and select **Add Computer Group**.

9. In the *Add Computer Group* dialog box beside **Name** type **XP Computers**. This will add a sub-group or node underneath the *Marketing* node. After creating this you should see our newly created computer group and its nested groups as shown in Figure 3.47.

Figure 3.47 Newly Created Computer Groups

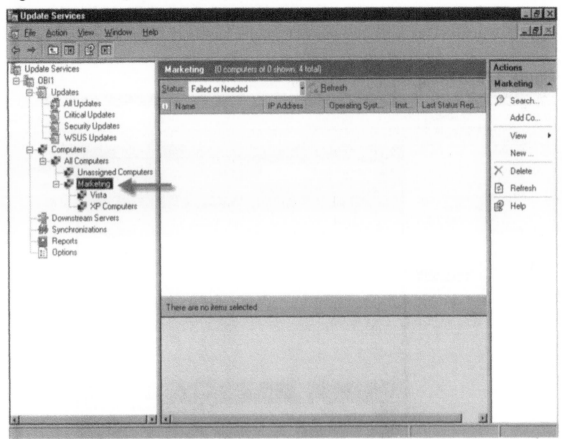

10. Now that our computer groups are created, we need to populate them. Go to the **Unassigned Computers** group and find all the computers running **Windows Vista** that are from the Marketing Department. If you need to you can go to the **Actions Pane** under **Computer** and select **Group By** and group the computers by operating system. In our example, we only have one computer that meets this criterion, but in reality this would be a more populated group.

11. In the **Details Pane**, right-click on the computer that you need to move and select **Change Membership**.

12. You will see the list of groups from *Marketing*. Put a check mark beside **Vista Computers** and press **OK.** Do the same thing for your Windows XP systems that are part of the Marketing Department and put them in the *XP Computers* group.

13.   After moving the computers to their respective groups, you can then go into each group and view the computers that you just moved. Figure 3.48 shows the Windows Vista system we moved from the *Unassigned Computers* top level group.

Figure 3.48 Viewing Computer in Computer Group

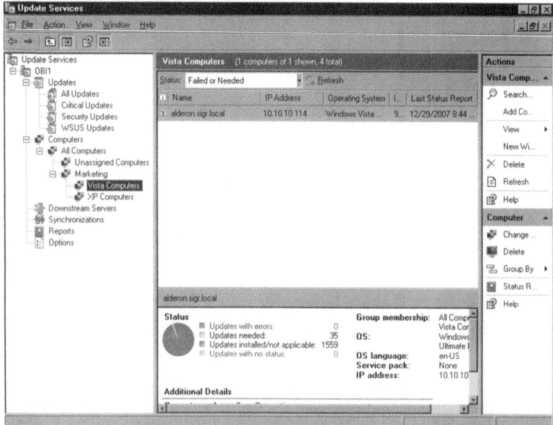

Now that you have created computer groups you'll be able to target updates to those specific groups instead of having them update all systems throughout the network at the same time.

Options

During the installation of WSUS 3.0, you are given the opportunity to provide information about any upstream servers, proxy servers, products you wish to download updates for, the update classifications, and even setup synchronization. You can change these settings after the WSUS configuration wizard is finished. To do this you need to go to **Options** in the WSUS Administrative Console.

In the Console Tree at the bottom you will see the **Options** node. This node allows you to configure settings on your WSUS server. The list of options that can be configured is shown in Table 3.5.

Table 3.5 Available Options in WSUS 3.0

Option	Description
Update Source and Proxy Server	Choose whether the WSUS server synchronizes with Microsoft Update or an upstream WSUS server
Products and Classifications	Specify the products and the types of updates you want
Update Files and Languages	Decide whether to download update files, the location to store them at, and which languages you need to support
Synchronization Schedule	Choose to synchronize manually or set a schedule for daily automatic synchronization
Automatic Approvals	Specify how to automatically approve installation of updates for selected groups and how to approve revisions to existing updates
Computers	Specify how to assign computers to groups
Server Cleanup Wizard	Can be used to free up old computers, updates, and update files from the WSUS server
Reporting Rollup	Choose to have replica downstream servers roll up updates and computer status
E-mail Notifications	WSUS can send e-mail notifications of new updates and status reports
Microsoft Update Improvement Program	Can join the Microsoft Update Improvement Program to improve quality, reliability, and performance of Microsoft software
Personalization	Choose how downstream server rollup data is displayed, which items are shown in the To Do list, and how validation errors are displayed
WSUS Server Configuration Wizard	Configure several of the basic WSUS settings

Figure 3.49 is a view of the Options node and its Details Pane.

Figure 3.49 Options in WSUS

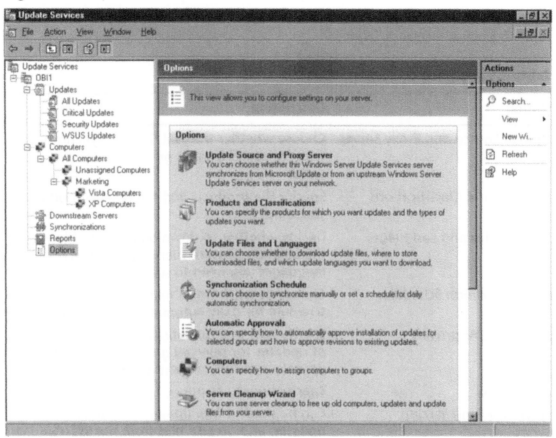

Update Source and Proxy Server

By default, WSUS 3.0 is configured to synchronize and obtain updates from Microsoft Update and to do so without going through a proxy server. If either of these settings need to be modified after installation, simply pull up the WSUS Administrative console and go to **Options | Update Source and Proxy Server**. The *Update Source and Proxy Server* setup screen is shown in Figures 3.50 and 3.51. Figure 3.50 is the **Update Source** tab where administrators can decide where they will obtain downloads. In our example, we will synchronize from Microsoft Update. However, we could change this to synchronize with another WSUS server. If we were to do that we would need to provide that server's name and the port number. We could use Secure Sockets Layer (SSL) to synchronize with an upstream WSUS server by putting a check beside **Use SSL when synchronizing update information**. We can also inform WSUS that this server is a replica of the upstream server. Doing this would prevent anyone independently approving updates on this downstream system. This is a good idea if we have a hierarchy server topology and a centrally located administrative staff.

Figure 3.50 Update Source Tab

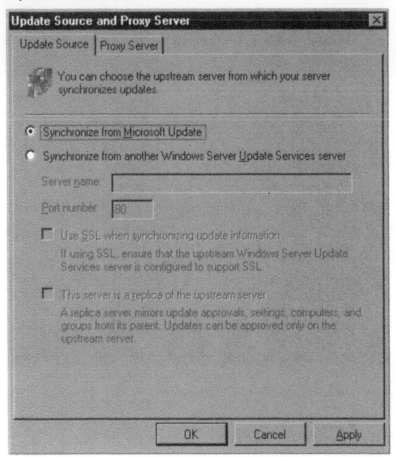

The proxy server settings can be changed by clicking on the **Proxy Server** tab in the *Update Source and Proxy Server* dialog box. In situations where a proxy server has been added since the installation of the WSUS 3.0, you will need to enter the proxy server's name, the port number, and any user credentials that may be required to allow the server to synchronize upstream with the Microsoft Update site.

Figure 3.51 Proxy Server Tab

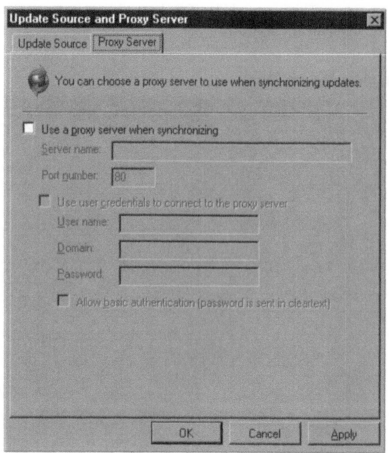

Products and Classifications

Products and classifications allow you to choose and/or modify which products you wish to download updates for. For instance, if you wanted to synchronize updates for all supported versions of Microsoft Office you would first go into **Options | Products and Classifications**. At the **Products** tab, scroll down the list of products and put a check mark in the box beside **Office**, as you see in Figure 3.52. This selects Office versions 2002/XP, 2003, and 2007.

Figure 3.52 Select a Product(s) to Synchronize Updates

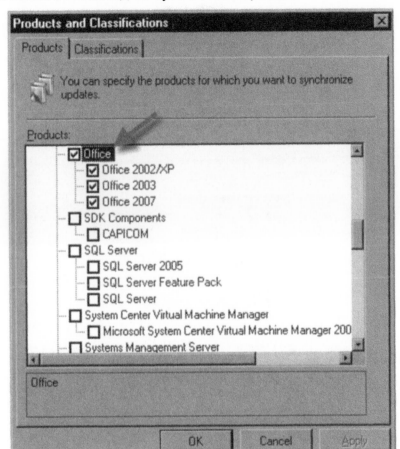

Classifications such as *Critical Updates*, *Definition Updates*, *Drivers*, *Feature Packs*, *Security Updates*, *Service Packs*, *Tools*, *Update Rollups*, and *Updates* can be selected by clicking on the **Classifications** tab and choosing the type(s) you wish to support.

Update Files and Languages

In *Update Files and Languages* an administrator can decide to store update files locally on the WSUS server or not. They can also decide what languages of the updates they need to support. Figure 3.53 shows the option to store updates on the WSUS server itself. If we want to store the update files locally then we would select **Store update files locally on this server**. We then would choose when we needed to download the files. We have the option to **Download update files to this server only when updates are approved**, meaning that we only download what we approve.

Figure 3.53 Update Files Tab

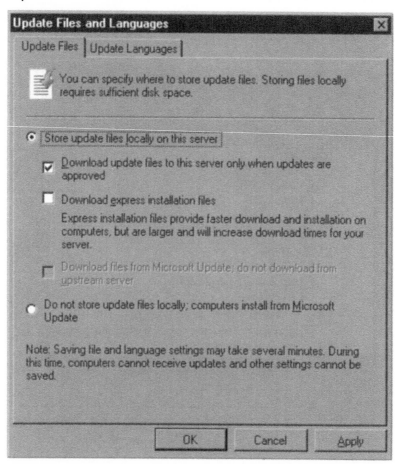

We can alternatively choose to **Download express installation files**. An express installation file is the delta or change between the version of a file that already exists on a system needing updated and the updated file itself. The advantage of this is that you limit the bandwidth consumed on the local network, but at the cost of bandwidth consumption on your Internet connection plus disk space on the server.

So why would this increase the amount of bandwidth used for the Internet connection? The files/updates downloaded must contain all the possible deltas of that file. You could end up doubling or tripling the size of an updates download using express installation files, but you gain on the cost of bandwidth when you install those updates.

Besides deciding whether or not to store updates locally, notice the option grayed out. That option is **Download files from Microsoft Update; do not download**

from upstream server. Since this is the only WSUS server on the network and it is already configured to download updates from the Microsoft Update site, we aren't provided this option. If we were a downstream server and we had permission to do so, we could download directly from Microsoft Update. This does not mean that the particular server would no longer be a downstream server, just that the updates that are approved from the upstream server would be downloaded directly from Microsoft Update.

In the **Update Languages** tab seen in Figure 3.54, you are given the option of downloading updates in all languages, including any new languages supported later, or choosing individual languages that are supported in your environment.

Figure 3.54 Update Languages Tab

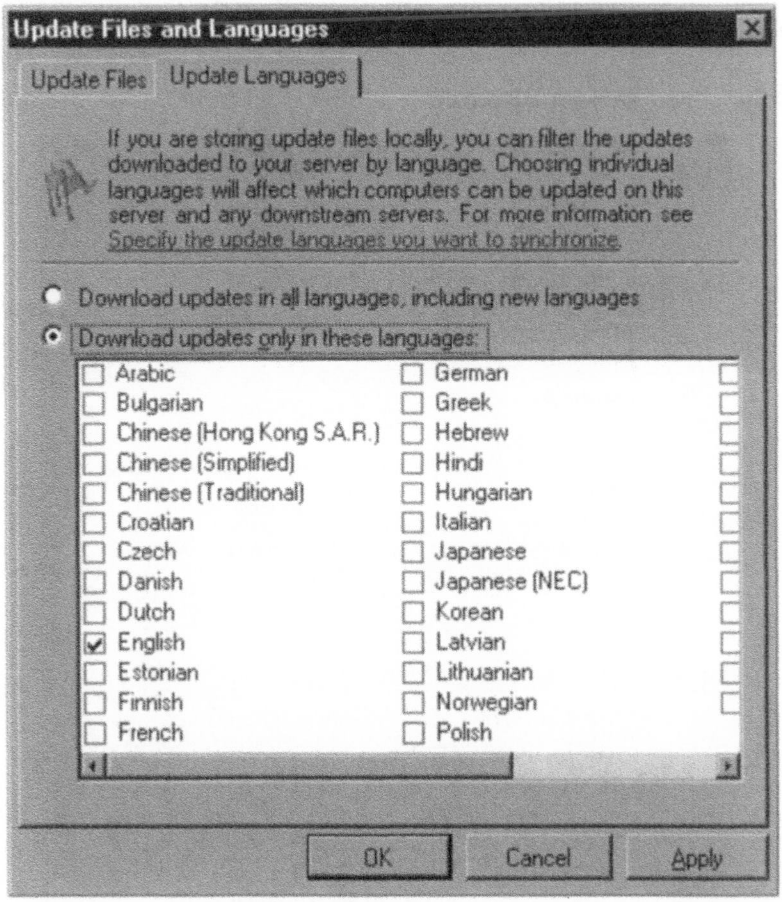

NOTE

As mentioned earlier in this chapter, it is highly recommended to choose **Download updates only in these languages** and select the language(s) used in your environment. Choosing to download updates in all languages will increase the amount of bandwidth used in downloading updates from Microsoft Update, the time needed to download the updates, and the amount of disk space used to store them.

Synchronization Schedule

The **Synchronization Schedule** option allows administrators to choose how they want to synchronize with Microsoft Update or an upstream server, when they want to synchronize, and how often each day. For our example, during setup we chose to **Synchronize automatically** at 12:12 A.M. and do so only once per day (Figure 3.55).

Figure 3.55 Synchronization Schedule

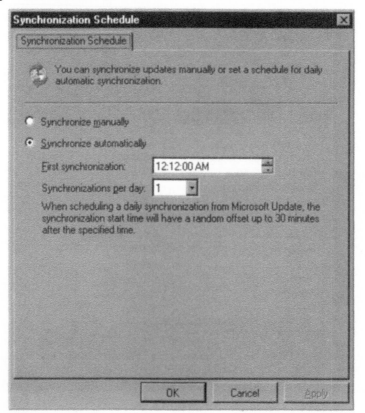

Automatic Approvals

The **Automatic Approvals** option allows an administrator to automatically approve updates to be installed based on product and classification, and gives the ability to target which computers to set the automatic approval(s) for. Automatic approvals are based on rules. For instance, we could create a simple rule to automatically update all computers in the Vista Computers group within the Marketing department for any Windows Vista updates.

1. To create a new rule, first click on **Automatic Approvals**, found in **Options**.

2. In the **Update Rules** tab, select **New Rule**, as shown in Figure 3.56.

Figure 3.56 Create a New Rule

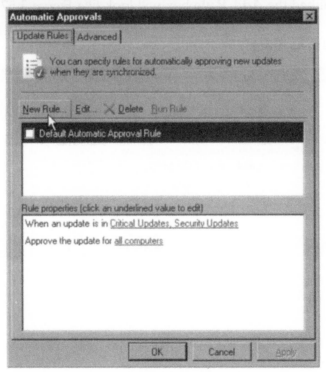

3. There are three steps in the **Add Rule** box. The first step is to select properties. For our example, we chose an update based on product, so we selected **When an update is in a specific product**. We could also specify a certain classification if we wanted to.

4. The second step is to edit the properties or values. Click on the link for **any product** and in the list of products remove the check from **All Products**. Now scroll down to the listing for **Windows** and select all the Windows Vista

selections: **Windows Vista Dynamic Installer, Windows Vista Ultimate Language Packs,** and **Windows Vista**. After doing this, click **OK**.

5. We are now back at the **Add Rule** box. Click the link for **all computers**, found within the line that reads **Approve the update for all computers**.

6. Now you should see the **Choose Computer Groups** list. The groups listed here are those we created earlier in this chapter. For our example we will go down to the **Marketing** group and put a check mark beside the group labeled **Vista Computers.** If any other groups have checks, remove the checks and click **OK**.

7. Back at the **Add Rule** dialog box, go to step three at the bottom and **Specify a name** for our rule; in this case it will be called **Marketing Vista Rule**. Once finished the **Add Rule** box will look like Figure 3.57. Now click **OK**.

Figure 3.57 Add Rule Steps

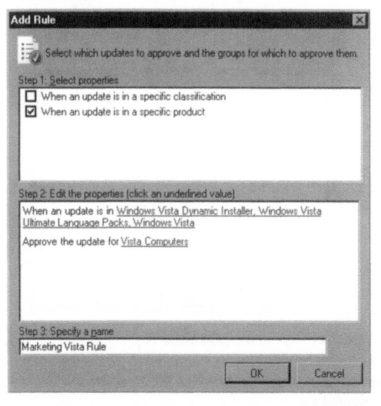

8. Back at the **Automatic Approvals** and **Update Rules** tab shown in Figure 3.58, you will now see the new **Marketing Vista Rule** listed, its rule properties, and a check mark beside it showing that it is enabled. Click **OK**.

Figure 3.58 New Rule Enabled

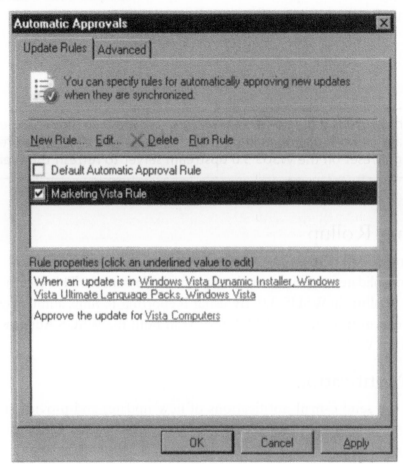

As you probably noticed there is an **Advanced** tab in the **Automatic Approvals** screen. This tab allows administrators to automatically approve updates for WSUS 3.0 itself, automatically approve new revisions of previously approved updates, and decline updates when a new one causes them to expire.

Computers

The **Computers** option allows administrators to specify how computers are assigned to groups. Computers can be added to groups using either **Group Policies (or registry settings)** or via the **Update Services console** but not both.

Server Cleanup Wizard

The **Server Cleanup Wizard** is used to help administrators manage their disk space by removing unused updates and revisions, deleting computers not contacting the server, deleting unneeded update files, declining expired updates, and declining superseded updates.

NOTE

If you have WSUS 2.0 downstream servers, you may see discrepancies in update metadata on both upstream and downstream servers. This can be resolved by running *iisreset* on the WSUS 3.0 upstream server to refresh the Web cache.

Reporting Rollup

In environments where there are multiple WSUS servers, administrators have the option to consolidate status information into a single console. This is done using **Reporting Rollup** in WSUS 3.0. By using Reporting Rollup, administrators can easily view downstream replica WSUS servers in both the WSUS Administrative Console and in WSUS reports themselves.

E-mail Notifications

WSUS 3.0 can send e-mail notifications of new updates and provide status reports to whomever an administrator feels needs this information. To set this up do the following:

1. Create a user account for the WSUS server to use as an e-mail account. For instance, in our example we created a user account with a mailbox in our domain called *WSUS*.

2. Now open the WSUS Administrative Console, go to **Options** in the Console Tree area, then in the Details Pane select **E-mail Notifications**.

3. In the **General** tab of E-mail Notifications, as seen in Figure 3.59, put a check beside **Send e-mail notification when new updates are synchronized** and type the e-mail addresses of the recipients. If you have more than one recipient, separate them by commas.

4. If you are sending status reports to these recipients, put a check beside **Send status reports**. Select the frequency with which each report is sent (**Weekly** or **Daily**) and the time the reports are to be sent, and type in the

names of the recipients. You can also select which language you wish the reports to be sent in.

Figure 3.59 General Tab of E-mail Notifications

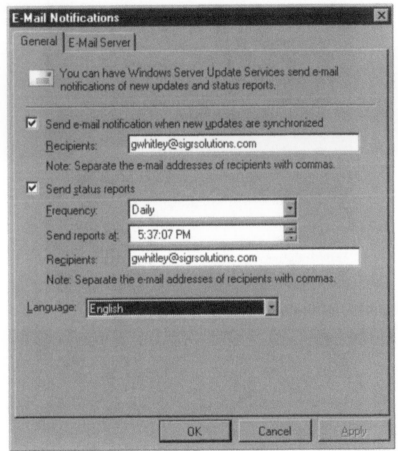

5. Now that the information on the General tab is complete, go to the **E-mail Server** tab and enter the information about the SMTP server, its port number, the sender's name and e-mail address, and the username and password of the user that you created for the WSUS account earlier. Figure 3.60 is an example of an E-mail Server tab with the pertinent information.

6. Once you've entered the correct information, click the **Test** button to verify your settings are correct. If everything looks correct, click **OK** and you're done. Figure 3.61 is an example of an e-mail report using **E-mail Notifications**.

Figure 3.60 E-mail Server Tab

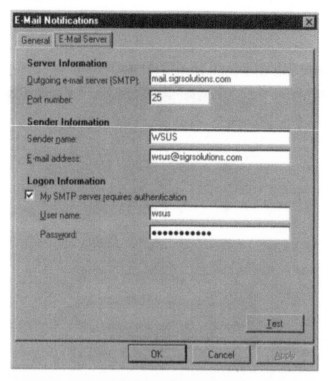

Figure 3.61 E-mail Notifications Example Report

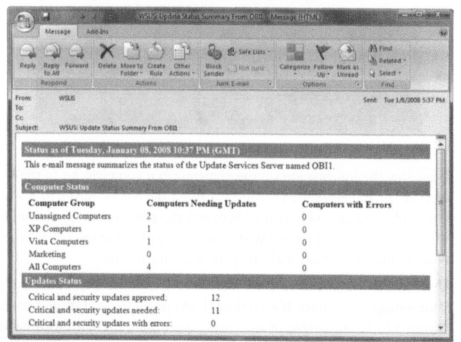

Microsoft Update Improvement Program

The **Microsoft Update Improvement Program** is used to improve the quality and reliability of Microsoft's updates. If you opt in to this program, your WSUS server will send information to Microsoft, such as the number of computers in the organization, number of computers that successfully install each update, and number of computers that fail installation. You are not forced to join. If you decide you want to, click on **Microsoft Update Improvement Program** within **Options**. Once there, check **Yes, I would like to join the Microsoft Update Improvement Program** and you're in.

Personalization

If you want to personalize the way information is displayed for a WSUS server you can do so by clicking on **Personalization** within **Options**. This option allows administrators to choose how server rollup data is displayed, what items will be listed in the To Do list, and how validation errors are displayed. Figure 3.62 shows the option to consolidate information from replica downstream servers to your WSUS 3.0 server.

Figure 3.62 General Tab of Personalization

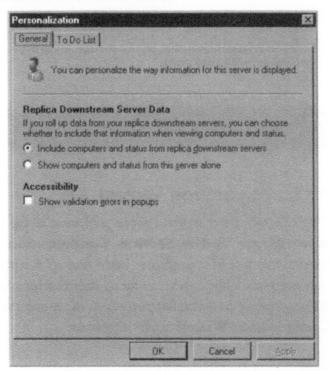

In the **To Do List** tab, you can choose which items will be shown in the To Do list for that server, as seen in Figure 3.63.

Figure 3.63 To Do List Tab of Personalization

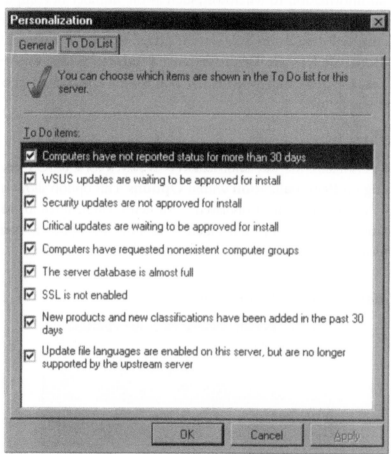

WSUS Server Configuration Wizard

After we installed WSUS 3.0 earlier in this chapter, the next thing we did was run through the **Windows Server Update Services Configuration Wizard**. This wizard allows administrators to easily configure basic settings for upstream server, proxy server settings, supported languages, products, classifications, and synchronization schedule. If for any reason an administrator needs to re-run this wizard, click on **WSUS Server Configuration Wizard** under **Options**.

Troubleshooting WSUS

As you've already seen, WSUS 3.0 has many components and therefore many potential areas for problems to occur. The key to troubleshooting any product such as WSUS is knowing where to begin. Many times this process starts with examining event logs via *Event Viewer* and then checking out Microsoft's Knowledge Base at http://support. microsoft.com, examining news groups on the Internet, and even using Google or Yahoo, to name a few options.

WSUS 3.0 provides even more help than its predecessors. It now includes a new health monitoring service that logs detailed status information to the **Application Event Log** in Windows. The source in event viewer found for WSUS events is **Windows Server Update Services.** This information is very helpful in troubleshooting problems in WSUS. When a problem occurs WSUS immediately writes an event and will continue logging updates until the problem is resolved.

WSUS Health Checks

The WSUS health check service has two cycles: **Detect** and **Refresh**. In the detect cycle, changes in the status of WSUS are logged. An example would be a service that was running and has stopped. The detect cycle will poll WSUS every ten minutes. With the refresh cycle, all warnings and errors are logged. The refresh cycle polls WSUS every six hours, but can be configured using the *wsusutil* tool, located on the WSUS server in the C:\Program Files\ update services\tools directory. The syntax for changing either the detect and/or refresh cycles is *wsusutil.exe HealthMonitoring IntervalsInMinutres <Detect interval> <Refresh interval>*. The WSUS components that are monitored by the two cycles are shown in Table 3.6.

Table 3.6 WSUS Components Monitored by Detect and/or Refresh Cycles

Component	Description
Core	Disk space, permissions, e-mail notifications, catalog and content synchronization
Database	Connectivity and availability
Web Services	Permissions and Web service health
Clients	Clients not reporting, client self-update, update agent, client inventory, client ability to install updates

Group Policy

Group Policies are the easiest way to configure automatic update settings for client systems in an Active Directory environment. We've already talked about how to enable these settings using GPOs. We also introduced you to examining the WindowsUpdate. log file, verifying that the new WSUS server is being used by client systems. One way to verify that the Group Policy is running on a client is by using the Resultant Set of Policy (RSoP). Although this isn't specific to WSUS troubleshooting, it is a place to examine whether the GPO you've created for configuring your update settings is running on your client systems. For this example, we've created a GPO called *Updates* that is set to use the server Obi1 as the WSUS server. Here is how to verify using the Group Policy Management Console (GPMC) and RSoP.

1. Click **Start | Administrative Tools | Group Policy Management**. The Group Policy Management Console will come up.

2. At the bottom of the Console Tree, you will see a node called **Group Policy Results**. Right-click on it and choose **Group Policy Results Wizard**.

3. It will come up to the *Welcome to the Group Policy Results Wizard* screen. Just click **Next**.

4. Now you will come to the *Computer Selection* screen. You have the choice of **This computer** or **Another computer**. In our example, we are choosing **Another computer** and have selected the computer named **Alderon** (Figure 3.64). Now click **Next**.

Figure 3.64 Selecting the Computer for RSoP

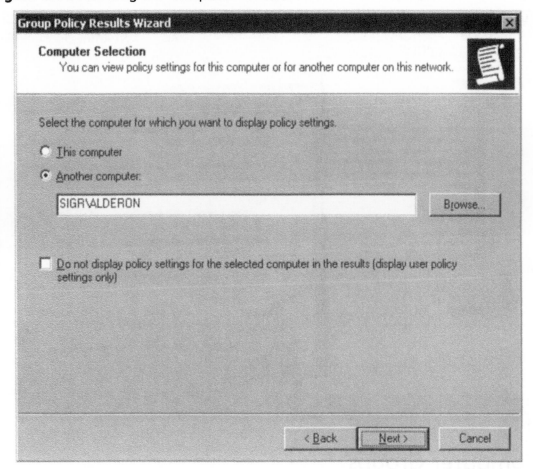

5. Now you can select a specific user or check **Do not display policy settings for the selected computer in the results (display user policy settings only)**. Since we are only interested in whether the Updates GPO has run, we will not select a user.

6. Next the *Summary of Selections* screen comes up, allowing you to review your selections. Once you've verified them, click **Next** and the *Completing the Group Policy Results Wizard* will come up. Click **Finish**.

Now RSoP will run and generate a report for our computer. In the details pane at the right, under **Summary**, click on **Group Policy Objects | Applied GPOs**. You should see the list of applied GPOs. In this case we are looking for the GPO *Updates*. In Figure 3.65, you can see our GPO at the bottom, so it has run.

Figure 3.65 Verifying GPOs via RSoP

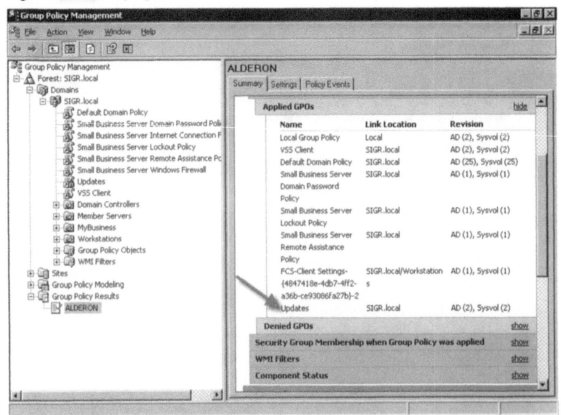

Computer Groups

As we mentioned earlier in this chapter, Computer Groups allows administrators to better manage updates going to specific/targeted machines. There are two distinct ways of assigning computers to groups in conjunction with WSUS. An administrator can do it through the WSUS Administrator's console which is referred to as *server-side targeting*, or by GPOs, referred to as *client-side targeting*.

One common issue is when an administrator has chosen to manage computer group populations via client-side targeting but never sees the changes made in the GPO. As we demonstrated in the last example, whether or not a GPO has executed can be verified by running through RSoP. When an administrator runs through RSoP and verifies that the GPO is being received, they may be confused. With WSUS 3.0, you must specify via the WSUS Administrator's Console that you are using *client-side targeting*. To do this, perform the following steps:

1. On the WSUS server, click **Start | Administrative Tools | Microsoft Windows Server Update Services 3.0**.

2. In the WSUS Administrator's Console, choose **Options** in the Console Tree. In the Details Pane, select **Computers**.

3. You will then come to the Computers screen at the General tab. You are shown on the screen that **You can specify how to assign computers to groups.** The default value is **Use the Update Services console**. To take advantage of client-side targeting, select **Use Group Policy or registry settings on computers**. Once this has been selected, click **OK**.

4. You should then be able to manage the Computer Group populations via Group Policies.

However, sometimes even that will fail. Another thing to check is to make sure that the Computer Group names specified in the GPOs match those on the WSUS console. If not then the modifications that an administrator tries to make to Computer Groups will fail. By making a change to group membership using client-side targeting, you can reset the automatic update client by issuing the command wuauclt.exe /resetauthorization /detectnow. The detection cycle will take about ten minutes to finish.

Although this is not every issue an administrator can run across working with Computer Groups, this is one of the most common and easiest to resolve. As we said earlier in the section, in troubleshooting errors with WSUS, start by examining the Event logs in Event Viewer. Then check the Microsoft Knowledge database, news groups, and engines such as Google or Yahoo. Most likely whatever issue you are working to solve, someone else has already done it and has posted the resolution on the Internet.

Summary

Microsoft's Windows Software Update Services 3.0 builds on the components and services that its predecessors did. WSUS is a free, robust, easy to deploy, and easy to manage patch/update management solution. Before setting up WSUS 3.0, administrators must decide which topology works/fits best with their environment(s). Choices can range from a single-server solution to an NLB failover design. WSUS 3.0 runs on both Windows Server 2003 Service Pack 1 or higher and Windows Server 2008. WSUS 3.0 can run on both 64 and 32-bit architectures. It supports clients such as Windows 2000 Service Pack 4 or higher, Windows XP Service Pack 1 or higher, Windows Server 2003, Windows Vista, and Windows Server 2008. Installation of WSUS 3.0 can be done with an administrator actively running through setup or it can be kicked off in a script making use of the WSUSSetup.exe command. Administrators are given the choices of what Microsoft Products they want updates for, what language packs they support, and what classifications they require. Using Group Policies is the easiest way to configure client systems to use WSUS 3.0. Two of the main settings that have to be enabled are: **Configure Automatic Updates** and **Microsoft Update Service Location**.

WSUS 3.0 does not support a Web-based administrator's interface. The administrator's console uses MMC 3.0 or higher and consists of three panes: a console tree, a details pane, and an action pane. The reporting capability of WSUS has improved performance and the level of detail provided with the support of the Microsoft Report Viewer 2005. As with WSUS 2.0, version 3.0 supports the use of computer groups, allowing administrators to better manage their update environments. One improvement in this area is that now administrators can have nested computer groups, thereby specifying computer groups to even lower levels.

Troubleshooting WSUS should always start off with examining the event logs in Event Viewer. Once the error is confirmed, then further investigation can take place in the knowledge base at http://support.microsoft.com along with checking out Internet news groups and querying Google and Yahoo for additional help. WSUS 3.0 also uses Health Monitoring to better check the health of WSUS servers.

WSUS has continued to grow more and more and become a viable product for companies of many sizes. It has allowed administrators to analyze and test updates before deploying them to the masses. With each version Microsoft creates a friendlier and more powerful product.

Solutions Fast Track

Using Windows Software Update Services

☑ WSUS is a robust, easy to deploy, and easy to maintain patch/update management system

☑ Four WSUS topologies include: single-server, hierarchy server, NLB failover, and roaming client

☑ WSUS 3.0 is supported on Windows Server 2003 SP1 or higher

☑ Clients supported by WSUS 3.0 are: Windows 2000 SP4 or higher, Windows XP SP1 or higher, Windows Server 2003, Windows Vista, and Windows Server 2008

☑ WSUS 3.0 can be installed interactively or through scripts using the WSUSSetup.exe file

☑ Administrators can choose which Microsoft products they want to maintain updates for and the classifications they need

☑ WSUS 3.0 can be set up to synchronize with an upstream server manually or automatically with a scheduled time

☑ Two Group Policy settings for WSUS are: Configure Automatic Updates and Microsoft Update Service Location

☑ TCP 8530 should be used whenever another website on the WSUS server uses TCP 80

☑ To force clients to check for new updates run the command wuauclt.exe /detectnow

Navigating the WSUS Console

☑ WSUS 3.0 administrative console makes use of MMC 3.0 or higher and no longer provides a Web interface

☑ The administrative console consists of a console tree, details pane, and an action pane

- ☑ Approving updates in WSUS 3.0 consists of going to the **Updates** node in the console tree, finding the specific update in the details pane, and clicking **approve** in the actions pane

- ☑ WSUS 3.0 uses the Microsoft Report Viewer 2005, which provides better performance and reporting detail then found in previous versions

- ☑ Three category of reports are: Update, Computer, and Synchronization reports

- ☑ Computer Groups in WSUS allow administrators to better organize their computer systems and how they want to deliver their updates

Troubleshooting WSUS

- ☑ Troubleshooting begins by examining event logs in Event Viewer and then checking external resources such as: Microsoft's Knowledge Base, Internet news groups, Google, and Yahoo

- ☑ Troubleshooting issues with GPOs can be tricky but with tools such as RSoP it becomes easier than ever before

- ☑ Computer Groups can also be an area where problems arise, such as how to manage group populations, especially when administrators make use of client-side targeting. Settings must be adjusted in both the WSUS Administrator's console and in the GPMC

Frequently Asked Questions

Q: What ports does WSUS 3.0 use?

A: In communicating with an upstream server or the Windows Update site, the WSUS server will usually use TCP port 80 or 443. When client systems communicate with the WSUS server, they either use TCP 80 or TCP 8530.

Q: In an environment where laptop users travel from office to office and site to site, what topology would help in guaranteeing these systems get their updates from the nearest WSUS server?

A: Using the roaming client topology will most likely be the best option.

Q: How do you force a WSUS client to look for new updates?

A: While logged on to the client, run the wuauclt.exe /detectnow command.

Q: Does WSUS 3.0 support a Web-based administrative interface like previous versions did?

A: No. It only supports an administrative console that uses MMC 3.0 or higher.

Q: What might be a good way to deploy and test updates on only a few client systems?

A: Create and use Computer Groups from within the WSUS Administrative Console.

Q: Where do you go to reconfigure the synchronization schedule for a WSUS server to either the Windows Update or an upstream WSUS server?

A: In the WSUS Administrative console on that server, go to the Console Tree, click Options, then go to the Details Pane and select Synchronization Schedule.

Q: Why would administrators use Internet news groups to troubleshoot issues with WSUS 3.0?

A: People in news groups can be your best asset in troubleshooting WSUS. Most likely someone there has seen your issue, resolved it, and is willing to share their solution.

Chapter 4

Observing and Maintaining Microsoft Forefront Clients

Solutions in this chapter:

- **Using the Microsoft Forefront Client Security Management Console**

- **Configuring Microsoft Operations Management**

☑ **Summary**

☑ **Solutions Fast Track**

Introduction

The Microsoft Forefront Client Security Management Console will allow a network administrator to effectively manage the Forefront Clients in the Enterprise. Centralized management is key when an organization has hundreds or thousands of computers. The Microsoft Forefront Client Security Management Console allows administrators to deploy a policy to computers within an organizational unit in Active Directory and to print reports on the security status of those computers. Finally, the network administrator can further utilize the Microsoft Operations Manager (MOM), to set up a system of alerting and reporting so the administrator is always kept in the loop.

The Microsoft Forefront Client Security Management Console's robust reporting feature will help administrators to ensure that their clients (and servers) are kept free of viruses, spyware, and malware. The Reporting feature will report critical issues to the network administrator and informs them of events such as malware and vulnerability detections. It is important for a network administrator to be aware of how to effectively use the Forefront suite as well as be able to effectively analyze reports that may indicate what type of threats are present in the network.

Using the Microsoft Forefront Client Security Management Console

A security professional needs to be able to deploy policies that will meet the requirements of the company or agency for whom they work. The Microsoft Forefront Client Security Management Console allows network operators to deploy policies to computers within an Active Directory Infrastructure. The console includes tools for editing, deleting, and troubleshooting these policies. The Client Security Management Console allows the network administrator to effectively manage Microsoft Forefront Clients in an enterprise environment. Let's now discuss some features of the Microsoft Forefront Client Security Management Console.

Dashboard

The Microsoft Forefront Client Security Dashboard is just like the dashboard in your car. By looking at it we can get a lot of very useful information quickly. Of course the difference is that instead of checking your speed and the fuel gauge, it is the first place to look when you need to find out the health and status of the computers in your network. The Dashboard provides a high-level overview indicating the number of computers being managed by Forefront, the percentage of computers that are reporting critical issues, computers reporting no issues, and computers not reporting. Additionally the dashboard provides quick access to more detailed reports and a 14-day history of malware activity. Finally, the Dashboard provides a list of alerts that can be interrogated for more information using the Microsoft Operations Manager console.

The Dashboard also features the ability to launch virus and malware scans on one or all computers with the Forefront Client agent installed by clicking **Scan Now**. This is useful if you suddenly need to scan all computers, for example to contain an outbreak. However, you should be careful using this feature, because scanning computers with Forefront can noticeably reduce the computer's performance. Doing this when users are working can cause disruptions and reduce productivity, so this should be done only when absolutely necessary.

In Figure 4.1, we can see the elements that make up the Dashboard. Notice that in this example there are two managed computers.

Figure 4.1 The Microsoft Forefront Client Security Dashboard

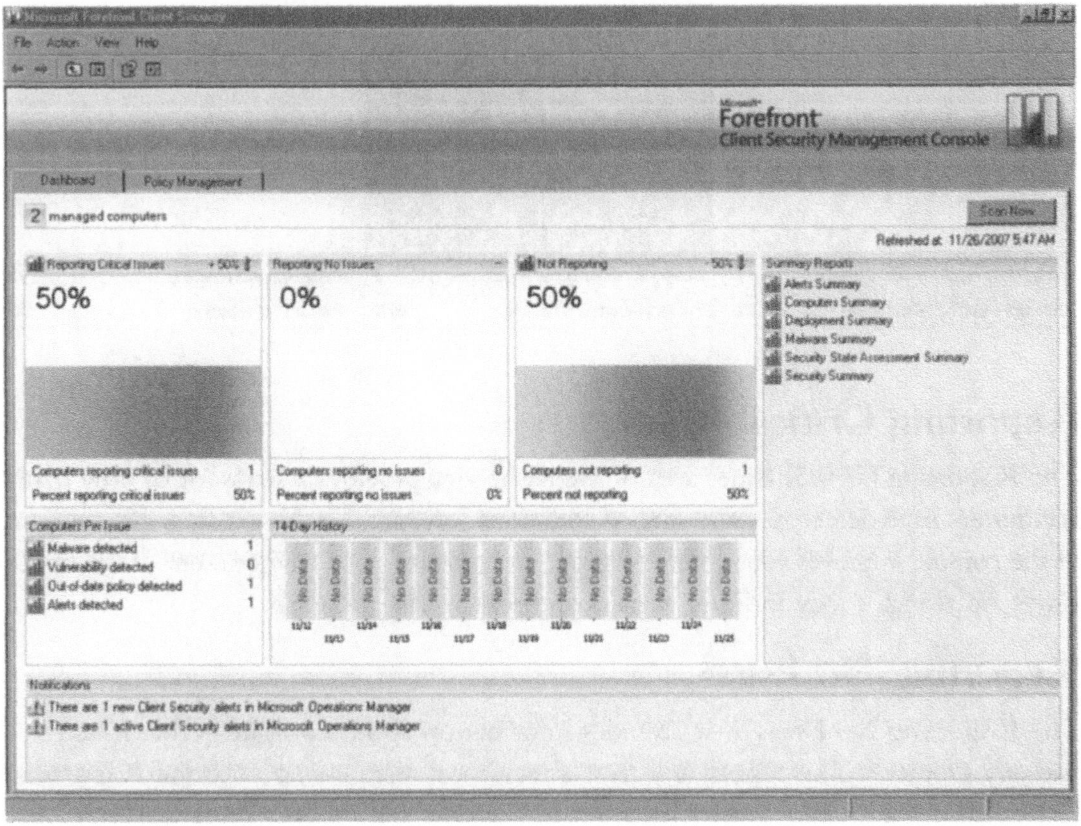

The predominant parts of the Dashboard are the three high-level reports. These reports all work in a similar fashion and provide important information when assessing network health. In the screen shot you can see that the title bar provides information about the percentage of change between 12:00 A.M. the previous night and the moment you opened or refreshed the console. In Figure 4.2, one computer has reported a critical issue. Since there are only three computers being managed, this represents a 33% increase in the number of critical issues. The arrow next to the percentage will indicate if the percent of critical issues has increased using an up arrow or decreased using a down arrow. If there has been no change, it will display a dash.

The main graph also indicates what percentage of computers are currently reporting critical issues, with the bottom of the graphic reporting the number of computers and the total percent reporting critical issues.

Figure 4.2 Reporting Critical Issues

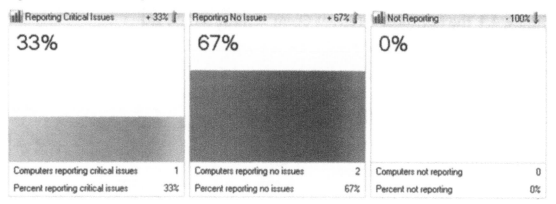

Reporting Critical Issues

The Reporting Critical Issues area of the dashboard provides a snapshot of how many computers have detected some sort of malicious software. Understanding this element of the console improves your ability to gauge the status of your environment. If the critical issues are rising, it may indicate a virus outbreak in the network.

Reporting No Issues

The Reporting No Issues area provides information about computers that haven't had any problems. This report will have a reciprocal relationship with the Reporting Critical Issues area. In a perfect situation this section should be reporting 100%.

Not Reporting

If the Forefront agent is stopped on a computer it won't report. This does not go unnoticed by Microsoft's Forefront Client Security Console. This is the final area of the dashboard that operates in the same way as the first two. It is a good idea to monitor this report as closely as the Critical Issues Report. Investigate any sudden or progressive changes such as a large number of clients that stop reporting, or if you notice that more and more clients stop reporting over a period of time. This behavior may indicate a threat that disables malware scanning agents.

Keep in mind that mobile users may cause this report to increase; make sure you know how many mobile users there are in your organization, and approximately how many will be disconnected from the corporate network at any given time. This should be taken into consideration when analyzing the Not Reporting status.

Computers per Issue

When a computer reports an issue the issue will fall under one of four categories (see Table 4.1). We can query these categories to determine which computers are being affected by the category.

Table 4.1 Categories of Computer Issues

Category	Description
Malware detected	Lists the number of computers that have detected malware.
Vulnerability detected	Lists the number of computers that are missing important patches or may be vulnerable to attack for various reasons.
Out of date policy detected	The Forefront Client Security Policy on the client is older than the one defined on the Forefront server.
Alerts detected	Computers that have had alerts triggered.

We will take a look at policies and alerts in more detail later in this chapter. What is really useful is the ability to launch a more detailed report by clicking on the Issue category. This report will list each computer that is experiencing the issue. You can then choose a specific computer in the report to get extensive details about that computer, including all the possible security issues detected by Forefront.

Summary Reports

Another set of reports that can provide more detailed insight into the state of the network are found under the Summary Reports section on the dashboard. Table 4.2 lists the types of categories about which these reports provide information.

Table 4.2 Summary Reports

Type of Report	Description
Alerts	Provides a summary of alerts that have occurred in the past 24 hours.
Computers	Provides a summary of computers that have experienced issues, such as malware detection, or vulnerability.
Deployment	Provides a summary of policy deployment, along with spyware, virus, anti-malware engine updates. It also reports on the status of the vulnerability detection signatures and engine.
Malware	Provides a summary report of the malware that has been detected on PCs in the past 24 hours.
Security State Assessment	Provides a summary report on the Security State Assessment.
Security	Provides a summary report of the security issues that may be affecting computers in the network.

These reports summarize a lot of information about the status of your network in relation to the malware and to the status of the computers. Each report links further to more detailed reports about each element found in the summarized reports.

Designing & Planning...

Security State Assessment

Before installing Forefront Client Security you will need to determine your Security State Assessment requirements. The security state assessment is based on the policy set forth by the organization on what is considered to be a secure state.

So if we consider a midsized company with 1000 managed computers, the security state assessment might dictate that we shouldn't have more than 10% of computers having issues within given time. This means that if more than 100 computers detect malware or experience some sort of security issue, the network Security State is not in compliance with the stated policy. This policy will naturally be different in each organization. It is important to know before you install and configure Forefront Client Security so you can appropriately gauge whether you are experiencing an outbreak, or if the level of malware activity is normal.

The Security State Assessment is based on what your organization defines as an acceptable level of malware activity and security issues over a defined period of time. There is a service on any computer that is running the Forefront client called the Microsoft Forefront Client Security State Assessment Service. This Service runs periodically to evaluate whether the computer is in a compliant security state. If the computer is found to be in a state that is not compliant with the configured policy it will generate an alert. This information is also stored in the Forefront database. If the Security State Assessment is enabled, the default interval is 12 hours.

Policy Management

The key method for configuring the behavior of Forefront Client Security is through the creation and deployment of policies. Policies can be associated with groups or Organizational Units (OUs); this means that it's easy to associate different policies for different types of users. For instance, you can create a policy that more closely monitors executive computers. This way if even a minor malware issue is detected, the security team knows about it right away. They can respond and make sure that critical data is not at risk.

Policies are based on an Administrative (ADM) template, which modifies registry keys. The ADM template is associated with an OU, or with a security group in Active Directory. Once a template has been applied using a GPO it can be viewed through the normal Group Policy Management Console (GPMC). The configurations apply only at the computer basis, and not to the user configuration.

Policies allow central administration of Forefront managed computers. It allows the administrator to reduce the task of managing thousands of computers to a minimal set of tasks. Configuring the policies is straightforward; defining the policy, however, is not trivial. It is important to understand the requirements of the target environments. Consider elements such as:

- Corporate policy
- User type
- User environment
- Administration model

We'll take a look at how these elements can affect administration as we take a look at Policy management and creation.

Creating a New Policy

Creating a policy is performed in the **Policy Management** tab in the Forefront Client Security console. Once you click **New Policy** you'll be presented with a tabbed configuration dialog. Click through the dialog to set the policy to meet your requirements. The first tab you'll see is the **General** tab; after filling in the name and description of the tab click the **Protection** tab.

Protection Tab

The **Protection** tab allows you to configure what malware protection is turned on, to schedule full scans, and to configure the interval for the Security state assessment (see Figure 4.3).

Figure 4.3 The Protection Tab

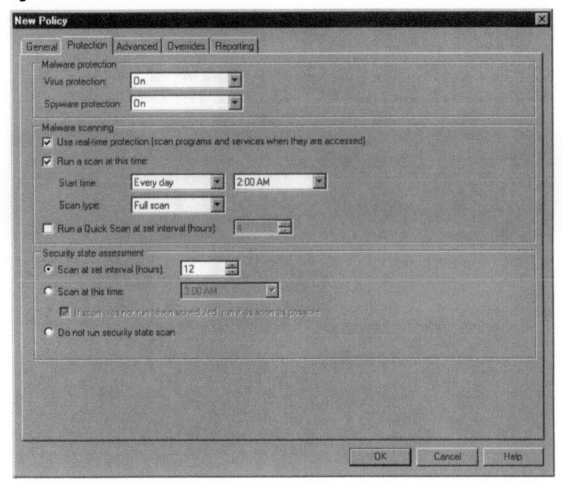

When configuring these options you should consider the clients who will receive this policy. For instance if you configure the client to run a full scan, make sure it is not during peak times. This could impact the performance of the machine and cause users to experience general system slowdown.

Advanced Tab

The **Advanced** tab allows you to configure several important options (see Figure 4.4). The first is Malware definition updates. This allows you to configure when to check for updates. A really important feature in this section is related to whether or not the client is allowed to check Microsoft Update if they cannot connect to WSUS. This is important because if you deploy this policy to mobile clients that often aren't connected in the corporate environment this can make sure the virus and spyware definitions are up to date.

Figure 4.4 The Advanced Tab

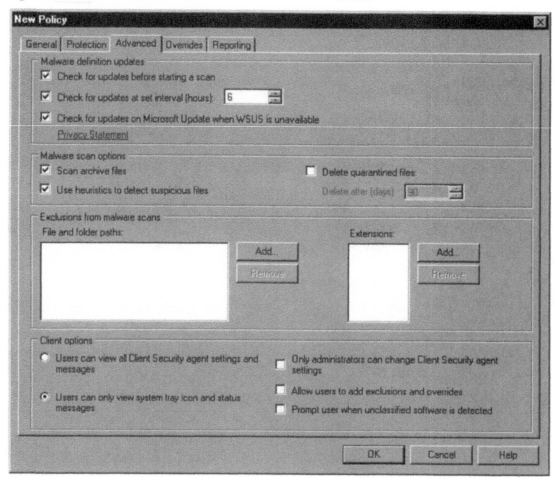

The next section allows you to fine tune several performance options. Scan Archive files will cause the Forefront engine to expand and scan into archives. Using heuristics to detect suspicious files allows for more chance of stopping malicious software. However it may also increase the possibility of a false positive.

The Exclusions from malware scans allows you to define files and folders that should be excluded by the real-time scanner. This is useful if the agent is running on a server or workstation that has another virus scanner built into another software package. You can also indicate extensions that should not be scanned.

Finally, Client Options, one of the most important options to configure, allows the administrator to configure how the end user will see the Forefront Client security client console on their workstation. The administrator can also configure which options the user may configure. Typically administrators will leave the default option, Users can only view system tray icon and status messages. Additionally, in a heavily locked down environment, the Only administrators can change Client Security agent option should be enabled. Because these setting are per policy, we can configure a locked down policy for users in an environment with limited computer access needs, whereas for users requiring more granular control of their environment we can allow the user to control the agent.

Overrides Tab

The **Overrides** tab allows for default configured behaviors to be modified when Forefront detects malicious software (see Figure 4.5). For example if the default behavior for a virus under the category MPSpyTestFile is to quarantine, that could be overridden to Remove. The initial behavior comes from the Forefront malware definition database.

Figure 4.5 The Overrides Tab

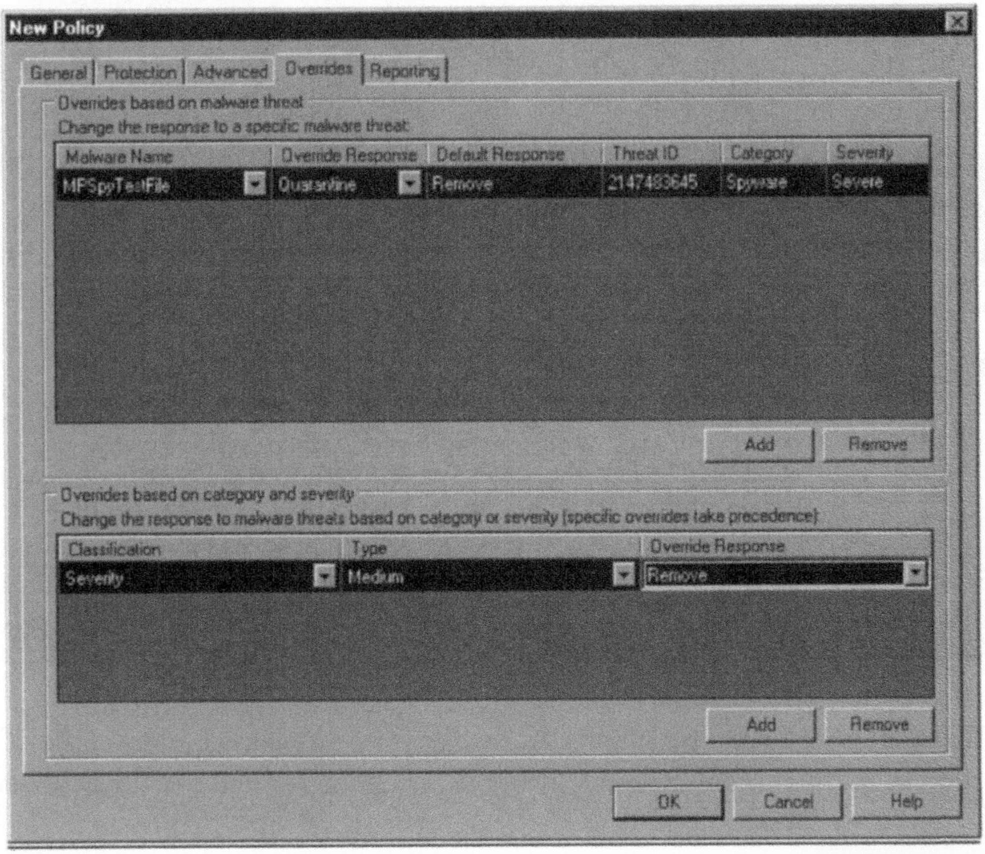

The override can be applied to a category of malware, or it can be applied to a classification and type of malware. This can be useful in some false positive scenarios, in particular when using remote access programs.

Reporting Tab

The **Reporting** tab is where you can configure what Alert level the policy will apply, as well as whether you want to participate in Microsoft's SpyNet (see Figure 4.6).

Figure 4.6 The Reporting Tab

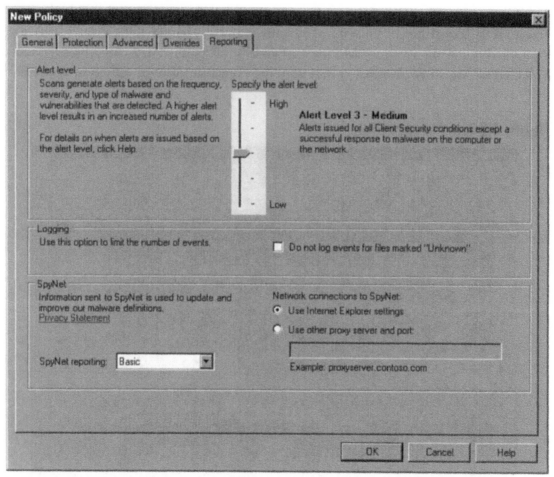

The Alert level for the policy will be configured based on the importance of the computer in question. If the computer is part of critical infrastructure or contains sensitive information, it may be desirable to use the highest Alert level. This will generate a considerable amount more Alerts than, let's say, level 3; however, if the computer detects and removes even one Trojan, we might want to know right away that somehow a Trojan attempted to infect the computer. Some examples of when you would use higher alert levels would be on executive workstations or laptops and critical servers.

SpyNet reporting allows Forefront Client Security to send threat information to Microsoft. This information then is used to track current threats, as well as assess and produce solutions for nondisclosed threats. This does not include any personal data, or information that can be linked to the computer.

Deploying a Policy

Once a policy is created; it needs to be deployed to computers. These computers can be associated to an Organizational Unit in Active Directory, a GPO, or they can be filtered using security groups.

Forefront Policies should be managed through the Forefront Client Security console. When you deploy a policy, Forefront adds unique data to the deployed policy so that it can be tracked and managed using Forefront. You can see this tagged data by opening the Group Policy Configuration Management console and noting the Globally Unique Identifier (GUID) that is attached to the GPO.

Editing a Policy

Editing a policy provides access to the same initial screens as when you create a policy. However in the general screen, information on when it was last edited and by whom, is displayed. Note that after editing a policy it must be redeployed.

Copying a Policy

Copying a Policy allows you to quickly replicate a given policy. You can then edit the properties to change to whom the policy is applied, and fine tune the settings for that policy. Remember each time you copy a policy you'll need to deploy it in order for it to be in effect.

Undeploying a Policy

When you want to stop applying a policy you can undeploy it. This causes the policy not to be associated with a GPO or a group; however it does not get deleted from the Forefront Client Security Console.

Deleting Policies

When a policy is no longer needed, and it is not in use, it can be deleted from the Client Security Console.

Viewing Reports

After a policy has been deployed you can review which clients have applied the policy. This can be accessed through the reporting section of the console. This report is very useful when it is important to keep track of which clients have deployed the policies. If you notice that the policy is not being applied by a workstation it should be investigated.

Viewing Extra Registry Settings in Group Policy Management Console

When you load the Group Policy Management Console, you can see the group policy objects that Forefront configured. The settings in these policies can be viewed by the normal reporting view for the GPMC. Notice that when you view the options you are shown the registry key that each section of the group policy is modifying. If you import the Forefront ADM template into Active Directory, the titles and names of the registry keys will be displayed.

FCSLocalPolicyTool

There will be instances where a computer will require a Forefront policy but the computer does not belong to a domain. Therefore the policy cannot be deployed using a GPO. In this case it is possible to export the policy as a .REG file, and then import the .REG file to the client computer. The client should use the FCSLocalPolicyTool tool to import the .REG file. This ensures that the Forefront client immediately restarts and applies the most up-to-date settings. It's important to note that the domain or OU-based policy will overwrite the local policy. Therefore this method of applying a policy will work only if the computer does not have a GPO being applied to it.

Configuring Microsoft Operations Management

Forefront Client Security (FFCS) comes with a built-in version of Microsoft Operations Manager 2005 (MOM 2005). This is a specialized version of MOM that has been customized to tightly integrate with FFCS. If you have worked with MOM before, a lot of the following elements will be familiar to you.

For those unfamiliar with MOM, you only need to know how to configure a few key areas in order to leverage the MOM with Forefront. First we need to understand a bit about MOM so you know where to find different elements of MOM.

MOM 2005 has two main Windows consoles: the operators console and the administration console. The operations console is where you can view and drill into alerts that have been fired from clients, and the administration console is where you can configure the fine grain details about the alerts. You can also configure notification groups and notification methods from the administration console. The following categories will elaborate on several areas that define the rules and alerts that have been customized to work with MOM.

MOM receives data from computers by an agent sending information to the MOM database. In a normal MOM installation you deploy MOM agents to computers. Microsoft has integrated a MOM agent into the Forefront client that is designed to report back to the Forefront MOM server.

Configuring & Implementing...

Forefront and MOM Agent on the Same Machine

It is very likely that you will end up deploying the Forefront agent on the same computer that already has a MOM agent installed. The Forefront server and agent have been customized so that the agent will report only to the Forefront server's version of MOM. It is possible to monitor the same events as Forefront using a normal MOM agent; however the MOM administrator would have to create a custom MOM management pack in order to do so. The reasoning for having a separate server for malware events is separation of job roles. MOM is concerned with much more than just malware, and typically in large organizations there are resources dedicated to handling malware issues. Normally administrators dealing with Forefront will not be concerned with issues such as memory usage and performance problems. Having all that information on top of the Forefront data can cause important malware alerts to be lost in the stream of normal day-to-day alerts when working with MOM.

To access the MOM administrative console on the computer where Forefront is installed, click **Start | Program Files | Microsoft Operations Manager 2005**, then click **Administrators Console**. Once the console is open, expand the Management packs Node, Expand Microsoft Forefront Client Security, and finally expand Rule Groups.

> **TIP**
>
> A Microsoft Management Pack is a package of Monitors and Alerts that is focused on monitoring a specific service or environment. MOM provides management packs for monitoring Active Directory and Exchange.

Common Rules

Common rules are rules that will be used by all Management packs. In most cases these rules do not need to be modified. The rules will typically provide basic information about the ability of the Forefront/MOM agent to communicate with the MOM server.

Distribution Alerts

Distributions alerts provide information on the status of the Forefront Product in regards to activation and licensing.

Host Alerts

Host alerts are generated by the agents installed on the computers in the network. They correspond to the different alert level in the Alerts tab in policy configuration. By modifying the settings in the host alerts you can change the type of activity that will cause different alert levels to be triggered. For instance, if you want to change the number of malware detections that cause a "Very Infected computer alert" to trigger in alert level 4 you can choose the alert, and change the Event Count Threshold parameter. The default is 5; if we decrease that to 3, the computer will trigger a level 4 alert, indicating that it is Very Infected after three infection events occur.

Host Behaviors

Host behaviors are a series of rules that MOM uses to collect information and maintain collection data on the client. These rules have been preconfigured to help keep the agent software running smoothly. In most normal situations the behaviors that are configured are adequate.

Management Alerts

Management alerts are generated by the Client Security Management Server. These alerts pertain to the health and functioning of the Management Server.

Reporting Alerts

Reporting alerts provide alerts on the status of the Microsoft Reporting services, and Microsoft Windows 2003. If there are any issues such as a problem with the server, activation report alerts will trigger a notification.

Server Alerts

These are alerts generated by the Forefront Client Security server. Note that this is different from Management alerts because server alerts provided notification to many other possible issues, including when the server detects malware.

Server Behavior

As with clients, the Server Behavior rules perform various actions to keep key data up to date, and detect various threats such as a malware flood.

Configuring Notifications

As with a normal MOM installation, you can set up notifications. Notifications allow you to associate an alert with a notification group. The notification group can be configured to be notified using various notification methods.

SQL Reporting Services

SQL reporting services is the foundation for all Forefront reporting. All reports are generated by predefined templates. The majority of the reporting that is necessary with Forefront will be available in the reports that come with Forefront.

Summary

Configuring policies in Forefront is one of the most important jobs for security administrators who manage a Forefront Client Security deployment. Aligning the Forefront policies with the organization's documented policies is a key step in implementing Forefront. Properly configuring policy deployment is also a crucial area of managing Forefront. Special care should be taken whenever a policy is deployed to make sure it complies with standards and best practices for deploying any group policy. Finally, monitoring and reporting on the various malware incidents and tracking computers that comply with the anti-malware policies is a key task that requires constant review. If you don't know whether your computers are protected, you don't have control of your environment. Forefront provides an extensive suite of tools for tracking and reporting the status of your environment.

Solutions Fast Track

Using the Microsoft Forefront Client Security Management Console

☑ The Microsoft Forefront Client Security Management Console is used to track malware and computer status at a glance.

☑ The Microsoft Forefront Client Security Management Console is provides quick access to general reports on the health of the network environment.

☑ The Microsoft Forefront Client Security Management Console is provides quick access to more detailed reports that can be queried further for more concise information.

☑ You can deploy policies through the Forefront Security Console by attaching custom GPOs to an OU or a user group.

☑ You should configure different policies for different groups. Make sure each group's policy reflects their needs. Adjust Alert levels, Malware detection levels, and the frequency that the Security State Analysis runs.

☑ You should use the FCSPolicyTool to deploy policies to workgroup computers.

Configuring Microsoft Operations Management

☑ Forefront Client Security's built-in version of Microsoft Operations Manager 2005 (MOM 2005) enables you to customize Alert levels and responses.

☑ Forefront Client Security's built-in version of MOM also enables you to configure notifications so that various groups can be notified via e-mail.

Chapter 5

Using Forefront to Guard Microsoft Exchange Server

Solutions in this chapter:

- Implementing Microsoft Forefront Server for Exchange

- Configuring Microsoft Forefront Server for Exchange

☑ Summary

☑ Solutions Fast Track

☑ Frequently Asked Questions

Introduction

Microsoft Forefront Server for Exchange (FSE) is a tool that will help companies deal with the threats associated with e-mail service. Microsoft Exchange is used in a large number of businesses for e-mail services. Microsoft FSE was not always so widely used, but its integration with Active Directory (starting with Exchange 2000) made it a more viable product for companies to use. The number of threats written to compromise these systems has increased as more companies implement Microsoft FSE in their infrastructure.

The importance of e-mail to productivity in most companies is the reason that extra security mechanisms, like Microsoft FSE, need to be in place. Attachments and phishing scams pose serious threats to companies. The Microsoft FSE gives companies extra mechanisms to filter attachments and scan for viruses.

The Microsoft FSE server allows network administrators to centrally manage the security of the exchange servers. Administrators using FSE can conduct filtering, scanning, and job scheduling of e-mail-related attachments from a central management console. Reports can give the security professional using FSE indication of what the real problems are and help them to discern from where they are originating. Using FSE can help companies effectively deal with security issues related to e-mail.

Implementing Microsoft Forefront Server for Exchange

When you are implementing FSE you should ensure that you carefully plan your deployment to ensure that the additional load placed on your FSE servers does not negatively impact performance and that you do not inadvertently block legitimate messages.

Due to the filtering abilities of FSE, it is very easy to block legitimate messages. This causes inconvenience for the recipient of the message, but also creates more work for administrators who either have to provide an alternative method of *sending* files to people or retrieve the files from quarantine and forward them to the recipient. Depending on the amount of legitimately blocked attachments, you may have to dedicate significant resources to review and deliver quarantined attachments.

It is common within companies to block executable attachments from being sent and received. This is done to protect the company's infrastructure from programs, which could potentially cause problems, and also prevent potentially dangerous attachments being sent to third parties. While this will help to protect your infrastructure, it can easily cause legitimate messages to be blocked causing inconvenience to the sender and the recipient.

Planning a FSE Deployment

The complexity of your FSE deployment will vary depending on the complexity of your FSE infrastructure and the types of message filtering you want to implement. In order to help with your planning it is recommended that you split this into two components, Antivirus (AV) scanning and message filtering.

When you are planning the deployment of FSE, it is important to understand the FSE infrastructure. It is assumed in the course of this chapter that an FSE 2007 infrastructure is being used.

In FSE 2007, the functionality has been split into five roles:

- **Client Access Server** Allows clients to access FSE.

- **Hub Transport Server** Transports messages between mailbox servers and to edge transport servers.

- **FSE** Stores users mailboxes.

- **FSE** Provides unified messaging capabilities.

- **FSE** Allows messages to be sent and received from external sources.

The first four roles can all be installed on a single server for small deployments. The Edge Transport Server has to be installed on its own server as it usually resides in a perimeter network.

This chapter will refer to different roles when indicating where to install or how to configure FSE. It is assumed that these are installed on separate servers.

Antivirus Scanning

FSE allows you to virus scan messages as they enter and transit through your FSE infrastructure. When they are in the user's mailbox, this is done by deploying FSE on your Edge and Hub Transport roles and on the Mailbox role.

It is recommended that you deploy AV scanning on all of your servers running the FSE. This ensures that messages are virus-scanned providing for a safe FSE infrastructure. You can use up to five AV engines to scan each message and then attempt to clean the message, remove the attachment, or log that a virus was detected, When messages are cleaned or removed, they can be quarantined allowing you to retrieve the files if required. You can specify different AV engines for each of the three Scan Job types—*Transport, Real Time,* and *Manual*—although it is recommended that you keep them the same.

On servers running the edge and hub roles, you can choose to scan internal, incoming, and outgoing messages. It is recommended that you choose to scan all three. This allows you to ensure that no virus-infected messages enter or leave your organization and that internal machines are not sending viruses to your own users. By default, FSE only virus scans a message once, which allows for the best use of resources across your FSE infrastructure. This means that if a message is scanned on an edge role, it will not be re-scanned on the hub role used to relay the message through your organization.

On servers running the mailbox role, you have more control over which messages are virus-scanned. You can perform real time scanning which allows for messages to be scanned as they are accessed. This will, by default, only scan messages that have not been scanned for viruses before. These are usually public folder posts, calendar appointments, and messages in folders like Sent Items, as these messages do not pass through the hub role. While there is an overhead to scanning messages as they are accessed in terms of both resources and a delay to the end user, the impact should be minimal due to the small amount of messages that will be scanned.

You can also configure messages to be background scanned. Background scanning allows you to re-scan messages that have been received or created within the last *x* days by re-scanning. It is likely that new AV definitions will have been released, meaning that any new viruses will be detected. This is the only AV scan that will, by default, re-scan messages that have been previously virus-scanned. Running this scan is a considerable overhead, so you should set it to run in off-peak hours.

The final option is to perform a *manual* scan, which can be scheduled to run at a specific time. This is most commonly used when you first install FSE, to allow you to scan and stamp all existing messages, ensuring that your infrastructure is virus free. AV stamping is used to indicate that a message has already been virus-scanned. This stamp is placed in the message header when it is being routed through the FSE infrastructure. Once the message have been accepted into a users mailbox, the AV stamp is converted into a MAPI property of the message.

For each of the Scan Jobs on the Mailbox Role, you can choose which mailboxes they scan. This can be useful if you have a large number of mailboxes and you want to use the Manual Scan Job to scan these in batches. For the Real Time Scan Job, it is recommended that you scan all mailboxes, which will ensure that your entire infrastructure is protected.

Once a message is detected as containing a virus, the recommended action is to delete the attachment. While you can opt to clean a message, this uses considerable resources and most attachments containing viruses are usually unsolicited. Therefore, there is no point in trying to clean them. Unsolicited messages are also known as spam. These messages usually have a commercial content where the recipient has not requested this information. It is common for these messages to contain misleading attachments that contain viruses.

When you are planning your AV protection, you should ensure that all of your messages are scanned at least once to ensure that they are free from viruses. You should do this not only for incoming messages, but also for outgoing and internal messages. By scanning these messages you are ensuring that you are not sending viruses to other companies and that your entire infrastructure remains virus free.

If you opt to quarantine detected viruses you should ensure that you clean out the quarantine area on a regular basis to prevent the quarantine database from being filled up and that disk space does not run out. You can opt to automatically purge this information after a number of days. It is recommended that you enable this and purge messages after 30 days. The purge setting will also affect messages quarantined due to messages filtering.

Message Filtering

Message Filtering in FSE allows you to filter messages based on attachments, message content, keywords, and who is sending the message. This filtering is in addition to filtering performed by the Exchange Edge role and is performed after the FSE filtering. Therefore, it is likely that a large amount of unsolicited e-mail will have been rejected by this stage.

FSE Message Filtering is a lot more flexible than the filtering offered in Exchange, and allows you to quarantine the messages you filter. This allows you to recover deleted messages and attachments if required, along with being able to create highly complex and customized filters to meet your company's requirements.

It is vital that you plan your filtering correctly, otherwise you could end up filtering messages that you never intended to. The Transport Scan Job allows you to filter messages based on their attachments and the contents of the message body. You can specify senders that you always want to receive e-mails from; these are known as *safe senders*. If you enable filtering on Real Time and Manual Scan Jobs, you can filter messages based on their attachments and against the contents of the Subject and Senders Domain.

It is recommended that you restrict all file filtering to the Transport Scan Job. This way messages are only scanned once before they are submitted for delivery. The reason for this is that if you enable filtering for executable files in the real time scan and a user attempts to send a message with an executable file attached, the message will be modified while it sits in the Drafts folder. This will result in an error when the user tries to send the e-mail. These error messages can cause confusion for the sender and may result in an increased number of calls to your Helpdesk.

By moving the file filtering to the Transport Scan Job, users will be able to send e-mails, but they will be checked during transit. This allows for the message to be filtered and for a notification e-mail to be sent if configured. While this has the same end effect as the message being filtered, the end user has a better experience.

When you configure file filtering you can do this based on extension, type, and file size. This provides you with a large amount of flexibility when configuring the file filters. It is recommended that you filter by file type wherever possible, as this prevents people from changing a file extension to bypass the filter. An example of file filtering will be provided in the configuration section of this chapter.

Once you have planned your file filtering, you will need to plan any other filtering methods you plan to use. If you need to check the body of the message for certain phrases, this can be done using the Transport Scan Job. Also known as *keyword* filtering, this filter provides more control than the content filter in FSE.

When you create a keyword filter you can configure logical operators. Logical operators allow you to specify that multiple words have to be in the message body or that words have to appear multiple times. Using this technique allows you to create complex filters.

The final set of filters you can create are *content* filters. These are available in the Real Time and Manual Scan Jobs and allow you to specify sender domains. This allows you to filter messages from certain e-mail addresses or domains. While you can perform the same functionality using sender filtering on an FSE Edge server, this filter has the added ability to quarantine messages and can be used if you have not deployed an Edge server.

Using the *content* filter you can also filter messages based on their subject. This allows you to filter on common unsolicited e-mail subjects, which may be useful if you are not running an FSE Edge server.

When you start to plan you FSE filtering, you should ensure that you are not duplicating workload if you are using the anti-spam filters on an FSE Edge server. You should not duplicate their work in FSE, as this places an additional work load on your servers. You should ensure that you test your filters before deploying them to make sure they only filter e-mail you want to filter (e.g., if you are only filtering incoming executables and not ones sent between internal recipients).

You should be aware that the more filtering you add, the higher the load on your servers. If you are using real time filtering this will also affect the access time for users when accessing messages.

Designing & Planning…

Exchange Hosted Service

When you are planning the protection for your FSE Infrastructure, you should also review Exchange Hosted Services (EHS). EHS provides a similar service to FSE, but on a hosted basis and only for incoming and outgoing e-mail.

EHS provides the same features as FSE, but does not provide for the pro-active scanning of mailboxes or for the scanning of internal-only messages. By using a hosted solution, you can remove a considerable processing overhead from your own infrastructure.

Many companies use the two systems together, using EHS to remove a large amount of messages with viruses and obvious unsolicited e-mail, and then using FSE to process the remainder of the e-mail which is more likely to be legitimate and also have the added advantage of being able to proactively scan internal e-mails.

Installing Forefront Server for Exchange

When you install FSE you can either install it locally on each machine or by performing a remote install. Remote installs are performed within the Forefront installer. When possible, it is recommended that local installations are performed. This section will take you through performing both a local and a remote installation along with how to install FSE on clustered mailbox servers.

When you install FSE you have the option to perform a full installation. This can be performed on Exchange servers running the Edge Transport, Hub Transport, and Mailbox roles or a Client Installation, which installation allows you to install the Forefront Server Administrator onto administration machines and can only be installed locally.

If you have clustered mailbox servers using either Single Copy Cluster (SCC) or Cluster Continuous Replication (CCR), the installation process will differ slightly to installing on other FSE servers. The process is different for both SCC and CCR clusters. If you are using Local Continuous Replication (LCR), the installation of Forefront Server for Exchange should be the same as a normal install.

If you are using Standby Continuous Replication (SCR), you should not install FSE unless this server becomes active. Once the server is made active, you will then need to configure it as required. Fortunately, to speed up the configuration, you can use configuration templates.

When performing a local installation you should be logged into the machine as a user that has administrative rights on the machine. As part of the installation, you may be required to restart some of the FSE services; therefore, it is recommended that installation is performed during off-peak hours.

To perform a local install:

1. Run the FSE Installer.
2. Click **Next**.
3. Accept the **License Agreement**.
4. Enter **User Name** and **Company Name** and click **Next**.
5. Select **Local Installation** and click **Next**.
6. For a full installation, select **Full Installation** and click **Next**.
7. Select **Secure Mode** or **Compatible Mode** and click **Next**. When you select Secure Mode, AV scan and filter messages are forwarded from quarantine. When you select Compatible Mode, AV scan messages are forwarded from quarantine.
8. Select up to four AV engines (see Figure 5.1) and click **Next**.
9. Click **Next**.
10. If you need to use a Proxy Server for updates, enter **Address** and **Port** and click **Next**. (If you need to use a username and password you can specify this under General Options once FSE is installed.)
11. Choose the **Installation Location** and click **Next**.
12. Choose the **Programs Folder** and click **Next**.
13. Review the **Installation Options** and click **Next**.

14. You may be asked if you want to restart Exchange Transport Service. If you want to restart this now click **Next**; if you want to restart this later click **Skip**.

15. If you choose to restart the service, click **Next** once the service has restarted.

16. You may be asked if you want to restart FSE Information Store. If you want to restart this now click **Next**; if you want to restart this later click **Skip**.

17. If you choose to restart the service, click **Next** once the service has restarted.

18. Click **Finish**.

19. For a Client installation **Select Client – Admin** console only and click **Next**.

20. Choose the **Installation Location** and click **Next**.

21. Choose the **Programs Folder** and click **Next**.

22. Review the **Installation Options** and click **Next**.

23. Click **Finish**.

Figure 5.1 Selecting the AV Engines

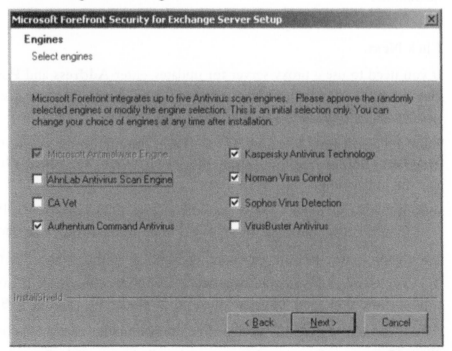

When performing a remote installation, the destination machine and the machine that you are to perform the install from need to be in the same domain. You should be logged in as an administrator of the remote machine. File sharing also needs to be enabled on the remote machine in order to allow for installation files to be copied over. The installation may also require you to restart some of the FSE services; therefore it is recommended that the installation is performed during off-peak hours.

To perform a remote install:

1. Run the FSE Installer.

2. Click **Next**.

3. Accept the **License Agreement**.

4. Enter **User Name** and **Company Name** and click **Next**.

5. Select **Remote Installation** and click **Next**.

6. Enter the **Server Name** and **Share Name** (see Figure 5.2).

7. Select **Secure Mode** or **Compatible Mode** and click **Next**. When you select Secure Mode, AV Scan and Filter messages are forwarded from quarantine. When you select Compatible Mode, AV Scan messages are forwarded from quarantine.

8. Select up to four AV engines and click **Next**.

9. Click **Next**.

10. If you need to use a proxy server for updates, enter **Address** and **Port** and click **Next**. If you need to use a username and password you can specify this under General Options once FSE is installed.

11. Enter the Installation Location into the Destination Directory field, enter the **Programs Folder** into the **Folder Name** filed, and click **Next**. This will start the installation.

12. You may be asked if you want to restart Exchange Transport Service. If you want to restart this now click **Next**; if you want to restart this later click **Skip**.

13. If you choose to restart the service, click **Next** once the service has restarted.

14. You may be asked if you want to restart FSE Information Store. If you want to restart this now click **Next**; if you want to restart this later click **Skip**.

15. If you choose to restart the service click **Next** once the service has restarted.

16. Click **Next** to perform another remote installation or click **Cancel** to exit.

Figure 5.2 Specifying Remote Server and Path

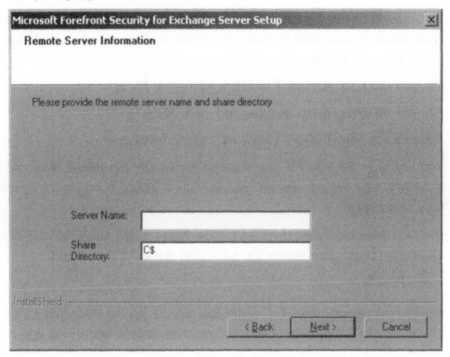

To install FSE on a CCR mailbox cluster you will need to install the FSE on to the Active node first and then, once the installation is complete, you will need to install FSE on to the Passive node. Each installation should be done locally.

To install FSE on a CCR node:

1. Run the FSE Installer.

2. Click **Next**.

3. Accept the **License Agreement**.

4. Enter **User Name** and **Company Name** and click **Next**.

5. Select **Local Installation** and click **Next**.

6. Select **Full Installation** and click **Next**.

7. Select **Secure Mode** or **Compatible Mode** and click **Next**. When you select Secure Mode, AV scan and filter messages are forwarded from quarantine. When you select Compatible Mode, AV scan messages are forwarded from quarantine.

8. Select up to four AV engines and click **Next**.

9. Click **Next**.

10. If you need to use a proxy server for updates, enter **Address** and **Port** and click **Next**. If you need to use a username and password, you can specify this under General Options once FSE is installed.

11. Choose the **Installation Location** and click **Next**.

12. Choose the **Programs Folder** and click **Next**.

13. Review the **Installation Options** and click **Next**.

14. You will now be asked if you want to restart the Clustered Mailbox Server (CMS). If you want to restart this now click **Next**; if you want to restart this later click **Skip**

15. If you choose to restart the CMS, click **Next** when the CMS has stopped, and click **Next** again when the CMS has started. Click **Next**.

16. Click **Finish**.

You should now perform the same procedure on the passive node. You should ensure that the CMS has not failed over. Any configuration information you enter such as proxy server, details will be overwritten with the configuration from the Active node.

To install FSE on a SCC Mailbox cluster you will need to install the FSE on to the active node first, and then once the installation is complete you will need to install FSE on to the passive node. Each installation should be done locally.

To install FSE on a SCC node:

1. Run the FSE Installer.

2. Click **Next**.

3. Accept the **License Agreement**.

4. Enter **User Name** and **Company Name** and click **Next**.

5. Select **Local Installation** and click **Next**.

6. Select **Full Installation** and click **Next**.

7. Select the **Cluster Drive** from the **Shared Cluster Volume List**, enter a Cluster Folder, and click **Next**.

8. Select **Secure Mode** or **Compatible Mode** and click **Next**. When you select Secure Mode, AV scan and filter messages are forwarded from quarantine. When you select Compatible Mode, AV scan messages are forwarded from quarantine.

9. Select up to four AV engines and click **Next**.

10. Click **Next**.

11. If you need to use a proxy server for updates, enter **Address** and **Port** and click **Next**. If you need to use a username and password, you can specify this under General Options once FSE is installed.

12. Choose the **Installation Location** and click **Next**.

13. Choose the **Programs Folder** and click **Next**.

14. Review the **Installation Options** and click **Next**.

15. You will now be asked if you want to restart the CMS. If you want to restart this now click **Next**; if you want to restart this later click **Skip**.

16. If you choose to restart the CMS, click **Next** when the CMS has stopped and click **Next** when the CMS has started. Click **Next**.

17. Click **Finish**.

NOTE

When you are installing Forefront Server for Exchange on a SCC, you are required to select the Cluster Drive, which is the shared volume used by the Cluster Service. If the drive you require is not listed, you will need to exit the installer and re-run it specifying the following. It is assumed the drive letter is S:

forefront_setup_file.exe /c S:

You should now be able to select the drive from the **Shared Cluster Volume** List.

You should now perform a standard local installation on the passive node. You should also ensure that the CMS has not failed over. Any configuration information you enter during the passive installation such as proxy server details, will be overwritten with the configuration from the active node.

Configuring Microsoft Forefront Server for Exchange

Once you have installed FSE, you will need to configure the various settings to ensure that messages are processed as required for your business.

There are two ways to configure FSE. The first option is to use the Forefront Server Security Administrator (FSA), which allows you to configure each server running FSE on an individual basis using the tool locally or remotely. The other option is to use Forefront Server Security Management Console (FSSMC), which allows for Forefront servers to be centrally administered (The Management Console is an additional product and is not included with FSE). For this reason, this section will focus on the FSA as the method used to configure FSE.

While the configuration information is stored in a number of different locations, the majority of the information is stored in a series of FDB files, which are located in the FSE installation directory. This information can also be stored in templates to allow for settings to be copied across servers. The remainder of the information is stored in the registry. This information is usually server specific, and the majority of the settings can be modified through the FSA.

When you are running clustered mailbox servers you should ensure you connect FSA to the Exchange Virtual Machine. The one exception to this is if you need to release quarantined files from a passive node. In that case, you should connect FSA directly to the passive node. All configuration information is replicated between the active and passive nodes ensuring that if a failover occurs the configuration information is available.

Settings

The Settings section allows you to configure the AV scanning options and server configuration for FSE along with the ability to create new configuration templates. Throughout this section there will be up to three available Scan Jobs for which you can modify settings. The Scan Jobs available are dependent on the Exchange Roles installed on the server.

If the server is running the Edge Transport or Hub Transport role, the Transport Scan Job will be available. If the server is running the Mailbox Role, the Real Time Scan Job and Manual Scan Job will be available. If you add roles to the server, you will need to re-run the FSE installer for the relevant Scan Jobs to be made available. Scan jobs are automatically removed if you install a role.

Scan Job

The Scan Job section allows you to configure which messages and mailboxes will be processed by the jobs (see Figure 5.3).

Figure 5.3 Scan Jobs

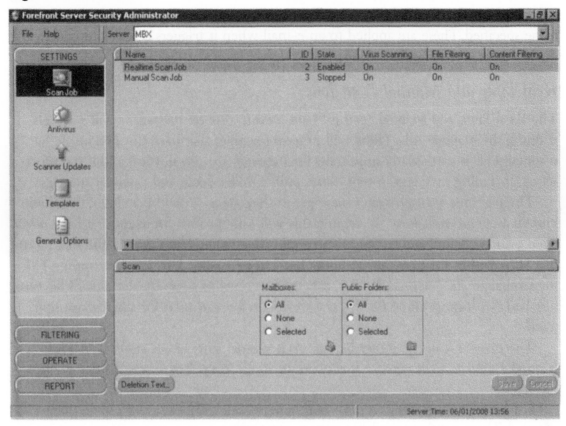

For each of the Scan Jobs, you can specify the deletion text that is used when an attachment is removed and replaced with a text file containing the specified text. To allow for e-mail-specific information to be entered, there are a number of keyword substitution macros available.

Keyword substitution macros can be inserted by right-clicking in the Edit Text field and selecting **Paste Keyword**, and then selecting the Macro to insert.

Transport Scan Job

The Transport Scan Job is used to process messages on servers running the Edge or Hub Transport Roles. This can be configured to process inbound, outbound and/or internal e-mail. The option to scan internal messages is available on servers running the Edge role, even though Internal mail should not reach the Edge.

The other configurable option is the *tag text,* which is used when keyword filtering is enabled for the Scan Job. Tag text allows for a subject line text and header tag text to be specified. These are applied to an e-mail when it triggers a keyword match, and the action is set to tag the message.

Real Time and Manual Scan Jobs

The Real Time and Manual Scan Jobs are used to process messages on the servers running the mailbox role. These will process messages that have not previously be scanned. This is particularly important for messages that do not use a hub transport server, including messages in sent items, public folder posts, and calendar messages.

The real time scan processes messages as they are accessed by a client; this is also known as an *on access* scan. By default, this will only process messages that have never been scanned before and are within a certain time range. This range in the first release of FSE is within the previous 24 hours but can be changed. If you are running FSE for Exchange 2007 Service Pack 1, this value is fixed to be every day since FSE was installed. Settings specified for the real time scan are also used for the background scans.

The manual scan can either be run on a manual basis or on a schedule. This is usually used to scan specific mailboxes or to clean up a mail server after a virus outbreak.

For both of these scans you can configure which mailboxes and public folders are scanned. There are three available options for each:

- **All** Scans all current and future mailboxes or public folders
- **None** Does not scan any mailboxes or public folders
- **Selected** Scans only the selected mailboxes or public folders

If you select *Selected* you will need to select which mailboxes or public folders to scan:

1. Select **Selected**.
2. Click on the **Mailbox** or **Public Folder** icon.
3. Check the mailboxes or public folders you want to scan; you can select an entire *store*. If you select a store, then only current mailboxes will be included. Any new mailboxes will need to be added as required. (See Figure 5.4.)
4. Click on the **Back Arrow** to exit the Selection List.
5. Click **OK** to save the changes.

Figure 5.4 Selecting Mailboxes

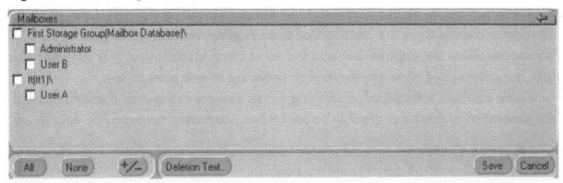

It is recommended that you leave the real time scan set to "All" as this will ensure that messages that have not been scanned are scanned to ensure they do not contain viruses.

Antivirus

The AV section allows you to configure which AV engines are used when scanning messages, how many engines need to be used for each message, and the action to take if a virus is detected (see Figure 5.5).

Figure 5.5 Antivirus Settings

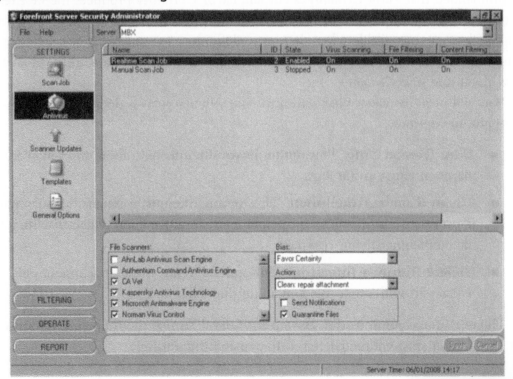

For each Scan Job, you can specify up to five AV engines to use. However, one of these engines has to be the *Microsoft Antimalware Engine*. You can select any of the four other engines from the list. Each of these engines are licensed as part of the FSE licenses, so select the engines that you feel most comfortable using. It is advisable that you research each of these engines before choosing which ones to use.

Once you have selected which AV engines to use you can specify the *bias*, which is the number of engines that need to be used when scanning a message. The options are:

- **Max Certainty** Use all selected engines. If an engine is not available, queue e-mail until all the engines are available.

- **Favor Certainty** Use all selected engines. If an engine is not available, continue to process e-mail with available engines.

- **Neutral** Scan each e-mail with at least half of the selected engines.

- **Favor Performance** Scan each message with between one and one-half of the available engines.

- **Max Performance** Scan each message with one engine.

The choice you make depends on your environment and requirements, but it is recommended that *Favor Certainty* is chosen. Favor Certainty produces the best results in terms of virus detection and also keeps e-mail flowing if an engine becomes unavailable. Engines become unavailable when their virus definitions are updated. Since each engine can be updated several times a day, this could cause significant interruption to e-mail flow if you use *Max Certainty*.

You will need to select what action to take when a virus is detected. There are three possible options:

- **Skip: Detect Only** This option leaves the infected file in the e-mail and places an entry in the logs.

- **Clean: Repair Attachment** This option attempts to repair the attachment. If a repair is not possible, the attachment is removed and replaced with a text file containing the *deletion text*.

- **Delete: Remove Infection** This options removes the attachment and replaces it with a text file containing the deletion text.

There is an exception to the above if in *General Settings* the following options are set. The attachments will be deleted if they match the setting:

- Delete Corrupted Compressed Files

- Delete Corrupted Uuencoded Files

- Delete Encrypted Compressed Files

The final two options are to *Send Notifications* and to *Quarantine Files*. The Send Notifications option allows for notification e-mails to be sent if a virus is detected. These e-mails are configurable and will be covered later in this section. The Quarantine Files option allows you to specify if attachments are quarantined when a virus is detected; this will occur no matter what you set the Action to be.

Scanner Updates

The Scanner Updates section allows you to configure the update source for the AV engines and how often they are updated. By default, all of the engines are updated on an hourly basis at 5-minute intervals of each other; this includes engines that are currently not being used.

For each of the engines, you can specify a primary and secondary update location. This can either be left at the default (which is the Microsoft Update Web site) or can be changed to point to an internal distribution server. Any FSE server can be set to be a redistribution server (covered later in this section). Alternatively, FSSMC can be used to distribute updates.

The choice of where to download updates from depends on your requirements. If your servers are able to access the Internet either directly or through a proxy server, then you may wish to leave the update location to be the Microsoft Update Web site.

To configure a Proxy Server:

1. Select **Settings** followed by **General Options**.

2. Check **Use Proxy Settings**.

3. Under **Proxy Server Name/IP Address** enter your **Proxy Server Name** or **IP Address**.

4. Under **Proxy Username** enter an **Account Username**, if required.

5. Under **Proxy Password** enter an **Account Password**, if required.

6. Click **OK** to save the changes.

If you choose to receive updates using a Redistribution Server you will need to enter the UNC path into the Network Update path. This will need to be done for each AV engine. If you have multiple redistribution servers you can enter a secondary Update Path by clicking on **Secondary** and entering the **UNC path**. Alternatively, the secondary Update Path could point to the Microsoft Update Site.

If you need to configure credentials in order to access the Update Path:

1. Select **Settings** followed by **General Options**.

2. Check **Use UNC Credentials**.

3. Under **UNC Username** enter an **Account Username**.

4. Under **UNC Password** enter an **Account Password**.

5. Click **OK** to save the changes.

The update interval for the AV definitions can be configured on a per-engine basis and can be performed once, every x hours per day, daily, weekly, and monthly. The start time for the updates can also be specified. This should be staggered for each engine to ensure that updates do not occur at the same time. It is recommended that you update the definitions once per hour, which is the default setting. This helps to ensure that you are running the latest definitions. By not updating the definitions regularly, you run the risk of detectable viruses not being detected.

It is also possible to configure updates to occur when FSE is started. This is useful if you have specified a long update window. If you use the default setting of hourly updates, then this is usually not required.

This can be configured by:

1. Select **Settings** followed by **General Options**.

2. Check **Perform Updates at Startup** (see Figure 5.6).

3. Click **OK** to save the changes.

If you want to be notified of update actions such as Update Success, Failure, and No Updates Available, these updates can be sent to the *Virus Administrator*. The address of the Virus Administrator is configurable and is covered later in this section. To enable notification:

1. Select **Settings** followed by **General Options**.

2. Check **Send Update Notifications**.

3. Click **OK** to save the changes.

Figure 5.6 Scanner Updates and General Settings

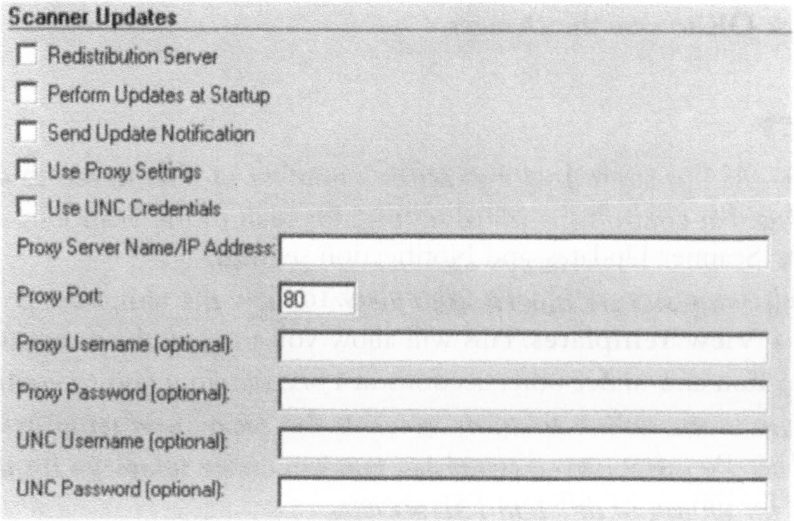

The remaining options are to force an update using the *Update Now* option and to disable updates for AV engines. This can be useful it you do not use some of the engines or do not want to keep up-to-date definitions for them. If you choose to change AV engines for Scan Jobs at a later time, you will need to ensure you enable updates.

WARNING

If you are using a proxy server or redistribution server and usernames and/or passwords become invalid, updates will fail. As a result, you could become vulnerable to new viruses.

Redistribution Server

A Redistribution Server allows a Forefront Server for Exchange Server to redistribute AV definitions to other FSE servers. This allows for updates to only be downloaded once from the Internet. This means that other FSE servers do not need access to the Internet. To configure an FSE Server to be a Redistribution Server:

1. Share the **Engines** folder located, by default, at C:\Program Files (x86)\ Microsoft Forefront Security\Exchange Server\Data.

2. In FSA, Select **Settings** followed by **General Options**.

3. Check **Redistribution Server** (see Figure 5.6).

4. Click **OK** to save the changes.

Templates

Templates are used to control settings across a number of FSE servers. A default template exists that controls the initial settings for each of the Scan Jobs along with the Antivirus, Scanner Updates, and Notification settings.

By default, templates are hidden from view. To view the templates, go to **File | Templates | View Templates**. This will allow you to view the templates under the Templates section and under other sections in FSA, allowing you to configure them.

In addition to the default template, you can also create new templates, known as *named templates*. By using named templates, you can create templates for different scenarios or for groups of different FSE servers.

These templates are stored in the *template.fdb* file along with the default templates, and can be applied to different Scan Jobs through the FSA. When you deploy the *template.fdb* file to other FSE servers, you can then apply these named templates to Scan Jobs on that FSE server.

When you need to create a new template there are four types of templates you can create. These are:

- Transport

- Real time

- Manual

- Filter Set

The first three templates are for each of the Scan Job types and the Filter Set template is used to create a set of filters. The Filter Set can then be applied to any of the Scan Job types, allowing for a single set of filters to be applied to both real time and manual Scan Jobs. For example:

To create a new named template, this can be seen in Figure 5.7:

1. Go to **File | Templates | New**.

2. Select the type.

3. Enter a template name.

4. Click **OK**.

Figure 5.7 Creating Templates

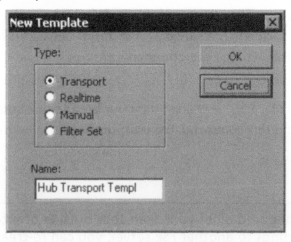

You can also rename and delete the templates by going to **File | Template** and choosing the appropriate option. If you are renaming the template, you will be asked to enter a new name. If you are deleting a template, you will be asked to confirm the deletion.

Once you have configured a template, you will need to apply it to a Scan Job. To apply a template in the Templates section, select the Scan Job, then select the template from the drop-down list under **Templates**. Once you have selected your template, click **Load From Template**. If you also need to apply a filter set, you can do this by selecting the Filter List from the drop-down list under **Filter Sets** (see Figure 5.8).

Figure 5.8 Applying Templates to Scan Jobs

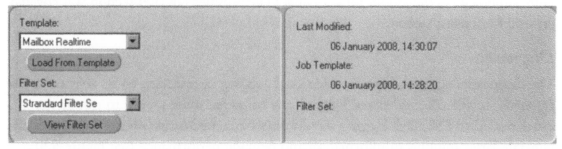

If you have applied a filter set to a Scan Job, these settings will be used first, followed by settings for the Scan Job.

Once you have configured your templates you will need to copy them to the other FSE servers. This can be done by either using FSSMC or by using the command line *FSCStarter.exe*.

To apply the templates to another FSE server, you should first copy the *template.fdb* file to the FSE server. This file is located by default in C:\Program Files (x86)\ Microsoft Forefront Security\Exchange Server\Data. Once you have copied this file, you should run the following at the command prompt:

```
"C:\Program Files (x86)\Microsoft Forefront Security\Exchange Server\FSCStarter" t
```

This command forces FSE to re-load the template file that you have just copied over. If you do not run this command, the templates will not be made available in FSE.

TIP

If you have configured all of your Scan Jobs outside of a template but want to copy the settings to another FSE server, you can re-create the default template based on the current configuration of your Scan Jobs.

This can be performed by deleting the *Template.fdb* file from C:\Program Files (x86)\Microsoft Forefront Security\Exchange Server\Data. Then, restart the FSC Controller service. This will re-create this file based on your current Scan Job settings. This will only re-create the default template. If you have any named templates, these will be lost.

General Options

The General Options section allows you to configure settings specific to the server. These settings are stored in the registry and include diagnostic and event logging along with additional configurations for scanning. (The Scanner Updates section was covered previously in this chapter).

Diagnostics

The diagnostic logging allows for additional logging information to be written to the *programlog.txt* file. The additional logging can be useful when trying to troubleshoot issues related to FSE. This logging should only be turned on when necessary, as it can generate large amounts of information and degrade performance (see Figure 5.9).

Figure 5.9 Diagnostic Logging

As part of diagnostic logging, you also have the option to archive messages. This option is only available on FSE servers with the Transport Scan Job. You have four options when configuring this:

- No Archive

- Archive Before Scan

- Archive After Scan

- Archive Before and After Scan

E-mails are archived into two folders—In and Out for inbound and outbound messages. By default, these folders are located at C:\Program Files (x86)\Microsoft Forefront Security\Exchange Server\Data\Archive. If you choose to archive messages before scanning, the messages may contain viruses. Be aware of the consequences to storing these e-mails. The archiving of e-mails can use up a significant amount of disk space and degrade performance. You should only enable this option when required.

You can opt to send notification to the Virus Administrator whenever the *Internet Scanner* starts. The Internet Scanner is used by the Transport Scan Job to process messages. It is recommended that this should only be enabled on servers running the Transport Scan Job if you wish to receive these notifications.

The final option is the Critical Notification List, which allows you to specify a list of addresses that Critical Notifications should be sent. A Critical Notification is defined as the failure of the FSE Services. Failure of these services would result in AV Scanning and Message Filtering failing. However, e-mail would continue to flow through FSE.

Logging

The Logging section allows you to choose which information is logged. It is recommended that these default settings be utilized, as this allows for basic logging of FSE activities along with Virus and Filter Notifications. The available settings are shown in Table 5.1. Settings marked with an * are dependent on which FSE Server Roles have been installed.

Table 5.1 Logging Settings

Setting	Description
Enable Event Log	FSE writes basic information to the Application Event Log, such as engine updates and Scan Jobs not running. These events can be monitored from systems like System Center Operations Manager.
Enable Performance Monitor and Statistics	Performance and statistics information can be made available to Performance Monitor; if these are not required this can be disabled.
Enable Forefront Program Log	The Program log provides information on FSE starting along with AV engine updates; this provides basic trouble-shooting information. This file is located in the Forefront Data folder and is called *ProgramLog.txt*.
Enable Forefront Virus Log	The Virus log allows for the logging of detected virus Infections to a text file *VirusLog.txt*. It is recommended that this be left disabled.

Continued

Table 5.1 Continued. Logging Settings

Setting	Description
Enable Incidents Logging – Transport* Enable Incidents Logging – Real Time* Enable Incidents Logging – Manual*	Incident logging allows for the actions taken on detecting viruses and filter matches to be logged into a database. This is covered later in this chapter. It is recommended that these options are not disabled.
Max Program Log Size	The Program Log file can grow to be large, especially if debugging is left turned on for any period of time. In order to ensure that it does not use up all the available disk space, a maximum size can be set the value is in KB with a minimum of 512. If you do not want to set a max size, enter a value of 0.

Scanning

This section allows you to modify settings relating to the virus scanning of messages. For the majority of companies, these default settings can be used. Due to the large amount of settings, only the most common are covered, as seen in Table 5.2. The FSE Help File provides extensive details on all settings. Settings marked with an * are dependent on which Exchange Server Roles have been installed.

Table 5.2 Virus Scanning Settings

Setting	Description
Body Scanning – Manual* Body Scanning – Real Time*	Enables the scanning of the message body instead of just the attachments. Transport scans always scan the body.
Delete Corrupted Compressed Files Delete Corrupted Uuencoded Files	If files are corrupt, virus scanning cannot always detect viruses. The safest option is to delete these files from the message. Since corrupted files are of no use to the recipient, there should be no issues with removing them.

Continued

Table 5.2 Continued. Virus Scanning Settings

Setting	Description
Delete Encrypted Compressed Files	Encrypted compressed files cannot be virus scanned. Allowing these through poses a significant risk. These files will be quarantined so they can be manually retrieved if required.
Scan Doc Files As Containers – Manual* Scan Doc Files As Containers – Transport* Scan Doc Files as Containers – Real Time*	This setting is relevant to Office Documents up to the 2003 release. These documents can contain embedded files. Enabling this will ensure that these files will be virus scanned.
Optimize for Performance by Not Scanning Messages That Were Already Virus Scanned – Transport*	When messages are virus scanned, an AV Stamp is placed in the message header during transport, then stored in the MAPI Properties of the message. If this is detected, the message will not be re-scanned. If you disable this option, the message will be re-scanned. If this tag exists, this can add considerable load. It is recommended that this be left enabled.
Scan on Scanner Update*	This setting indicates that messages should be re-scanned if newer AV definitions are available. This only effects the On-Access scanning on the Mailbox servers. If you run Outlook Clients in Cached Mode, an On-Access event will not be triggered when accessing cached items. If an update occurs when a background scan is running, this will be restarted. This could continue to restart if updates keep occurring. It is recommended that this setting is not enabled as it can add a considerable load to your servers.
Enable Forefront Security for Exchange Scan	This gives you the option to enable only parts of FSE. You can Disable All, Enable Store Scanning, Enable Transport Scanning, and Enable All. By configuring this option, you can prevent the scanning process from

Continued

Table 5.2 Continued. Virus Scanning Settings

Setting	Description
	being loaded allowing for resource saving. You need to restart FSE after modifying this setting.
Transport Process Count* Real Time Process Count*	You can specify how many processes are available to process messages. This setting can be between 1 and 10. It is recommended that you do not enable more than 2 for each processor core in the server. There is also a large memory overhead for each process. For most companies four processes will suffice.
Quarantine Messages	When messages are quarantined due to content or file filters, they can be stored as an EML file, which keeps the attachment and message in a single file. Or, the attachment and message can be stored separately. If you store messages as an EML file you will need an application that is capable of viewing them.
Deliver From Quarantine Security	This setting controls how messages are handled when they are delivered from quarantine. If this is set to Compatible, messages will be virus scanned. If this is set to Secure, messages will be virus scanned and filters will also be applied.
Internal Address	In this field you should enter all of the domain names hosted on your FSE servers. This will be used to indicate who internal notifications should be sent to. You do not need to enter sub-domains. Domains should be separated by semicolons with no spaces.
Transport External Hosts	You should enter the Internet Protocol (IP) address of each of your Edge Servers. Addresses should be separated by semicolons with no spaces.

Background Scanning

Background Scanning is only available on servers running the Mailbox Role. This allows for messages to be re-scanned based on their age. This also allows for scanning with updated AV definitions, ensuring that new viruses are detected. This scan in enabled as a Scheduled Job and is covered later in this chapter (see Table 5.3).

Table 5.3 Background Scanning Settings

Setting	Description
Enabled Background Scan if 'Scan On Scanner Updated Enabled'	This setting is conditional on "Scan on Scanner Update" being enabled.
Scan Only Messages With Attachments	By scanning only messages with attachments, you reduce the total number of messages to scan.
Scan Only Unscanned Messages	Scan only un-tagged messages. This setting is not recommended as it prevents new viruses from being detected.
Scan Messages Received Within The Last *x* Days	The available time intervals are Anytime, 4, 6, 8, 12, and 18 hours, and 1, 2, 3, 4, 5, 6, 7, and 30 Days.

By default, the scan interval is set at 2 days. For most companies, this should be sufficient to ensure that the job completes within a number of hours. If you host a large amount of mailboxes on your Mailbox server and receive large amounts of messages daily, you should reduce the interval to a value appropriate for your company.

Filtering

The filtering section allows you to configure message filters for each of the Scan Jobs.

When you configure the filters, you are able to select the *action* to take if the filter matches. While the options vary depending on the filter type, there are four available:

- **Skip: detect only** This option leaves the attachment in the message and places an entry in the logs.

- **Delete: remove contents** This option removes the attachment and replaces it with a text file containing the deletion text.

- **Purge: eliminate message** Remove the entire message.
- **Identify: tag message** Place a tag in the subject and/or message header.

You will also be able to choose if the files or messages should be quarantined. If you enable this option, the file will be quarantined if you choose the Delete or Purge action. You will also be able to enable Notifications, which will allow you to send notifications to the sender and/or recipients.

Content

Content filters allow you to filter messages based on the Sender or the Subject Line. These filters can be used by the Real Time and Manual Scan Jobs. When setting up a Subject Line filter, it will only match against the entire subject unless you use wildcards. For example, if you specify *make money* as the subject line it will only match if "make money" is the subject. If you specify "*make money*," it will match as long as "make money" appears somewhere in the subject. If "you can make money now" is the subject, it will be a match and that message will be filtered. Similar wildcards can be used for the Sender Domain, for example, *testuser@fse.syngress.local* or **@fse.syngress.local*.

When you create a Content filter, you can either enter the Sender Details or Subject Lines directly into the filter, or you can use a Filter List. It is recommended that you use Filter Lists because this allows you to put a meaningful name against the list. Using Filter Lists makes things easier when you are reviewing your settings at a later time.

To create a Content filter (not using a Filter List):

1. Go to **Settings | Filtering | Content**. If this is grayed out, select the **Scan Job** or **Template** first.
2. Select the **Scan Job** or **Template**.
3. Select **Sender-Domains** or **Subject Lines** from **Content Fields**.
4. Click **Filters**.
5. Click **Add**.
6. Enter the **Subject Line** or **Sender E-mail Address** or **Sender Domain** you want to match.
7. Under **Filter** select **Enabled**.
8. Select the required **Action**.
9. Select if you want to **Send Notifications** or **Quarantine Files**.

To create a Content filter using a Filter List, you first need to create the Filter List. To do this, refer to the Filter List section. Once you have created the Filter List you can create the Content Filter (see Figure 5.10):

1. Go to **Settings | Filtering | Content**. If this is grayed out, select the **Scan Job** or **Template** first.

2. Select the **Scan Job** or **Template**.

3. Click **Lists**.

4. Select the **Filter List**.

5. Under Filter select **Enabled**.

6. Select the required **Action**.

7. Select if you want to Send Notifications or Quarantine Files.

Each Content filter can be disabled by selecting **Disabled** from the Filter List. If you need to edit or delete a Sender-Domain or Subject Line, you can do this by selecting it and clicking **Edit** or **Delete**.

Figure 5.10 Configuring Content Filter

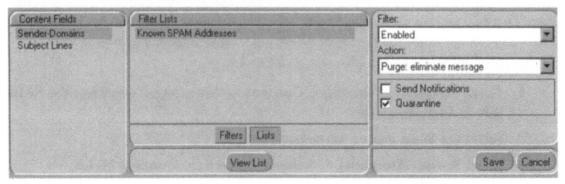

Keyword

Keyword filters are used by the Transport Scan Job to process the body of a message. If the message body matches the criteria of the filter, the defined action will be applied to the message.

When you create a Keyword filter you first need to create a Filter List. This Filter List can contain multiple items, and each item should be the word or sentence you want to match against.

This filter can contain logical operators that allow for more control over the matching. These are (there must be a *space* between the word and the underscore):

- **word1_AND_word2** Logical AND operator, message must contain *word1* and *word2*.

- **word1_NOT_ word2** Logical NOT operator, message must contain *word1* but not *word2*.

- **word1_ANDNOT_word2** The same as _AND__NOT_.

- **word1_WITHIN[#]OF_word2** *word1* has to be within # words of *word2*, where # is a number.

- **_HAS[#]OF_ word** The body has to contain # of the word, where # is a number.

The filter will match if a single item in the list is matched. You can increase this by changing the *minimum number of matches required*.

To create a Keyword filter, you first need to create the Filter List. To do this, refer to the Filter List section. Once you have created the Filter List, you can create the Keyword filter (see Figure 5.11):

1. Go to **Settings** | **Filtering** | **Keyword**. If this is grayed out, select the **Scan Job** or **Template** first.

2. Select the **Scan Job** or **Template**.

3. Select **Message Body** under **Keyword Fields**.

4. Select the **Filter List**.

5. Under Filter select **Enabled**.

6. Select the required **Action**.

7. If you set an Action of Tag, click on the **Identify** tab and check the **Subj Line** and/or **Msg Hdr** boxes.

8. Select if you want to **Send Notifications** or **Quarantine Files**.

9. Select which messages the filter should effect; **Outbound**, **Inbound**, or **Internal**.

10. Specify the Minimum Unique Keyword Hits.

Each Keyword filter can be disabled by selecting **Disabled** from the Filter List.

Figure 5.11 Configuring Keyword Filter

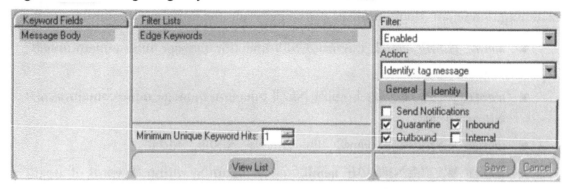

File

File filters are used to control the types of files sent through your FSE infrastructure. These filters can be applied on any of the Scan Jobs, but it is recommended that you do not use File filters on the Real Time Scan Jobs.

When you create a file filter, you can either enter file names directly into the filter or you can use a Filter List. It is recommended that you use Filter Lists, because this allows you to put a meaningful name against the list and when reviewing settings later, this can make things clearer.

For each of the entries, you need to specify an extension. Extensions can include wildcards, along with a file type and an action to take. You can also specify if the filter should be applied to inbound and outbound messages, and if it should only affect files of a certain size.

To limit the effect of a filter, it can be preceded by either *<in>* or *<out>*. This will limit the filter to either inbound or outbound messages. To limit the filter by size, you should place a comparison operator followed by the size. For example:

```
<in>*.exe>500KB
```

This will limit the filter to inbound files with an *.exe* extension that is over 500 Kilobytes in size.

To create a File filter (not using a Filter List):

1. Go to **Settings | Filtering | File**.
2. Select the **Scan Job** or **Template**.
3. Click **Names**.
4. Click **Add**.

5. Enter the **Extension** along with any limitations.

6. Under File Filter select **Enabled**.

7. If you need to choose specific file types, uncheck **All Types**, accept the warning, and check the **File Types** required.

8. Select the required **Action**.

9. If you set an Action of Tag, click on the **Identify** tab and check the **Subj Line** and/or **Msg Hdr**.

10. Select if you want to **Send Notifications** or **Quarantine Files**.

To create a File filter using a Filter List, you first need to create the Filter List. (To do this, refer to the Filter List section.) Once you have created the Filter List you can create the File filter (see Figure 5.12):

1. Go to **Settings | Filtering | File**.

2. Select the **Scan Job** or **Template**.

3. Click **Lists**.

4. Select the **Filter List**.

5. Under File Filter select **Enabled**.

6. If you need to choose specific File Types, uncheck **All Types**, accept the warning, and check the **File Types** required.

7. Select the required **Action**.

8. If you set an Action of Tag, click on the **Identify** tab and check the **Subj Line** and/or **Msg Hdr**.

9. Select if you want to **Send Notifications** or **Quarantine Files**.

Figure 5.12 Configuring File Filtering

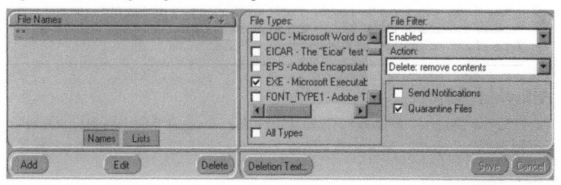

Each File filter can be disabled by selecting **Disabled** from the File Filter List. If you need to edit or delete an extension from the File Names List, you can do this by selecting the **filename** or **extension** and clicking **Edit** or **Delete**. If you need to modify the order that the Files Filters are evaluated, you can use the up and down arrows to change the order. Filters higher up the list are evaluated first. Once a match has been made, no other filters will be evaluated.

For example, if you wanted to disable the ability for users to receive incoming executables you would configure the following:

1. Create a Filter List called **Executables**.

2. Add an item to that filter as **<in>***.* This will check all incoming attachments irrelevant of name or extension.

3. Go to **Settings | Filtering | File**.

4. Enable the **Executables** Filter List for the **Transport Scan Job**.

5. Specify a File Type of **EXE – Microsoft Executable File**.

6. Set an action of **Delete: remove contents**.

7. Under the **General** tab select **Quarantine Files**.

By configuring the above, you have told FSE to scan all incoming attachments to see if it contains an executable file, and if it finds one to delete it from the e-mail and place it in quarantine. When the end user receives the e-mail, it will contain a text attachment explaining that the file had been removed. If you choose to modify the Deletion Text you could instruct them to contact the Helpdesk for their attachment.

NOTE

This will also remove executable attachments in ZIP files. If you wanted to allow these, you would need to create another entry above the one to remove executables that has an action of *Skip: detect only* and has a *File Type* of *ZIP – Compressed file created by* PKZip.

Allowed Senders

The Allowed Senders tab allows you to specify that messages from specified senders should not be subject to Keyword, File, or Content filtering. This could be useful if you generally block Visual Studio source files, but you need to ensure you receive them from a development company.

Before you configure the Allowed Senders, you need to create a Filter List. To do this, refer to the Filter List section.

Now that you have created the Filter List, you can enable it for a Scan Job. You can also specify which filters should be skipped when messages are from the specified senders:

1. Go to **Settings | Filtering | Allowed Senders**.

2. Select the **Scan Job** or **Template**.

3. Select the **Sender Filter List** from Sender Lists.

4. Under **List State** select **Enabled**.

5. Under **Skip Scanning**, select the **Filters** you want to skip.

If required, you can enable multiple Allowed Senders for each Scan Job, or they can be disabled by selecting **Disabled** from the **List State**.

Filter Lists

Filter Lists are used to create groups of settings for the filters. These lists allow for settings to be created under a meaningful name. This also means that the same list can be used by multiple Scan Jobs. Filter Lists are all created, edited, and deleted in the same manner as when you add items to a Filter List. There is no checking performed on the entries to ensure that they are valid; therefore, if you are creating an Allowed Sender List, you are able to enter invalid e-mail addresses, such as addresses missing the @ symbol. If you find that a filter is not acting as you would expect, you should ensure that you have not entered any information incorrectly.

To create a Filter List:

1. Go to **Settings | Filtering | Filter List**.

2. Select a **List Type**.

3. Click **Add**.

4. Enter the list name, which should be something meaningful.

Once the list has been created, you can delete it by selecting the list from List Names and clicking **Delete**. Adding items to a Filter List is done through editing the list.

To edit a Filter List:

1. Select the **List Type** followed by the **List Name**.

2. Click **Edit**.

3. An Edit Filter List window should open.

4. Under **Include in Filter** click **Add**.

5. Enter the item text (e.g., an e-mail address or a file extension).

6. To add multiple items click on **Add** again. If you need to **Edit** or **Remove** an item, select it from the list and click the appropriate button.

7. Click **OK**.

Operate

The Operate section allows you to choose which Scan Jobs are enabled along with settings related to these jobs. You can also specify schedules for scans and initiate a quick scan.

Run Job

The Run Job section allows you to:

- Enable or disable Scan Jobs

- Specify if the Scan Job scans for viruses or filters messages

- View logs for each Scan Job

By default, each of the Scan Jobs are enabled. If you need to disable them for any reason, it can be done by selecting the Scan Job and selecting **Bypass** (see Figure 5.13). You can re-enable the job by selecting **Enable**.

Figure 5.13 Enabling Scan Jobs

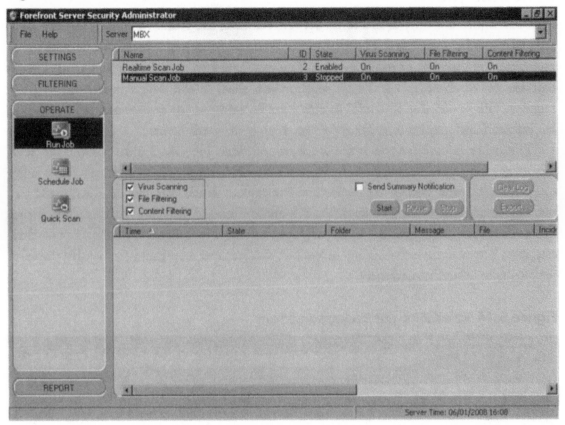

For each of the Scan Jobs, you can also specify if the job carries out virus scanning and filtering. This is configured through a series of checkboxes. For Transport Scan Jobs, you can enable or disable File and Keyword filtering. For Real time or Manual Scan Jobs, you can enable or disable file and content filtering. These settings take effect immediately, and affect the job even if it is running.

You are also able to view the incidents for each Scan Job. This information is the same as the incident information shown in the Report section, but is specific to the selected Scan Job. You also have the option to export the incident information or to clear the log, or you can also delete individual log entries if required.

Schedule Job

Scheduled jobs are only available on servers running the Mailbox role. There are two jobs that can be scheduled. The first is the Manual Scan Job, which can be run on a one time, daily, weekly, or monthly basis. This can be useful if you want to scan mailboxes that are not covered by a real time scan or you want to use different settings or AV engines. This could also be useful to run after an outbreak to ensure that no mailboxes are infected and can be scheduled to run during off-peak hours.

The other Scheduled job is the Background Scan Job (see Figure 5.14). This Scan Job allows for recent messages to be re-scanned using newer AV definitions. This helps to ensure that new viruses are located and removed. While this can be configured to run one time, daily, weekly, or monthly, it is recommended that you run this daily during off-peak hours. (Background Scan Jobs are discussed in greater detail earlier in this chapter.) You also have the ability to enable, disable, and stop these Scan Jobs; these settings take effect immediately.

Figure 5.14 Scheduling the Background Scan

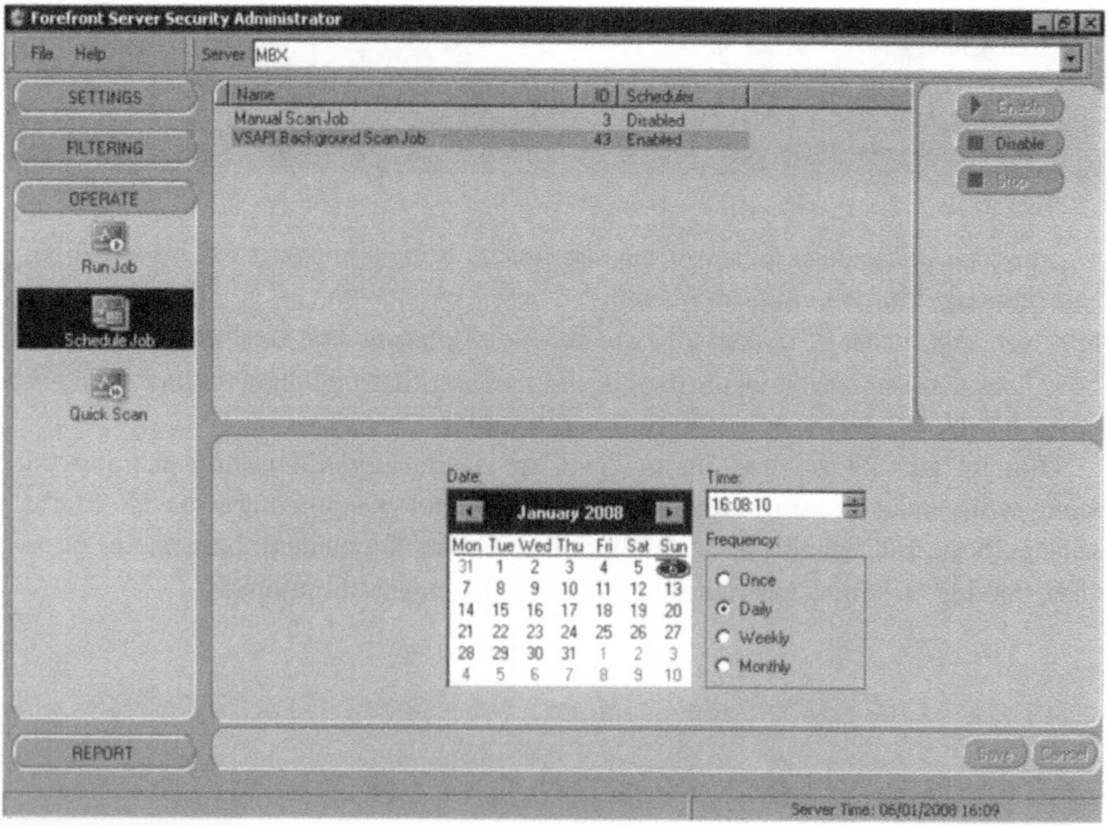

Quick Scan

A Quick Scan allows for the ad-hoc scanning of mailboxes and public folders, and is available only on servers running the Mailbox role. This is configured in the same manner as other Scan Jobs in terms of AV engines to use along with the bias and actions.

You can specify which mailboxes and public folders are scanned. This allows you to select mailboxes that you suspect have been infected. For example, a Quick Scan can only perform AV scanning and cannot be used to apply filters to messages. Depending on the number of messages within the selected mailboxes and public folders running, a Quick Scan could put a considerable load on the server. It would be wise to be careful to ensure that this does not adversely affect performance for day-to-day operations.

Report

The Report section allows you to view the Incident Logs and the Quarantined Messages. You can also configure E-mail Notifications.

Notification

The Notification section allows you to configure who receives e-mail notifications, along with the contents of the e-mails. Most of the e-mails have pre-defined recipients and contents, If needed, these notifications can also be enabled and disabled (see Figure 5.15).

Figure 5.15 Enabling Notifications

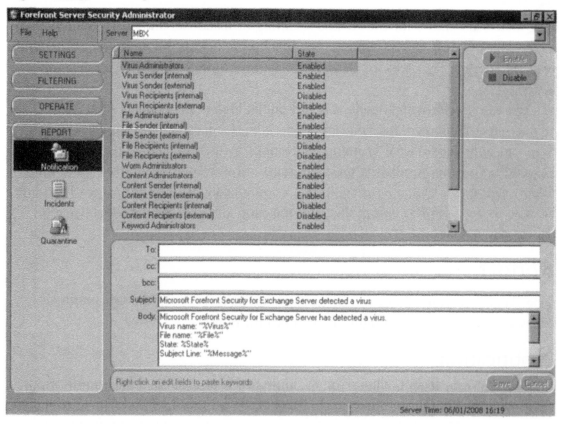

The notifications you should modify are the Administrator e-mails, as these are used to notify you of issues. They are also used to notify you of viruses and filter matches if notifications for these have been enabled. You should specify whom these are sent to. This could be individual recipients or distribution lists (multiple addresses should be separated by semicolons).

The other available notifications are for alerting either the sender or recipient that there was an issue with a message. These notifications are further separated into external or internal parties. By default, only the sender is notified. Recipient e-mails are disabled but you may choose to enable or disable these depending on the requirements for your company. By allowing different messages for external and internal parties, you can tailor messages to the intended audience (e.g., an internal recipient may be instructed to contact the IT Helpdesk).

The final part to consider is the sender of the Notifications. By default, this is ForefrontServerSecurity@*ServerName*.com. It is recommended that this be changed to something more meaningful (e.g., the postmaster address for your company or the address for your IT Support desk).

These settings are configured through the registry:

1. Go to **Start | Run**, enter **regedit**, and click **OK**.

2. Navigate to **HKEY_LOCAL_MACHINE\SOFTWARE\Wow6432Node\Microsoft\Forefront Server Security\Exchange Server**.

3. Locate the **ServerProfile** key.

4. Modify the key and enter an e-mail address.

5. Close **regedit**.

Incidents

The Incidents section allows you to view the incidents that have occurred. Incident entries are created when a virus is detected or a filter is matched. The information displayed includes the recipients and sender along with the action taken. It is possible to perform the following actions:

- Delete individual incidents (using the Delete key)
- Clear the log
- Export the log
- Purge incidents after a number of days
- Apply filters to the log
- View statistics
- Clear statistics

The incident log is stored in an Access Database and has a file limit of 2 GB. If the Notification Log grows to more than 1.5 GB a notification will be sent daily to the Virus Administrator. To clear the log you can click the **Clear Log** button. This command will be queued and the messages will be cleared when the database is compacted which is at 02:00 daily.

An alternative to this is to automatically purge messages when they reach a certain age. For example, after 30 days the rate at which incidents are generated depends on how busy your e-mail servers are and how many viruses or filter actions are received. Configure this to match the requirements for your company.

Quarantine

The Quarantine section allows you to view the messages that have been quarantined. You can also choose to deliver these messages to the intended recipients. While this may not be of use for viruses, it can be useful for messages that have been quarantined due to matching a message filter. It is possible to perform the following actions:

- Delete individual messages (using the Delete key)
- Clear the log
- Export the log
- Save attachments to the file system
- Deliver messages to the intended recipient
- Purge messages after a number of days
- Apply filters to the log

If you choose to save attachments to the file system, this will allow infected files to be saved. Therefore, you should ensure that you have a current virus scanner running on the machine and that you understand the consequences of doing this.

If you want an attachment to be delivered to either the intended recipient or to another address, this can be done using the Deliver option. When you select this option, you will be given the option to send to the original recipients and/or to new recipients (see Figure 5.16). If you have selected a virus to be delivered, you will be warned that the file is infected but you will still be able to submit the message for delivery. This message will be treated the same as any other new message and will be subject to the same AV scanning as any other new message. This may result in the message being quarantined again.

Figure 5.16 Delivering a Quarantined Message

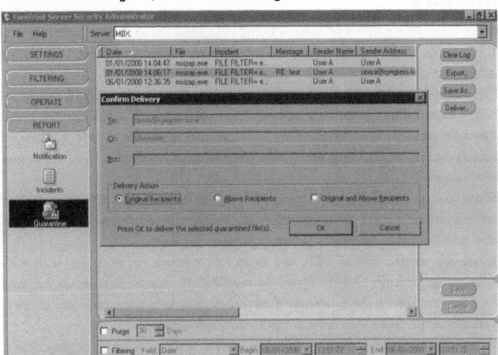

If you choose to deliver a message that was quarantined due to a filter match, this will be handled in one of two ways depending on the Deliver from Quarantine security setting. If this is set to Secure Mode, messages will be processed against the message filters. If this setting is set to Compatible Mode, messages will not be checked against filters.

NOTE

If you are often in a position where you need to deliver legitimate files that have been quarantined due to a filter match, you will either need to set the *Deliver from Quarantine Security* to Compatible Mode to deliver them through e-mail, or use an alternative method by saving them to the file system and then transporting them to the recipient.

The Quarantine database has the same limitations as the Incidents database, and only the log details are stored in the database. The actual messages are stored as individual files on the file system.

Summary

With the increasing number of viruses being circulated through e-mail, it is becoming more important to ensure that your FES infrastructure if fully protected against viruses and other threats that threaten your infrastructure.

FSE allows you to virus scan messages as they transit through you FSE infrastructure and when they are in the user's mailbox, ensuring that your infrastructure remains virus free. In addition to virus scanning, you can also apply filters, which allow you to proactively protect against unwanted attachments, along with checking the contents of the messages

When you are considering deploying FSE, you should carefully plan your deployment to ensure that you do not adversely affect the performance of your Exchange servers and that you do not accidentally delete legitimate messages.

When you start to deploy FES, you should do this out of hours and start with the Edge Transport Servers first, followed by the Hub Transport Servers and then the Mailbox Servers. This helps to ensure that you do not introduce any new viruses to your infrastructure once you have started your deployment.

In order to effectively manage FES across your entire Exchange deployment, you should consider using FSSMC, which allows you to centrally manage the configuration and the quarantine databases.

When deploying security products, it is possible to over-engineer their design and deployment. This can often cause unforeseen issues and a level of complexity that is not always necessary. Your initial deployment should provide the basics for what you require. You should then add additional scanning and filtering as required while ensuring that you do not overload your infrastructure, and that the end user's experience is not adversely affected.

Solutions Fast Track

Implementing Microsoft Forefront Server for Exchange

☑ FSE can be deployed on servers running the Edge Transport, Hub Transport, and Mailbox roles.

☑ You can use FSE to scan for viruses and filter messages.

☑ You should ensure that you carefully plan your FSE deployment so that you do not accidentally delete legitimate messages, and so that you do not place too greater load on your Exchange servers.

Configuring Microsoft Forefront Server for Exchange

☑ Configure the AV engines to use, along with the Bias and Action.

☑ Configure message filtering if required.

☑ Schedule and enable the background Scan Job.

☑ Configure administrator notifications.

Frequently Asked Questions

Q: I have installed FSE and am trying to send the Eicar test virus to a user as a test. While the message is rejected, I am not seeing anything in the FSE logs. My infrastructure includes an Exchange Edge server and a combined Hub and Mailbox server.

A: I am assuming you are using a file called *eicar.com*. The Exchange Edge server automatically rejects *.com* files along with a number of others. Exchange filters are evaluated and actioned before those of FSE. If you want to test FSE with the Eicar virus rename the file to something like *eicar.test*. To view the extensions that the Edge servers block, run *Get-AttachmentFilterEntry* within the Exchange Management Shell.

Q: Since installing FSE and configuring File filters I am unable to receive some Office 2007 documents; however, I am able to receive Office 2003 documents without any issues.

A: In Office 2007, a new document format was used known as Openxml, which is actually a zip file that contains your document in XML format along with any embedded files such as pictures and audio files. Due to this it is possible that you have configured a filter to block one of these embedded files, which is causing the document to be rejected. In order to accept these files you should create a new File filter with a file type of OPENXML and an action of Skip and place this at the top of your File List. You should now be able to receive these files.

Chapter 6

Managing Microsoft SharePoint Portal Securely Using Forefront

Solutions in this chapter:

- Implementing Microsoft Forefront Server for SharePoint
- Configuring the Forefront Server Security Administrator for SharePoint

☑ Summary

☑ Solutions Fast Track

☑ Frequently Asked Questions

Introduction

Microsoft Forefront Server Security for SharePoint Services is a tool that will help network administrators prevent vulnerabilities that can occur within SharePoint workspaces. SharePoint workspaces are areas on the network where users can create, edit, and save files and folders. If these storage locations on the network are used in a malicious manner, an enterprise can be vulnerable.

SharePoint Services, replacing the less robust and discontinued SharePoint Team Services, is a relatively recent addition to Microsoft's line of products. SharePoint Services has become increasingly popular among companies where employees need to collaborate on documents and spreadsheets. The explosion in popularity of Share Point Services means that additional security mechanisms need to be in place in order to prevent the network from becoming vulnerable.

The Microsoft Forefront Server Security allows network administrators to centrally manage the security of the SharePoint servers. Administrators using Forefront Server Security can conduct filtering, scanning, and job scheduling of SharePoint repositories from a central management console. Reports can give the network engineer using Forefront Server Security Administrator an indication of how end users are utilizing the SharePoint workspaces. If end users are improperly utilizing SharePoint Services, additional filters can be added. Using Forefront Server Security can help network administrators deal with vulnerabilities related to SharePoint Services.

Implementing Microsoft Forefront Server for SharePoint

Microsoft's SharePoint server provides a collaboration environment that allows people to share documents and contacts, and it provides a single place for project management. While antivirus software on the server can scan files for viruses, Forefront Security for SharePoint allows for a higher level of integration, including real-time scanning and the ability to use up to five scanning engines at once for maximum protection.

Implementation of Forefront Security for SharePoint can be broken into two components: installation and configuration. The installation of Forefront must be planned ahead of time to ensure all of the requirements are met. If they are not, both hardware and software upgrades may be required. A thorough implementation plan will allow you to determine if upgrades are needed. Once installed, you must configure Forefront properly in order to provide the security and protection planned for during the design phase. The ability to customize Forefront to fit different corporate models is a key strength that allows every installation to be optimized to fit goals decided during the design phase.

Installing and Configuring Forefront Security for SharePoint

Microsoft has made the installation of Forefront Security for SharePoint quick and straightforward, allowing you to begin configuration as quickly as possible. Once you have the installation media, it is only a matter of minutes to install Forefront. While the installation itself is straight forward, don't be fooled into thinking you don't need to plan. The decision to do a local installation or remote installation will require the installer to have account information readily available with the proper access to the target server.

ForeFront Security for SharePoint Requirements

Before we start the installation, let's take a look at the minimum server requirements to install Forefront Security for SharePoint. It is also important to make sure that the software requirements for Forefront security have been met. If they have not, you will be notified upon installation with a dialog box and the installation will stop.

- Processor: Dual-processor computer rated at 2.5 GHz or higher
- Operating System: Microsoft Windows Server (Standard, Enterprise, Datacenter, or Web Edition) with Service Pack 1
- Hard Disk: 550MB of available disk space
- SharePoint Requirement: Microsoft Office SharePoint Server 2007 or Microsoft Windows SharePoint Services, version 3
- Microsoft Windows Workflow Foundation Runtime Components
- Microsoft .NET Framework
- Internet Information Services 6 in worker process isolation mode
- NTFS file system
- MAPI client such as Microsoft Outlook

Installation

Forefront Security for SharePoint has the option to install on the local server or on a remote server. To initiate either installation, you will need to log on to the server with an account that has administrative rights. For an installation on a remote server, the local account you use to log in needs to have administrative rights on the remote server. This is usually accomplished by using a domain account that is the administrators group of both computers. Because the installation registers services on the target server, it requires administrative access.

A great new feature of Forefront for SharePoint is the ability to use Hot Upgrade technology (see Figure 6.1). This allows installations of Windows SharePoint Services without interrupting existing SharePoint service because a restart of the Windows SharePoint Services is not needed.

Figure 6.1 Forefront Security for SharePoint Hot Upgrade Feature

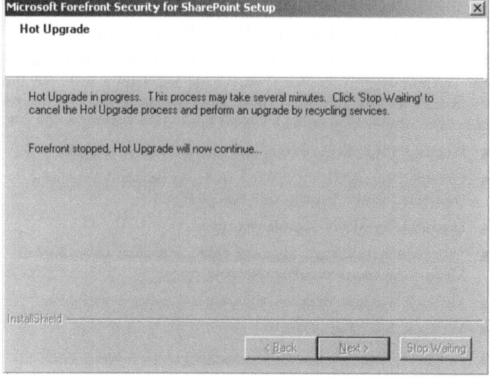

Forefront installs two main components that service the requests from the Forefront administrator and control all of the back-end functionality. The FSCController is installed as a service and coordinates all scanning activities within Forefront Security for SharePoint Server. The FSSPController is also an installed service, which communicates between Forefront and the SharePoint SQL server database.

Configuring & Implementing...

Command Line Utilities

Most of the configuration of Forefront Security for SharePoint will be done through the administrator console. Two utilities run from the command line can be helpful when dealing with the Forefront installation. These two command line utilities are FSCDiag.exe and FSCstarter.exe.

The FSCDiag utility is a diagnostic tool that gathers information about the installation that can be sent to Microsoft if you run into a problem with the installation. The tool is located in the installation directory and will prompt you to add various pieces of information to a single file. If you execute this file by double-clicking, you can answer the questions and it will generate the file, but the window will close and you will not be able to see if there were any errors. Once all the information is gathered, it is compressed and a new file is generated in the Log\Diagnostics folder. The format for the file is FSCDiag-servername-date-time.zip.

The FSCstarter utility is used to disable and enable scan jobs. This is done to unload the engines from memory so that the DLL can be updated. FSCstarter allows for the jobs to be stopped without recycling the SharePoint services; however, once the scan jobs are disabled, data flow will be halted for ten minutes. This can be run locally or on a remote server. FSCstarter is located in the Forefront installation directory.

1. To begin installation, insert the Forefront Security for SharePoint CD or download the installation file from the Microsoft Download Center.

2. At the initial **Welcome** screen, select **Next**.

3. At the **License Agreement** screen, read the agreement and if you accept the terms, click **Yes** to continue.

4. At the **Customer Information** screen, enter the **User Name** and **Company Name** for the installation and click **Next**. Both are needed for the **Next** button to be active.

5. At the **Installation Location** screen, you will select the type of installation you wish to perform, **Local** or **Remote**, and then click **Next**.

6. This step is only for Remote Installations. If you are completing a local install, go to step 7. At the **Remote Server Information** screen, enter the target **Server Name** that you want to install Forefront Security for SharePoint on and the **Share Directory** (see Figure 6.2). The default Share Directory is C$.

Figure 6.2 Remote Server Setup Screen

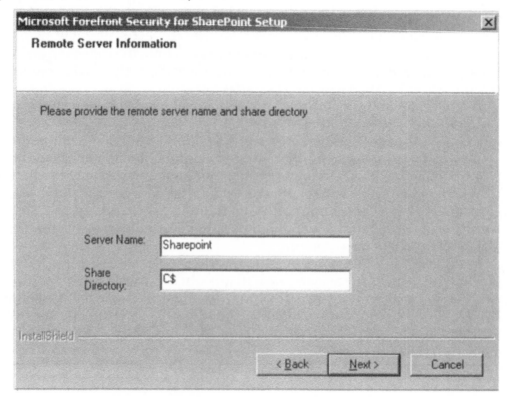

7. At the **Installation Type** screen, you can select **Client—Admin Console Only** or **Full Installation**. To install the Forefront Security for SharePoint application on the server, you will need to select **Full Installation**. The **Client— Admin Console Only** installation type only installs the administrator console to manage the server remotely.

8. At the **Engines** screen, you will see eight antivirus scan engines that Forefront Security can use to protect the server (see Figure 6.3). **Microsoft Antimalware Engine** is selected by default and cannot be changed, allowing for you to select between the remaining seven scan engines. A maximum of five engines can be used, so you will be able to select four of the seven available to you. Just remember

that each antivirus engine you select will require more memory to be dedicated to Forefront. If you have a server without the minimum amount of memory, you may want to select fewer antivirus engines. The installation automatically selects four engines randomly which you can keep or change. Once you have determined which antivirus engines you will enable, click **Next**. You can find out more about the scan engines by going to the following the Web sites:

1. **AhnLab Antivirus Scan Engine** http://global.ahnlab.com

2. **CA Vet** www.ca.com

3. **Authentium Command Antivirus** www.authentium.com/command

4. **Kapersky Antivirus Technology** www.kaspersky.com

5. **Norman Virus Control** www.norman.com

6. **Sophos Virus Detection** www.sophos.com

7. **VirusBuster Antivirus** www.virusbuster.hu

Figure 6.3 Scan Engines (Randomly Selected) Screen

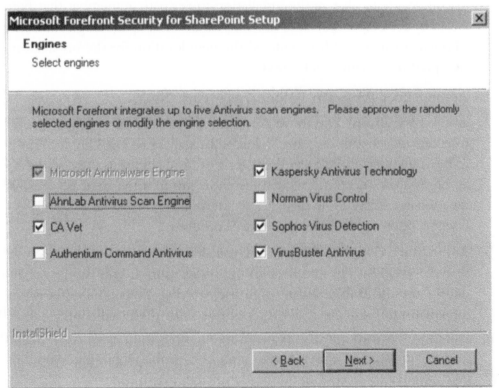

9. At the **Engine Updates Required** screen, click **Next**. Forefront Security for SharePoint Server will automatically search and update the virus definitions hourly starting five minutes after the service is started. This is necessary to ensure the antivirus engines are up to date, protecting the server from the latest threats.

NOTE

If a proxy server is used in your organization, the antivirus engine updates may fail. You will need to enter the proxy information using the Forefront Server Security Administrator console. Once you have entered the proxy information, use the **Update Now** button to immediately download the latest engine updates. If this is not done, you will not have an up-to-date virus engine and will be leaving your server vulnerable to viruses and other malicious code.

10. At the **Choose Destination Location** screen, select the destination folder for the installation. The default installation folder is C:\Program Files\Microsoft Forefront Security\SharePoint, which should be suitable for most installations. If you decide to change the installation folder path, remember that Forefront Security for SharePoint does not support an install path length over 170 characters. Once you have entered the new location for the installation or accepted the default, click **Next**.

11. At the **Select Program Folder** screen, click **Next**.

12. At the **SharePoint Database Account Information** screen, you will need to enter the account used for SharePoint database access. This account needs to be a member of the SharePoint server's local administrators group as well as the database server's local administrators group if the database was installed on a separate server. The format for entering the username is Domain\UserAccount or Machinename\UserAccount.

13. At the **Start Copying Files** screen, you should review your settings to ensure that everything is correct prior to the installation. If you want to change a setting, use the **Back** button to go back to that screen and enter the new information. If you are ready to continue with the installation, click **Next**.

14. Forefront Security for SharePoint is now going to install on your SharePoint server. This process can take a few minutes, during which time you will see a few command screens pop up as part of the installation.

15. Once installed, you will have the option to view the README file and click **Finish**. The installation is complete and you can now move on to configuring Forefront.

NOTE

The FSSPController service is configured with the account information provided in step 12. If you change the password for the account used, you will need to change the password for the FSSPController service also.

Configuring the Forefront Server Security Administrator for SharePoint

Once you have installed Forefront Server Security for SharePoint, start the administrator and connect to the server you will be managing (see Figure 6.4). You will be able to configure all of the SharePoint settings from this console. There are four general areas of configuration: Settings, Filtering, Operate, and Report. We will go over the configuration options of each section to make sure you understand all of the settings available to you.

During the configuration of Forefront for SharePoint server, you will notice that there are three different panes (see Figure 6.5). The left pane contains the different areas that Forefront can configure. The work pane appears on the top right of the administrator console and provides the administrator the ability to select which job or setting you will be configuring. The bottom pane has the settings available for configuration. This setup can take some time to get used to but as you browse through the different areas of the console, it will become clear.

Figure 6.4 Forefront Administrator Connection Dialog Box

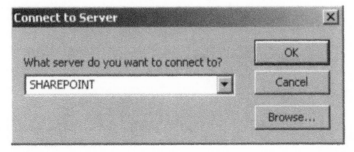

NOTE

The Forefront Server Security Administrator tool can be run from a remote machine to configure Forefront Security for SharePoint. To make the connection, however, the Anonymous Logon group must be granted remote access permission. To ensure that Anonymous Logon has the correct permissions, run dcomcnfg and browse to **My Computer** under the **Component Services** group. Right click on **My Computer** and select **Properties**, go to the **COM Security** tab and select **Edit Limits** under **Access Permissions**. Make sure **Anonymous Logon** is set to **Allow Permission for Remote Access**. If you want to secure the administration by not allowing remote management of Forefront for SharePoint, you can set **Anonymous Logon** to **Deny**.

Figure 6.5 Forefront Administrator Main Console

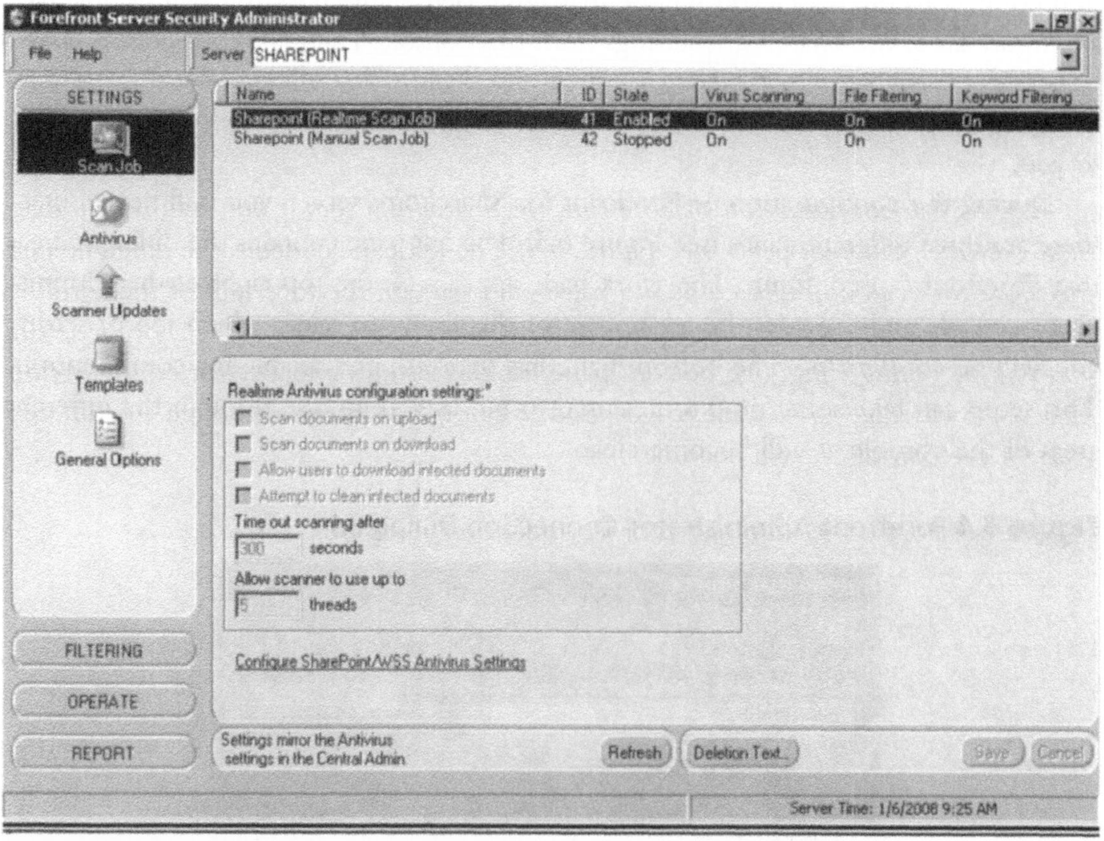

Settings

Configuring the settings for Forefront Security scan jobs provides the foundation for the level of depth at which the scan job detects files. In this section you will be able to control the antivirus engines used, how often they are updated, the level of logging generated, and many other important options. It is also important to consider consistent settings between different SharePoint servers. If there are requirements to have individual settings based on content or function, then a baseline template with all the basic scanning options is a good idea.

Scan JobForefront Security for SharePoint allows for real-time and manual scans. Manual scans are customizable and allow you to scan a document library or the entire SharePoint site with different settings or a different antivirus engine than the real-time scan job uses. It is recommended that after the installation of Forefront, a full manual scan be completed on the server.

The *Scan Job* setting provides a job list in the work pane on the top right of the console. You can select which job you wish to modify by clicking on it.

Real-Time Scan Job

Real-time scanning will be the first job in the list. By default, the state of the real-time scan job is *Enabled* with virus scanning, file filtering, and keyword filtering all set to *On*. Once you select SharePoint *Realtime Scan Job* the bottom pane will change to display the *Realtime Antivirus* configuration settings. These settings are grayed out because they cannot be modified at the Forefront Security Administrator Console. To change the *Realtime Antivirus* settings, click on the **Configure SharePoint/WSS Antivirus Settings** link in the bottom pane. A browser will open that connects to the SharePoint administrator site. Once you are logged in, click the **Operations** tab and select **Antivirus** under the **Security Configuration** section. Any changes to the Antivirus settings in this section will be reflected in the Forefront Server Security Administrator console.

The default settings for real-time scanning are to scan documents on upload, scan documents on download, and attempt to clean infected documents. These settings allow for the most secure real-time scanning environment. The **Deletion Text** button at the bottom of the console allows you to customize the message the user will see if they open a file that is deleted by an antivirus engine.

Manual Scan Job

Manual scanning allows you to scan a specific location or file to determine if there are any infected files. While the real-time scan job will catch the majority of infected files, there are still situations where a manual scan would catch a malicious file that was not caught by the real-time scan. For example, if a malicious file was uploaded prior to the antivirus engines being updated about it, it would be on the server and not detected until it was accessed, even after the engines were updated. Depending on your *Realtime Scan Job* settings, you may not be properly secure. Periodically running a manual scan with different scan engines than the *Realtime Scan Job* will ensure the maximum protection.

With **Manual Scan** highlighted, select the SharePoint locations you wish to scan in the tree view located in the bottom pane. You can select an entire site or specific libraries to scan. The **browse** and **find** buttons under the tree view can also help you locate a specific folder or file to scan. Once the location for the scan has been selected, choose the scan engine from the Antivirus settings.

NOTE

Prior to installing Forefront Security for SharePoint with Service Pack 1, make sure the latest Microsoft Windows SharePoint Service 3.0 Hotfix is installed. Failure to do so may generate errors (see Figure 6.6) during the later stages of configuration or with the SharePoint sites on the server.

Figure 6.6 Error Message if Service Pack 1 for SharePoint Is Not Applied

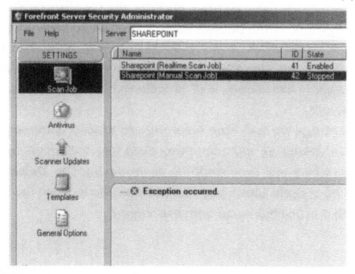

Antivirus

The antivirus settings for the jobs in the Job List can be set independently, allowing for different scan engines to be used for different scan jobs. The five File Scanner engines listed are the ones that were selected during the initial installation. You are not required to only use these engines; you can select any five or fewer engines to complete the scan.

The *Action* setting configures how Forefront will handle infected files during the scan. The default setting is to *Clean* and repair the document. You can also *Skip* (detect) or *Delete* (remove) the files that are infected during the scan.

The Bias setting allows you to set how many engines will be used to determine if a file is clean or infected. The more *Certainty* that is used, the bigger the hit on system performance as more than one of the engines will scan the files, providing a greater chance of catching all viruses. If *Performance* is favored, the scanning will be done with a single scan engine or fluctuate between single scan engines. This setting can greatly impact the performance of the server and should be configured cautiously.

- **Maximum Certainty** Scans each file with all selected engines
- **Favor Certainty** Scans each file with all available engines
- **Neutral** Scans each file with half of the selected engines
- **Favor Performance** Scans each file with between one and half the engines selected
- **Maximum Performance** Scans each file with only one engine

NOTE

If you manage the Forefront Server Security Administrator console with an account that does not have SharePoint Administrative rights, the Antivirus Settings pane will be disabled.

Configuring & Implementing...

Scanning Files by Type

As a Forefront Administrator, you will be constantly balancing server performance with enhanced security controls. Many of the settings like *Bias* can directly impact the performance of the server. Finding the proper balance will ensure that server security is not impacting user productivity. During the Planning and Design phase, it will be important to understand that every setting can have an impact on the server. Even a simple change can adversely impact the performance of the server.

One of the things that Microsoft has done to increase performance and speed up scans is to only scan files that typically contains viruses. Microsoft realized that using the file extension alone to determine the file type was not sufficient. Instead, Forefront looks at the file header, a more secure way to detect file type, even if the extension is spoofed. This allows for a secure environment without wasting resources on unnecessary files.

If you want to scan all attachments, no matter the file type, a registry key change must be made to the *ScanAllAttachments* key. Changing the value from 0 to 1 will ensure that Forefront scans all files.

The registry key can be located at:

For 32 bit systems: HKLM\Software\Microsoft\Forefront Server Security\ SharePoint

For 64-bit systems: HKLM\Software\Wow6432Node\Microsoft\Forefront Server Security\SharePoint

Scanner Updates

Updating the scanning engines is one of the most important functions for Forefront. Without up–to-date scan engines, you are at risk. The most dangerous viruses are the ones that cannot be detected. That is why Forefront updates scan engines hourly, starting five minutes after the service is started.

Selecting the different scan engines displays their schedule in the bottom pane. This is where you can configure the engine to update on any schedule and check the current status. If you have an engine that has not been updated recently, click the

Update Now button on the work pane. You can also **Enable** or **Disable** a scan engine. If your server makes a connection through a corporate proxy, the updates will fail. You can change the proxy configuration in the *General Settings* section.

Templates

Templates can be used to provide consistent scan settings to multiple Forefront Security for SharePoint installations. If you have an existing template, you can select it from the drop-down menu. To create a new template, select **File | Templates | New** and you will be prompted with a dialog box on which type of template you would like to create. The options are **SP Realtime**, **SP Manual**, and **Filter Set**. Enter the name of the template and click **OK**.

To modify the new template, select **File | Templates | View Templates**. The templates will now appear in the work pane with the Jobs List. With the new template selected, you can change and save scan job settings which can be distributed to other Forefront servers. The next time you select the *Templates* settings, you can choose the new template and click **Load from template**. This will change all scan settings to the settings saved to the template.

All templates are saved to template.fdb, located in the data subdirectory of the SharePoint installation location. You can use the Forefront Server Security Management Console to deploy the templates remotely. Then use the command line utility *fscstarter* to install the templates to the server locally.

General Options

The *General Options* settings are broken up into four sections (see Figure 6.7): *Diagnostics*, *Logging*, *Scanner updates*, and *Scanning*. These settings impact how Forefront operates. It is important to understand what each setting does and how it will impact the server. Once you make a change to the General Options, you must click the **Save** button at the bottom of the Administrator Console.

The *Diagnostics* section allows you to gather more information about scanning that is being done on the server. The *Additional Manual* setting logs every file that is scanned by the manual scanner. The *Additional Realtime* setting logs every file that is scanned by the Realtime scanner. This additional diagnostics information is located in the ProgramLog.txt file. If you are scanning a lot of files or running a lot of scans, this file can get quite large. You should only enable this level of diagnostic if you are encountering a problem with Forefront. The *Notify on Startup* generates an email to the Virus

Administrators list every time a scan is started. This will enable you to track when scans are being kicked off and if there are any conflicts.

The *Logging* section allows you to customize the type and size of logs generated by Forefront. By default, the following settings are selected: *Enable Event log*, *Enable Forefront Program log* (ProgramLog.txt), and *Enable Performance Monitor and Statistics*. The max program log size is also set to 0 (unlimited). If you are running short on space, you may want to enter a maximum log size. You can also enable the Forefront Virus Log (VirusLog.txt) to log all viruses found on the server.

The *Scanner Updates* section allows for configuration of the scan engines. In this section, you can configure the server to be a redistribution server or a spoke server that connects to another server for updates. Using this setting allows you to designate one server that will be configured to download all the updates from Microsoft and the others to connect internally to get updates. To configure a server to be the Redistribution server, enable the **Redistribution Server** option. If you need to use a proxy to get updates, enable **User Proxy Settings** and enter the **Proxy Username** and **Proxy Password** information in the appropriate text fields. If the server will be getting updates from another forefront server, enable **Use UNC Credentials** and enter the **UNC Username** and **UNC Password** in the appropriate text fields. To send a notification every time a scan engine is updated to the Virus Administrator, select **Send Update Notification**.

The *Scanning* section allows for detailed configuration of scanned files. The *Block/ Delete Corrupted Compressed Files* is enabled by default and will take its action based on the *Action* setting for the job that is being run. Forefront can scan the first file of a multiple-file RAR compressed file. The remainder of the multiple files will be treated as a Corrupted Compressed file and the *Delete Corrupted Compressed Files* setting will be followed. Similarly, the *Block/Delete Corrupted Unencoded Files* will follow the instructions based on the *Action* setting for the job that is being run if enabled. Enabling the **Scan Doc files as Container** setting will ensure that embedded files in documents such as Microsoft Word, Excel, and PowerPoint are scanned as well. This setting can be enabled for real-time and manual scans. You can also enable **Case Sensitive Keyword Filtering** and a re-scan of files after a scanner is updated. The rest of the options detail the size or number of items that Forefront will use when scanning a document. Raising these numbers may impact performance so you will want to test any changes in a test environment where you can simulate a production load. In most production environments, the default settings are sufficient.

Figure 6.7 Forefront Security for SharePoint General Options

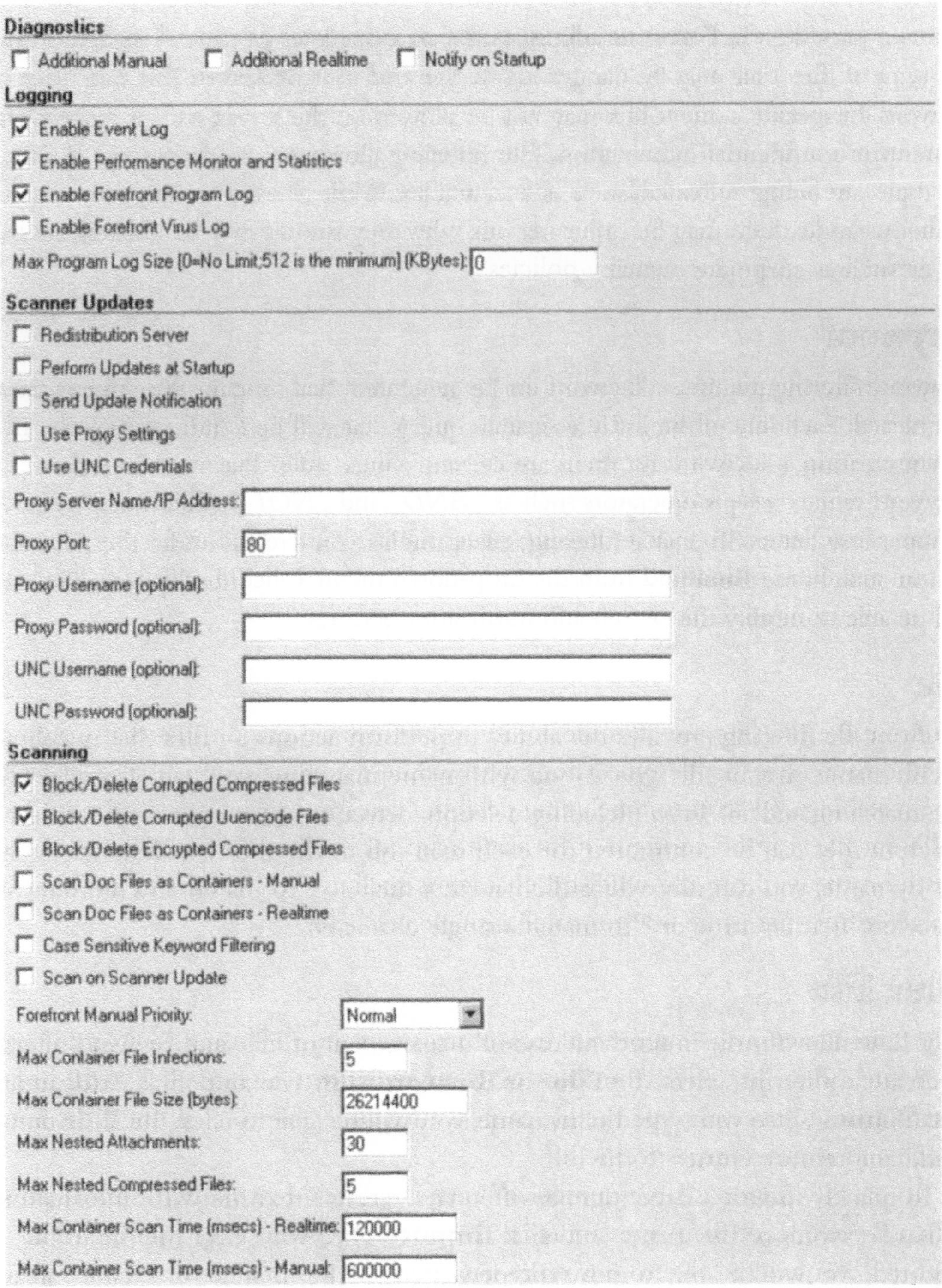

Diagnostics

☐ Additional Manual   ☐ Additional Realtime   ☐ Notify on Startup

Logging

☑ Enable Event Log

☑ Enable Performance Monitor and Statistics

☑ Enable Forefront Program Log

☐ Enable Forefront Virus Log

Max Program Log Size [0=No Limit;512 is the minimum] (KBytes): `0`

Scanner Updates

☐ Redistribution Server

☑ Perform Updates at Startup

☐ Send Update Notification

☐ Use Proxy Settings

☐ Use UNC Credentials

Proxy Server Name/IP Address: `_____`

Proxy Port: `80`

Proxy Username (optional): `_____`

Proxy Password (optional): `_____`

UNC Username (optional): `_____`

UNC Password (optional): `_____`

Scanning

☑ Block/Delete Corrupted Compressed Files

☑ Block/Delete Corrupted Uuencode Files

☐ Block/Delete Encrypted Compressed Files

☐ Scan Doc Files as Containers - Manual

☐ Scan Doc Files as Containers - Realtime

☐ Case Sensitive Keyword Filtering

☐ Scan on Scanner Update

Forefront Manual Priority: `Normal ▼`

Max Container File Infections: `5`

Max Container File Size (bytes): `26214400`

Max Nested Attachments: `30`

Max Nested Compressed Files: `5`

Max Container Scan Time (msecs) - Realtime: `120000`

Max Container Scan Time (msecs) - Manual: `600000`

Filtering

Filtering provides the Forefront administrator an extra level of control in determining the type of files that may be dangerous to the end user or server. You can filter on keyword for specific content that may not be allowed on the server, such as inappropriate content or confidential information. File filtering allows you to determine if specific file types are being uploaded, such as executables. While these files may not contain malicious code, there may be other reasons why they should not be allowed on the server, such as corporate security policies.

Keyword

Keyword filtering requires a keyword list be generated that contains the information to be queried. Each line of the list is a separate query that will be conducted by the filter. When creating a keyword list, there are certain syntax rules that must be followed. Keyword syntax accepts operators such as _AND_ and _NOT_, which must be entered in upper case letters. To enable filtering, select the list you created under the *Filter Lists* section and choose **Enabled** from the drop-down menu. Once the list is enabled, you will be able to modify the action and notification settings.

File

Forefront file filtering provides the ability to perform actions on files that match a specific name, size, or file type. Along with name matching, you can also select file type matching and an *Action* including deletion, detection, quarantine, and notification. Different files can be configured for each scan job in the Jobs list. When selecting files by name, you can use wildcard characters such as * to match any number of characters in a file name or ? to match a single character.

Filter List

Filter Lists allow for the import and ease of management of File and Keyword filtering. To create a filter list, select the **Files** or **Keywords** list type and click **Add** under **List Names**. Once you type the list name, you will be able to click the **Edit** button to add and remove entries to the list.

To quickly import a large number of entries, create a text file with information such as keywords or file names and click **Import**. Once you select the file to be imported, you will be able to move the new items to the Include or Exclude areas (see Figure 6.8). After you have moved the items, click **OK**.

Figure 6.8 Forefront Security Filtering Import Screen

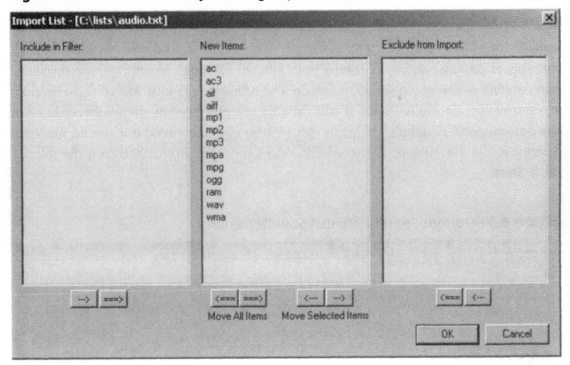

NOTE

Forefront Security does not accept import filter lists that are UTF-8 formatted. To change the file type of the filter list, you can open the list in Microsoft Notepad and click **Save As**. On the **Save As** screen, you can change the Encoding to **Unicode** to ensure that it will be accepted by Forefront.

Operate

The *Operate* section of the Administrator Console is where the scans are started, either by selecting the job and starting it manually or scheduling it for a later time. Once you have completed configuration of a job, this is where you will ultimately end up to run it.

Run Job

The *Run Job* selection provides a list of jobs in the work pane that are available to run instantly (see Figure 6.9). The state of the job tells you if it is currently enabled, stopped, running, or paused. Typically Realtime Scan Jobs are running constantly in the Enabled state, waiting to detect viruses upon upload. The Manual Scan Jobs will be the ones that are initiated by the administrator. If you have already run the scan, the results are listed in the bottom pane. Highlight the Scan you wish to run and check if it should use Virus Scanning, File Filtering, or Keyword Filtering. Once you are ready to run the job, click **Start**.

Figure 6.9 Forefront Security Manual Scan Detection

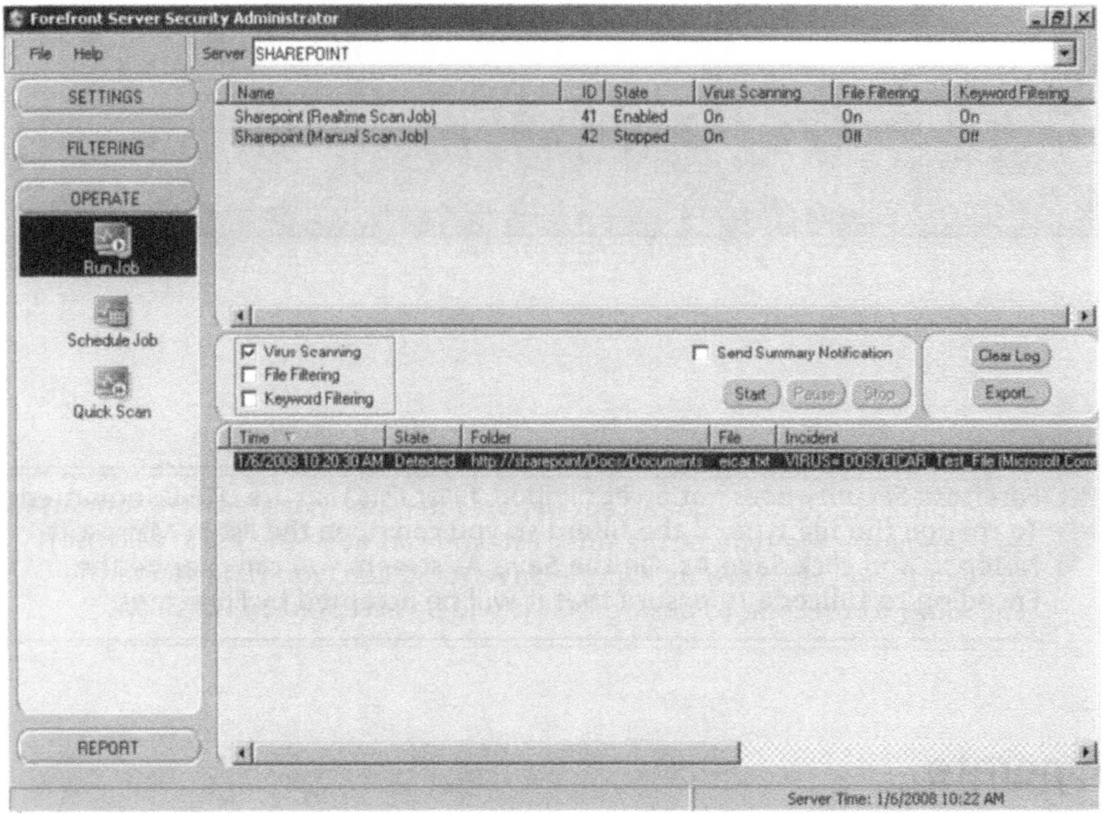

Schedule job

Any manual scan job that is created can be scheduled by going to the *Schedule Jobs* settings under the *Operate* section. Select the job that you would like to schedule and you will see a calendar in the bottom pane. Once you put in the date, time, and frequency of the scan, click **Save**. The scan will be ready to execute at the specified time.

Scheduling manual scan jobs on a periodic basis is a good practice ensuring that all files are being scanned on a continuous basis. As we learned earlier, manual scan jobs can also be configured to use different scan engines, allowing for maximum protection of every file on the server. Be sure to schedule these scans during "off hours" to minimize any performance issues.

Quick Scan

If a quick scan of a document library or SharePoint installation is required without needing it to be reoccurring, the Quick Scan section is where you will run it. The Quick Scan allows you to select any location you would be able to select with a manual scan, the file scanners to use, and the Bias, Action, and Notification settings mentioned previously. All the key options are available in one place for ease and speedy configuration with the results showing up in the bottom pane. Once you initiate the scan, it can also be stopped or paused from this window.

Report

Now that we have configured the scans, set up filtering, and set them to run, we will need to take a look at how the data will be presented back to us. The *Report* section provides three different views into the results of the scans that have been run. We will take a look at the settings used for notification of successful detection during the scanning process along with a historical look at past scanning results that can be exported and reviewed during standard incident response procedures.

Notification

The notification settings allow the Forefront administrator to be alerted instantly of any files that are malicious on the server and what action was taken against the file.

Organizations will have varying response procedures dependent on the type of information on the SharePoint system and the importance of securing the specific server. The great thing about the notification section is that the alerts can be customized. You will be able to add SMTP email addresses for each of the notifications listed in the work pane, as well as customize the individual subject and body fields. If you do not want a specific type of notification to be sent, you can also disable it by selecting the notification name and clicking the **Disable** button.

TIP

To access other keyword variables when customizing the notification message, right click in the field and highlight **Paste Keyword**. You will see a listing of all available keywords that will provide additional information to the recipient.

Incidents

The incidents section (see Figure 6.10) provides a historical look at the files that triggered an alert during a scan. The work pane has the name of the scan job that generated the alert along with the location, specific file, the triggering event, and specifics about the author of the file and who last modified the file. Analyzing this data will enable the Forefront administrator to quickly identify a threat to the server with detailed information about the source of the incident.

The option to purge the logs after a set number of days allows you to keep the incidents database maintained for quick queries. Filtering the results will allow you to focus your search to specific areas, which will aid in determining who may be infecting the server. All files that were flagged will show up in the incidents list, whether it was flagged for a virus, keyword violation, or file type violation. These incidents can be filtered by any of the columns shown in the incidents list. Once you input the filtering criteria, select **Save**.

Figure 6.10 Forefront Security Incident Reporting

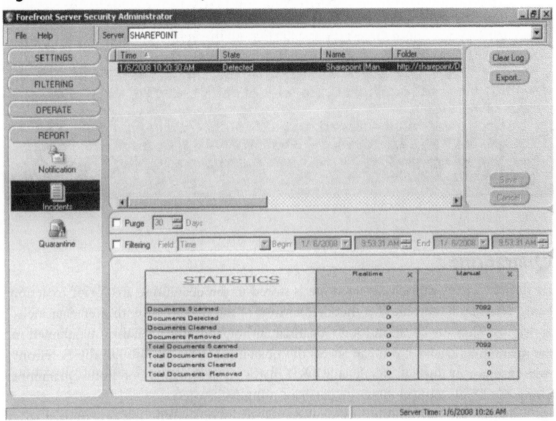

Maintaining the Incident and Quarantine Databases

All incidents are stored in a database called Incidents.mdb located in the installation folder of Forefront Security for SharePoint. The quarantine database is called Quarantine.mdb and is also located in the installation folder. These databases each have a 2GB limit. When the database reaches 75% full, a notification is sent to the Virus Administrators that the database is near the limit and that maintenance is needed. If events are not purged, future incidents may not be saved.

Continued

> There are two ways to clear the log; the first is to the right of the list of incidents where you are provided the option to save the log and to clear the log. When you choose **Clear Log**, it will clear all the events listed in the incident section. The second way is to go to the individual scan that was run in the *Operate* Section and select **Clear Log**. This will only clear events associated with that specific scan. If there are a lot of entries selected, this process can take a long time.
>
> Once the events are cleared, they do not show up in the Administrators console, but they have not yet been removed from their respective database file. They will be removed the next time the database is compacted, which is typically at 2:00 A.M. daily.

Quarantine

By default, a copy of each detected file is stored in the quarantine area prior to action being taken by Forefront. The encoded version of the files along with metadata such as original filename, location found, original author, and other details is maintained in the quarantine database. You can access the quarantine database through the Forefront Administrator or through the default DSN that is created named Forefront Quarantine. Using the DSN, you can view the database using MS Access.

Using Forefront Administrator, you can clear the quarantine log or export it to a text file. To extract a copy of the file that was quarantined, select the file to be extracted and use the **Save as** button. You will then be prompted for a location to save the file in question. Like the incidents section, the quarantine section provides the ability to purge after a specific number of days as well as filter the quarantine list by any of the columns listed in the work pane.

Summary

As collaborative, document-sharing environments such as Microsoft SharePoint become more prevalent, the need to provide a high level of security with minimal impact to the user community is more necessary. Forefront Security for SharePoint provides a way to eliminate malicious files and questionable content. The ability to use real-time and manual scanning in an integrated environment greatly decreases the chances that virus outbreaks will occur, which is critical when many users have access to the same data sources such as documents, spreadsheets, and Web pages.

To provide the greatest level of certainty that any and all malicious files will be detected, Microsoft provides the ability to choose from eight different leading antivirus vendors, with up to five selected at one time. Combined with the ability to customize the level of analysis that each file gets by selecting the Bias, you are able to provide a safe working document sharing library. For any business, the ability to balance security and performance is a priority, which we will need to constantly reassess as Forefront Administrators of the SharePoint collaborative environment. As more documents are loaded, more sites are created, and performance loads on the servers adjust, we too must reevaluate how Forefront is installed and maintained.

During the installation of Forefront Security for SharePoint, it is important to remember that SharePoint be updated to the latest Service Pack and hot fixes. If it is not, you may see exception errors after installation. With the Microsoft's Hot Upgrade technology, Forefront installation is made easier because SharePoint services do not need to be restarted, resulting in no downtime or loss of productivity for the system users.

After the initial installation, Forefront must be configured and optimized for your business requirements. More security requirements will set the framework for higher Bias and increased scanning whereas performance concerns will drive minimal scanning with limited antivirus engines. With a total of five antivirus engines available to scan at any time, it is important to remember that each vendor releases updates on different schedules, some more frequently than others. It is a good idea to research which antivirus vendor best suits your need.

Providing a consistent scanning environment should also be considered if installing Forefront Security for SharePoint on multiple SharePoint servers in an organization. Forefront allows the ability to save and load scanning configuration templates, which can be copied to all Forefront servers and imported, ensuring that the same keywords, files, and file types are scanned.

Solutions Fast Track

Implementing Microsoft Forefront Server for SharePoint

☑ Verify that SharePoint Service Pack 1 has been installed prior to installing Forefront Security for SharePoint. If SharePoint has not been upgraded to the latest version, errors will be generated when you try to manage the installation.

☑ Prior to installing, make sure you know what accounts you will be using and verify that they have the proper authorization. If the SharePoint database is located on a separate server, you will need to have the account and password available during installation. The account that is logged in to do the install must also have administrative privileges on the target server.

☑ Ensure that the hardware requirements of the server can support the planned configuration. If required, upgrade the memory of the server prior to the installation to support the increased load from configuring multiple scanning engines.

Configuring the Forefront Server Security Administrator for SharePoint

☑ Determine the antivirus strategy you will be implementing and ensure that you have the proper scans to provide coverage for all document libraries and SharePoint sites. Configuring scans that overlap may cause unnecessary performance issues or having document libraries or SharePoint sites that are not covered may leave your SharePoint installation vulnerable.

☑ Understand how Bias affects the antivirus engine scan process and can impact server performance. This setting directly impacts how much attention files receive, from one scan engine to all five.

☑ Use Filter lists to detect files that may not be malicious but violate confidentiality or inappropriate content restrictions. These lists can be important to ensure consistency throughout the organization.

☑ All files that are detected are maintained in their original form in the quarantine areas. For submission to antivirus vendors or for further research in the security department in your organization, you can export the original file to a shared location.

☑ Use the Reporting tools in Forefront Administrator to provide analysis on files that may contain malicious content or break keyword or file type restriction. You can export these reports for later analysis.

Frequently Asked Questions

Q: What access is required of the account that is used during installation?

A: During the installation, you will be prompted to enter an account that is a member of the SharePoint server's local administrators group as well as the database server's local administrators group if the database was installed on a separate server. Also, the account that you are logged in with will need administrative rights on the target installation server.

Q: If you install Forefront Security for SharePoint and receive an exception error when in the Administrator console, what is the first thing you should check?

A: Service pack 1 for Windows SharePoint Server is required for Forefront Security for SharePoint. If you receive an exception error when managing Forefront using the console, verify that the latest service pack and hotfixes have been applied by running Microsoft Windows Update.

Q: If you change the password for the account used during setup to connect to the database server, do you need to update Forefront?

A: Yes, the *FSSPController* service is configured with the account information provided during setup and can be changed in the **Services Management Console**. If the password is not changed, the *FSSPController* service will fail.

Q: Is it required to select all five antivirus engines to perform scanning?

A: The more antivirus engines you have scanning the files on the SharePoint server, the bigger the performance hit will be. Only one scan engine is required and the addition of each additional engine should be reviewed as additional server memory will be allocated to it. You can also choose more than one antivirus engine and configure the **Bias to Favor Performance**, which will scan the file with between one and half the number of engines selected.

Q: What command line utility can be used to disable and enable scan jobs in Forefront?

A: FSCstarter.exe, located in the Forefront installation directory, can disable or enable scan jobs from the command line. This is often done to unload scan engines from memory so they can be upgraded without having to stop the Forefront Services.

The command line utility works on the local server as well as on remote Forefront for SharePoint installations.

Q: How can I control the level of scanning the antivirus engines will complete on the files within the SharePoint server?

A: The Bias setting allows for a scalable implementation of the antivirus engines that goes from scanning with only one engine (Maximum Performance) to scanning with the five selected antivirus engines (Maximum Certainty). There are a total of five levels available that let you control more specifically how Forefront handles scanning with regard to the antivirus engines.

Q: Does Forefront Server for SharePoint detect files based on their file extension?

A: No, Forefront looks at the header of each file that is uploaded to determine the type of file that it is. Changing file extensions was an easy way to get past antivirus scans in the past so Microsoft has implemented a more sophisticated approach. For example, if you were to change the name of a zip file from SharePoint.zip to Sharepoint.txt, Forefront would still be able to determine that it was a zip file and deal with it according to the scan settings.

Q: Does every Forefront Server for SharePoint need to have access to the Internet to download engine updates?

A: Antivirus engine updates can be downloaded by connecting to Microsoft over the Internet or by connecting to a redistribution server on the local network. This allows for the configuration of one server to connect to the Internet and download the updates, and the other servers to connect to it.

Chapter 7

Managing and Maintaining Microsoft Forefront Servers

Solutions in this chapter:

- Implementing a Backup Strategy
- Utilizing the Microsoft Forefront Server Security Management Console

☑ Summary

☑ Solutions Fast Track

☑ Frequently Asked Questions

Introduction

Centralized Management is one of the major benefits of the Microsoft Forefront products. The Microsoft Forefront Server Security Management Console (FSSMC) is a Web-based interface that allows an administrator to centrally manage all of their Microsoft Forefront Exchange and SharePoint servers. Servers can be grouped and managed from a central location to further simplify administration. And, for the sake of simplification, global configurations can also be invoked.

Most administrators will appreciate the Microsoft FSSMC for its ability to run reports and manage jobs for Forefront servers in an easy-to-use Web interface. The network administrator can also use the Alert feature to stay on top of problems or activities that are occurring on any Forefront servers on the network. Using these alerts along with the reporting feature, will keep a security professional informed about security-related issues on the network.

The implementation of Microsoft Forefront servers on the network results in the additional workload of monitoring these extra servers. Microsoft has created the Web-based FSSMC to give network administrators the flexibility to manage all Forefront servers from a central location. This Web-based console makes it easy for security professionals to manage and maintain the Forefront servers on the network.

Implementing a Backup Strategy

FSSMC can be installed in a stand-alone mode or in a primary backup mode to ensure high availability. Deploying primary and backup servers ensures information such as engine updates and signature updates. When the primary goes offline, the backup server takes over and performs the functions of the primary server. Information that is replicated between the primary and backup servers includes the managed server list and user data such as templates and jobs.

The FSSMC console screen of the backup server differs from that of the primary server. On the backup server you will find the link to configure replication (see Figure 7.1).

Figure 7.1 Forefront Security Management Console of a Backup Server

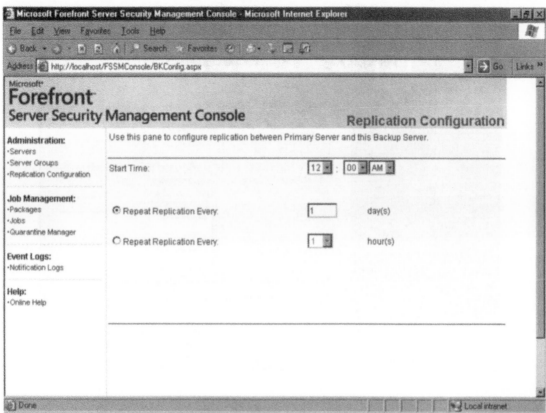

When you execute the setup utility to install FSSMC, you have the option to choose from a stand-alone, primary, or backup installation (see Figure 7.2) If you select the primary server role option, you need to provide a password, which ensures secure communication between the primary and backup servers. You need to provide the same password while installing the backup server. Please ensure the password meets the complexity requirements (combinations of characters, numbers, and symbols), otherwise you will get an error message.

Figure 7.2 FSSMC Installation Options

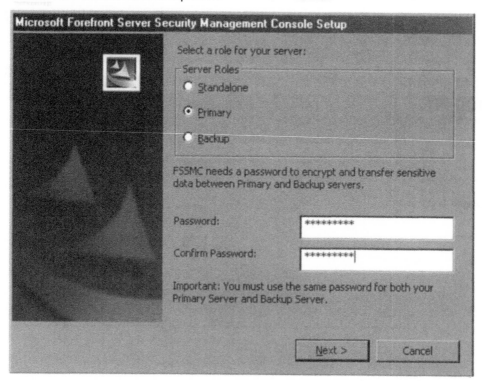

Designing & Planning...

FSSMC

FSSMC cannot be installed on a domain controller, Exchange server, or a SharePoint server. FSSMC should be installed on a member server (Windows 2003) by a domain user with local permissions on the server. Also, FSSMC should not be installed in a demilitarized zone (DMZ).

Internet Information Server (IIS) 6.0, ASP.Net 2.0, and Structured Query Language (SQL) Server 2005 Express Edition are the prerequisites to install the FSSMC. FSSMC setup installs SQL Server 2005 Express automatically. However, if you plan to install the FSSMC in a multiple-server environment or for a large enterprise, it's recommended to install SQL Server 2005 standard edition.

Figure 7.3 shows a typical setup with an Exchange server, SharePoint server, Forefront Security server, and FSSMC servers.

Figure 7.3 Typical Forefront Security Servers and FSSMC Setup

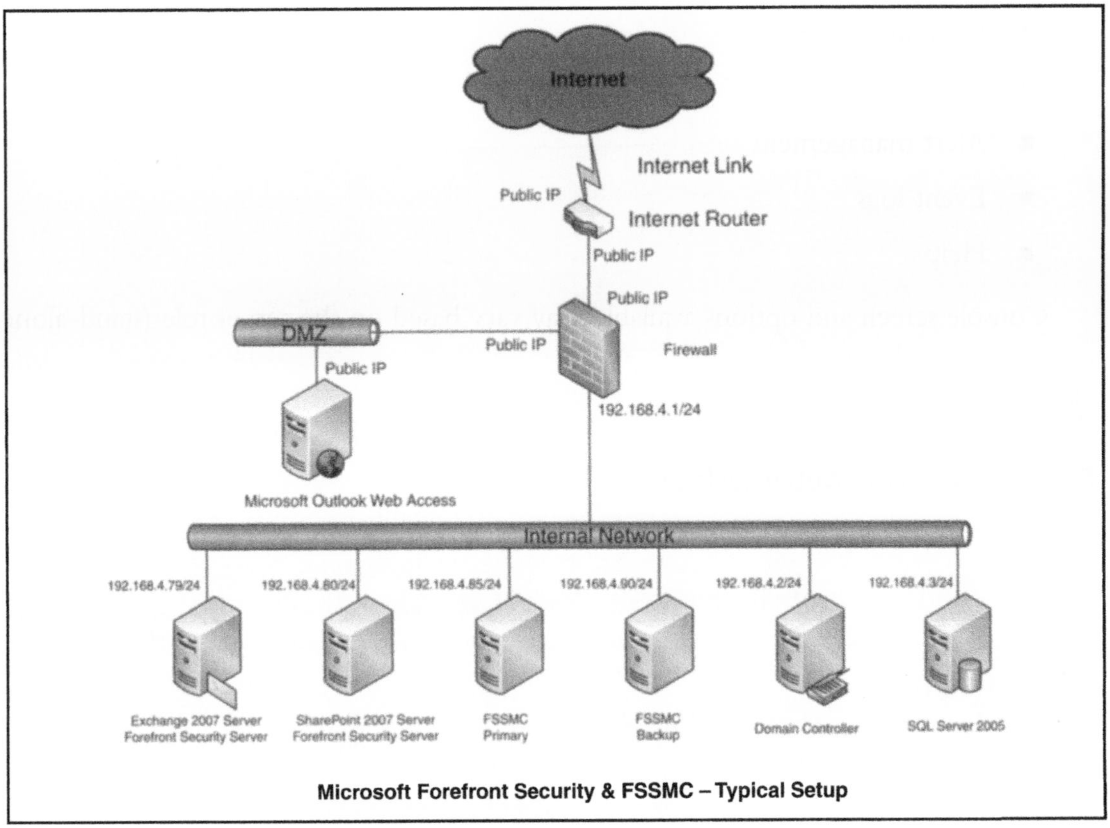

Microsoft Forefront Security & FSSMC – Typical Setup

Utilizing the Microsoft FSSMC

FSSMC deployed on a Windows 2003 server (non-domain controller) provides you the ability to deploy and manage Forefront Security for Exchange and SharePoint servers. You can maintain the antivirus (AV), anti-spam scan engines and versions, hot fixes, and quarantine data, and generate reports with the FSSMC. In addition, packages can be deployed, templates and reports can be created, and alerts can be configured in the FSSMC. In summary, the FSSMC is really a "one stop shop" where Forefront Exchange and SharePoint servers can be managed.

FSSMC can be installed locally or remotely. It provides an easy-to-use Web interface to perform Forefront security management tasks. FSSMC is a background operation and runs regardless of whether the Web interface is kept open or not.

Main Console Page

FSSMC's Web interface (see Figure 7.4) has the following components:

- Administration
- Job management
- Reports
- Alert management
- Event logs
- Help

Console screen and options available may vary based on the server role (stand-alone, primary, or backup).

Figure 7.4 FSSMC Web Interface

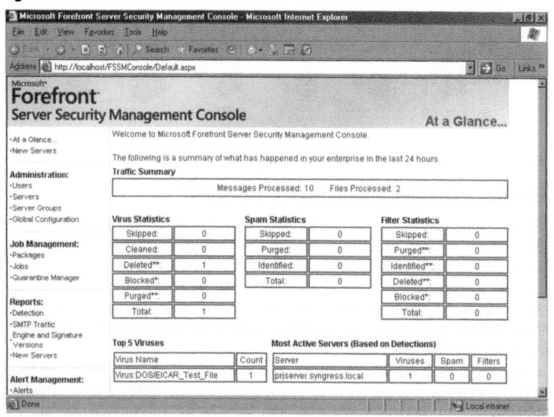

FSSMC also provides a link referred to as "At a Glance," which provides summary information gathered from the managed servers. The link "New Servers" displays servers that are either discovered automatically or added manually. Table 7.1 describes the FSSMC Web interface and its components.

Table 7.1 FSSMC Web Interface and its Components

Component	Link	Description
Main Console	At a Glance	View the traffic summary, virus statistics, spam statistics, filter statistics, top five viruses, and most active servers.
Main Console	New Servers	View the new servers in your network that are discovered through auto-discovery.
Administration	Users	Create user accounts to manage the FSSMC from **Manage Users** work pane.
	Servers	Add or remove servers from the FSSMC from the **Manage Servers** work pane. You can deploy the FSSMC agent on the servers. This agent enables communication between the console and the managed servers.
	Server Groups	Group servers from the **Manage Server Groups** work pane. Grouping the managed servers simplifies the way you can manage the servers.
	Global Configuration	Configure Simple Mail Transfer Protocol (SMTP) and polling intervals from the **Manage Global Configuration** work pane. FSSMC uses SMTP server settings to send notifications.
Job Management	Packages	Deploy Forefront Security images, templates, and product activations from the **Manage Packages** work pane. You can create and configure packages and deploy it through the FSSMC.
	Jobs	Create, modify, delete, or view FSSMC jobs from the **Manage Jobs** work pane.

Continued

Table 7.1 Continued. FSSMC Web Interface and its Components

Component	Link	Description
	Quarantine Manager	Retrieve, filter, and analyze quarantine information from the FSSMC database. You can also view and delete quarantine messages from the **Quarantine Manager** work pane.
Reports	Reports	Generate reports on detected viruses and spam from the **Select Detection Reports** work pane.
	SMTP Traffic	Generate reports on the number of messages and the size of the messages sent and received from the **SMTP Traffic Reports** work pane.
	Engine and Signature Versions	View the reports that are related to signature and engine versions of various AV engines on Forefront Security servers.
	New Servers	Generate reports on the number of servers added during a specific period from the **Select New Servers Report** work pane.
Alert Management	Alerts	Configure alerts to monitor virus and spam activity in your environment from the **Manage Alerts** work pane.
Event Logs	Alert Logs	View alert events.
	Notification Logs	View FSSMC activity logs such as deployment, general options, log retrieval, manual scan, and redistribution jobs from the **Notification Logs** work pane.
Help	Online Help	FSSMC help.

Configuring & Implementing...

FSSMC Primary and Backup Servers

Modification to servers or servers groups is not possible through backup servers. Only Windows authentication is allowed for primary and backup mode installations.

The FSSMC on a backup server may look different from the console of primary servers. The console on the backup server gives you the ability to view servers and server groups, view or copy template packages, and add template packages. The FSSMC on the backup server also allows you to copy, rename, or edit template packages or deployments if they were created on the backup servers. Template packages and jobs that are created on the primary server cannot be modified on the backup servers.

Traffic Summary

The Traffic Summary on the main console screen displays the number of mail messages and files processed. The files processed are attachments of the mails from Exchange or documents in a SharePoint environment.

Virus Statistics

The Virus Statistics (see Figure 7.5) on the main console screen displays information about the viruses processed by the AV engines. Information displayed includes skipped, cleaned, deleted, blocked, and purged. A single asterisk (*) symbol next to deleted, blocked, or purged indicates the Forefront Security for SharePoint. Double asterisk (**) symbols next to these parameters indicate Forefront Security for Exchange servers.

Figure 7.5 Virus Statistics

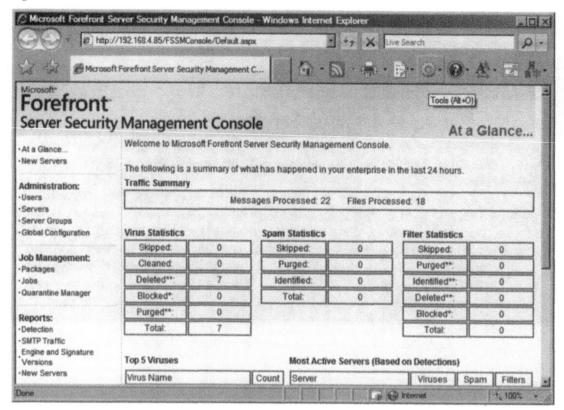

Spam Statistics

The Spam Statistics section of the FSSMC displays skipped, purged, and identified spam. As an experienced administrator, I cannot emphasize enough how management has communicated their feelings about not wanting to receive spam in their inbox, especially if the content is inappropriate or offensive. Be sure to watch these statistics carefully for that reason. Be cautious, because even if the FSSMC is displaying a total of zero spam messages, this will not guarantee a network is spam free. Also, be careful to make sure that e-mail messages from legitimate businesses wind up in the inbox of your employees. You will find that spam settings will need to be adjusted over time, because spammers become more creative in the ways that they are able to penetrate systems through e-mail.

Filter Statistics

Filtering is possible on files, content, and keywords. The Filtering Statistics section of the FSSMC displays skipped, purged, identified, deleted, and blocked messages based on the filters configured.

As mentioned in Chapter 5, you can use filters to perform specific actions such as delete, quarantine, notify, or report whenever the file filter finds attachments matching a specific name, size, or type within a message.

Use file type filters when you want to identify e-mail attachments sent with the *.com* or *.exe*. extension. Attachments with such extensions could obviously harbor malicious code. Filtering by file type helps you to quickly identify attachments with these extensions that are trying to enter the company network.

Obviously, files with extensions other than *.com* and *.exe* also need to be filtered. Use extension filters when you want to identify attachments with specific extensions. As an administrator, you will notice over time that the number of extensions that are blocked by copy policy usually increases. This is because over time new file types are developed and the number of threats continue to rise. Often, these settings are tweaked over time by administrators and/or company policies. When people are unable to conduct legitimate business, restrictions on file extensions will either need to be tightened or loosened.

Use name filters to identify file attachments with a specific name. Name filters can be used to block files containing certain key words or to block identified malicious attachments. Once again, filters such as these can be used to block offensive or inappropriate content. However, these filters can at times block legitimate messages.

The FSSMC also displays the total number of messages that meet the specifications defined by all the filters applied on the messages and documents.

Top 5 Viruses

The Top 5 Viruses section (see Figure 7.6) on the FSSMC main console screen displays the virus name and number of times (count) the virus has been identified. This will help you to understand the types of viruses your network is vulnerable to and allow you to apply appropriate defense mechanisms.

Figure 7.6 Top 5 Viruses

Top 5 Viruses

Virus Name	Count
EICAR_Test_file_not_a_virus!	6
Virus:DOS/EICAR_Test_File	1

Most Active Servers

In a multiple Forefront Security servers' environment, you may also want to know which of these servers are active in identifying viruses and spam. The Most Active Servers section of the FSSMC displays information about the servers based on the maximum detections. This section displays information about viruses, spam, and filters per server. This section will have more significant implications on enterprise networks with a large number of servers.

Administration

You can configure users, servers, server groups, and global configuration under the Administration section.

Users

The installation administrator is the user account utilized to install the FSSMC. It is important to note that there are limitations on where FSSMC can be installed. The FSSMC cannot be installed on a domain controller, DMZ server, or the same server on which you have installed Forefront Security Server. The FSSMC should be installed on a member server by a domain user with local permissions on the server. The user account utilized to install the FSSMC is automatically granted permissions to access the FSSMC. However, you may want to assign permissions to additional users to perform routine management tasks. FSSMC users are linked to the domain user accounts.

Adding/Removing Users

To add or remove users:

1. Click **Start | All Programs | Microsoft Forefront Server Security | Forefront Server Security Management Console** to start the FSSMC. If you are on a different computer then you can type the URL *http://ip_address/FSSMConsole/* on the browser's address bar to access the console.

2. Provide the username and password to authenticate as the administrator.

3. Click **Users** under **Administration** on the navigation area (left) of the FSSMC.

4. Click **Add Users**.

5. Click **Browse** to locate the users.

6. Click on the drop-down button to choose your domain (if not selected already by default). You will find the list of users of the domain on the left pane.

7. Click on a particular user or select multiple users (CTRL + click) and press the >> button to add the users.

8. Click **Add**.

9. Click **Add Users**. Now you will find the users added to the **Manage Users** work pane screen (see Figure 7.7).

10. You may also delete the users from the **Manage Users** work pane by clicking on ☒ **Delete Users**.

Figure 7.7 User Administration

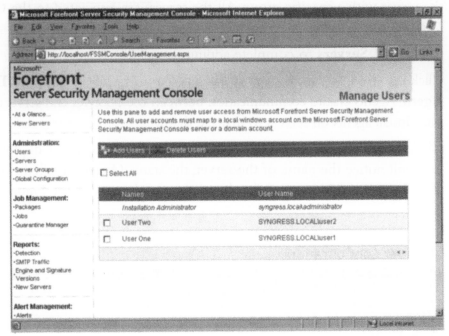

Servers

Forefront Security servers are installed on the Exchange 2007 and SharePoint servers. These servers are managed by the FSSMC. The FSSMC deploys agents to communicate with the Forefront Security servers. You need to add the servers before you can deploy the packages, run jobs, or generate reports.

Adding/Removing Servers

To add or remove Forefront Security Servers to the FSSMC:

1. Click **Servers** under **Administration** on the left navigation area of the FSSMC.

2. Click **Add Servers**.

3. Click **Browse**.

4. Click on the drop-down list to select the **Domain**.

5. Click **Find Now**.

6. Select the servers you want to add from the left pane and press **>>**.

7. Click **Add**.

8. You can also choose a server group from the **Apply Groups** section to associate the server with a specific group. All the servers are associated to the Group *Default* automatically.

9. Click **Add Servers** to complete adding the server.

10. Click the check box on the left of the server you just added and click **Deploy Agent**. Agents ensure communication between the FSSMC and servers. You must install agents on servers to manage them.

11. Click **Deployment Status** to know the status of the agent deployment. You will notice the name of the server, the status (Agent installed), version (Forefront 10.1.0746.0) and the description of the server (see Figure 7.8).

Figure 7.8 Server Configuration

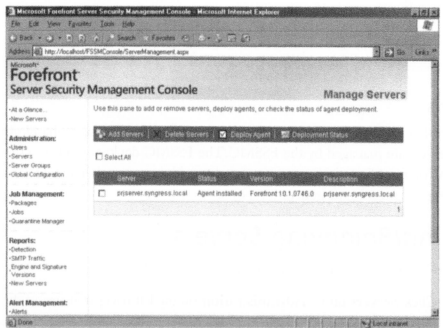

Server Groups

Servers can be grouped and managed from a central location to further simplify administration, and, for the sake of simplification, global configurations can also be invoked. You may add servers to one or more groups.

To add or remove servers from the Server Groups:

1. Click **Servers Groups** under **Administration** on the left navigation area of the FSSMC.

2. Click **Add Group**.

3. Type a name and click **Add**. You may notice a folder-like icon displaying the newly created group. When you add new servers you may assign the same to this group to manage multiple servers.

4. Click **Assign Servers**.

5. Choose the servers by selecting the check boxes and press the **Assign** button to complete the server assignments.

You may use the Manage Server Groups work pane to rename, delete, and move groups. You may also delete the servers from this work pane (see Figure 7.9).

Figure 7.9 Server Group Configuration

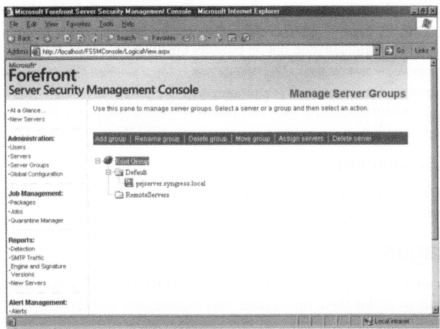

Global Configuration

Global configuration is one of the main tasks you need to perform after implementing the FSSMC. Adding servers and users and configuring jobs are the other important tasks you need to perform.

The Global Configuration section includes SMTP server, statistics polling, and download configuration options.

You need to provide the SMTP Server (Internet Protocol [IP] address or fully qualified domain name) from the address, user name, and password. If your mail server is configured to check SMTP authentication, you need to select the checkbox **Require SMTP Authentication**. This information is used by the FSSMC to send notifications and alert messages. You may create a user in your Active Directory called *fssmc_alert* instead of using any regular user accounts. You can send a test mail to confirm that you receive e-mails from the FSSMC. You can also create a Distribution group in Active Directory and assign individuals within your organization responsible for forefront to that group. That way, all individuals responsible for the FSSMC will be alerted when there are any issues.

In a multiple Forefront security servers environment, you may have a considerable amount of traffic between the FSSMC and managed servers. FSSMC periodically retrieves historical data from these managed servers to generate reports. The default interval is set to 240 minutes. A shorter value may provide accurate reports but result in increased network traffic. A larger value will generate less network traffic, but may result in less accurate reports. You may tweak this value to optimize the polling interval specific to your environment.

The download configuration option provides the site from where FSSMC downloads the latest signatures and updates. The default site is *http://forefrontdl.microsoft.com/server/scanengineupdate*. If your network is configured to use proxy servers, provide the proxy server IP, port number, user name, and password. If you use proxy servers in your environment and have not supplied this information, FSSMC updates may fail.

Job Management

Through Job management you can deploy the packages, schedule jobs and maintain the quarantine database.

Packages

Packages are used to upload software, hot fixes, and templates. You may also upload licenses files to deploy them throughout your organization. You can add, copy, rename, edit or delete packages from Manage Packages work pane.

To add a package:

1. Click **Package** under **Job Management** on the left navigation area of the FSSMC.

2. Click **Add**.

3. Type the name of the Package you want to deploy.

4. Click **Browse** to locate the setup file from the local computer. You may choose an installation package or a Forefront security template. Based on the file size you load, it may take time as FSSMC adds the file to its database. Uploading files from a remote computer may amount to additional time to upload.

After you upload the package, the Configure Installation Package work pane appears (see Figure 7.10). You have the following options:

- **Target Folders** Provide the installation folder and start menu folder information.

- **Product Key** Provide the license key or product key.

Figure 7.10 Package Configuration

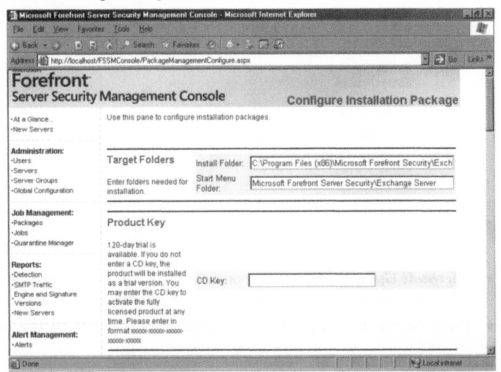

- **Engine Selection** You can integrate the package deployment with five AV scan engines. The Microsoft Antimalware Engine is selected by default. Other options include AhnLab V3 Engine, CA Vet, Command, Kaspersky, Norman Data Defense, Sophos Anti-Virus, and VirusBuster. The engine selections can also be changed at a later stage (see Figure 7.11).

- **Enable Anti-Spam Updates** Microsoft Update offers anti-spam updates apart from the regular product updates. You can enable this checkbox to automatically update the anti-spam components for the Exchange servers.

Figure 7.11 Package Configuration Options

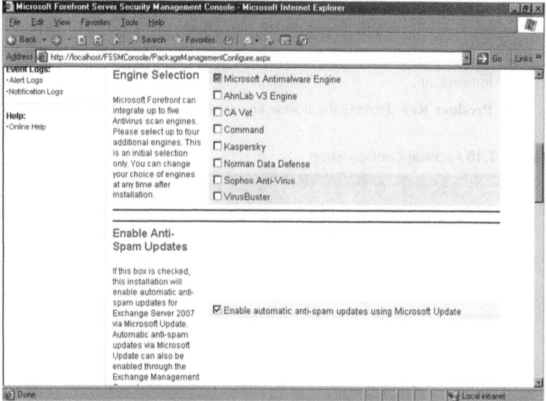

- **Microsoft Update** You have the option to use Microsoft Update or not. Select from the drop-down list if you do not want Microsoft updates.

- **Proxy Server** Provide proxy server information if your network uses proxy servers.

- **Quarantine Security Settings** Secure mode allows applying filters on messages delivered from the quarantine. The other mode is the Compatibility mode, which you can choose from the drop-down list.

- **Hot Upgrade Critical File** You can choose between Recycle services or Abort upgrade. The Recycle services option allows upgrades without stopping the services (see Figure 7.12).

Figure 7.12 User Administration

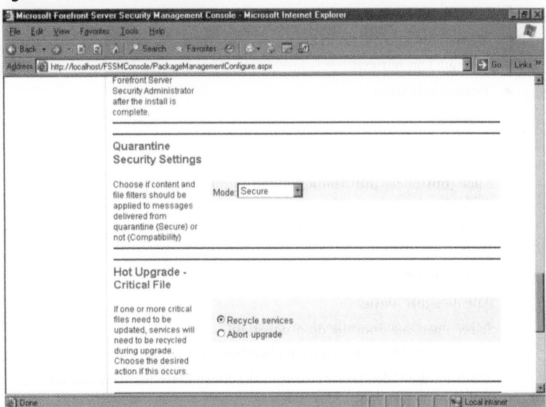

- **Hot Upgrade-mail Flow** During the upgrades of services, e-mails to be scanned will be queued. Recycle services, Disable scanning, or Abort upgrade are the three actions FSSMC can perform on the e-mail flow. Recycle services is the default and recommended option to ensure e-mails are not passed without scanning.

Jobs

From the Manage Jobs work pane, you can create, edit, copy, delete, check status, and run various jobs. You can also roll back from a previously executed job. Run Now allows you to manually execute the task immediately. You can create the following jobs:

- Deployment
- Signature redistribution
- Schedule report
- General option
- Manual scan
- Remote logs retrieval
- Product activation
- Operation

To create a job:

1. Click **Jobs** under **Job Management** on the left navigation area of the FSSMC.
2. Click on the type of job from the tree displayed on the **Manage Jobs** work pane.
3. Click **Create**.
4. Provide a **Job name**.
5. Select a package from the drop-down list.
6. Deselect the **Do not schedule** checkbox. This activates the calendar.
7. Click on the Calendar icon next to the **Start Date** text box and select a date to schedule a job.
8. Select the **Start Time**.
9. Type an e-mail address and click **Add**. Notification of the success or failure of the job will be sent to this e-mail address.
10. Click **Next**.
11. Select the Forefront Security server to which you want to assign this job.
12. Click **Finish**.

You will find the job listed under the specific category you chose earlier (see Figure 7.13) when you return to the Manage Jobs work pane.

Figure 7.13 Job Management

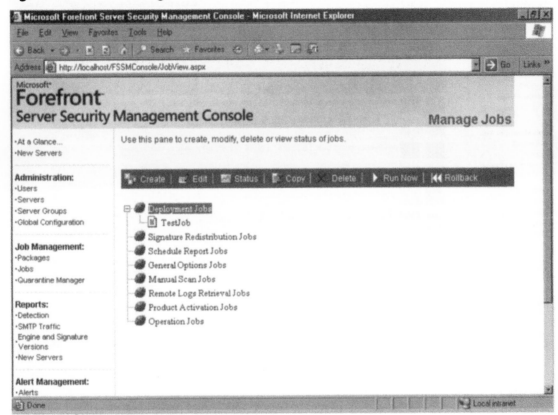

Quarantine Manager

You can analyze and manage quarantine data using Quarantine Manager (see Figure 7.14).

The Retrieve Data tab allows you to import data from Forefront Security servers. You can select the start date from when you want to import the data for analysis.

The View Filter tab allows you to filter the imported data with parameters such as host (all machines or specific server), sender, sender address, recipients, recipient address, file, incident, CC (carbon copy), CC address, message, BCC (blind carbon copy), and/or BCC address. You can use *and/or connector* to apply different combinations of the filters.

You can sort the information in ascending or descending order and by all parameters available in the filter. You can also sort the information by date and time.

A single asterisk (*) refers to entries for Exchange server.

Figure 7.14 Quarantine Manager

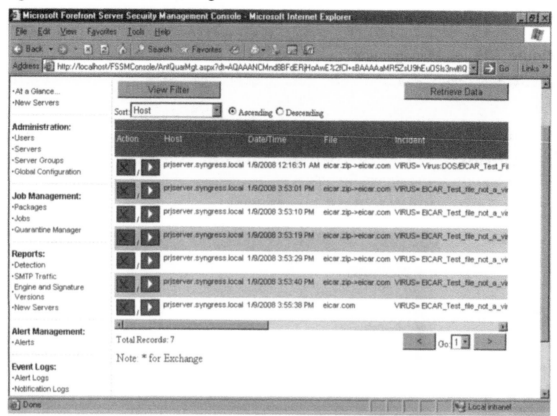

Reports

The Reports section, as seen in Figure 7.15, allows to you to generate various reports on the virus and spam detections, SMTP traffic, engine, and signature versions and new servers detected.

Figure 7.15 Reports

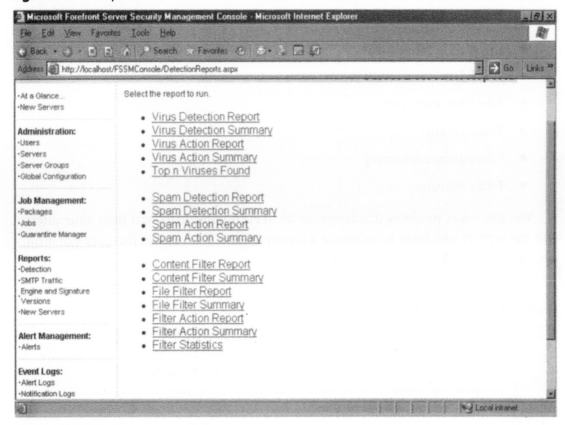

Detections

From this section of the FSSMC you can generate various types of detection reports. The report types include:

- Virus detection
- Virus detection summary
- Virus action
- Virus action summary
- Top *n* viruses found
- Spam detection
- Spam detection summary
- Spam action

- Spam action summary
- Content filter
- Content filter summary
- File Filter
- File filter summary
- Filter action
- Filter action summary
- Filter statistics

You can select products (Exchange or SharePoint), start date and time, time interval, and the servers you want to generate a report. Figure 7.16 shows the configuration options for Virus Detection Report.

Figure 7.16 Virus Detection Report

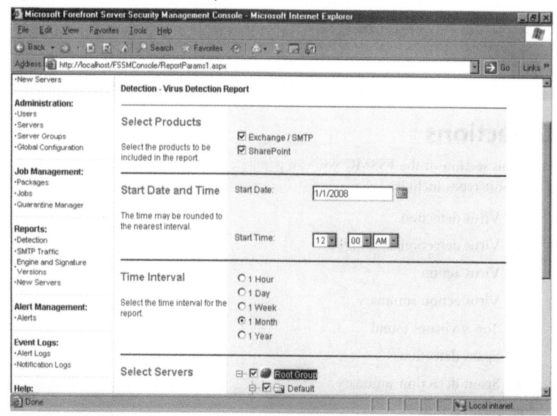

SMTP Traffic

From this section of the FSSMC you can generate various types of SMTP traffic reports. The report types include:

- SMTP messages processed
- SMTP messages processed summary
- SMTP bytes processed
- SMTP bytes processed summary

Figure 7.17 displays the SMTP messages process summary report.

Figure 7.17 SMTP Messages Process Summary Report

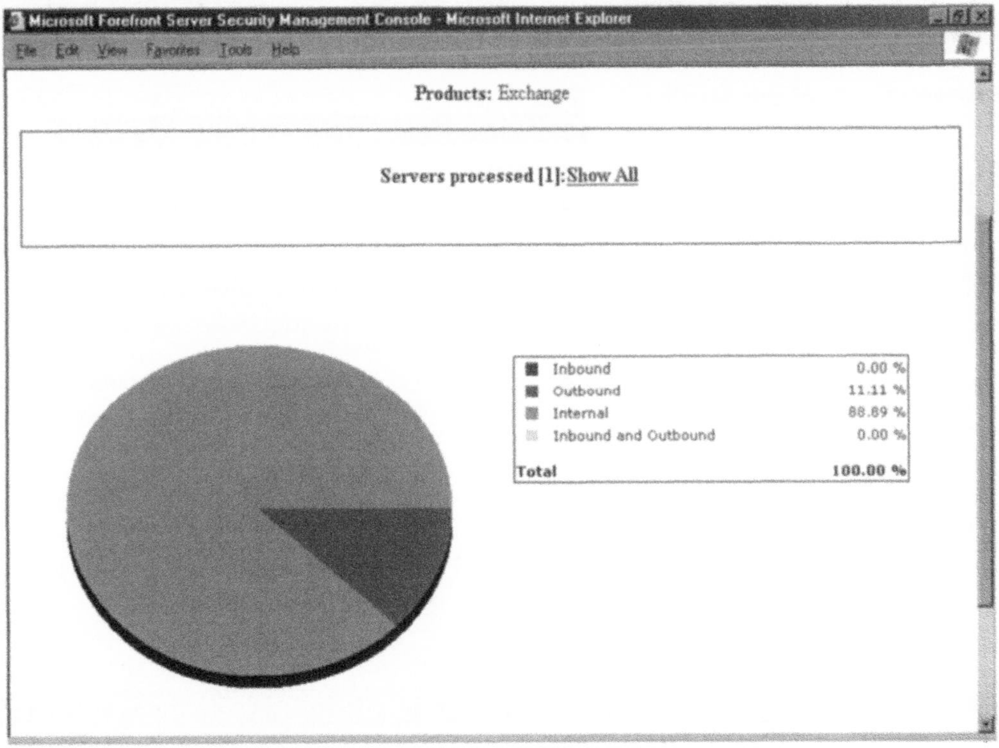

Engine Versions

From this section of the FSSMC, you can generate out-of-date engine, signature versions full engine, and signature versions. Knowing the current version and the version deployed in your network is very important. Monitor whether your network has the latest AV and anti-spam measures in place. Microsoft Forefront Security server supports engines from several vendors. Response time from anti-virus vendors to an outbreak varies. A vendor's approach to resolving a virus issue can vary. Customers can greatly benefit from this multi-vendor protection approach. This approach works better than a single engine approach, as single engine approaches will not work if that particular vendor fails or delays to respond to a virus. Figure 7.18 shows various engines supported by Microsoft Forefront Security.

Figure 7.18 FSSMC Engines

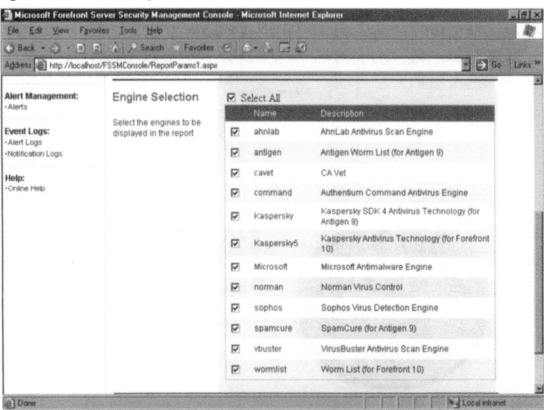

You may also generate the list of engines along with the current signature version report. Figure 7.19 shows the server name, update, engine, and signature versions, and the last checked and last updated details of all engines.

Figure 7.19 Engine and Signature Version Report

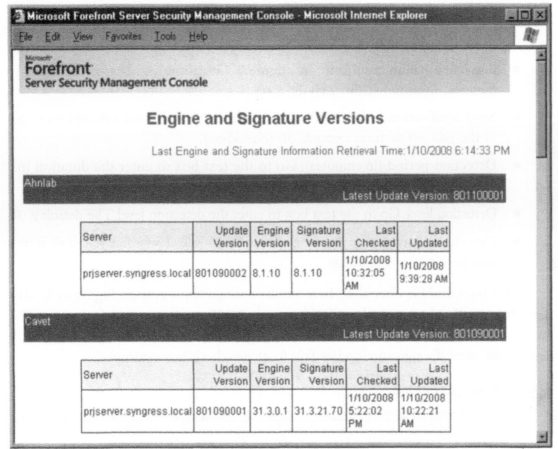

Alert Management

Through Alert Management, you can configure various alerts options available with the FSSMC. Alerts help you to notify critical events occurring in your network. You can configure alerts for a single server or server groups.

Alerts

The types of alerts include virus, spam, filter, file filter, and signature update alerts. In the Configure Virus Alerts work pane you can enable alerts, configure outbreak settings, e-mail and Simple Network Management Protocol (SNMP) notification (see Figure 7.20).

Under Enable Alerts you can configure the following:

■ Send notification if no detections have been reported for infected messages in the past *60* minutes (checkbox).

■ Suspected malfunction time (in minutes). Go to the text box to enter the duration in minutes. The default is *60*.

■ Send notification if the number of detections reported for infected messages in the past *60* minutes exceeds *30* (checkbox).

■ Detection period (in minutes). Go to the text box to enter the duration in minutes. The default is *60*.

■ Detection level. Go to the text box to enter the detection level. The default is *30*.

■ Detection Units. Go to the drop-down list to select whether the unit is in a number or in a percentage.

Spam, filter, and file filter alerts have similar configuration options. Signature Update alerts have enable alerts, e-mail notification, and SNMP notification configurations. The Enable Alerts options include send notification when signatures update successfully and send notification if a signature update fails (both are check box options).

Figure 7.20 Alert Configuration

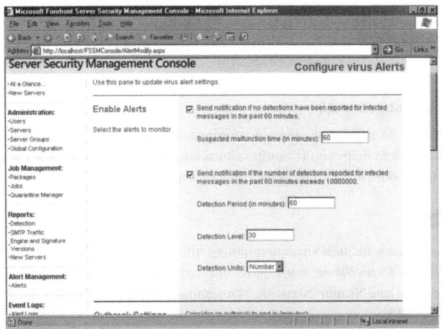

Event Logs

Alerts logs and notification logs are the two options available from the Event logs section of the FSSMC. Event logs can provide deployment, log retrieval, manual scan, and redistribution information. Monitoring logs is a regular activity of an administrator to understand the network and step up the security measures on a proactive basis.

Alert Logs

The Alert logs option allows you to generate real time alerts. The information available includes the host name, the date and time, and a descriptive message. Figure 7.21 shows an Alert log. You can press the Purge button to purge the logs. On top of the screen you have the option to choose a particular server or all servers to view Alert logs from.

Figure 7.21 Alert Logs

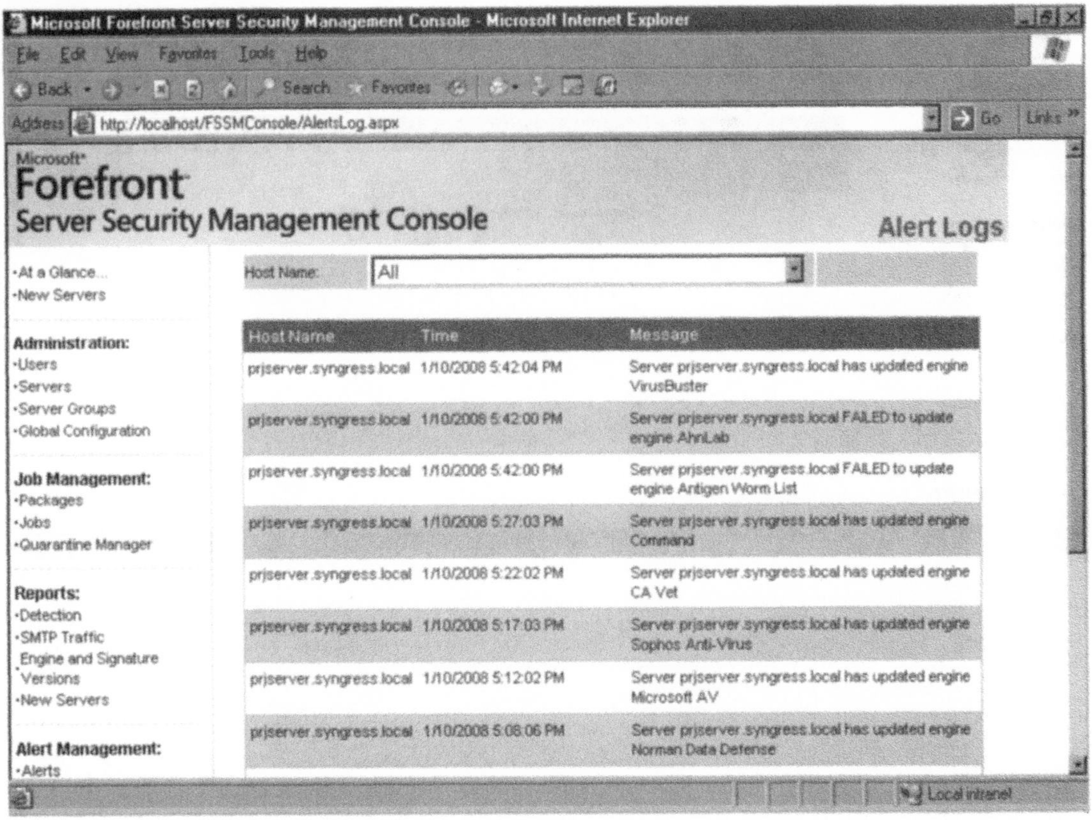

Notification Logs

The Notification logs option allows you to generate logs based on the job type, job name, and host name filters. You can generate logs for deployment, general options, log retrieval, manual scan, and redistribution. Figure 7.22 shows the Notification log configuration screen.

Figure 7.22 Notification Logs

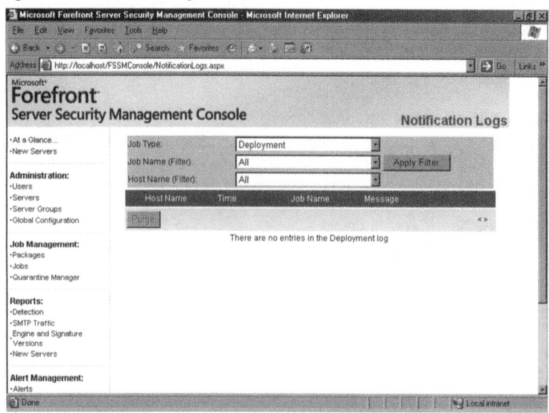

Summary

The FSSMC is a centralized Web-based management tool to manage Forefront Security servers deployed on the Microsoft Exchange 2007 and Microsoft SharePoint servers. AV, anti-spam, and content filtering are the key functionalities of Forefront Security servers. FSSMC provides a simplified mechanism to deploy packages across the enterprise, generate alerts and reports, schedule jobs, and manage servers.

FSSMC is installed on a non-domain controller server running Windows 2003. FSSMC should not be implemented in the demilitarized zone. You can increase redundancy in your network by implementing FSSMC on two servers: primary and backup. The backup server delivers all the functions of primary server, when the primary server goes offline. Critical data such as scan engine updates, templates, and server information are replicated between primary and backup servers.

Logs and reports are two primary benefits administrators can readily realize from deploying FSSMC. You have a wide range of reports to keep yourself updated on the events and engine status on the network.

Solutions Fast Track

Implementing a Backup Strategy

- ☑ FSSMC can be deployed in a stand-alone mode or in a primary-backup mode.

- ☑ Deploying FSSMC in a primary-backup mode offers high availability.

- ☑ A password is required to encrypt communications between the primary and the backup server. The backup server takes over when the primary server goes offline.

Utilizing the Microsoft FSSMC

- ☑ The FSSMC consists of administration, job management, reports, alert management, and event logs and help sections.

- ☑ Global configuration, adding users, adding managed servers, and scheduling jobs are the four important tasks you can perform through the FSSMC.

- ☑ Alert and notification logs provide you with a variety of information of your Forefront Security servers and helps you to analyze and manage the events occurring in your network.

Frequently Asked Questions

Q: What are the hardware requirements to install the FSSMC?

A: The following hardware requirements are listed by Microsoft:

- Microsoft Windows Server 2003 (x86).

- At least 128 MB of RAM (the more the better).

- 183 MB of disk space for the software components required to install the FSSMC.

- 65 MB of disk space for the FSSMC.

Q: What are the software requirements to install the FSSMC?

A: The following software components must be present before you install the FSSMC:

- IIS 6.0.

- ASP.NET version 2.0.

- SQL Server 2005 Standard Edition, SQL Server 2005 Express, or SQL Server 2000.

In addition to this, the following components are required. However, if you have not installed the same before, the FSSMC setup utility will automatically install the following:

- .NET Runtime version 2.0.

- Microsoft Message Queuing (MSMQ).

- MSXML 6.0.

Q: I am getting the error message "*FSSMC Cannot be installed on a Domain Controller. Setup will now exit.*"

A: You are trying to install the FSSMC on a domain controller. You can install the FSSMC on a server that is not a domain controller, and that doesn't have the Exchange 2007 or SharePoint server. You need to install it on a Windows 2003 server with a domain user account.

Q: I can see a list of scan engines during installation. How many of these can I deploy in my environment?

A: You can deploy a maximum of five scan engines. However, the engine types can be changed at any point in time.

Q: I am unable to create a new Deployment job.

A: Check whether you have uploaded any packages prior to this. After you upload the packages you can create a Deployment job.

Chapter 8

Using Intelligent Application Gateway 2007

Solutions in this chapter:

- Implementing an Intelligent Application Gateway 2007

- Configuring the Whale Communication Intelligent Application Gateway 2007

- Configuring ISA Server to Allow Communication Between the Two Servers

- Utilizing the Whale Communication Intelligent Application Gateway Tools

☑ Summary

☑ Solutions Fast Track

☑ Frequently Asked Questions

Introduction

The Whale Communication Intelligent Application Gateway 2007 is used in conjunction with Microsoft Internet Security and Acceleration (ISA) 2006 Server and Microsoft Internet Information Services (IIS). Microsoft acquired Whale Communications in May 2006 and shortly afterwards added the Intelligent Application Gateway to their suite of security products. When combined with virtual private networks (VPN), secure sockets layer (SSL) connections, endpoint policies, and compliance checking, the Whale Communication Intelligent Application Gateway 2007 will allow users to securely connect to servers where Web-based applications are stored.

End users are able to securely connect to a Web portal through the Whale Communication Intelligent Application Gateway 2007. Security over the Web is paramount for companies; important data about users and the organization can be exposed when mail is sent via the Web in plain text format. Network users are able to connect to Web-based applications, such as Outlook Web Access and Lotus Notes (IBM).

In summary, the Whale Communication Intelligent Application Gateway 2007 is a component of Forefront Edge Security and Access. The Intelligent Application Gateway (IAG) allows users to connect servers through portal Web sites. When users are connected to Web-based applications using Secure Sockets layer traffic, they are less likely to encounter the vulnerabilities associated with Web sites and portals whose traffic is not encrypted. The Whale Communication Intelligent Application Gateway 2007 with ISA 2006 Server, secure endpoints, virtual private networks, and compliance checking can help companies avoid the common vulnerabilities associated with remote clients connecting to their networks.

The History of SSL VPNs

Organizations were looking to utilize the global connectivity aspects of the internet to provide access to corporate resources. It started with customers and, of course, employees traveling to do business between national or international sites, as the productivity gains were both obvious and immediate.

There were few technologies that could provide this functionality.

The first to arrive was dial-up access, which was rather costly. Dial-up is sometimes the only choice available for most rural or remote areas where broadband provision is unlikely due to low population and demand. Low access speeds mean that users have a limited remote access experience connected to the corporate servers.

Next, there was a wave of reverse proxies, publishing Web-based applications to the outside world. An example of this would be the ISA Firewall's Web Publishing feature set. This delivered value but was limited to Web-based applications. However, it did add an additional layer of defense and encryption compared to previous remote access solutions.

There followed a wave of IP security (IPsec) VPN solutions that transitioned from the normal site to site solution to an encrypted client/server VPN. Employees got complete access to the company network, as they had when sitting in front of their corporate desktops. When connected over a faster Internet connection (for example, an ISDN 128 Kbps line), the connected experience was immensely superior to dial-up modem connections. End user experiences improved again when high-speed Internet connections (broadband, cable Internet, leased lines) from 1 Mbps upwards became available from home, hotels, and conference centers across the world.

The IPsec VPN solutions had its limitations; for one, it lacked security. The other significant problem was that the IPsec VPN client required to connect to the VPN became large and difficult to roll out. This was due to its requirement for client firewalls and antivirus inspection in order to make up for the lack in security. IPsec VPNs, while widely implemented, rarely gets used for end-to-end protection of application protocols. It is mainly used today as an "all or nothing" protection for a VPN.

One of the things that SSL VPN brings to the table is taking all of these current solutions and consolidating them into one platform. SSL VPN means access for:

- Any user
- Any location
- Any application

The current wave is focused on application intelligence; this is what is needed to ensure access for any user from any location to any application stays secure without the very large IPSEC VPN client tool. This has led to the current generation of SSL VPN features that are present in every SSL gateway. All these features are implemented at both the client and gateway:

- **Client side security** Endpoint security or endpoint policies
- **Tunneling** Tunnel non-Web and Web applications
- **Pre-authentication** Authenticate before contacting corporate servers

- **User Portal** Made available after the user has logged on; this is where access to published applications is found

- **Authorization** Allow and Deny access to the portal or the applications hosted in the SSL VPN portal

- **Application Layer Inspection** Some form of application layer inspection needs to be provided in order to qualify as an enterprise grade SSL VPN gateway.

Implementing an Intelligent Application Gateway 2007

History shows that if you want to implement a secure and stable firewall, remote access, or an enterprise resource planning (ERP) product, such a product must be the only hosted solution on an extremely security-hardened appliance.

With this in mind, Microsoft has partnered with original equipment manufacturers (OEMs) to bring Microsoft's Intelligent Application Gateway (IAG) and Microsoft Internet Security and Acceleration (ISA) server-based security appliances to the market. These two solutions combined bring IAG 2007 and the best of ISA 2006 Server, with a comprehensive-hardened configuration of Microsoft Windows Server 2003, configured on optimized hardware so that the appliance is ready to be rolled out straight from the box. IAG 2007 cannot be installed; it is only supplied preinstalled in an appliance form.

For client access, IAG has two types of license: the client access licenses (CAL) and the external connector (EC) license. With the EC license, there is no need to buy individual IAG 2007 CALs. An EC license is not mandatory; it's a license that can be used by business partners or customers instead of using CALs. License types are available through a network of channel partners, resellers, and Microsoft's volume licensing program.

The implementation stage and the ability of IAG 2007 to be adapted to a multitude of environments within an enterprise makes for easy deployment, even when expanding existing SSL VPN implementations within the organization. The ease of deployment goes hand in hand with the ease of implementing popular enterprise applications, hence the current focus on Application Intelligence in SSL VPNs.

Unlike other SSL VPNs where administrators have to do complicated technical configuration in order to get popular internal applications published onto a Web portal, the IAG 2007 administrator simply selects from a list of "out of the box" applications provided by Microsoft. IAG 2007 then performs most of the setup automatically. The hard work has been done by Microsoft; they have put together all the popular applications available and compiled a list of security considerations linked to each application. This is made available as automatic rule sets within IAG 2007 and ISA 2006. IAG 2007 then has the capacity to be manually changed to comply with nonstandard back-office systems and policies. This means that security can be tweaked to match complex security policies with organizations.

The major gain derived from implementing an SSL VPN is enabling access from computers which are not under company control. Taking this into consideration, the organization will need to implement endpoint policies to control access to corporate servers from unmanaged devices. Endpoint policies need to be implemented to state which conditions must be met by managed or unmanaged devices to gain access to the organization's SSL VPN and or applications made available on the Web portal. Until now, SSL VPNs did not have the ability to fully enforce such policies. These policies can be anything from a personal firewall that needs to be installed and up-to-date on end-user computers to a specific operating system that is not allowed on the SSL VPN.

ISA Server runs on the IAG server. The ISA configuration is maintained by IAG. Figure 8.1 shows a typical IAG SSL VPN.

Figure 8.1 A Typical IAG SSL VPN

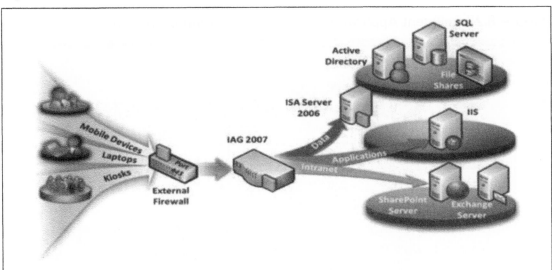

Configuring the Whale Intelligent Communication Application Gateway 2007

Configuring IAG 2007 to be a working SSL VPN out of the box, is a very easy process to follow, not only for the already experienced SSL VPN administrator, but also by an

SSL VPN administrator new to the world of VPNs. Once such a working gateway has been configured it can be tweaked in such a way as to become a very powerful and secure globally-used and standardized solution for an organization. Customizing IAG 2007 to fit with nonstandard organization-wide policies has never been easier, and enabling users to utilize well known internal applications from managed or unmanaged devices has never been as simple as with the IAG 2007 and ISA 2006 Server combination.

In this section we will be looking at not only running an out-of-the-box solution but also fully customizing a standard IAG 2007 solution. This will include creating a portal trunk, which will provide access to multiple applications via a single Web portal, and all of the steps necessary to complete and activate the portal in order to use nonstandard organization-wide policies on a secure SSL VPN.

Configuration Page

The IAG Configuration page is where most of the SSL VPN creation and configuration takes place. This is also where application access and endpoint policies are configured. From this configuration window, portals can be created, applications added, and necessary security changes made (see Figure 8.2).

Figure 8.2 Intelligent Application Gateway Configuration Screen

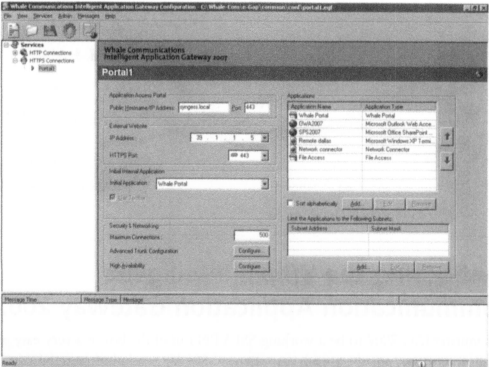

This page and all configuration changes made on this page are secured by a passphrase, which is set up during the initial IAG configuration procedures.

NOTE

For more information on passphrase and passphrase encryption, refer to the section "Passphrase" later in this chapter.

From here, additional changes can be made. For example, you can create a highly available IAG portal when expanding an existing SSL VPN implementation and make the necessary advanced trunk configuration changes when security policies need to be altered. Examples of changes to security policies include changing the Web server certificate, making authentication changes, changing session settings, tweaking URL inspection, and customizing an application.

From here, the portal backup can also be run, procedures restored, and IAG user access completely monitored.

Application Access Portal

End users will connect to a privately developed and owned, closed-system architecture, a Web-based application access portal to a variety of centralized resources, ranging from traditional client/server applications to Web and intranet applications by using the following URL based on Figure 8.3: *https://syngress.local.*

All transmissions between IAG and the local machine are encrypted using SSL (secure socket layer) technology, while site authenticity is assured through built-in digital certificate support. End users will only be able to see and log in to this page based on endpoint policies defined on the Web portal or application. The port defined here is the port number of the external Web site.

Figure 8.3 Application Access Portal

External Web Site

Figure 8.4 shows the external Web site where the open port and the IP address are configured and changed to connect to the Web portal. This is typically the external network cards IP address of IAG appliance. This IP address is configured during the portal trunk configuration.

Figure 8.4 External Website

A list of IP addresses and port numbers can be created by using the Service Policy Manager to control the IP addresses and port numbers that are used to access the internal network This step is needed to enforce the selection of predefined IP addresses and port numbers during trunk configuration.

NOTE

For details of the Intelligent Application Gateway Service Policy Manager, refer to the section at the end of this chapter titled "Intelligent Application Gateway Service Policy Manager."

Initial Internal Application

Figure 8.5 shows the initial internal application section on the configuration page. This is where the internal application to be displayed on the Web portal can be specified after the user has successfully logged on. The default setting is "Web Portal," which will display a list of available applications published by the organization.

Figure 8.5 Initial Internal Application

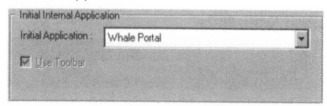

However, any of the applications published can be selected to be the initial internal application; when choosing anything other than the default, the Use Toolbar tick box will become available. In the scenario where the administrator selects OWA to be the initial internal application and to the Use Toolbar option, the end user would have the following toolbar when logged on to the Web portal (see Figure 8.6).

Figure 8.6 Web Portal

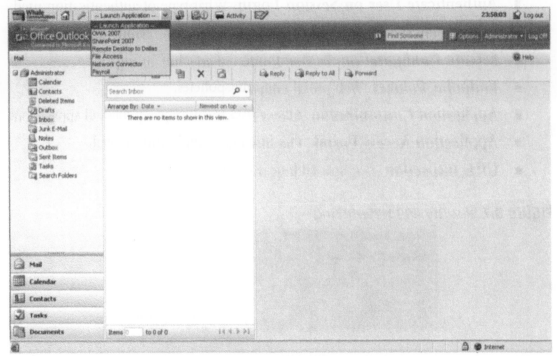

The result would be that when an end user logs on to the Web portal, the first thing to be loaded will be the end user's OWA. To continue the user can choose from any of the available published applications on the toolbar.

This will be the only way that the user will be able to navigate around the Web portal. The "Whale Portal" will no longer be available. In this scenario, when clicking on the IAG homepage icon on the toolbar, OWA will open as it is in the initial internal application.

Security and Networking

Figure 8.7 shows the Security and Networking section on the configuration page, where advanced trunk configuration and high availability can be modified. More high availability servers can be added to the configuration by navigating to the Admin High availability servers menu in the menu bar of the IAG Configuration page.

The advanced trunk configuration section allows the SSL VPN administrator to configure options otherwise left unconfigured by default. These options include:

- **Server Certificate** Certificate issued to the external site.

- **Website Logging** Enable detailed Web portal logging.

- **Authenticate User on Session Login** What type of authentication used.

- **Logoff Scheme** Logoff URL, message, and session termination.

- **Session Configuration** Session limits and attachment wiper.

- **Endpoint Policies** Web portal endpoint policies.

- **Application Customization** Allows IAG to customize published applications.

- **Application Access Portal** The intelligent application portal.

- **URL Inspection** See host address translation (HAT).

Figure 8.7 Security and Networking

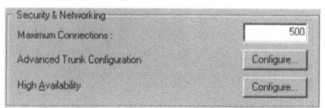

The major technical challenge SSL VPN administrators face regarding providing access to internal applications across the Internet is within the applications internal references. IAG 2007's host address translation (HAT) engine encrypts and translates any number of internal host names to a single external host name. End users will never have the ability to launch attacks based on what they see in the Web portal. In other words, http://internalservername:80/application will become https://external. hostname/whalecom/whalecom0/application.

IAG 2007 delivers data over a standard browser for end users to securely access sensitive information by overlaying industry-standard 128-bit encryption SSL. This prevents hackers intercepting and reading data. Only one-time authentication or one certificate is necessary, despite the user accessing a number of different published applications and server resources.

To prevent logon credentials or any other information from being cached on managed or unmanaged devices, IAG 2007 utilizes patent-pending Secure Logoff technology. This proprietary and innovative mechanism eliminates the possibility of malicious users reinstating user sessions.

Attachment Wiper

Upon completion of the end user SSL VPN session, the attachment wiper will remove all traces left on the unmanaged or managed device that was created during the session. This is triggered by the following:

- When a user logs off from the session.
- The computer browser is closed down.
- The computer browser experiences a crash.
- The managed or unmanaged device is shut down.
- The session logoff threshold passes.

Upon any of the above occurrences the attachment wiper removes the following:

- AutoComplete entries in the computer browser address bar and form field contents.
- Attachment temporary files.
- User credentials.
- Computer browser cookies downloaded during the user session.
- Computer browser history generated during the user session.
- Any temporary downloaded or created files generated during the user session.
- All computer browser cache entries.

Endpoint policies can be created to administer the attachment wiper. The attachment wiper will remove the listed information above, created when an end user's SSL VPN session is active.

The hard drive clusters on the unmanaged or managed device on which the end user has stored files will be overwritten with other data by the attachment wiper seven times to make it technically impossible to undelete or reinstate those files. Thus, the attachment wiper conforms to the DoD-acceptable way of sanitizing magnetic media. The attachment wiper functionality is only available with Internet Explorer 5.5 and higher.

Applications

Publishing internal applications is in the center of the new application intelligence wave of SSL VPNs. Microsoft's IAG 2007, together with ISA 2006, has made publishing an internal application one of the easiest processes.

Exercise: Adding a published application to the Web portal.

1. In the Application section in the IAG portal click Add, which will bring up the Add Application Wizard (Figure 8.8), giving you the choice of what kind of application you want to publish.

Figure 8.8 Add Application

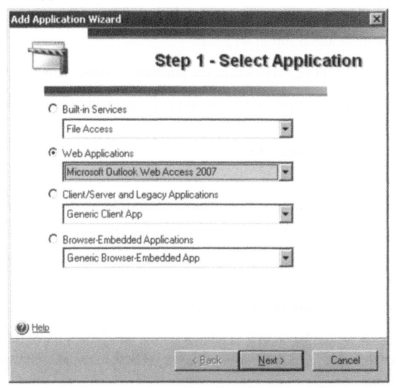

2. In this example we are going to add Microsoft Outlook Web Access 2007 Web Application. Click Next. In the wizard (Figure 8.9), name the application "OWA 2007". You can specify whether all users are authorized and you can set endpoint policies. Click Next.

Figure 8.9 Application Setup

3.   Add the name of the internal exchange server, choose port numbers (Figure 8.10).

Figure 8.10 Web Servers

4. Choose the Authentication Servers (Figure 8.11).

Figure 8.11 Authentication

5. Add the link to the portal and toolbar and click **Finish** (see Figure 8.12).

Figure 8.12 Portal Link

Figure 8.13 shows a typical list of Web portal published applications. From this window the SSL VPN administrator can add or remove applications. This window is also where the sort order for applications listed on the Web portal can be chosen.

Figure 8.13 List of Published Applications

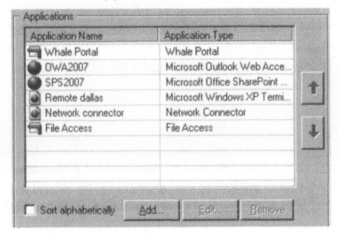

Limiting Applications on Subnets

Figure 8.14 shows where the SSL VPN administrator can restrict any of the applications made available on the SSL VPN Web portal so that only servers within the defined subnets are enabled for use from the Web portal. Once the trunk is activated and an end user requests a URL from the Web portal, the filter will first check the URL against the application list. If the application is listed, then the filter will check on the URL against the subnet list. Only if the URL passes both checks will the application be enabled to the user.

Figure 8.14 Subnets

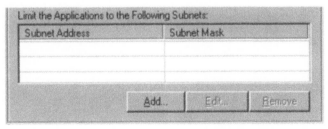

NOTE

For each application added, make sure that the application is listed in the IAGs DNS or HOSTS file.

Subnets are configured in the main window of the Configuration program, in the "Applications" area.

Creating a Trunk

When a new trunk gets created, the Configuration program activates the Create New Trunk Wizard (see Figure 8.15). This enables the administrator quick auto-complete of the initial trunk setup, external Web site, authentication, application customization, and URL inspection rules. A trunk can be made under the HTTP and the HTTPS services.

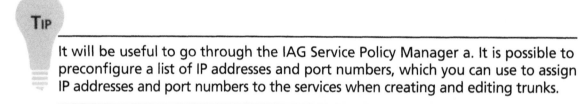

TIP

It will be useful to go through the IAG Service Policy Manager a. It is possible to preconfigure a list of IP addresses and port numbers, which you can use to assign IP addresses and port numbers to the services when creating and editing trunks.

Figure 8.15 Create New Trunk Wizard

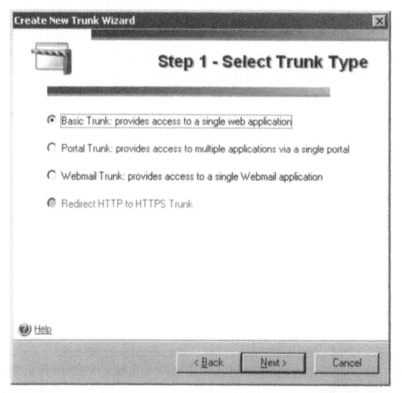

Basic Trunk

Basic trunks enable the establishment of a one-to-one connection, where one IP address routes to a single generic Web application. This type of trunk will be used in a scenario where the organization has a single Web application, which will be of benefit to be published to a Web portal.

During the setup process, select the public host name, external IP address of the portal, and the ports used. Next, setup authentication by choosing the appropriate certificate for this application and pointing to the actual application server with an optional path to the application. Then set up optional application authentication and, lastly, the endpoint policies.

Portal Trunk

An HTTP or HTTPS trunk has incoming and outgoing channels, allowing for bidirectional data flow. Unlike the other trunks a portal trunk is a one-to-many connection, where the same IP address is used to access multiple applications. It can be used to enable Web and non-Web applications, generic and out-of-the-box applications.

To create a portal trunk:

1. In IAG, right-click HTTPS Connections and choose New Trunk. From the options, choose Portal Trunk, and click Next.

2. Give the trunk a name and enter the Public Hostname/IP address of the Web portal. Add the IP address of the external Web site and choose which port you want to use for HTTP and HTTPS.

3. Select Servers for Session Authentication, click Add, and set up the needed type of authentication. During this process, select whether end users will need to authenticate only once or for each selected server.

4. Configure the Server Certificate by choosing the certificate that will secure the SSL Web portal. For the certificate to show in this window, it must be issued to the IAG server. The certificate manager can be launched for the local computer from this window in order to do local certificate management.

5. Session Access Policy controls access to the trunk, depending on endpoint policies. Privileged Endpoint Policy defines a policy for endpoints that enjoy session privileges. The necessary policies can be edited from this window. Click Finish.

Webmail Trunk

Webmail trunks are dedicated trunks for a single Webmail application, and are automatically created with authentication, application customization, and URL inspection rules that are optimized for the specific Webmail application being run on this trunk.

When creating Webmail trunks, it is recommended that the HTTPS Connections service be used.

Redirect HTTP to HTTPS Truck

It is very easy for an end user to use HTTP instead of HTTPS by accident. The SSL VPN administrator has to make sure that HTTP requests made to the Web portal are redirected to HTTPS by the organization and not by a third party with malicious intentions. When an HTTPS request is made to the Web portal, the request will be handled by the HTTPS trunk. If the requirement is there to redirect HTTP requests to the HTTPS trunk, it can be done by creating an additional redirect trunk.

The redirect HTTP to HTTPS Trunk option in Figure 8.16 will only become available if you select to create a new trunk by right-clicking on HTTP connections.

NOTE

A trunk can be deleted in the Configuration program by selecting the trunk in the list pane, and then selecting DELETE from the right-click menu.

Activating an IAG Configuration

Configuration changes on the IAG need to be implemented in various scenarios. Starting with when IAG is being set up in the initial stages of SSL VPN rollout. In the scenario where large organizational security policy changes or a small configuration change to the IAG configuration needs to be implemented, the configuration needs to be activated.

Saving and activating an IAG configuration enable the changes in the Web portal. This step also provides you with the option to back up the configuration and to apply the changes to external configuration settings (see Figure 8.16).

Figure 8.16 Activate Configuration

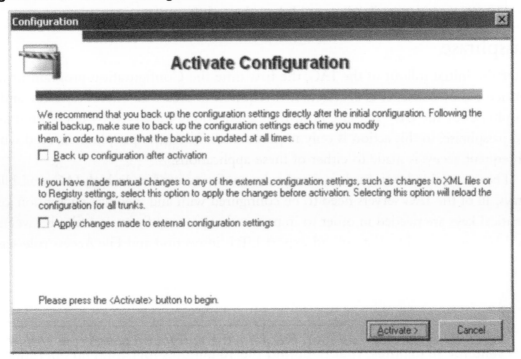

Backing up the IAG configuration can be done from this window so that configuration settings are backed up and changes are activated in one step. During a backup procedure, the IAG will make use of the Windows makeab.exe utility to archive the necessary files and Registry values in a .cab file. By default, the backup is created under the IAG installation path: …\whale-Com\e-Gap\Backup.

The name of the backup file that is created in the defined backup folder is *whlbackup.<host_name>.cab,* where *host_name* is the name of the IAG.

Restore from Backup in the IAG Configuration program from uses the Windows extract.exe utility to restore the files.

To restore the configuration in the configuration program:

1. From the Admin menu, in the Configuration program, click **Restore** from **Backup**.

2. Then activate the Configuration, to make the restore configuration. Then activate again.

Once the configuration is activated, the following message is displayed: IAG configuration activated successfully.

The trunk is now operational. All users who authenticate to the Web portal will be able to access the applications published through it.

Passphrase

After the initial rollout of the IAG, the first time the Configuration program or the Service Policy Manager is accessed, it is required to create an encryption key and passphrase for the IAG. Because both IAG applications are served by encryption key and passphrase, so this action is only required once. The same passphrase is used when subsequent access is made to either of these applications.

The encryption key is used to encrypt the configuration data. In high IAG availability arrays, all of the IAG servers need to be configured with and identical encryption key. Identical keys are needed in order to import and export configuration files between the IAG servers and to import and export URL inspection and File Access rule sets.

Tip

When using the Configuration program, the encryption passphrase entered is valid for 10 minutes. That is, during the 10 minutes following an operation that requires access to the configuration files, the files can be accessed again without having to reenter the passphrase.

Note

If different keys have already been defined on different IAG servers and they need to be unified, these steps can be taken:

To export the encryption keys, run the following utility in a command line, on one of the IAG servers …\whale-com\e-gap\common\bin\exportkeys.exe.

To import the encryption keys to the other IAG servers, run the following utility in a command line, on each of the servers …\whale-com\e-gap\common\bin\importkeys.exe.

Internet Information Services Manager

In addition to the first portal trunk created, the Create New Trunk Wizard automatically creates an external Web site on the Internet Information Services (IIS). IAG creates and maintains the configuration of the Web portal site.

In some circumstances you might need to restart the IIS Web Service on the IAG server, as described in the following steps:

1. Click **Start | All Programs | Administrator | IIS Manager**.

2. Select the **Local** server. Right-click and choose **All Tasks | Restart IIS**.

3. From the available choices, start, stop or restart IIS.

The port numbers IAG use to communicate with the IIS default Web site is port 6001 for HTTP and port 6002 for HTTPS (see Figure 8.17). If an application published by IAG is using one or both of these ports, the port number can be changed, as described below.

■ From the Admin menu in the Configuration program, click **Advanced Configuration**.

Figure 8.17 Advanced Configuration

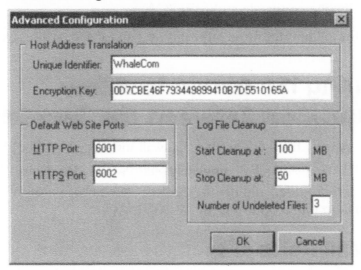

1. In the Default Web Site Ports area, replace the default HTTP or HTTPS port numbers, as required, and click **OK**.

2. Activate the configuration.

Viewing Remote Computer Certificate

Once an end user is connected to the newly created Web portal, making sure the session is secure before logging on is one of the most important steps because the end user wants assurance that his logon username and password are encrypted.

First, the SSL VPN administrator must keep in mind is that the HTTPS Web portal needs a valid and secure enough certificate attached to it. The way to do this is to make sure the new IAG gateway has a new certificate attached to it and that the certificate is valid for a long period. It is suggested to request a certificate be issued for a two-year period or longer. Second, the administrator should make provision for users accidentally connecting to the Web portal with HTTP instead of HTTPS. The way to do this is to create a Redirect HTTP to HTTPS Trunk in the IAG.

Depending on the end user's Internet browser, the certificate will be accessible when the end user browses to the IAG Web portal. A padlock will be displayed and double clicking the padlock will display the remote computer's certificate. By doing this the end user can see the following options:

- Issued to: this will display the public host name to which the certificate is issued.

- Issued by: the certificate authority (CA).

- Valid from: The valid from and valid to date of the certificate.

Configuring ISA Server to Allow Communication Between the Two Servers

The IAG 2007 actually has the 2006 ISA Firewall installed on it. The ISA configuration is maintained by IAG, making it a completely appropriate edge device. The ISA firewall has never been compromised and has no security issues; because of this, it makes sense to design an organization's SSL VPN on an IAG server.

IAG Firewall Rules (13)

With the IAG and ISA server so closely joined together, Microsoft has made creating a portal with published applications and the related firewall changes in ISA server into one process. When the IAG configuration is changed and the configuration activated, IAG will update the related firewall rules in ISA.

The first thirteen rules allowed in ISA were created during the installation of IAG. Figure 8.13 shows the list of firewall rules created in ISA server by the IAG after the configuration was activated. For example, rule 11 shows protocol UDP on port 53 is allowed to enter the firewall and go through to an internal server for all users.

Portal Trunk Configuration Rules (2)

The portal trunk configuration "allow" rules were created when the portal trunk was activated. After portal trunk activation, testing can start and the portal Web page can be used.

The second of the two allow rules is the Whale::Auth#001 rule (see Figure 8.18). This is the rule that allows connection to the Domain Controller, which in turn allows the Active Directory to authenticate the session. This rule is also the rule that will be used for whatever authentication setup during the configuration of the portal.

Figure 8.18 ISA Server

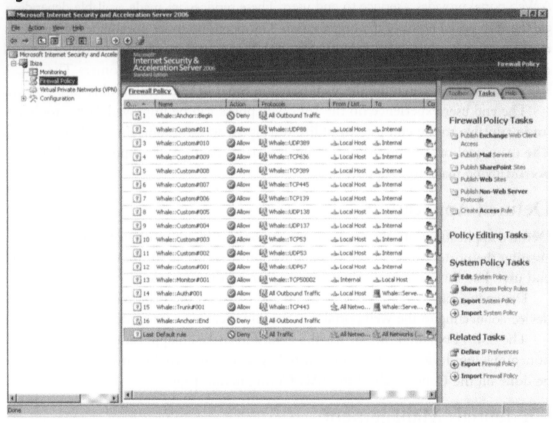

Utilizing the Whale Communication Intelligent Application Gateway Tools

One of the most important jobs the SSL VPN administrator is to make sure that the IAG gateway continues to run in good health even if it experiences unexpected high volume of requests. In a support environment around the IAG, it is very helpful to have a full range of tools to aid the administrator in resolving either potential disastrous events or small end user problems.

With IAG it has been made even easier to support such a VPN solution. It is recommended that the IAG configuration and security policies be documented; this will aid troubleshooting problems which might occur with IAG or an end user session.

Whale Communication Intelligent Application Gateway 2007 Web Portal

A Web portal provides a service to end users. These services are made available depending on the Web portal needs of the organization. This opens up more possibilities of problems that can arise from the use of the Web portal. These services could be a list of defined applications made available to employees on the road, and even customers. The SSL VPN administrator could use the Web portal in order to resolve a number of problems.

The end user experience on the IAG Web portal can be improved. Some tools are made available to the end user to utilize during an active session on the Web portal. The main goal of these tools is to eliminate a large portion of support calls that can potentially be made to a support desk.

Defined Applications

Defined applications are the applications the SSL VPN administrator published after creating the portal trunk. This list of applications is available in the Web portal to the end user. The list is also available in the toolbar on the Web portal.

Depending on endpoint policies set up and based on the managed or unmanaged device connecting to the Web portal will the end users see a list of defined applications.

The SSL VPN administrator has the ability to make an application portal link on noncomplying devices in the endpoint policy show up grayed or invisible. This can be done on the General tab of the IAG Configuration page.

Credentials Management

Working in an environment where there are potentially hundreds or even thousands of end users who not only work in the office or at home, but also work on the road or remote offices, user password management issues will arise. IAG Portal has added a feature to the Web portal so the user can experience a one-stop shop for credential management.

The SSL VPN administrator can enable the "Credentials Management" option in the Portals Advanced Trunk area of the Authentication tab.

When this option is activated (applicable for portal trunks only), a "Credentials Management" button is automatically added to the Web portal homepage, enabling end users to initiate the following options any time during a session:

- **Add authentication credentials** This option is accumulative. If the end user enters two sets of authentication credentials, then both sets are applicable to that session. Each set is then used for the relevant applications.

- **Change their password** This option is applicable only when the option "Enable Users to change their passwords" is activated on the Authentication tab during the portal configuration.

NOTE

Credential Management can only be accessed if the remote user has successfully logged into a Web portal session. Only then can the user make changes to passwords or add authentication credentials.

System Information

The system information window can be accessed from the Web portal by the end user. The information on the page will give the end user a better idea of what has been installed on the managed or unmanaged device (see Figure 8.19).

If the end user is experiencing difficulty doing something in particular on the Web portal, the system information will aid the SSL VPN administrator when supporting the end user and the certified endpoint status determination.

End users can check whether the Whale client components are installed on their system. They can also:

- **Uninstall Whale client components.**

- **Restore component defaults** End users can restore the Whale client components settings on their computer to the default values.

- **Delete the user-defined trusted sites list** Once users add a site or a number of sites to the list, they can remove them from the list via the System Information window.

Figure 8.19 System Information

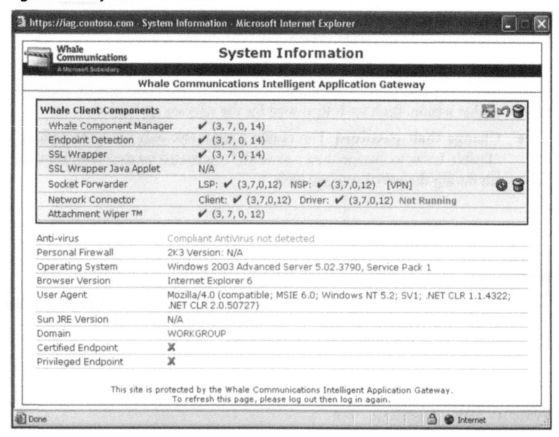

Activity

The portal activity window will be available in a portal trunk and a Webmail trunk. To open the portal activity window double click the portal activity icon in the windows system tray (to the right of the taskbar).

- **Connections area displays** The active channel and the connections. Double clicking the connection will show the number of bytes sent.

- **Application area displays** The list of application launched.

The end user can also disconnect a session from the Activity window.

Email System Administrator

Email System Administrator is another tool available on the IAG Web portal. This will open a new email message with the Administrators email address predefined in the "TO" field.

Strategically placed on the Web portal, end users can easily come into contact with the system administrator in order to raise a help desk call or even to suggest changes.

Whale Communication Intelligent Application Gateway Editor

If wanting to encrypt or decrypt any of the IAG files that are encrypted during day-to-day operation, the editor is the interface to use (see Figure 8.20). It enables easy editing, sorting, and conversion of any text file, including encrypted files and Base 64–encoded text. The editor can be opened by navigating to **Start | All Programs | Whale Communications IAG | Additional Tools | Editor**.

Figure 8.20 Editor

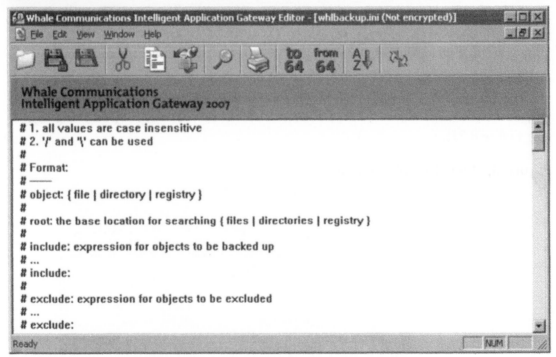

Using the Editor program, it is possible to:

- Save and encrypt files.
- Open multiple files simultaneously.
- Decrypt and edit encrypted files.
- Open and edit text (ASCII) files.

- Use the sort and find to locate the required text.

- Convert a text selection to and from Base 64 format.

TIP

Once the file is open, the title bar indicates whether the file is encrypted or not.

Whale Communication Intelligent Application Gateway Service Policy Manager

A list of IP addresses and port numbers can be created by using the Service Policy Manager. This is done to preconfigure the IP addresses and port numbers for HTTP and HTTPS connection services, which are used to access the internal network. This is needed to enforce the selection of preconfigured IP address and port number during trunk configuration.

The Service Policy Manager can be opened by navigating to **Start | All Programs | Whale Communications IAG | Additional Tools | Service Policy Manager** (see Figure 8.21).

Figure 8.21 Service Policy Manager

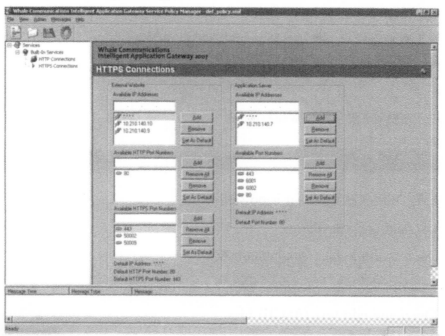

Whale Communication Intelligent Application Web Monitor

The Web Monitor is a complete solution for the SSL VPN administrator to monitor all user session events (see Figure 8.22). It is integrated within the system as a SSL VPN–supported application with its own Intelligent Application Optimizer. It allows the administrator to zoom into a user's Web portal session in real-time. Users with application access problems will be easily identified and solved with IAG working at the application level. The Web Monitor is essential in the administrators day-to-day support functionalities. The Web Monitor also gives the administrator event filtering and analyzing capabilities.

The Web Monitor can be opened by navigating to **Start | All Programs | Whale Communications IAG | Additional Tools | Web Monitor**.

If an IAG high availability array is deployed in an organization, one can make use of the Web Monitor to monitor all the IAG servers that are part of the array.

Redirect trunks are not monitored by the Web Monitor.

Figure 8.22 Web Monitor

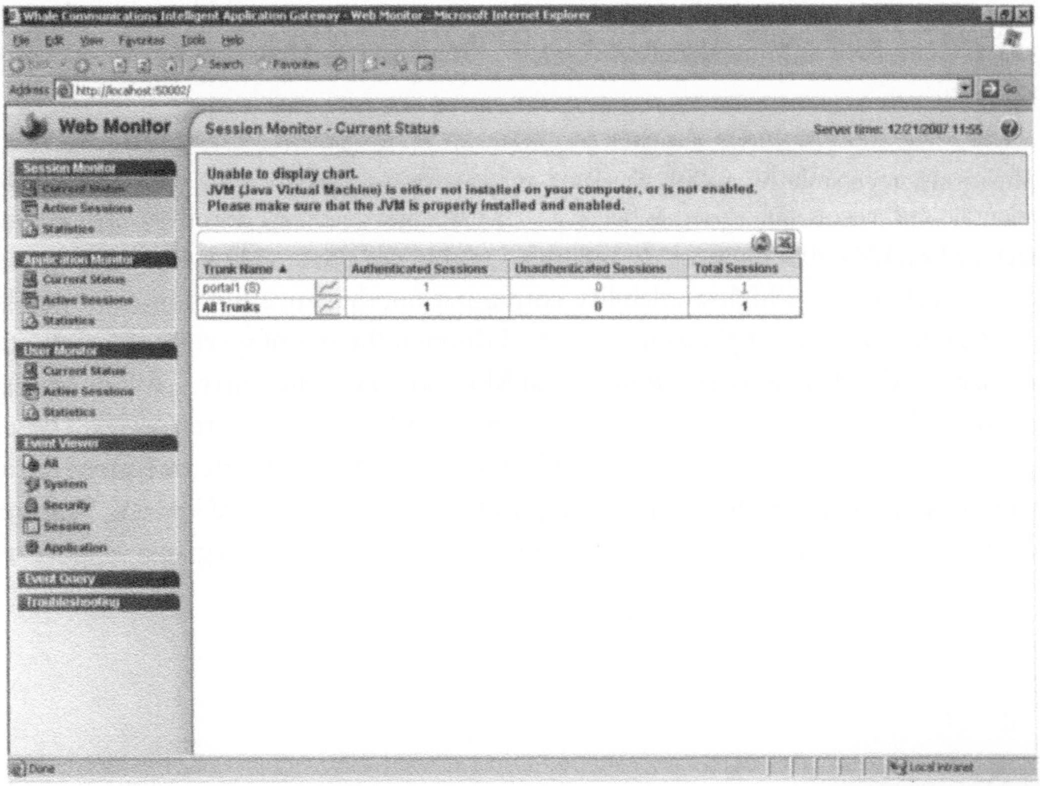

Creating and Managing Intelligent Application Gateway Endpoint Policies

Microsoft's Intelligent Application Gateway 2007 (IAG) is a hardware appliance that integrates technology purchased from Whale Communications in the summer of 2006 and the vendor's own Internet Security and Acceleration (ISA) Server.

IAG 2007 is ideal for IT managers, network administrators, and information security professionals who are concerned about the security, performance, manageability, and cost of network operations.

IAG 2007 combines an SSL VPN with endpoint security checks and firewall features, enabling the creation of policy-based remote access controls to a network and its individual applications. This "access portal" features three levels of policy-based traffic filtering at both the packet and application layers. End users access the platform through their Web browsers with communications being protected via SSL encryption; and policies can be defined specifying which users and/or machines are enabled access to which network resources.

Access to the IAG appliance from remote locations is accomplished with any Web browser. Microsoft lists multiple browsers as compatible; however, Internet Explorer has components that enable specific features of the gateway that are available only as ActiveX controls. Therefore, full functionality requires a Windows and Internet Explorer based endpoint.

The IAG 2007 provides a means to create an access portal to corporate network applications, accessible by a Web browser, which allows end users to authenticate their credentials and access only those applications and features that their administrators' defined policies allow. IAG 2007 supports an unlimited number of users, and up to 64 IAG nodes can be combined in a high-availability configuration, thus meeting corporate needs.

Access to corporate applications is assisted through the use of specialized "application optimizers," which are available from several Microsoft and third-party software offerings, including Microsoft Exchange server and Microsoft SharePoint portal server. These application optimizers consist of integrated software modules with preconfigured settings designed to allow access to the target applications through the IAG portal. Features provided by the optimizers to the target applications include single-sign-on support with the ability to apply certain granular rights assignments per user policy, and support for "attachment wiper," which removes and scrubs temporary session data from the client, including browser history files and pages, auto complete form contents, temp files, cookies, history, browser closure, and system shutdowns such as logoff and browser failure. Last but not least, the optimizers also even blocking file uploads if an approved virus scanner is not present on the endpoint machine. For example, the systems administrator could define a policy that if a remote user does not have the latest version of the corporate anti-virus solution, the user(s) will not be allowed to upload any attachment to their mailboxes.

IAG Server simply eliminates the risk of network attacks and operating system vulnerabilities as it only provides a means to access specific applications (or some of the features only) to approved users from approved machines.

Another notable feature includes the capability to have individual client tools that can be downloaded to the endpoint, enabling additional features of the portal. (Again, many of these features require a Windows-based endpoint and browser.)

Some of these features include:

- **End Point Detection** The ability to examine the endpoint's anti-virus checking capabilities. End point detection can work in combination with policy-based access; that is, a user can be allowed or disallowed to perform certain functions depending on their endpoint posture.

- **SSL Wrapper** The ability to transport certain network protocols (terminal services, RPC, terminal emulation) over an SSL connection via port-forwarding or socket-forwarding models.

- **Network Connector** The ability to enable full networking connectivity from the client via a bidirectional VPN tunnel. The network connector provides remote users with a local IP address as if they were directly connected to the corporate network.

Together these technologies provide mobile and remote workers with easy and flexible secure access from a broad range of devices and locations, including kiosks, PCs, and mobile devices anywhere the road warrior or remote user is based.

Summary

In this chapter, we reviewed the history and basics of the Intelligent Application Gateway. Understanding the history of SSL VPNs will help you get closer to the goals we defined at the beginning of this book. The design and planning stages are just as important as planning any other business-critical solution in the organization. Configuring IAG to be a secure application-sharing and robust SSL VPN tool will prove priceless for any sized organization.

Publishing business-critical applications has never been easier, and has never been as comprehensive as with Microsoft's combined IAG and ISA Servers. SSL VPNs not only brings the organization closer to a standardized way of accessing applications "on the road", but also moves the organization forward. Building a robust organizational SSL VPN has numerous benefits to employees and even customers.

We looked at creating different types of trunks for different scenarios, all the rules that apply to activating a trunk, and we discussed the importance of backups. The Web portal has all the relevant tools needed by the end user, and is a complete experience.

From a security perspective, it is important to remember that IAG with the built-in ISA Server is a complete, secure solution in one appliance on a hardened operating system. The importance Microsoft has put on security combined with the ease of creating firewall rules restricting access to only published applications and using endpoint policies together makes IAG a proven solution.

Solutions Fast Track

Implementing an Intelligent Application Gateway 2007

- ☑ For client access, IAG has two types of license: the client access license (CAL) and the external connector (EC) license.

- ☑ Application intelligence.

- ☑ Endpoint policies.

Configuring the Whale Communication Intelligent Application Gateway 2007

- ☑ Configuration screen.

- ☑ Publishing an application.

☑ Creating a trunk.

☑ Activating configuration.

Configuring ISA Server to Allow Communication between the Two Servers

☑ Firewall rules.

☑ Portal trunk firewall rules.

Utilizing the Whale Communication Intelligent Application Gateway Tools

☑ Credential management.

☑ System information.

Creating and Managing Intelligent Application Gateway Endpoint Policies

☑ IAG 2007 combines an SSL VPN with endpoint security checks and firewall features, enabling the creation of policy-based remote access controls to a network and its individual applications.

☑ Access to the IAG appliance from remote locations is accomplished with any Web browser.

☑ IAG 2007 supports an unlimited number of users, and up to 64 IAG nodes can be combined in a high-availability configuration.

Frequently Asked Questions

Q: Is it possible to limit the Web portal to a certain network segment for testing purposes?

A: By default all subnets are open to the published applications. However, the portal can be set up to limit the published applications to a set of subnets. It can be beneficial to implement this, as isolating certain applications during testing periods is necessary in order to make sure all endpoint policies are configured correctly.

Q: A few end users have reported that some published applications are grayed out on the Web portal and they cannot click to use the application.

A: Endpoint policies have been designed to govern which rules on managed or unmanaged devices the end user must adhere to. The "access" endpoint policy has two options for noncomplying clients: grayed or invisible. This can be achieved by accessing the published applications property page.

Q: Why should I choose IAG Server instead of an ISA server only?

A: On top of all the advantages ISA server will bring to the organization, IAG has the added advantage of granular policy control, advance security and manageability control, access from unmanaged PCs or mobile devices on unknown networks, and strong endpoint security.

Chapter 9

Using Outlook Web Access through the Intelligent Application Gateway

Solutions in this chapter:

- **The Importance of Securing Outlook Web Access**

- **Publishing Outlook Web Access in the Internet Application Gateway**

- **Securing the Outlook Web Access Interface**

☑ **Summary**

☑ **Solutions Fast Track**

☑ **Frequently Asked Questions**

Introduction

In just the last few years, Microsoft Exchange seems to have matched and possibly eclipsed IBM's Lotus Notes in terms of market share. Using an Exchange server makes sense for a lot of companies that already have a Microsoft infrastructure, because it integrates with Active Directory, and especially for smaller companies, allows them to use network administration staff with Windows expertise to manage their messaging infrastructure as well as other server components and desktops.

Exchange 2007 is Microsoft's newest e-mail server offering, which allows integration with voicemail and SharePoint services. Improved message retrieval options are available to users as well. They can dial in to have messages read back to them over the phone, and there is improved integration with wireless devices. It also provides new security enhancements including several antivirus options, the ability to send encrypted e-mail between servers running Exchange Server 2007, and improved secure Outlook Web Access (OWA) deployments.

OWA has actually been around since the days of Exchange 5.5. Many of the features of the regular Outlook program are available to users who utilize the Web-based application. Given the potentially sensitive information often sent over e-mail, it is considered a best practice to secure OWA using encryption. Since it is really just a Web application, using Secure Sockets Layer (SSL) to encrypt connections to OWA is the most logical way to provide this protection. OWA can be added to the Microsoft Intelligent Application Gateway (IAG) as a secure Web-based application providing not only SSL access to OWA, but unified management with other remote access technologies for an organization through Microsoft Internet Security and Acceleration (ISA) Server.

The Importance of Securing Outlook Web Access

More and more, users rely on e-mail in today's busy world. Unfortunately for many administrators, users have turned e-mail into a critical file storage repository as well as a preferred method of communication. However, with an inability to function without e-mail, and with the ever increasingly mobile workforce, administrators have been forced to provide remote access to e-mail. Numerous protocols exist for providing this functionality including:

- Post Office Protocol 3 (POP3)
- Simple Mail Transfer Protocol (SMTP)

- Internet Message Access Protocol (IMAP)
- Hypertext Transfer Protocol (HTTP)

Traditionally, POP3 and IMAP have been the most widely used standard protocols for providing remote mailbox access. However, with the introduction of OWA in Exchange 5.5, OWA has been an appealing option. It is fairly simple to deploy, and for organizations already opening port 80 for other Web services, it does not require exposing new protocols to the public. Many organizations began using OWA as an easy way to fix the functionality issue, allowing users to access their e-mail over a service they already allow and monitor.

The Security Problem

As many of you know, Microsoft's OWA has some serious security issues that hackers love to exploit. Exchange administrators worry daily over these possible security breaks. One of the security issues dealt with the fact that an OWA user's cached credentials can easily be used to gain unauthorized access to an Exchange mailbox from the local Internet browser. Another problem was that because an OWA session does not time out if the user forgets to logout and close the browser window, an intruder can gain access to the Exchange mail system simply by browsing to the open OWA session. Finally, OWA user ID's and passwords are stored in the browser cache for subsequent use, and remain in the cache as long as a browser session is active.

Most organizations know to use SSL to encrypt data transferred to and from the OWA client and the Exchange server, thus making it impossible to "sniff" the contents of a user's e-mail. But what some organizations do not understand is that SSL will not prevent an intruder from gaining access to the Exchange server via an OWA session. If SSL is used in conjunction with other security products such as the IAG, this reduces the risks by introducing policies that are related to certain rules that are created by the corporate security practices.

NOTE

Windows NT Challenge/Response (NTLM) is the authentication protocol utilizing the integrated single sign-on mechanism, also known as the Integrated Windows Authentication.

With the Integrated Windows Authentication, the user name and password (credentials) are hashed before being sent across the network. When you enable Integrated Windows Authentication, the client browser proves its knowledge of the password through a cryptographic exchange with your Web server, involving hashing. However, all of the information transmitted over HTTP is sent in the clear, and OWA is no exception.

The problem is that most information contained within an organization's e-mail system is sensitive and confidential and should be encrypted. The username and password are just the tip of the iceberg.

Users simply do not understand that e-mail is a fundamentally insecure communication method. In my experience as a System Engineer, I have witnessed users sending sensitive information such as their credit card information and social security numbers over e-mail, and then argue with System Administrators when they tried to inform them that e-mail was not secure method for transmitting such information. This type of activity also exposes security concerns on a company-wide level that a diligent hacker could use to their advantage. Some of the consequences could include stealing great deals of sensitive proprietary company information, including information about employee salaries, disciplinary actions, terminations, and company intellectual property information. In this day and age, it is difficult to believe sensitive information would be transmitted in clear text.

While securing an OWA deployment certainly will not solve every security issue related to e-mail, it can address those related to providing remote access to e-mail. With any remote e-mail access solution, the organization should be primarily concerned with connections from public networks, especially those from public wireless access points. A few places that are inherently problematic to have users connecting from include coffee houses, Internet cafés, technical conferences (kiosks), and international airports, all breeding grounds for sniffers. The logon credentials and all e-mail messages transmitted in these environments can easily be sniffed and captured by malicious eavesdroppers.

Similarly, there are situations where some corporations do not maintain a local Exchange Mail system on site, choosing to lease e-mail systems from local Internet Service Providers (ISPs), but still use OWA or other remote access methods to access their e-mail when on the road. Some people prefer OWA over the regular Outlook clients.

Users may also use remote e-mail access from their homes. While this seems private enough, there are plenty of users who have turned on and deployed unencrypted wireless access points in their homes. Even those connecting over hard-wired connections may be susceptible to snooping, especially if they receive service from their cable company, and are on a shared connection with several of their neighbors.

The threats to remote e-mail access are numerous because of the vast amounts of organizational data e-mail presents.

Some of the following threats will likely consider e-mail a prime target for attack:

- Entities engaged in corporate and industrial espionage
- Entities engaged in extortion
- Curios hackers
- Phishing Scams
- Worst-case hackers using e-mail to crash servers, thus stifling the corporation's communication

The Security Solution

In short, e-mail is potentially the most appealing target in your organization. Additionally, it is a requirement to provide remote access to the service; however, it provides an attack means for hackers, and there is no shortage of hackers who have the motivation, resources, and skills to penetrate the security of the network and e-mail system. Therefore, it is absolutely essential that when implementing OWA, the entire remote access session is encrypted.

Since OWA is a Web-based application, it makes sense to use SSL, which is also referred to as Transport Layer Security (TLS), which came out with Windows 2003 Server to provide the confidentiality and security required.

Configuring & Implementing...

SSL/TLS

So what exactly is SSL/TLS? The Secure Sockets Layer (SSL) protocol v.3 and Transport Layer Security (TLS) protocol, v.2 are the same protocols with a new name. The protocol is based on public key cryptography. SSL/TLS is used to authenticate servers and clients and then encrypt messages between the

Continued

authenticated parties. In the authentication process, a SSL/TLS client sends a message to a SSL/TLS server, thus responding with the information that the server needs to authenticate itself. The client and server perform an additional exchange of session keys, ending the authentication dialog. When authentication is completed, secured communication can begin between the server and the client using the symmetric encryption keys that are established during the authentication process.

Securing Your OWA Connection

- OWA sessions aren't encrypted by default, and the communication between the Exchange server and the end-user browser is in clear text. Adding SSL to your OWA sessions ensures end-to-end encryption for the duration of the session.

- Use the SSL/TLS support that is built into most current Web-browsers. If the user has access to a Web browser and an Internet connection they can connect securely.

- Establish an SSL connection between the OWA client and the ISA server firewall.

- Establish an SSL connection between the ISA server firewall and the OWA server.

Publishing Outlook Web Access in the Internet Application Gateway

One day you are minding your own business at your desk and your IT director approaches you and asks you to clarify why the company should consider using the IAG and why should they choose it over ISA 2006?

Designing & Planning…

OWA Server Placement

Although the main goal in this chapter is to show you how to use the IAG feature in ISA Server 2006 to secure OWA, it is important to consider the other aspects of securing the deployment. You should make sure you put your OWA server in a demilitarized zone (DMZ) separate from your mail servers and other systems. As with any service or application you are making public, you want to provide separation from your internal systems. This can be an especially sensitive consideration for an application that provides Web-based access to your organization's e-mail store.

Your comments should be easily explained by setting up a basic planning explanation. ISA server should be used when you need:

- Branch office gateway for site-to-site connectivity and security

- Data center Internet access control and Web caching

- Advanced security with inbound and outbound firewall

- Publishing, securing, and pre-authenticating access to specific Web services such as Microsoft Exchange server and Microsoft SharePoint server (when more advanced client options aren't required)

- Full network connectivity for managed PCs (via Virtual Private Network [VPN])

- High-security client access via Windows 2000 or Windows XP that needs host checking and quarantine and Internet Protocol Security (IPSec) (or other) encryption and authentication

To augment and enhance the ISA server, it recommended adding the Intelligent Application Gateway when you need to do the following in the corporate world.

- Browser-based clientless access with granular policy control of data and application components

- More advanced security and manageability control over the client when accessing Web- and non-Web-based resources

- Remote access to a broader range of third-party and line-of-business applications

- Access from unmanaged PCs or mobile devices on unknown networks

- Strong endpoint security verification

- No IPSec VPN clients available for the target host platform

- Extend policy-based access to partners and customers if warranted

Adding OWA to the IAG (Portal)

The first step before adding the OWA to the IAG is to verify that your portal Web site is up and operational. If not, you will not be able to proceed with the OWA installation. Creating the portal Web site is out of the scope of this chapter.

IAG 2007

Microsoft offers the Intelligent Application Gateway (IAG) 2007 as a high-performance application access and security appliance integrated with ISA Server 2006. IAG 2007 provides SSL VPN, a Web application firewall, and endpoint security management that enables access control, authorization, and content inspection for a wide variety of line-of-business applications. These technologies provide remote workers with easy and flexible secure access from a broad range of devices and locations including PCs and mobile devices. IAG also enables IT administrators to enforce compliance with application and information usage guidelines through a customized remote access policy based on device, user, application, or other business criteria. See Figure 9.1 for a basic idea of how the IAG could fit within your environment.

Figure 9.1 Infrastructure Cloud

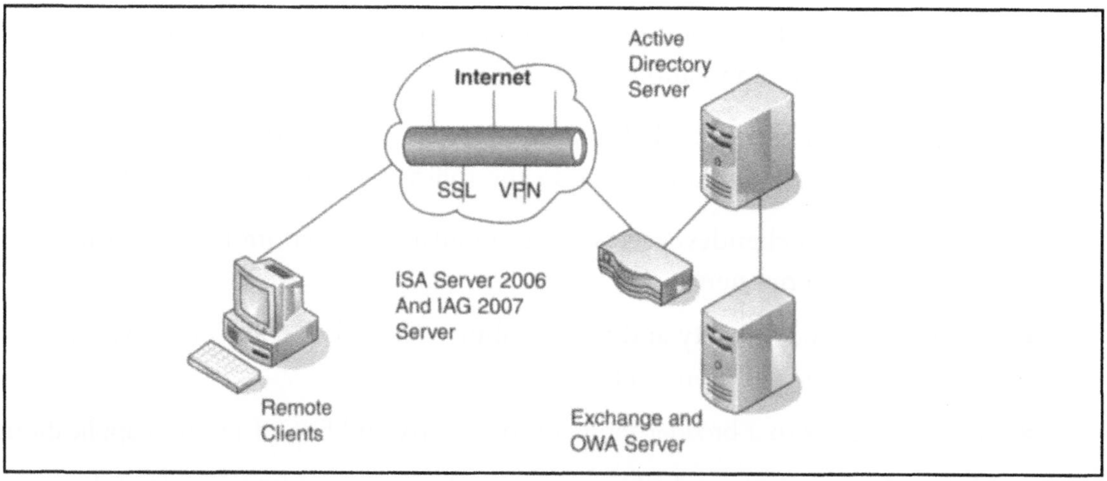

The following configuration steps provide you with a step-by-step process to add the OWA to the IAG gateway, otherwise known as the IAG Portal.

NOTE

Some assumptions need to be understood before the following steps can be implemented.

In adding to the following steps, it is understood that the IAG gateway is configured and running within your infrastructure. Only the following steps are needed to add the OWA.

Server Roles

Table 9.1 represents the server names and roles used as my examples for the successful install.

Table 9.1 Table of Computer Names Used in Demonstration

Computer Name	Role
"HQ"	Represents a Windows 2003 server R2 DC for the demo.com domain, and an exchange/OWA server
"SRV1"	Represents a Windows 2003 server R2, IAG 2007 and ISA 2006
"Client"	Represents a client computer on the internet; note that a client authentication certificate is installed
"Portal1"	Represents your company's infrastructure portal name

1. On the SRV1 computer, in the IAG Configuration console, under **HTTPS Connections**, select **Portal1** (see Figure 9.2).

Figure 9.2 IAG Configuration Console

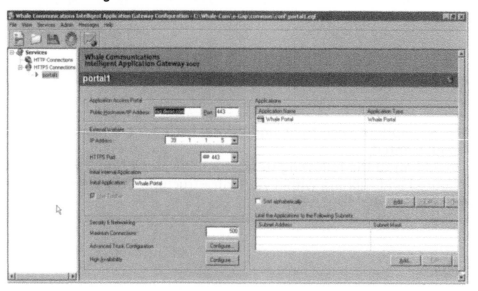

2. In the right pane, in the **Applications** section, click the top **Add** button. Note that depending on the window size, you may have to scroll through the IAG configuration pane to see the Add button.

3. On the Step 1-Select Application page in the **Web Applications** drop-down box, select **Microsoft Outlook Web Access 2007** and then click **Next** (see Figure 9.3).

Figure 9.3 Add Application Wizard-Select Application

4. IAG contains application-specific settings for many well-known applications.

5. On the Step 2-Application Setup page, in the **Application Name** text box, type **OWA2007** and then click **Next** (see Figure 9.4).

Figure 9.4 Add Application Wizard-application Setup

6. On the Step 3-Web Servers page, notice that IAG has already preconfigured the paths that OWA 2007 uses (see Figure 9.5).

Figure 9.5 Add Application Wizard-Web Servers

7. On the Step 3–Web Servers page, double-click the first row in the **Addresses** text box, and then in the new text box, type **hq.demo.com**, press **Enter**, and then click **Next** (see Figure 9.6).

Figure 9.6 Add Application Wizard-Web Servers

8. On the Step 4–Authentication page, click **Add**.

9. In the Authentication and User/Group Servers page, select **AD**, and then click **Select**.

10. IAG will authenticate requests for the OWA2007 application against the AD authentication server.

11. On the Step 4–Authentication page, click **Next**.

12. On the Step 5-Portal Link page, in the **Application URL** text box, change the URL to use HTTPS instead of HTTP - **https://hq.demo.com/owa/**, and then click **Finish** (see Figure 9.7).

The revised URL will appear under the Portal Link tab in the Application Properties (Microsoft Outlook Web Access 2007) page (see Figure 9.8).

Figure 9.7 Add Application Wizard-Portal Link

Figure 9.8 Application Properties (OWA 2007)

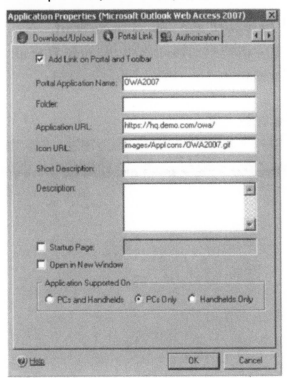

13. Later in this exercise, you will create a Redirect Trunk, which will automatically forward non-secured request to http://hq.demo.com and to https://hq.demo.com.

14. A window with an application-specific note for OWA 2007 appears.

15. Close the **Note** window.

Activating the Configuration

1. On the **File** menu, click **Activate**, or on the toolbar, click the gear icon.

2. In the **Passphrase** dialog box, type **password**, and then click **OK**.

3. On the Activate Configuration page, click **Activate**. (wait a few moments for the configuration activation to complete).

4. On the Configuration Activation Completed page, click **OK**.

Client to Connect to the IAG

The following represents the steps on the client computer:

1. Open Internet Explorer, and then on the **Favorites** menu, click **IAG Portal**.

2. On the IAG logon Web page, complete the following information:

   - User Name: **Administrator**

   - Password: **Password** and then click **Submit**.

3. You will see that the IAG Portal Web site now contains an entry for the OWA2007 application (see Figure 9.9).

Figure 9.9 IAG Portal Web

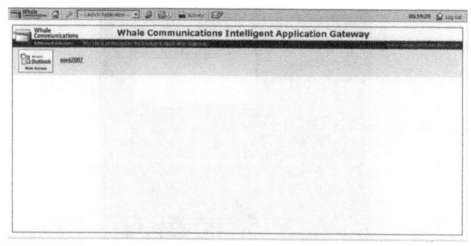

4. In the IAG Portal Web site, click **OWA2007**

- At this point, you should notice that you do not have to authenticate again when connecting to the OWA Web site. IAG handles the single-sign-on authentication.

NOTE

The first time any OWA Web site is opened, it may take a few seconds before the OWA screen appears and the OWA displays the inbox of Administrator.

---

5. On the IAG toolbar, click the home icon to go back to the IAG Web portal. Close the IAG portal Web site.

IAG Portal Web

In the next tasks, you will configure the IAG portal Web site to automatically redirect HTTP requests to the HTTPS trunk. This allows users to use the address http://iag. demo.com, and still connect to the HTTPS portal Web site.

Now let's attempt a connectivity test. In your Web browser connect to the IAG Portal Web site at **http://iag.demo.com**. (Remember do not use https.)

1. Open Internet Explorer, and then in the **Address** text box, type **http:// iag.demo.com**, and then press **Enter**. You should see the browser attempt to connect to the IAG portal Web site, without using HTTPS. After a few moments, the browser will display an error page as shown in Figure 9.10. (The page cannot be displayed).

Figure 9.10 HTTP Error Status Page

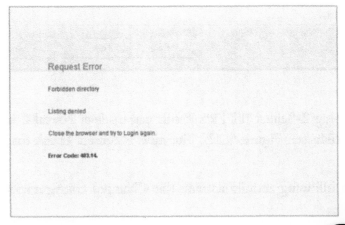

2. Close Internet Explorer.

Redirect the Trunk on SRV1

On the SRV1 server, create a Redirect Trunk for **Portal1**.

1. On the SRV1 Server, in the IAG Configuration console, right click **HTTP Connections**, and then click **New Trunk**.

2. On the Step 1-Select Trunk Type page, select **Redirect HTTP to HTTPS Trunk**, and then click **Next** (see Figure 9.11).

Figure 9.11 Create New Trunk Wizard - Select Trunk Type

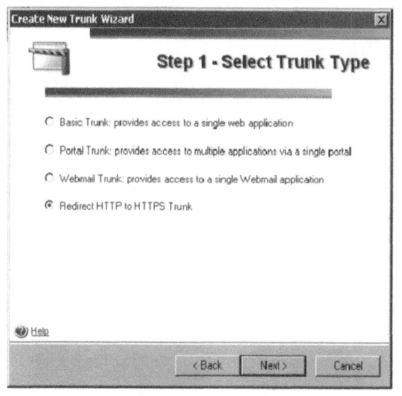

3. On the Step 2-Select HTTPS Trunk page, select **Portal1**, and then click **Finish** (see Figure 9.12). The new Redirect Trunk for Portal1 is created.

  ■ The following should activate the Changed configuration.

Figure 9.12 Create New Trunk Wizard- Select HTTPS Trunk

4. On the **File** menu, click **Activate**, or on the toolbar, click the gear icon.

"Client" to Connect to the IAG

The following represents the steps on the client computer. Also, the first time a client PC attempts to connect to the IAG portal Web site, some client computers may require components to be installed. Don't forget to click the Information Bar and then Click **Install ActiveX Control** and install when and if prompted.

1. On the Client computer, connect to the IAG portal Web site at http://iag.demo.com (Remember do not use HTTPS.)

2. On the Client computer, open Internet Explorer, and then in the **Address** text box, type **http://iag.demo.com**, and then press **Enter**.

3. Internet Explorer connects to http://iag.demo.com. The IAG server responds with HTTP status code 302-Object moved, and informs Internet Explorer to reconnect to https://iag.demo.com.

4. The IAG logon Web page opens, using an HTTPS connection. This result confirms that the Redirect Trunk successfully redirected the initial HTTP request to the HTTPS trunk (see Figure 9.13).

5. Close the IAG logon Web page.

Figure 9.13 IAG Portal Web Logon Page

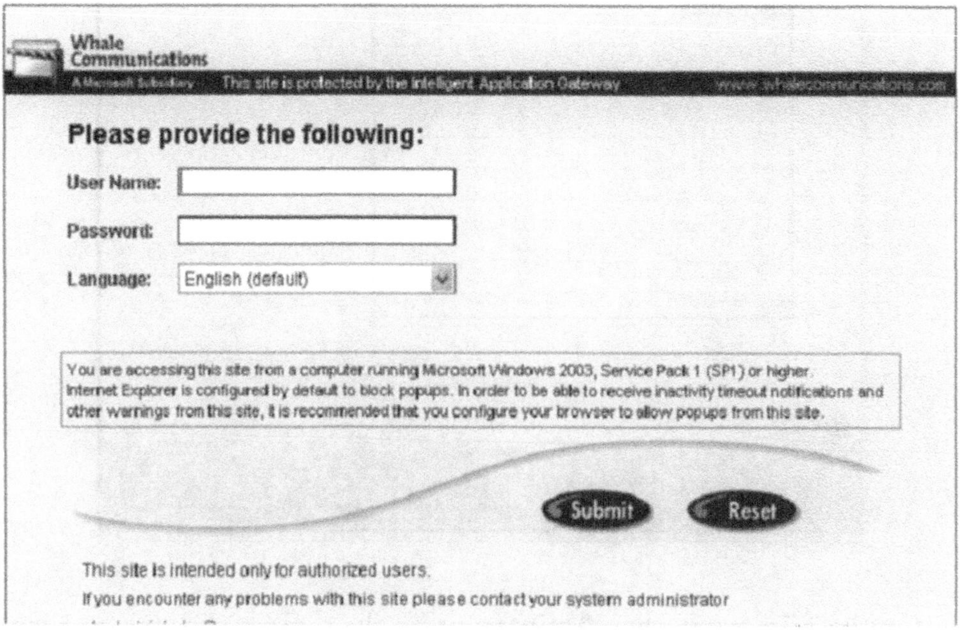

You have just successfully installed the OWA Web application.

Examining the Rules Added to the ISA Configuration

Any time the IAG has a configuration change and when the "activate the configuration" button is depressed, IAG will update the related ISA firewall rules.

In our demonstration for this chapter, both ISA 2006 and IAG 2007 are installed on the same server (SRV1). In the process of adding the OWA application and configuring the IAG, some 13 new rules are created on the ISA 2007 server. Also, additional "ALLOW RULES" are created when you update the portal trunk configuration.

ISA Rules

One newly created firewall rule on the ISA server called AUTH#001, allows network traffic from the IAG server to the domain controller. This new rule is for authentication purposes only.

The next rule, Trunk#001, allows network traffic from client computers to the IAG server on HTTPS port 443, which is the IAG portal Web site.

These rules and many more can be reviewed in the ISA Server Manager console.

Securing the Outlook Web Access Interface

Securing the OWA is straightforward with no hidden complicated procedures, and can be accomplished in approximately 5 minutes or less in most circumstances.

In this demonstration, you will define endpoint policies. "Endpoint policies" is another term for client computers. Endpoint policies allow you to specify required security configuration settings on the client computers. The IAG Client Components verify these client-side configuration settings when a user connects to the IAG portal Web site.

At this stage, you will define the criteria for your clients to be allowed to enter the portal Web site. Only if the client computer(s) meet certain configuration criteria will it be allowed access to the IAG portal Web site.

IAG Server

On the IAG server, session policies are needed to be configured to allow the corporate client PC's to connect to the AIG portal.

1. On the SRV1 server, in the IAG Configuration console, under **HTTPS Connections**, select **Portal1**.

2. In the right pane, in the **Security & Networking** section, after **Advanced Trunk Configuration**, click **Configure** (see Figure 9.14).

Figure 9.14 IAG Configuration Console - Security & Networking

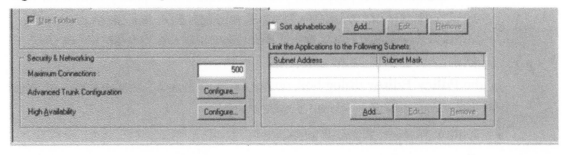

3. In the **Advanced Trunk Configuration (Portal1)** dialog box, on the **Session** tab, click **Edit Policies** (see Figure 9.15).

Figure 9.15 Advanced Trunk Configuration - Session Tab

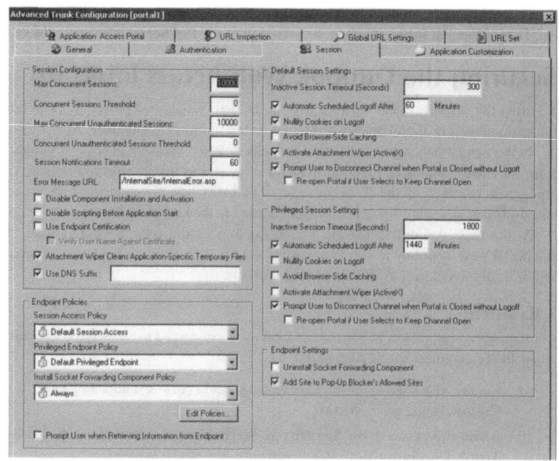

4. In the **Policies** dialog box, click **Add**.

 - For demonstration purposes, you will create a new policy definition to verify whether the Windows Firewall is enabled on the client computer. Instead of creating a new policy definition, you can also use any of the predefined policy definitions.

5. In the **Policy Editor** dialog box, on the General Policy Settings page, complete the following information (see Figure 9.16):

 - **Policy Name:** Firewall is enabled

 - **Category:** Policies

 - **Explanatory Text:** Windows Firewall must be enabled on network connection.

Figure 9.16 Advanced Trunk Configuration - General Policy Settings Editor

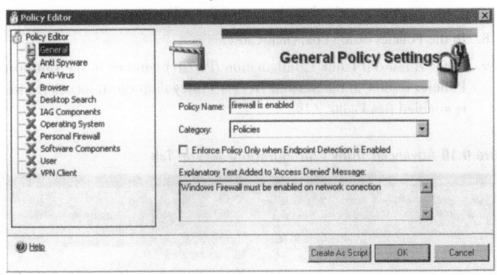

6.   On the left side, select **Personal Firewall** (see Figure 9.17).

7.   On the right side, on the **Personal Firewall** page, complete the following information:

   ■   **Enable Group:** enable

   ■   **Windows XP SP2 Personal Firewall:** enable

   ■   **Windows 2K3 SP1 Personal Firewall:** enable and then click **OK**.

Figure 9.17 Advanced Trunk Configuration- General Policy Settings - Personal Firewall

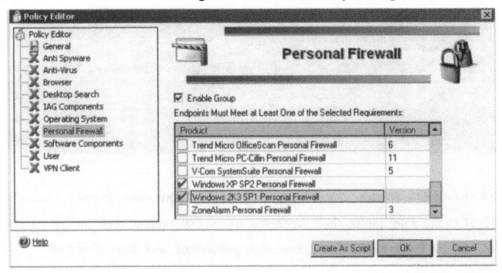

- You have just added a new policy definition named "Firewall," which is enabled and is added to the end of the policies list.

8. In the Policies dialog box, click Close.

9. In the Advanced Trunk Configuration (Portal1) window, in the **Endpoint Policies** section, in the **Session Access Policy** drop-down list, select **Firewall is enabled** (see Figure 9.18).

Figure 9.18 Advanced Trunk Configuration- Session Tab

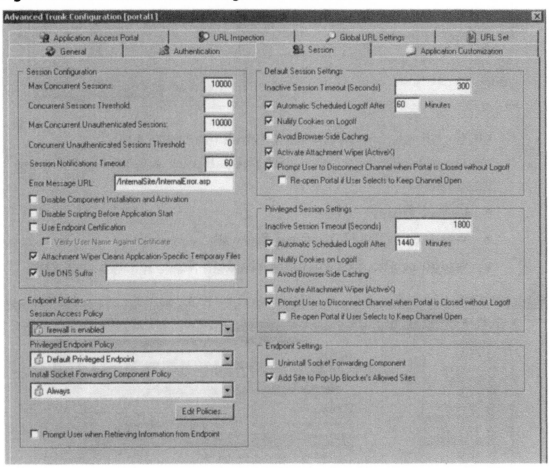

10. Click **OK** to close the Advanced Trunk Configuration (Portal1) dialog box.

11. On the **File** menu, click **Activate**, or on the toolbar, click the gear icon.

12. In the **Passphrase** dialog box, type **password**, and then click **OK**.

13. On the **Activate Configuration** page, click **Activate**. This activation can take a few minutes to complete.

14. On the Configuration Activation Completed page, click **OK**.

Configuring & Implementing...

"Client" Computer

This is close to the final stages of making sure the firewall is enabled. This is one of the policies described above to meet the requirements to connect.

15. On the "client" computer, open your browser., and then on the **Favorites** menu, click **IAG Portal**, or type **https://iag.demo.com**.

   ■ At this point, IAG checks the client compliance with the access policies. Because Windows Firewall is not enabled on the client computer, the user cannot access the IAG portal Web site (see Figure 9.19).

Figure 9.19 IAG Portal Web Warning Page

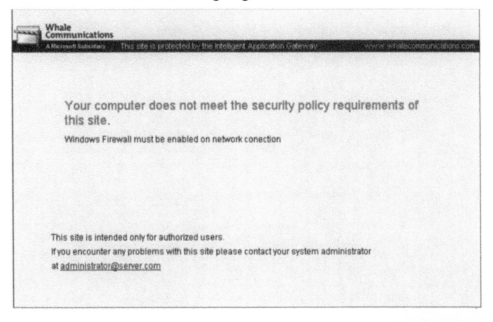

16. Close Internet Explorer.

   ■ Now to verify the connection with the firewall turned on, go the **Start** menu, click **Control Panel**, and then click **Windows Firewall**.

17. In the **Windows Firewall** message box, click **Yes** to confirm that you want to start the Windows Firewall/ICS service.

18. In the **Windows Firewall** dialog box, select **On**, and then click **OK**. Windows Firewall is enabled on the "Client."

19. Now having the Client firewall enabled, open Internet Explorer, and then on the **Favorites** menu, click **IAG Portal**.

   ■ Because Windows Firewall is enabled, the client computer meets the access policy, and IAG allows access to the portal Web site. Connection complete.

20. Close the IAG logon Web page.

Summary

The intent of this chapter is to give you a better understanding of how to install the Microsoft Outlook Web Access mail program through the newly acquired IAG 2007 appliance, that was turned into a software form of a gateway by Microsoft within the past year. The IAG is a comprehensive and secure remote access gateway that augments an ISA 2006 security, providing a SSL protection with endpoint security to protect all Web-based applications such as Microsoft OWA.

Solutions Fast Track

The Importance of Using HTTPS for Outlook Web Access

☑ HTTPS is a secure version of the HTTP, a secure means of transferring data using the HTTPS protocol on the World Wide Web where secure e-mail, e-commerce transactions, company sensitive information, and transactions are involved.

☑ HTTPS encrypts the session with a digital certificate (i.e., HTTP over SSL), which can be used by Web browsers.

Solution Publishing Outlook Web Access in the Internet Application Gateway

☑ Utilize HTTPS (port 443) packets to the internal IP address of the Exchange server.

☑ Make sure that your user's browsers have an appropriate URL to use for Outlook Web access. You can use a fully qualified domain name (FQDN), or even an IP-based URL such as https://xxx.xxx.xxx.xxx/abcdef. If you use the former, make certain that mail.yourdomain.com resolves to the appropriate IP address.

Securing the Outlook Web Access Interface

☑ Use the Integrated Windows authentication, which is enabled by default. Login names and passwords are not prompted, which allows for more of a secure interface by having the client and server to negotiate.

☑ Utilize the digital certificates; either create your own or purchase from a third-party vendor.

Frequently Asked Questions

Q: Why is it necessary to use SSL/TLS to secure access to my Outlook Web Access deployment?

A: To reduce the risk of exposing great deals of sensitive personal and/or proprietary company information that is sent daily via the corporate e-mail system across corporations.

Q: My system keeps prompting me that my encryption is not correct when I initiate the OWA login process. How can I fix this prompt?

A: The Web browser must be running 128-bit encryption.

Q: What's the most critical security issue I need to be concerned about when it comes to setting up OWA on my Exchange server?

A: Authentication! OWA can perform authentication either by clear text mode or utilizing the Integrated Windows Authentication by default. Obviously the clear text mode is not recommended.

Q: Why do I get the following error message when I try to connect?

HTTP 403.4 – Forbidden:

SSL required

Internet Information Services

A: After the Outlook Web Access user receives the error message, the user must manually type https:// at the start of the URL to connect to the Exchange Server computer. You may want to configure Internet Information Services (IIS) to automatically redirect the Outlook Web Access user's HTTP request to HTTPS, to minimize user interaction and to make sure that all incoming requests are enabled for SSL.

Chapter 10

Configuring Virtual Private Network Traffic Through the Intelligent Application Gateway

Solutions in this chapter:

- Setting up the Network Connection Server

- Connecting Through the Virtual Private Network

☑ Summary

☑ Solutions Fast Track

☑ Frequently Asked Questions

Introduction

As part of the Forefront infrastructure, virtual private network (VPN) traffic can be configured to pass through the Intelligent Application Gateway (IAG) using a Secure Sockets Layer (SSL) connection. VPNs allow remote users to securely connect to internal networks to gain access to resources. Previously, VPN traffic was encrypted using Layer 2 tunneling protocol (L2TP) or point-to-point tunneling protocols (PPTP), resulting in support problems such as problems with application compatibility, setup complications, and difficulty when being used over networks that use Network Address Translation (NAT).

Using encrypted VPN traffic to connect to the application gateway will help prevent data from being compromised. Using IAG 2007 Network Connector SSL VPN, this traffic is tunneled using a SSL connection. Company employees will establish connections from remote locations, such as their home or a branch office. Client computers will install a Network Connector Client application when they reach the Whale Communication IAG 2007 Portal, allowing them to connect to the internal network using SSL, and eliminate the usability problems that were previously caused by L2TP or PPTP connections.

A large number of companies are allowing employees to do work from home. Allowing employees to access the internal resources of the company's infrastructure can benefit the productivity of a company. When users connect to the internal network using an insecure network (the Internet), there are security risks involved. In addition, the client's computer may be in an unknown security state creating additional security risks. Using VPN, which encrypt the traffic, has helped to reduce the vulnerabilities associated with remote connection. Network administrators can use Microsoft Forefront to provide this functionality in environments and for applications for which it was previously unavailable using tunneling SSL connections through the Whale Communication IAG. Administrators can also require compliance with Windows updates, antivirus, anti-spyware, and/or other applications prior to allowing a client VPN access to the corporate network. Figure 10.1 shows the network path for a client connected using the IAG 2007 Network Connector SSL VPN.

Figure 10.1 Connecting a Client via the IAG 2007 Network Connector SSL VPN

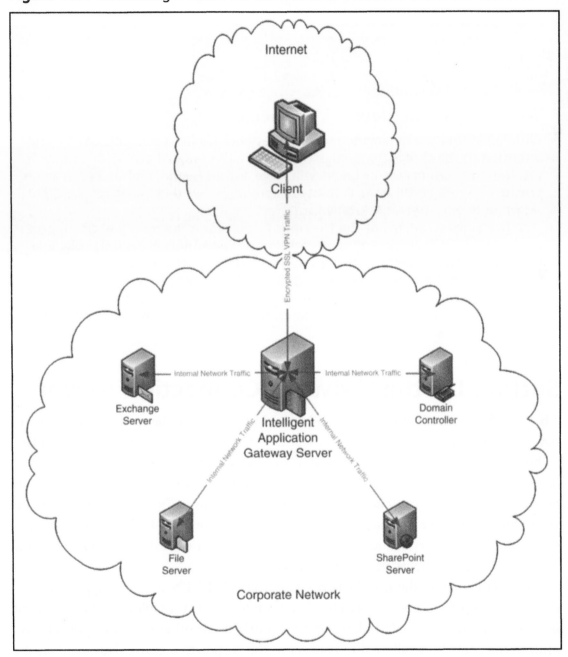

Designing & Planning…

When to Use the Network Connector

When planning the deployment of IAG Network Connector client, pay careful attention to the clients that you allow to have this level of access. Clients with the Network Connector installed will have full network-level access to your private network and the same ability to spread viruses and malware as a client attached to your network locally.

The biggest benefit of the Network Connector is it allows you to support applications and clients on networks that were not previously possible. Previously used on home or remote networks that used NAT or had strict firewall implementations may have been unable to create a LT2P or PPTP VPN connection. By using the Network Connector, you can now eliminate these restrictions and provide access to your clients to all applications without regard to their location or local network configuration.

Setting Up the Network Connection Server

The IAG Network Connector SSL VPN would be used for clients that you want to have full network-level access to the corporate network from remote clients. Similar to how LT2P and PPTP VPNs worked in the past but it will allow you to connect from network locations that were not previously possible. Some of these environments include connecting from a client that is behind a router using NAT or in environments with highly restrictive firewalls. The Network Connector also allows you to specify networking parameters including Domain Name System (DNS), WINS, Gateway, and Domain Name for clients after they connect.

Another benefit of the IAG Network Connector SSL VPN is that it supports IAG Access Policies prior to connection. This allows you to confirm compliance with important security measures, such as Windows updates, antivirus, or other software applications prior to the client being allowed to connect to the corporate network. This is a dramatic security improvement over L2TP and PPTP VPNs of the path. To begin configuring the IAG 2007 Network Connector SSL VPN, you would open the IAG Configuration Console and select **Admin | Network Connector Server**. The following tabs are displayed that allow you to configure the Network Connector to your specific needs.

Network Segment

The Network Segment tab is where you would go to define the network interface connector (NIC) for use by IAG. This dialog will display all of the server's network interface connections and allows you to select the one that will be used to access the corporate network. This NIC should be the one that is connected to the internal corporate network and it will display the current networking parameters that are active for this NIC on the server. Figure 10.2 shows this configuration page and the different options.

Figure 10.2 The Network Segment Configuration Page

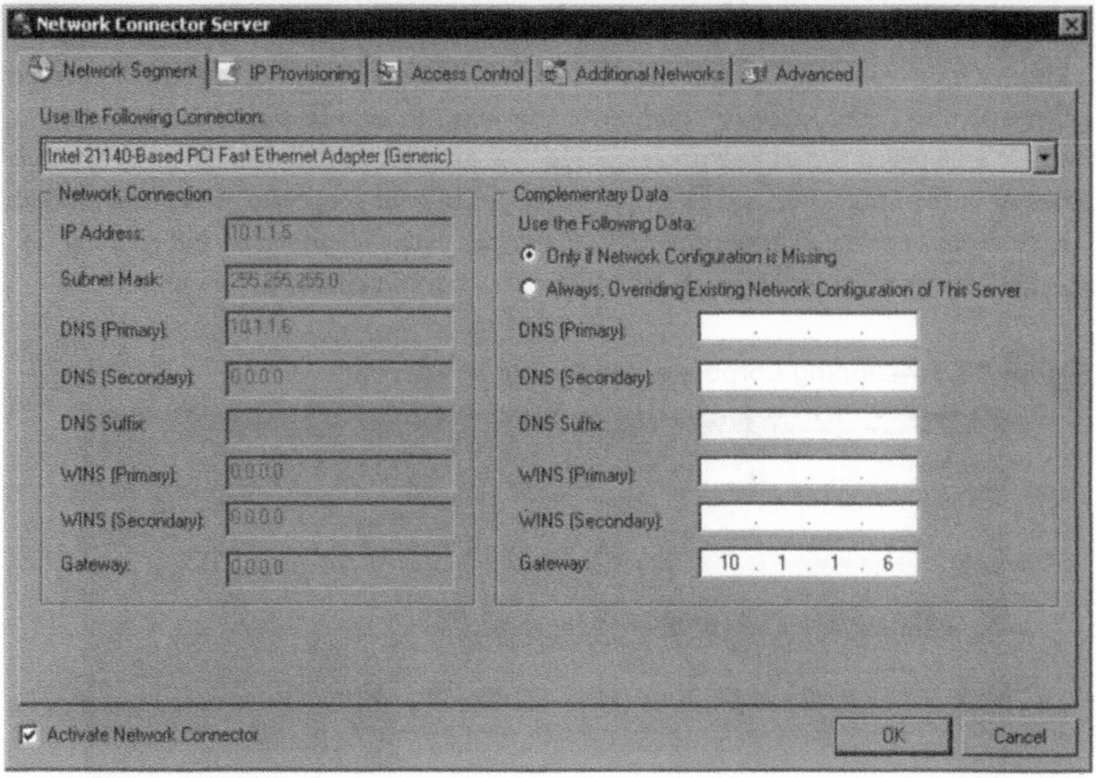

This tab also included a Complementary Data area, which allows you to define networking parameters including DNS, WINS, and the network gateway. You can specify that these settings override the server's own settings, or have them only apply to the server that doesn't have these settings configured. These are the settings that will be provided to clients after they connect using the Network Connector. This might be needed if you want to provide your client different settings, such as a specialized

WINS server or a special remote client DNS server that only includes name resolution for specific computers and applications.

IP Provisioning

The IP Provisioning tab is where you would go to define the different Internet Protocol (IP) ranges that will be given to clients when they connect using the Network Connector. All of the address ranges listed will need to be either corporate IP Addresses or private IP Addresses as a mixture of addresses is not supported. If your corporate network uses 10.1.0.0/255.255.0.0 as its corporate IP address space, you may decide to dedicate 10.1.254.2-10.1.254.254 as the corporate address pool for use by the Network Connector SSL VPN. For a private address pool, you may choose to use 192.168.254.2-192.168.254.254. If you specify corporate addresses, you will need to exclude these addresses from your corporate Dynamic Host Configuration Protocol (DHCP) server; otherwise, you could cause IP conflicts. If you select Private IP addresses you will also need to ensure that the address pools specified are properly routed through your network gateway to the IAG server and properly configured in your corporate firewalls. With both corporate and private addresses, the DHCP service needs to be installed and running on the IAG server in order to assign IP addresses to remote clients (see Figure 10.3).

Figure 10.3 Assigning Corporate and Private IP Addresses

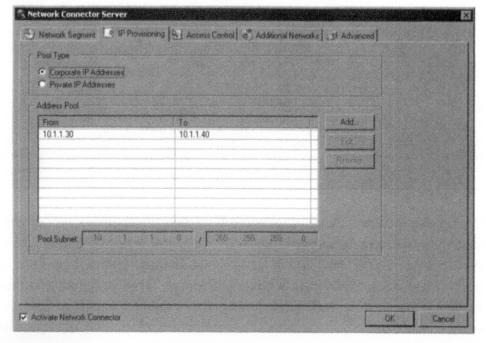

Designing & Planning...

Private IP vs. Corporate IP Address Pool

When you are planning the IP ranges to use for the IP pool, it is important to think about the level of access you want to provide to the users of the Network Connector. If you select Corporate, it is an easier configuration as you have more options regarding Internet access and additional networks. There is also significantly less router and firewall configuration required, since the addresses are already set up on your corporate network and firewalls. The trade off is you get less security, because clients will be assigned IP addresses on your corporate network. If you are unable to modify the corporate network routing and firewalls to support the private address pool, this is generally a preferred configuration. You would then also select split tunneling under Internet access on the Access Control tab. This configuration allows the users of the Network Connector access to the corporate network applications without the risk of them having access to your entire network traffic, and routing their Internet traffic through your corporate network. If you are unable to make the network routing and firewall changes required for a private address pool or are interested in a simpler configuration, selecting Corporate IP Address pool is the best option.

Access Control

The Access Control tab allows you to set the access restrictions that will apply to the clients that are connected via the Network Connector. The Internet Access section allows you to define how a client will connect to the Internet. This can be either Split Tunneling Mode, where Internet Traffic bypasses the VPN, Non-Split Mode, where Internet traffic is routed through the corporate connection, or No Internet Access, where the client allows access to only resources defined on the Network Connector server (see Figure 10.4).

Figure 10.4 Access Control

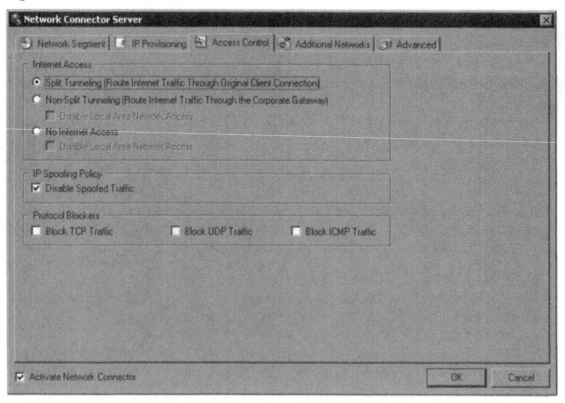

Additional Networks

The Additional Networks tab is where you would select any other networks that should be available to the Network Connector clients when they connect to the Network Connector SSL VPN. In addition, you will need to determine how client IP conflicts are handled. The choices are Fail, Prompt, and Skip. These options determine if a client is open on a Network Connector SSL VPN connection even if they are presently on one of the additional networks. The IP Pool does not need to be included, as that is done automatically. Take special care to include any addresses that your users may need to be able to contact, including infrastructure servers such as DCS, WINS, and DNS, in addition to any application server that they may need to access such as file, print, e-mail, and the location of their desktops for Remote Desktop Protocol (RDP) access. You should also take care to not be overly broad when you define your additional networks, since unmanaged clients may be able to access them and perhaps launch attacks against them. Only seven IP address ranges can be specified as additional networks (see Figure 10.5).

Figure 10.5 Defining Additional Networks

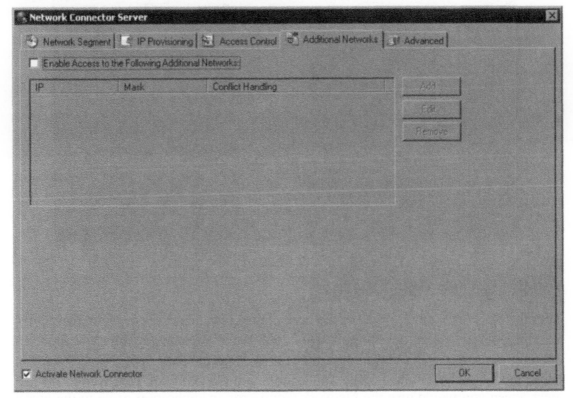

Advanced Tab

The Advanced tab allows you to set three groups of settings (see Figure 10.6). The first is the Network Connector Listener protocol and port. The default is Transmission Control Protocol (TCP) and Port 6003. The second group of settings is related to the log settings including the log level and location. The log levels range from 1 (minimal) to 5 (verbose). Be careful when increasing the log level as the logs can be extremely large when in verbose mode and affect system performance. The third group of settings allows you to modify the number of threads per central processing unit (CPU), buffer levels, and timeouts.

Figure 10.6 The Advanced Tab

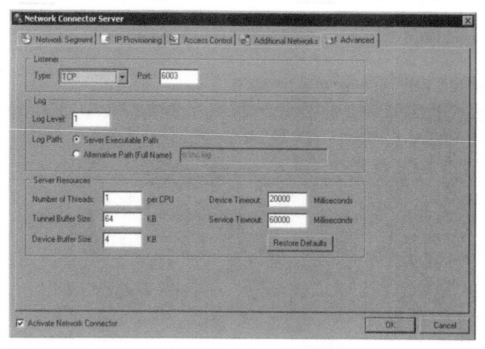

Adding the Application

After the Network Connector server has been configured and activated, you will need to add the application as an option in the IAG 2007 Portal. You can add the application by opening the IAG Configuration Console and running the Add Application Wizard, selecting Client/Server and Legacy Applications and the Network Connector. On the next screen you would give the Network Connector an application name in the portal, and define who is authorized to use the application and the access policy. The next screen displays the settings configured under the Network Connector server configuration and it also allows you to select Launch Automatically on Start, which launches the Network Connector Client upon login to the Portal. The final wizard screen allows you to organize the application in a folder and provide a short and full description for the application.

Connecting Through the Virtual Private Network

When clients first connect to the IAG 2007 Server Portal, they will be asked to download the Whale Communications' Client Components v3.7 if they are on machines that support ActiveX (see Figure 10.7).

Designing & Planning...

Supporting Non-Windows Operating Systems and Non-IE Browsers

IAG 2007 supports the option of a Network Connector Java client in addition to the Network Connector ActiveX client. The advantage of using this client is you will be able to support remote access for a wide range of operating systems and browsers besides Internet Explorer (IE). While the Java client does allow you to support additional browsers and operating systems, certain security features are unavailable when using non-IE browsers. If you wish to support non-IE browsers, you will need to disable Endpoint Detection and Policy Enforcement. By not supporting these features, clients will be able to connect to the corporate network without having their endpoint security and software applications validated. The decisions to support non-IE browsers and non-Windows clients is a decision that will need to be made early in the planning process to make sure access polices are created and applied properly.

Figure 10.7 Whale Communications Client Components v3.7

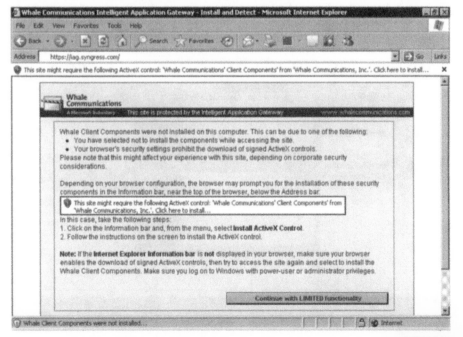

After installation of this ActiveX software package, the IAG portal will run a client compliance check against the connecting client. This compliance check will determine if your client has the software components required to access the portal. These components may include the presence of Windows updates, anti-spyware, antivirus software, and/or any other compliance requirement that is specified by the administrator of the IAG server. Once this compliance check has completed successfully, the logon screen will be displayed. If the client does not support ActiveX, the user will be taken directly to the login screen and no compliance check will be performed. After successfully logging into the server, you will be presented with a list of applications that are available for your use. One of these applications may be the Network Connector, which is the SSL VPN that operates at the network layer. Depending on the configuration, this Network Connector could also be automatically activated when you login to the portal. If the client supports ActiveX, a second installation will occur for the Network Connector client components. If the client does not support ActiveX but does support Java, a Java install of the Network Client will begin. You can determine the status of the Network Connector by selecting its icon in the system tray for the ActiveX version or a second Web page for the Java version. You can see the icon for the network connector and the status screen in Figure 10.8.

Figure 10.8 Portal Activity

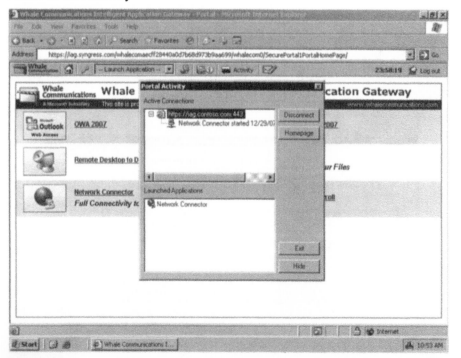

Once the Network Connector has successfully connected, you will be able to access your private corporate resources just as if you were located at the network. If you are using the ActiveX version, all internal and SSL wrapper-based applications will be tunneled through the network connector. If you are using the Java version, only Internet applications will be tunneled through the network connector. SSL Wrapper applications launched through the portal will use a separate SSL connection and not be tunneled over the Network Connector.

Configuring & Implementing...

Enabling Network Connector Logging

While the Network Connector should be very reliable, there will occasionally be a need to perform troubleshooting. The error messages displayed by the Network Connector Error Notification client are often very cryptic and you may need to enable client side logging to identify the problem. Below is the registry key and value options that allow you to enable detailed logging. Be careful when setting high logging levels, as the logs can be quite large and impact system performance.

Key   HKEY_LOCAL_MACHINE\SOFTWARE\WhaleCom\Client\
                    Networ Connector
Value   Log
Value Type   REG_DWORD
Value Data   C:\Program Files\Whale Communications\Client
                    Components\3.1.0\whlioc.log
   Location of where the log file data will be saved
Value   Log/Sniff
Value Type   REG_DWORD
Value Data   0
   Disable Logging
Value Data   1
   Enables logging of low level network traffic to and from the virtual network.
Value Data   2
   Enables logging of tunneled network traffic to and from the virtual network.

Continued

Value Data   3
Enables logging of both low level and tunneled network traffic to and from the virtual network.

The network dumps will be saved in the save folder as the Network Connector Software. The default location is C:\Program Files\Whale Communications\ Client Components\3.1.0\whlioc.dmp.

The IAG 2007 Network Connector SSL VPN has different versions for two different types of clients. The ActiveX version is available for Windows-based machines while the Java version is available for any machine that can run JRE 1.4 or higher. For MAC OSX, the Java Embedding Plug-In may also need to be installed. In order for the Network Connector to be made available to Java clients, the access policy for the Network Connector must be set to "Enforce Policy Only when Endpoint Detection is Enabled." This is because the Java client does not support endpoint detection. You would not want to disable policy enforcement for clients that do support endpoint detection. While the Java Network Connector is able to tunnel internal application traffic, it is unable to tunnel Web applications, and will instead open up a new SSL Wrapper Java Applet for each Web Application that is launched from the IAG 2007 Portal. This is different from the ActiveX Network Connector, which will tunnel all traffic. While this is different, it shouldn't cause any operational difficulties. If you have to enable client logging, the data recorded by the Java client will be different from the ActiveX client.

Summary

The Network Connection server provides your users with a new option for secure remote connectivity. The SSL VPN improves upon LT2P and PPTP by allowing connectivity in network environments where it was not previously possible, such as homes, hotels, or sites with highly restrictive firewalls. It will also allow you to access your clients as if it were on the local network, which can be useful for things such as software distribution and remote control. Unlike LT2P and PTPP connections, the SSL VPN can be configured to confirm client compliance prior to allowing a connection. This ensures that the client meets a minimum security standard prior to being allowed to connect to the corporate network. This is extremely important with the increased utilization of remote access on unknown computers of questionable security.

The following network diagrams will show how data is transmitted by the client, over the Internet, and into the corporate network when the network connector is connected.

Solutions Fast Track

Setting Up the Network Connector on a Corporate Network with Split Tunneling Internet

☑ The IAG Network Connector SSL VPN would be used for clients that you want to have full network-level access to the corporate network from remote clients.

☑ The Network Segment tab is where you would go to define the network interface connector for use by IAG.

☑ The IP Provisioning tab is where you would go to define the different IP ranges that will be given to clients when they connect using the Network Connector.

Connecting Through the Virtual Private Network

☑ IAG 2007 supports the option of a Network Connector Java client in addition to the Network Connector ActiveX client.

☑ If you are using the ActiveX version, all internal and SSL wrapper-based applications will be tunneled through the network connector.

☑ SSL wrapper applications launched through the portal will use a separate SSL connection and not be tunneled over the Network Connector.

Frequently Asked Questions

Q: What advantage does the IAG 2007 Network Connector SSL VPN have over PPTP and/or L2TP VPNs?

A: The IAG 2007 Network Connector SSL VPN eliminates many of the problems with application and network compatibility that can occur with PPTP or L2TP VPNs. In addition, there is no configuration required to set up the VPN; the client just logs into the portal and launches the Network Connector application. An additional benefit of the IAG 2007 Network Connector SSL VPN is that it allows administrators to set up software compliance rules for clients that apply prior to the connecting to the VPN. This ensures that the connecting clients meet the security requirements, such as current antivirus and patches, to ensure that clients will not cause security issues on your corporate network.

Q: Why would you choose to use the IAG 2007 Network Connector SSL VPN over the IAG 2007 SSL Application Wrapper?

A: The Network Connector SSL VPN is a good choice when you are working with applications that are not directly supported by the IAG 2007 SSL Wrapper. These may include File Transfer Protocol (FTP), Voice over Internet Protocol (VOIP), and video conferencing. It is also useful for people who need access to a large variety of corporate applications and/or file shares that are not defining as applications in the IAG 2007 Portal. In addition, the Network Connector SSL VPN also allows administrators access to the remote machine just as if it were on the corporate network. This can be extremely useful for software or patch installation and troubleshooting.

Q: Which IP provisioning pool method should you choose?

A: The IP Provisioning Pool Method is a difficult decision that is highly dependant on your network configuration as well as your desire to separate internal corporate traffic from Internet traffic. If you select Corporate Network, the clients will appear to be the same as any other client on your internal corporate network. If you select Private Network, the clients will connect to a private IP segment and traffic is routed through the IAG server.

Q: Which Internet Access method should you choose?

A: There are three options for Internet Access Methods for Network Connector Clients. The first option is Split-Tunneling, which is generally the preferred option. This option allows clients to bypass the Network Connector when they access the Internet. This increases their speed, as they have a direct connection to the Internet that is not slowed down by encryption. This also removes the traffic from your corporate network. The second option is Non-Split Tunneling. In this option, all Internet access is routed through the corporate network. The advantage of this method is you can monitor and secure this access using your corporate firewall. The disadvantage is it will be a slower access method for your user and increase the traffic on your corporate network. The third option is No Internet Access, which removes a client access to any part of the Internet. This option increases security because it prevents a client from being connected to the Internet and your corporate network at the same time. The second and third options also have an additional selection for Disable Access to Local Network. This can increases security even more by preventing access between the local network of the client and your corporate network. This last option will also disable access to local network printers when a user is connected to the corporate network. This may be desired or undesired depending upon your security and usability requirements.

Q: Is the IAG 2007 Network Connector SSL VPN compatibly limited to Windows and IE?

A: The Network Connector is compatible with a number of operating systems and browsers. For Windows, using IE the Network Connector will use an ActiveX-based installation of the client components. For other browsers, the Java-based client will be installed. The Java Runtime Environment version 1.4 or higher is required for the installation of the client component. On Mac OSX, you will also need to install the Java Embedding Plug-In in order for the Network Connector to work. On any computer, only one version of the Network Connector can be running at any one time.

Chapter 11

Configuring Microsoft Internet Security and Acceleration Server 2006

Solutions in this chapter:

- Installing Microsoft Internet Security and Acceleration Server 2006

- Configuring Microsoft Internet Security and Acceleration Server 2006

- Monitoring Microsoft Internet Security and Acceleration Server 2006

☑ Summary

☑ Solutions Fast Track

☑ Frequently Asked Questions

Introduction

Microsoft's first attempt to enter the firewall market, Proxy Server, was a rather rudimentary product with only basic packet filtering capabilities and some fairly serious security issues. This may be partially due to the fact that it was designed to be more of a proxy for Internet connections than a full-fledged enterprise-level firewall. The two releases of Proxy Server also came a decade ago when security was not the hot issue it is today. However, in 2001 Microsoft began the effort to provide a secure, efficient, and user-friendly software firewall product under the Internet Security and Acceleration Server product name.

Microsoft Internet Security and Acceleration (ISA) Server 2006 is the latest release of Microsoft's perimeter protection product. It should make sense that as Microsoft bundles and markets a suite of security products they are calling Forefront, ISA Server is considered an integral part of the product family. Windows administrators will find that Microsoft ISA Server comes with a familiar interface, which will hopefully ease the learning curve for this product. This chapter will outline some of the main features of Microsoft Internet Security and Acceleration Server 2006, and provide administrators with an overview of some of the key tasks they will need to perform using the product.

It is important to note here that personnel with network security responsibilities really do need to have a strong understanding of the basics of TCP/IP. Without a clear technical understanding of routing, firewalls, and application proxies, all based on deep technical knowledge of TCP/IP, the ISA management interface will only provide a quick way for administrators to create security holes in their networks. This chapter assumes that you have an understanding of these low-level network fundamentals.

Installing Microsoft Internet Security and Acceleration Server 2006

The ISA Server installation routine is one of the simpler and quicker Microsoft product installations I've come across in quite a while. I think it actually might be easier than installing Microsoft Office. However, there are some fairly complex pre- and postinstallation configuration options that need to be considered as well. Ensuring that the preinstallation configuration gets done, and that you are at least aware of the postinstallation options that will need to be considered, will ensure that the deployment goes smoothly.

Preliminary Configuration of Windows Server 2003

Before installing ISA Server 2006, you need to configure several settings on the server. This chapter was written based on Windows Server 2003 R2, but most of the issues covered here are not specific to this version of Windows, and therefore should be applicable across a variety of Windows platforms. I try to point out where this is not the case.

Designing & Planning...

Subnets and Your TCP/IP Configuration

For all but the most experienced packet junkies, subnetting is never quite second nature, and many people attempting to deploy ISA Server will be part of a very small IT staff trying to wear several different hats while protecting users and organizational data. Getting the fundamentals right is most often going to be the difference between success and failure, though, because no amount of fiddling with the ISA Server management console is ever going to overcome a fundamentally unroutable packet.

With this in mind, I would suggest that before you being the installation and configuration of ISA Server, that you take a look at a good subnet overview as either an introduction or a refresher. A decent one can be found here: www.networkcomputing.com/unixworld/tutorial/001.html. Additionally, when it comes time to plan out the network, it is always useful to have a subnet calculator on hand. There are thousands of these online, but this one is pretty easy to use: www.subnet-calculator.com/.

Hardware Considerations

The system requirements for ISA Server are pretty modest. When you compare the critical role ISA Server will play in your network against the role Windows Vista might play it is astonishing to see the antiquated hardware requirements ISA Server needs in order to function. Microsoft lists the minimum requirements for ISA Server 2006 as shown in Table 11.1.

Table 11.1 Minimum Hardware Requirements for ISA Server 2006 Standard or Enterprise Edition

Processor	733 Mhz Pentium III
Memory	512 MB
Disk Space	150 MB (NTFS formatted)

The only caveat here is that this is for the basic firewalling functionality of ISA Server. Most administrators will want to make use of the web proxy and caching functionality. For anyone who has dealt with any caching web proxy, you know that this function can be extremely demanding (especially in terms of memory requirements). Keep this in mind when planning your deployment. It is a good idea to do some research based specifically on your target uses of ISA Server as well as your estimated workload.

TIP

There are plenty of users who can provide feedback especially in the isaserver. org forums. However, in order to get good answers based on your capacity needs, you should do some baselining of your environment to make sure that your estimated workload is not just a wild guess.

Designing & Planning...

Network Topology and Networking Hardware Considerations

It is always a good idea to consider not only the ISA Server configuration, but the details around it as well. Whenever possible the ISA Server should be deployed inline to provide the highest level of security. This is not a best practice that is unique to ISA Server, but to all firewalls. Although ISA Server and many other firewall technologies support deployments with a single NIC, this means that the firewall will need to be attached to a switch or router, and you are relying on this surrounding infrastructure to pass packets to ISA Server for inspection before they are allowed to go to other hosts. Although this should work, it can be circumvented, and this is why it is considered almost mandatory to use an inline deployment scenario.

By extension, this means that your ISA Server will need to have at least two NICs—one for the Wide Area Network (WAN) interface and the other for the Local Area Network (LAN) interface. For higher availability it is a good idea to place redundant NICs into the server.

Configuring TCP/IP Settings

Even for those who have configured Network Interface Card (NIC) settings in Windows thousands of times over the course of the last several years, this part can be tricky. I am assuming that you have a fairly simple network layout, and you are deploying the ISA Server as your main perimeter protection device with a single internal network segment behind it. In this scenario, we have two NICs to configure.

The trick is that we only want to configure a single default gateway and a common DNS server setting for all interfaces. In the lab I have an ISA Server that needs to have the IP addressing information configured based on the information in Table 11.2.

Table 11.2 Overview of TCP/IP Information

External IP Address	192.168.1.72
Internal IP Address	10.0.1.1
Primary DNS Address	10.0.1.5
Secondary DNS Address	192.168.1.1
Upstream Router Address	192.168.1.1

In order to implement these settings properly on the external NIC, I would use the settings shown in Figure 11.1.

In order to implement these settings properly on the internal NIC, I would use the settings shown in Figure 11.2.

Figure 11.1 TCP/IP Configuration for External NIC

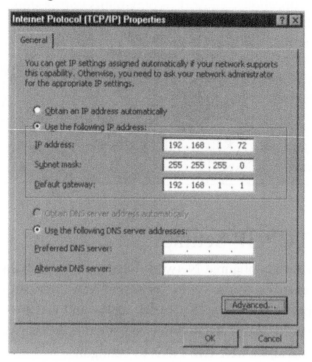

Figure 11.2 TCP/IP Configuration for Internal NIC

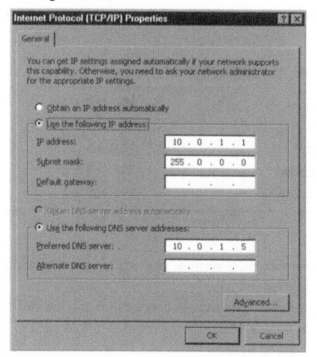

TIP

Collect all of the pertinent network information you can before you begin installing and configuring your ISA Server. For existing networks, collect network address, subnet mask, and default gateway information for each subnet as well as the IP addresses of existing servers providing network services such as DNS and DHCP. It is a good idea to have a diagram of the network layout as well. Bring all of this documentation with you when you go to install and configure the ISA Server.

Domain Membership

Although the debate has not been won outright by either side, it is generally considered a best practice to make the ISA Servers domain members. The ISA guru, Thomas Shinder, has written a good article covering the pros and cons of making your ISA Servers members of your domain or a workgroup (www.isaserver. org/tutorials/Debunking-Myth-that-ISA-Firewall-Should-Not-Domain-Member. html), so I won't try to outdo him in a couple of paragraphs here.

I do think it is worthwhile to discuss one of the points in his article further, though. He argues that although the Active Directory Domain Admins group will be added to the local Administrators group on each ISA Server device, you should be able to trust your domain admins with permissions on these systems. However, the basic principles of least privilege and separation of duties hold that you absolutely should *not* give your Windows domain administrators unrestricted permissions on the firewalls unless they require it, part of the reason being provided in the disclaimer I placed in the introduction: Very good Windows system administrators with years of experience configuring permissions, performance options, and security options throughout a variety of Microsoft Windows server infrastructures do not necessarily have the detailed technical knowledge of the TCP/IP stack required to be firewall administrators.

Some may find this to be a paranoid attitude. However, the entire reason that we, as security professionals, have jobs, and that Microsoft is bundling a suite of security products together is that it helps to be paranoid in this industry. In fact, least privilege and separation of duties are far from requirements of a paranoid data owner. They are security fundamentals as recognized by the National Institute of Standards and Technology (NIST) in their security-related publications, the International Information Systems Security Certifications Consortium, and numerous best-practice whitepapers. Perhaps the primary reason for relying on these principles is that insiders are still the number one threat that organizations face.

For small to mid-sized organizations where fewer than a dozen IT personnel control the infrastructure, and must be able to cover for each other on various tasks, this separation of duties may not be feasible. However, for numerous enterprises with multiple sites, thousands of nodes, and well-defined roles within the IT group, separation of duties and least privilege are the norm.

This point aside, the argument Thomas Shinder has provided for making your ISA Servers domain members is a valid one. You may find it necessary to fix the issue of having the Domain Admins group with local Administrators privileges though depending on the expertise of the people in your organization, and the need to provide technical controls providing this separation of duties. You could easily implement this separation by creating an ISA Firewall Admins group in Active Directory, placing the appropriate users in the group, and giving the ISA Firewall Admins group administrative rights on the ISA firewalls. Then remove the Domain Admins group from the local Administrators group on the devices running ISA Server. Be aware that this may impact your particular setup in unforeseen ways, and as with any configuration changes, you should test this in a lab before deploying it in production.

System Hardening

Any device at the perimeter of your network should be locked down as much as possible. Even the ones inside the perimeter should be locked down, but for your firewall you need to take special care to harden the system. Since ISA Server runs on top of a Windows operating system the following main ideas should be kept in mind:

1. Use the most secure version of Windows available.
2. Disable all unnecessary services.
3. Apply additional system hardening parameters.

The first point means you should probably not be running ISA Server on older versions of Windows Server. Even though Windows Server 2000 is not exceedingly old, numerous security enhancements were made to Server 2003, and default installations of Windows Server 2003 will be somewhat less susceptible to attack than default installations of Windows 2000 Server. In addition to simply using a newer version of Windows Server, the first point means that you must be religious about applying security patches to your firewalls. As always, patches should be tested in a lab before being placed into production, but patching and updating must be done in a timely manner for these perimeter devices. This point cannot be stressed enough.

The second point is equally important, but a bit more complex. Primarily, the ISA Server system should be running the most basic installation of the Windows operating system possible. All unnecessary system software should be unchecked during installation. For most software there is going to be an associated service or set of services created in Windows, and these need to be disabled. If the software is not installed in the first place it means less work because the services that come with the installed programs will not have to be disabled. It also means there is less software that will require a hotfix later. The only piece of software that really needs to be installed on this system is ISA Server, and if ISA Server relies on another piece of software to function it will let you know when you install it. So during the installation of the operating system (OS) use this rule: when in doubt, leave it out.

NOTE

The National Institute of Standards and Technology (NIST) has developed secure configuration checklists for most versions of Windows and secure deployment guidelines for most network services. It is worth checking out these resources at checklists.nist.gov and csrc.nist.gov before getting started.

Once the system is installed as you like, unnecessary services should be disabled using the Services Management Console. Some examples of services you should consider disabling are:

- Computer Browser
- Terminal Services
- Remote Registry
- Print Spooler
- TCP/IP NetBIOS Helper

Lastly, there are some hardening options that fall outside of the scope of the first two categories. One primary precaution that should be taken is to disable NetBIOS on the WAN adapter. In addition, I would recommend that NetBIOS be disabled on all adapters unless it is absolutely necessary.

This can be done in this way:

1. Right-click the WAN adapter and select **Properties**.

2. Select **Internet Protocol (TCP/IP)** and click **Properties**.

3. Click **Advanced**, and then select the **WINS** tab.

4. Select the radio button option to **Disable NetBIOS over TCP/IP** as shown in Figure 11.3.

Figure 11.3 Disabling NetBIOS

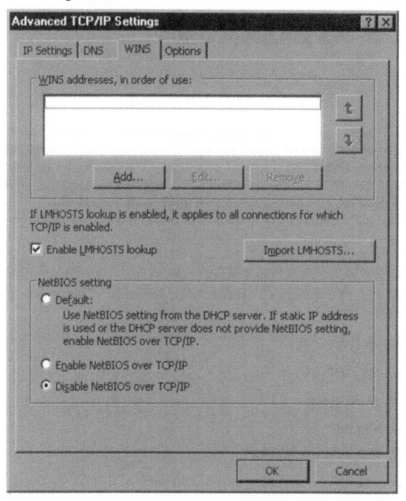

My last system hardening recommendation also happens to be the one I can't adequately cover in a small section here. It involves locking down various aspects and functions of Windows, user capabilities, and other components of the system, and requires a great number of settings to be configured. The best education I got on locking down a Windows Server was when I attempted to remove any peripheral functionality from a Terminal Server deployment using Group Policy Objects in Active Directory so that all users could do was log on, use applications, and then log off. I strongly recommend that you check out this whitepaper on locking down terminal servers from Microsoft: www.microsoft.com/windowsserver2003/techinfo/overview/ lockdown.mspx. The basic goal here is to use Active Directory to manage some low-level security settings across all ISA Servers in the enterprise. Some of the restrictions that can be implemented this way are:

- Preventing password hashes from being stored locally.

- Preventing remote users from shutting the system down.

- Defining the minimum session security for authentication.

- Restricting access to various services and parts of the operating system.

Configuring & Implementing...

Configuring Multiple WAN Addresses

Organizations that have at least a business-class DSL or cable connection or better often have more than one IP address provided by their Internet Service Provider (ISP). Setting up multiple WAN addresses in Windows is actually quite easy. With your set of IP addresses in hand, enter the Network Connections interface, and complete the following:

1. Right-click the **WAN adapter** and select **Properties**.

2. Select **Internet Protocol (TCP/IP)**, and click **Properties**.

3. Click **Advanced** to open the **Advanced TCP/IP Settings** dialog box.

4. On the **IP Settings** tab, under IP addresses you should see the first IP address you have assigned to the WAN interface. Click **Add**.

5. Simply enter the IP address and subnet mask you want to add, and click **Add**. Repeat as many times as necessary until you have added all of your IP addresses. The **Advanced TCP/IP Settings** dialog will look similar to the one in Figure 11.4.

Figure 11.4 Entering Multiple IP Addresses for a NIC

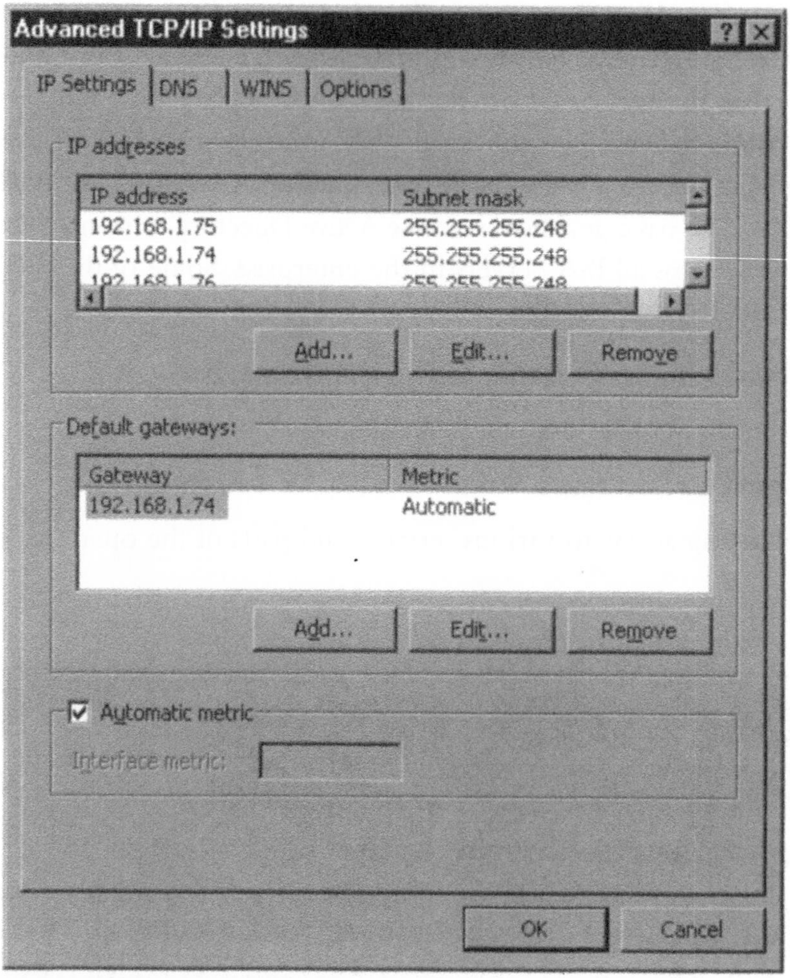

Installation of ISA Server 2006

Once you have implemented the necessary network configuration, and have hardened the base operating system (OS), it is time to install ISA Server. This part should be pretty straightforward.

1. Start the ISA Server installation.

2. Once the ISA Server installer checks some settings the ISA Server installation wizard will appear. Click **Next**.

3. On the license agreement screen, select **I accept the terms in the license agreement** and click **Next**.

4. Enter your customer information including product license key, and click **Next**.

5. On the following screen you will be able to select the installation type, either **Typical** or **Custom**. Choose your installation preference and click **Next**.

   ■ If you opted for the Custom installation option you will be presented with only three easy-to-understand options—ISA, Advanced Logging, and ISA Management—as shown in Figure 11.5.

Figure 11.5 Custom Installation Options

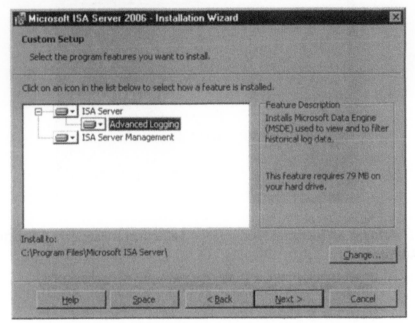

   ■ Select which options you prefer (I recommend selecting all of them), and click **Next**.

6. On the following screen you will be prompted to enter the network address ranges ISA should consider as internal networks. Click **Add**.

7. On the dialog box that opens up (as shown in Figure 11.6), you can add internal networks by either selecting the NIC in the machine that is associated with the internal network, selecting from a default list of internal address ranges, or by specifying the network range. If you have already configured your NICs properly it is probably best simply to click **Add Adapter**.

8. You will see a screen similar to the one shown in Figure 11.7. Select the adapter you wish to use and click **OK**. Click **OK** again to close the **Add Networks** dialog box.

Figure 11.6 Adding Internal Networks

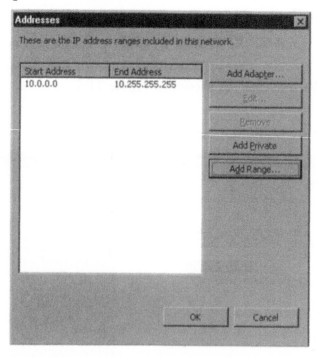

Figure 11.7 Adding an Internal Network by Selecting a Properly Configured Network Adapter

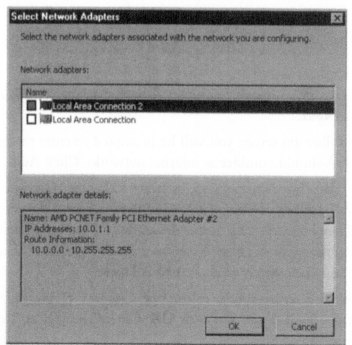

9. On the next screen you will be asked if you wish to support older ISA Firewall Client software. Unless it is mandatory that you do so, it is recommended that you leave the **Allow non-encrypted Firewall client connections** checkbox unchecked, and click **Next**.

10. This screen will warn you that some services will be restarted during installation while others will be disabled. Click **Next**. On the following screen click **Install** to begin the installation.

   ■ After a short wait the installation will finish, allowing you to enter the ISA Management interface to configure the firewall.

Configuring ISA Server 2006

The configuration of ISA Server 2006 is done in the usual Microsoft style using a Microsoft Management Console (MMC). The ISA Server Management console contains a tree-style navigation pane on the left side, which enables access to various areas of the software, and a pane on the right, which is split into two areas. The left side of the details pane contains tabs of subcontent related to the configuration item you select in the left navigation pane. The right side of the details pane lists tasks that you may complete related to the tab you are viewing. See Figure 11.8.

Figure 11.8 The ISA Server Management Console

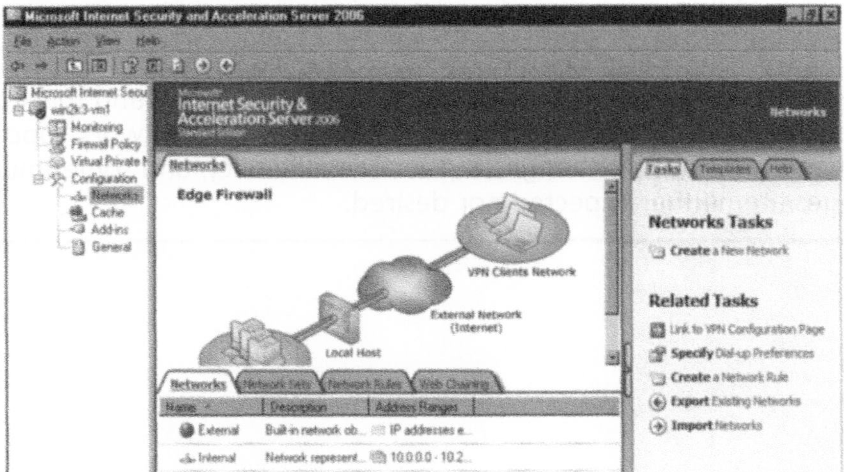

Configuration

The Configuration node in the navigation pane of the ISA Server Management console is probably going to be the most frequently used area of the console for every administrator. It provides you with an interface into configuring almost every underlying aspect of the software including setting the network topology, enabling and disabling various application proxy filters, setting how user authentication should occur, designating cache space for the web proxy to use, and even routing rules. We will cover all these items in the following sections.

Networks

This is probably the most user-friendly and useful node in the ISA Server Management interface. Microsoft has done a good job of taking one of the more complex aspects of deploying any firewall, and simplified it by including network templates for you to use. If you entered the right information during installation you probably don't need to do any further configuration here, but if there are changes to the network topology you can simply select a new network template from the template pane on the right as shown in Figure 11.9. A wizard will then walk you through applying the necessary changes.

Warning

Take caution when applying network topology changes, and thoroughly review and test the firewall afterward. Changing the network topology on this page can result in changes to the Firewall Policy, and sometimes these changes are neither expected nor desired.

Figure 11.9 The Networks Configuration Pane with Network Templates

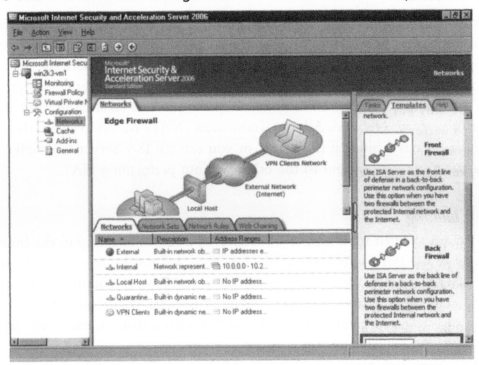

It is good to see that the first task the wizard allows you to perform is to export your current configuration in case you wish to revert back to it. This should be a mandatory step that cannot be bypassed, but since it is not, I recommend you take a moment to do this. The configuration will be saved as an XML file wherever the user chooses.

Network Sets

The idea behind the tab under the Networks node is to just group networks together as a named grouping, so that when you need to create rules you can refer to the Network Set instead of having to call out multiple network names. A simple wizard allows you to select a new name for a network set, and then assign networks to the set. It is also possible to alter the properties of existing Network Sets here, but I strongly recommend that you do not change any of the predefined Network Sets because there are already predefined rules built around them. Changing these sets could, therefore, have pretty substantial negative effects on your network.

Network Rules

It is important to understand the function of the Network Rules as compared to the Firewall Rules. Network rules generally are not used to determine what packets are passed through or dropped by the firewall. Instead, this is where the network administrator will define the way packets are routed between network segments. There are only two options available for the rules you can create. You can tell ISA Server to perform Network Address Translation (NAT) on the packets, thereby obfuscating the real internal IP address, or you can tell ISA Server to simply route the packet from one segment to the other without performing NAT.

Web Chaining

Large enterprises that must support thousands of nodes connecting to the Internet, and want to use ISA Server's web proxy functions will not be able to build a single super server that can proxy all connections. However, these organizations will certainly want to conserve Internet bandwidth whenever possible. Web chaining allows these organizations to deploy a hierarchical array of ISA Servers that can effectively distribute the proxying workload among each other.

The caching web proxy functionality of ISA Server 2006 will be covered in more detail in Chapter 14; look there for further details. However, it is useful to understand how Web Chaining rules interact with the web proxy function. The basics of web chaining require that you understand that a downstream server is closer to the inside of the network where the client nodes are. Upstream servers are out on the perimeter, closer to the Internet. As a network node makes a request to the local web proxy server, that downstream server will evaluate its proxy and web chaining rules as follows:

1. ISA Server will check to ensure that the request is allowed.

2. If the request is allowed, the server is set to cache content, and a valid version of the object exists in the cache, then the server will return the content to the requestor.

3. If the server could not fulfill the request, it will check the Web Chaining rules to determine where to forward the request.

4. The next server upstream will perform the same steps to attempt to fulfill the request. If no caching proxies can fulfill the request it will eventually be forwarded to the Internet.

Cache

As we just noted, the caching web proxy functionality of ISA Server will be covered in greater detail in Chapter 14. Basically, caching web proxies provides administrators with a good way to conserve precious bandwidth for critical network services without having to take draconian measures with regard to users' ability to access the web. Often users request the same resources and content from the web. Caching web proxies will download and save this content while retrieving it for the client that requested it. When subsequent requests for this same content are made, the content can be returned by the proxy without having to download it from the Internet again, thus conserving bandwidth. Of course, web content does not remain static so it is important to tune caching rules so that the proxy eventually identifies its local copy of the content as stale, and again retrieves an updated copy from the Internet.

Add-ins

The Add-ins node in the ISA Server Management Console allows administrators to access application-level filters. These are separated into two groups and displayed on two tabs in the interface, and the distinction between these is a bit confusing at first. The first tab shows Application Filters, which are dynamic link libraries (DLL) that proxy a number of different traffic protocols including:

- Domain Name Service (DNS)
- File Transfer Protocol (FTP)
- Remote Procedure Call (RPC)
- Point-to-Point Tunneling Protocol (PPTP)
- Simple Mail Transfer Protocol (SMTP)

There are a few other application filters provided as well, including one labeled Web Proxy Filter. This filter is one of the more important in the set as it will be most used. Although many people will not be interested in proxying or perhaps even allowing the H.323 protocol for multimedia content, almost everyone using ISA Server will want to proxy traffic to the web. To do this, you need to use the Web Proxy Filter.

The Web Filters tab shows a set of filters that are actually Internet Server Application Program Interface (ISAPI) plug-ins to the Web Proxy Filter. In other words, these are all dependent on the Web Proxy Filter, and allow for the tweaking of some functionality of this filter.

The trick to understanding these filters is to know that the configuration of these filters is not actually done in this area. The only thing you can do under this node is to enable and disable filters. Configuring settings for these is done throughout the rest of the ISA Server Management Console interface. For example, under **Configuration | Add-ins | Web Filters** you can enable or disable the **Caching Compressed Content Filter**. However, in order to set what or how much compressed content can be cached by the web proxy, you need to go to **Configuration | General | Define HTTP Compression Preferences**.

One final note needs to be provided on these filters. In environments where there is a lot of traffic, and system resources on the ISA Server Firewall need to be conserved, administrators should look to disable any filters not in use. Each one loads into memory, and consumes processor and memory resources.

General

There are a great number of administrative settings available in this section broken into three separate sections:

- ISA Server Administration
- Global HTTP Policy Settings
- Additional Security Policy

Despite the large number of configuration areas in this section of the interface, there are really only a few of them that require coverage here. For example, some simply allow you to add user accounts that are allowed to administer the ISA Server Firewall. This should be straightforward and basic enough for anyone who has ever set permissions on a Windows box before so we won't spend time on it. However, we will cover the finer points.

Specify RADIUS and LDAP Servers

If you want to control network access, including access to different content on the web, or simply access to the web based on what user is making the request, you will need to authenticate each user in order to do so. Authentication can be performed through a Lightweight Directory Access Protocol (LDAP) or Remote Authentication Dial-In User Service (RADIUS) server.

For RADIUS, perform the following steps (see Figure 11.10).

1. Click **Specify RADIUS and LDAP Servers**.

2. On the **RADIUS** tab, click **Add**.

3. Enter the IP address or DNS name of the RADIUS server you want to use.

4. Change the port number if you've configured the RADIUS server to use a different port, and change the timeout if need be.

5. Enter the shared secret if one is required.

6. Click **OK**.

Figure 11.10 Adding a RADIUS Server to Authenticate Users Attempting to Send Traffic through the Firewall

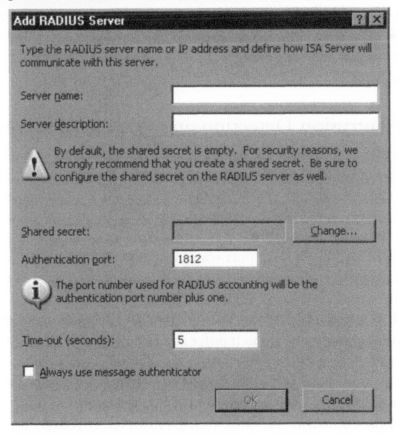

For LDAP, perform the following steps.

1. Go to the **LDAP** tab, and click **Add**.

2. Here you will enter a "set" of LDAP servers. Enter the name you want to use for the server set.

3. Click **Add** to add the IP address or DNS name of the LDAP server you want to add to the server set.

4. Enter the fully qualified domain name for the domain being authenticated to.

5. Check whether ISA Server should use the global catalog to perform the authentication.

6. Check whether ISA Server needs to make a secure connection to the LDAP server.

7. Click **OK**.

8. Click **Add** to enter a login expression if you like, or leave it blank. This setting can be used to have some wildcard matching done on the authentication credentials so that basically instead of a user having to enter *domain\username*, they can just enter *username*.

9. Click **OK**.

Enabling Intrusion Detection and DNS Attack Detection

Intrusion detection is enabled by default. However, you can select which types of attacks ISA Server watches for and alerts on. Port scans are the only attack type listed that is not enabled by default. It is debatable whether this is really something useful to alert on. In reality, any system on the Internet is being port-scanned numerous times each day, and if you do not tweak the alerting for this type of attack you will pick up false positives in addition to real port scans. It may be better to keep the logs fairly clear so that when one of the other attack types is detected, it will clearly be visible in your alerts.

DNS attack detection is also enabled by default, and three types of attacks are enabled. One important one, zone transfer attack detection, is disabled by default. If your company does not have DNS servers that should legitimately be making zone transfers on the external side of the ISA firewall, then by all means enable the zone transfer attack detection. This type of attack is very dangerous. A malicious party will request to download the entire zone file from your DNS server, effectively capturing your entire internal network layout.

This section is moderately helpful in keeping firewall administrators abreast of potentially malicious events occurring at the perimeter. However, there is not enough flexibility to configure attack detection to make this a really robust Intrusion Detection System (IDS). Unfortunately, if you wish to monitor for potential zone transfer attacks and have DNS servers outside the firewall that are allowed to make zone transfers, there is no perfect solution for your situation. Either the events fire or they do not. The IDS settings are not granular enough to allow administrators to configure a set of IP addresses that are legitimate, and have ISA Server log an alert any time an IP *not* in the set attempts a zone transfer.

Similarly, the other intrusion detection settings lack flexibility. Other IDS systems allow you to configure alerts for basically any event for which you can define a rule. Here, however, the administrator has the ability to select from six different attack types, most of which are quite frankly a bit dated. Although the IDS capabilities in ISA Server are better than nothing, it is hard to believe anyone who actually wanted to monitor potential intrusions would find this to be a suitable replacement for Snort or other full-featured IDS solutions.

Configuring IP Protection

The IP Protection function can be useful. By clicking **Configure IP Protection**, you will open the IP Preferences dialog box shown in Figure 11.11.

Figure 11.11 Configuring IP Protection

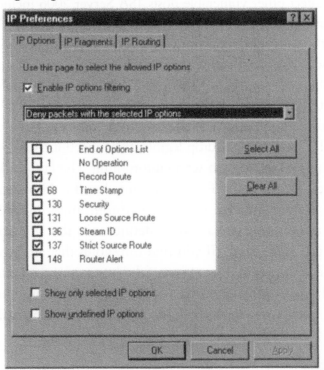

The IP Options tab can be an effective deterrent for maliciously crafted packets. IP packets have a field for IP options, but these are generally not used a great deal for legitimate use. Some of the options can, in fact, be used effectively for information gathering so it is nice to be able to configure ISA Server to filter these types of packets. This being said, there really should not be any configuration that needs to occur here. ISA Server comes with a sensible configuration in this area out of the box.

The other two tabs should be left at their default settings. The only configuration option available on the IP Fragments tab is to filter fragmented packets. This should not be enabled unless you are on a controlled network segment and because packets are often legitimately fragmented during transit. Enabling this would cause network connectivity issues.

The other tab, IP Routing, is set to use kernel mode for routing. This should provide maximum routing performance, and therefore should be used unless you come across an issue that requires you to disable it.

Configuring Flood Mitigation Services

Flood mitigation options allow you to combat attacks that are manifested primarily as a large amount of traffic of one kind or another. Generally, you will see a lot of this sort of thing from worms as they infect a host, and then begin flooding the network with attempts to infect other vulnerable hosts. ISA Server 2006 includes settings specific to a number of different types of traffic floods. When working with the flood mitigation options, you set the maximum amount of that type of traffic ISA Server will accept and evaluate in detail before all subsequent traffic from that host is dropped. This helps to avoid denial of service conditions that may occur when your firewall has become overwhelmed with traffic.

When configuring flood migration services, make sure you don't tighten things down too much or the ISA server might drop legitimate connections. One way to ensure that legitimate traffic is not denied is to set a custom limit. The custom limit will generally provide a more lenient threshold for the unwanted traffic. Also, you can define a list of IP exceptions that are hosts to which the custom limits apply. So basically, the IP exceptions and custom limits are a way to define hosts that you trust more. I do not recommend using IP exceptions. If you find thresholds that are unwanted for traffic then they are generally unwanted regardless of the host, and the minute you start trusting a system it will become infected with a worm that will abuse your custom limits. The traffic flood options are shown in Table 11.3 with an explanation of each.

Table 11.3 Flood Mitigation Options

Potential Flood Attacks	Description
Maximum TCP connect requests per minute per IP address	This setting defines how many SYN packets a host can send per minute.
Maximum concurrent TCP connections per IP address	This defines the maximum number of TCP connections a host can have open at once.
Maximum half-open TCP connections	This defines the maximum number of TCP connections that have gone halfway through the TCP three-way handshake (in other words the offending host has sent a SYN packet and the destination host has replied with a SYN-ACK packet) a host can have open at once.
Maximum HTTP requests per minute per IP address	This setting defines how many HTTP requests a host can send per minute.
Maximum new non-TCP sessions per minute per rule	This setting defines how many sessions that are not TCP-based a host can initiate per minute even if they are allowed by a rule.
Maximum concurrent UDP sessions per IP address	This defines the maximum number of UDP connections a host can have open at once.

In order to use this service effectively, I recommend that you begin with the ISA Server defaults set by Microsoft. Configure the alerting to your liking. Then, you will need to monitor traffic in your environment for a while in order to determine what is and what is not normal. Begin tightening the thresholds from there, and try to make them as strict as possible without adversely affecting normal traffic flows.

Firewall Policy

Given the configuration options we've already covered, it should not come as too much of a surprise that the Firewall Policy node in the navigation pane of the ISA Server Management console offers relatively few management options. The main tasks you will do here are opening and closing ports and protocols.

The first thing you need to know when dealing with any firewall is whether the firewall uses a first match or last match rule processing engine. ISA Firewall uses a last match rule policy, and comes with a last rule that blocks all traffic. Therefore, you will need to open the services and protocols you want to enable in rules ahead of this last rule so that they are passed by ISA Server. When the firewall rule engine gets to the last rule, if the traffic has not matched any rules yet it will be dropped.

Wizards allow you to easily open traffic into and out of your network. One of the first things you will need to do here after setting up ISA Server as your perimeter firewall is to create a rule that allows some common protocols from your internal network out to the Internet. To do this, follow these steps:

1. Click **Create Access Rule** in the **Task** pane on the right.

2. Enter a name for the rule, for example Outbound Connection, and click **Next**.

3. Since we want this rule to allow traffic that matches to pass through the firewall, select **Allow** and click **Next**.

4. Leave the **Selected Protocols** option selected, and click **Add**.

5. ISA Server will provide you with protocols grouped into various categories to make it easy to find the ones you wish to add. You can find the ones we will select in the Common Protocols category. Either select and then click **Add** or simply double-click HTTP and HTTPS to add them. Click **Close** and then click **Next.**

6. On the **Access Rule Sources** screen, click **Add**. Then use the dialog box to add the Internal network. Click **Close**, and then click **Next**.

7. On the **Access Rule Destination** screen, click **Add**. Then use the dialog box to add the External network. Click **Close**, and then click **Next**.

8. On the User Sets screen leave it set to **All Users** unless you wanted to limited access to the web to a specific set of users, and then click **Next**.

9. Click **Finish**.

The rule you have just created will appear in the Firewall Policy tab as shown in Figure 11.12.

Figure 11.12 Your New Firewall Rule

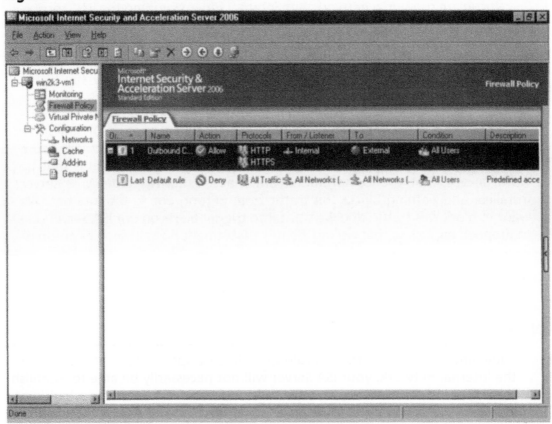

If you are running a network with internal servers running the DNS service, then these are the only devices that should be allowed to be the source for outbound DNS queries. We will need to create a second rule that is similar to the first except that we will set the source as only the list of internal DNS servers. We will want to make an identical rule for SMTP that has only the list of outbound mail relays as the source.

Keeping our outbound traffic locked down as much as possible like this is good practice. We could allow all internal hosts to send outbound DNS or SMTP traffic, but this opens the possibility that our internal hosts can actually cause some havoc if they are ever compromised. A great deal of e-mail is sent by workstations that are compromised and have a lightweight SMTP server installed, and nothing blocks this traffic from getting out to the Internet. We want to block this traffic, and we want it to trigger alerts on our ISA Server due to dropped packets so that we can identify problematic hosts as soon as possible.

NOTE

Remember that if you create a rule that allows a specific type of traffic from the internal network, your ISA Server will not necessarily be able to establish these types of connections. In order to include your ISA Server as a legitimate source of traffic you need to include "Local Host" in the **Access Rule Sources** selection. Another option is to enable the system rule related to the protocol you want to enable since system rules are generally rules that enable certain forms of traffic to and from the ISA Server. Although you shouldn't allow the ISA Server to be used for web browsing it may need to log to a remote host, fire e-mail alerts, and download Microsoft updates from an internal server.

There is one very big gotcha with this part of ISA Server. The Firewall Policy screen shows only the rules we've created as well as the last default block all rule, but there are actually 30 other rules in place from the time of installation. If you click **Show System Policy Rules** in the Task pane you will suddenly see the additional rules as shown in Figure 11.13.

Figure 11.13 The–Firewall Policy Rules Screen

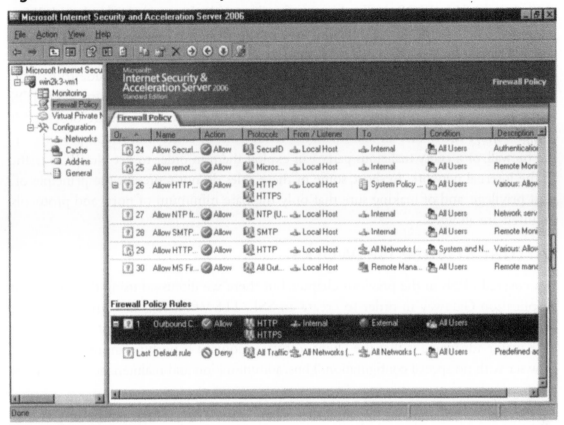

Not all these rules are enabled, and some actually pass no traffic in their default state. Some require internal destinations or service configurations on the ISA Server to be defined, and all are defined to allow protocols to and from the local host. However, it is troubling that Microsoft would hide these rules from the management interface by default. Firewall administrators should have a clear and accurate understanding of the entire rule set at all times, but ISA Server comes with these 30 rules hidden. Additionally, for some firewall administrators these rules represent too loose of a configuration.

There will obviously be those that argue that the rules found here pose little or no risk, and are needed for minimal functionality of the firewall. However, firewall administrators need to be a cautious bunch in order to survive, and these rules do not adequately represent this sort of cautiousness. There are two separate rules related to the passing of NetBIOS traffic. Anyone familiar with the myriad of vulnerabilities associated with NetBIOS and the numerous worms that have preyed on ports 137, 138, and 139 should be concerned that these rules exist.

These rules do not specifically allow NetBIOS traffic from the outside to pass the firewall and reach the inside. However, because these rules exist allowing NetBIOS traffic from ISA Server to the internal network, and because the rules are obscured it is much more likely that an administrator-made rule, or some minor compromise on the firewall, or a crafty malicious party can exploit them in order to get NetBIOS traffic to the internal network. In short, some of these rules do not represent the principle of least privilege, and of making sure that only the bare minimum of ports and protocols required are allowed.

Virtual Private Networks

We covered VPNs in the previous chapter, but there we discussed using the Intelligent Application Gateway in order to create an SSL/TLS VPN. This has quickly become the preferred method of allowing VPN traffic into the network for most enterprises. The major advantage is that the client software required is nothing more than a web browser with no special configuration. Thus, administration and maintenance of the VPN is infinitely less time consuming.

ISA Server still contains the ability to create IPSec VPNs. These can be site-to-site VPNs that connect geographically separated offices, or they can be VPNs used by remote workers to connect to the office network. Remote site VPNs are covered in detail in Chapter 13 so we will not spend more time on those here. In order to create a VPN for your remote users you will need to perform the following basic tasks:

1. Configure the way IP addresses will be assigned to VPN clients

2. Configure authentication for VPN users

3. Enable VPN access

4. Create the VPN client

5. Test the VPN

The options for IP address assignment are too numerous to cover here, but you will either want to configure the VPN clients to use DHCP or a pool of static addresses. You can set either option using the Configure Address Assignment Method link on the VPN Clients tab. Once you have configured addressing, you simply need to point the ISA Server to your internal RADIUS server that will handle client authentication. This is configured in the same dialog box as the IP addressing.

Once you have completed these key steps, you need to enable the remote access using the Enable VPN Client Access link on the VPN Clients tab. You can control how many concurrent VPN clients can connect to the ISA Server as well as what type of VPN is used. It is recommended that you use IPSec if possible over PPTP for enhanced security although PPTP is still a generally accepted VPN protocol.

Once you have configured the ISA Server you need to configure the VPN client on the Windows device you want to connect from. This configuration and the deployment of these clients requires some overhead, and more importantly can cause some remote connectivity issues that require troubleshooting over the phone. These are the reasons why network administrators have favored SSL/TLS VPNs in recent years. Once the client is configured you test access to the ISA Server before deploying clients to the user machines that require them.

Monitoring ISA Server 2006

Once the initial configuration of the ISA Server is done, the Monitoring node in the Management interface will become the most useful destination for administrators. Firewalls should generally not require a great deal of configuration changes after the initial setup. This is because modifications to the basic services and protocol support required do not change that frequently and partially because changes to these devices can have catastrophic consequences when performed without proper testing.

However, firewall administrators must remain in a constant state of vigilance. Firewalls are the primary protection device at the network perimeter, and many user services depend on having constant and efficient access to the Internet. Therefore, firewall administrators always need to have a clear understanding of what is happening on the firewalls from the perspective of both performance and security. The Monitoring node in the ISA Management interface provides a great deal of options.

Dashboard

The Dashboard is basically just the splash page for the Monitoring portion of the ISA Management application. It contains summary views of the information found on other tabs in this section as well as links to those tabs. It also contains two simple network performance indicator graphs. The Dashboard for a fresh install of ISA Server should look very similar to Figure 11.14.

Figure 11.14 The Monitoring–Dashboard Screen

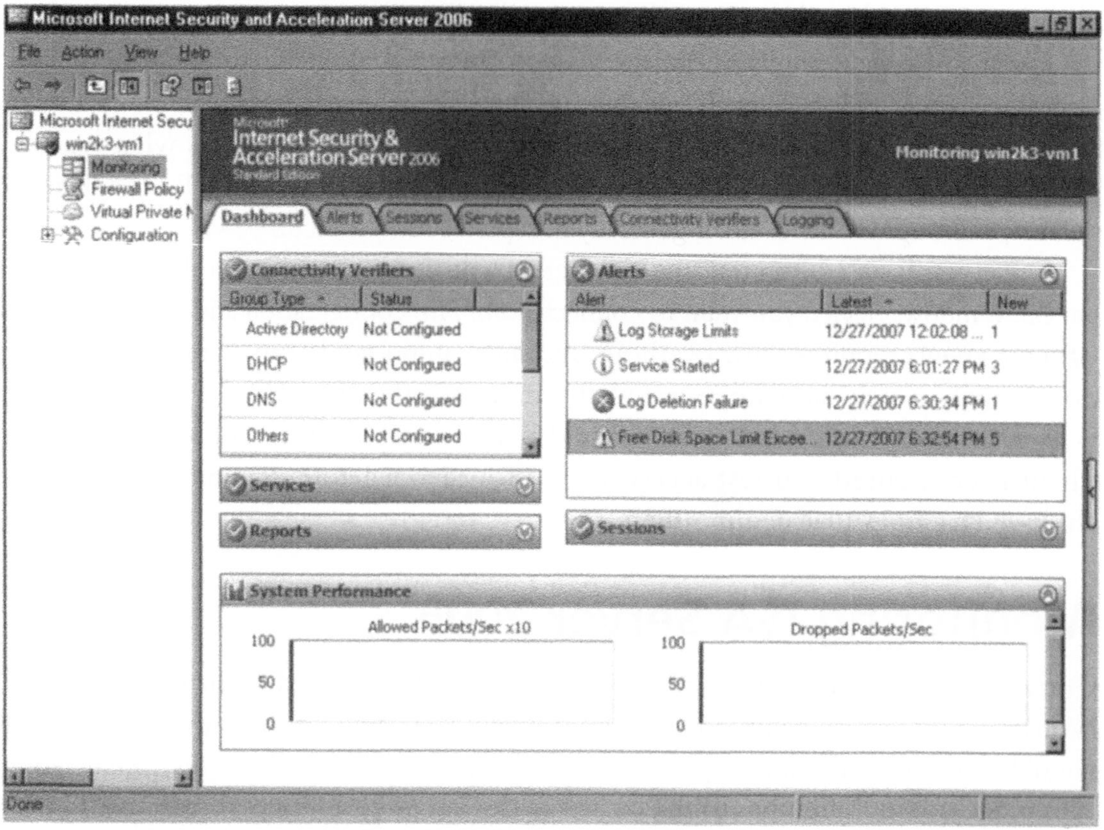

Alerts

The Alerts tab allows the user to view event log information categorized as an information, warning, or alert item. Elsewhere in the management interface there are options to configure events to trigger alerts. Some of the events that you can configure alerts for include web proxying events, caching, the firewall, and other parts of the system. Doing so will allow you to see these events consolidated in the Monitoring–Alerts area.

Sessions

The Sessions tab allows the user to view information about the current open sessions as shown in Figure 11.15. This is what you would typically call the state table. Any open connections traversing the firewall will show up on this tab. The tab allows the administrator to configure filtering options in order to reduce the amount of sessions shown. For instance, if you are trying to take a closer look at a single machine, you can filter to see only sessions that involve that system. You can also right-click on a session and select Disconnect Session in order to clear the session from the state table, and effectively kill the connection.

Figure 11.15 Viewing Active Sessions

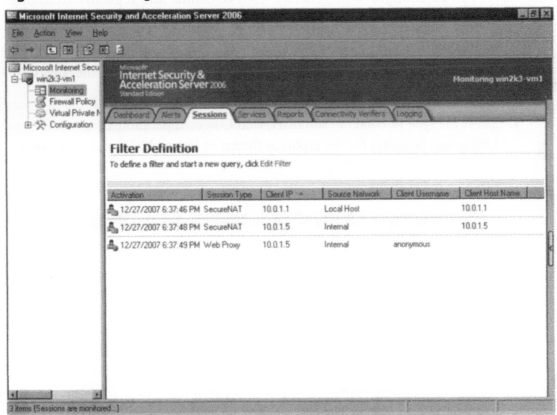

Services

The Services tab allows the user to view information about what services currently are running on the firewall, as well as allowing them to stop and start these services. However, you will see only services specific to ISA Server here. This can give a deceiving sense of security to administrators who have numerous other services running on the system. Although they may have a variety of services on the machine, this tab will show only:

- Microsoft Data Engine

- Microsoft Firewall

- Microsoft ISA Server Job Scheduler

Reports

ISA Server can be configured to generate both one-time and regularly recurring reports, which contain a variety of information on the firewall. In order to create a new one-time report:

1. While in the **Reports** tab, click **Generate a New Report** in the **Tasks** tab.

2. Enter a name for the report and click **Next**.

3. Select the type of content (Summary, Web Usage, Application Usage, Traffic and Utilization, Security) for the report as shown in Figure 11.16, and click **Next**.

Figure 11.16 Report Creation Wizard Content Selection Options

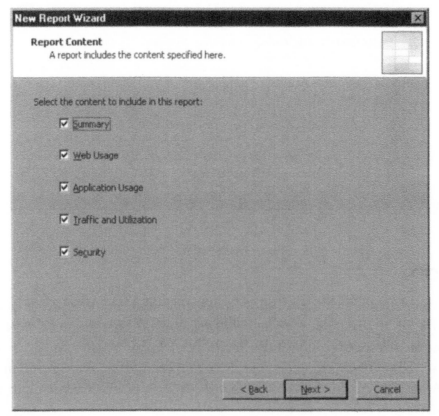

4. Select the reporting period you wish to view information about, and click **Next**.

5. The next screen allows you to publish the reports to a directory. This can be useful for those who wish to maintain reports in a central location off of the ISA Server itself. Set the desired options, and click **Next**.

6. The next screen allows you to configure an e-mail to be sent when the report is generated, and a link to the report can be included. Set the desired options, and click **Next**.

7. Once the report is generated it should show up under the **Reports** tab as shown in Figure 11.17.

Figure 11.17 The Monitoring–Reports Tab

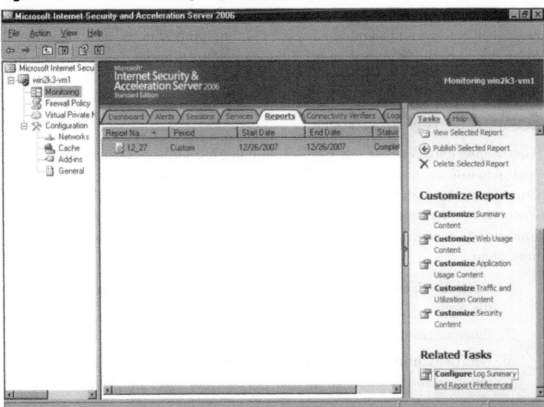

You will notice that there are options for customizing the report content for each individual report category (Summary, Web Usage, Application Usage, Traffic and Utilization, Security) in the Task pane. Unfortunately, the configuration options are incredibly limited. As an example, the Security content for reports is limited to dropped packets and authorization failures. The configuration options for each of these just allow the administrator to set the number of clients or users who registered one of these problems. As a firewall administrator, personally, I am not as concerned about when a user fails to authenticate properly and gain access to their blog. I would be much more concerned about a flood of packets that hit the external interface between 1:05 A.M. and 1:07 A.M. the previous night.

Although it is nice to see that reporting has been included, most administrators are going to find this functionality severely lacking. However, ISA does have the ability to log to a central database. Reporting could certainly be enhanced by utilizing either a Microsoft Operations Management Server or a custom web-based application. However, the primary drawback with those options is that adding those additional pieces will require more administrative overhead up front. With the next iteration of ISA Server, it would be nice if more of this type of functionality is included out of the box.

Connectivity Verifiers

The Connectivity Verifiers tab can be configured to display information about what network services are online. You can configure a connectivity verifier for basically any service imaginable, although there are some things to be cautious of when setting them up. We'll cover that right after we walk through setting up a connectivity verifier. In order to configure a connectivity verifier simply follow these steps:

1. Click the **Create New Connectivity Verifier** task in the **Task** pane on the right.

2. Enter a name for the connectivity verifier and click **Next**.

3. On the **Connectivity Verification Details** page you can enter detailed information about the connection you want to verify. See Figure 11.18.

Figure 11.18 Configuring the Connectivity Verifier Details

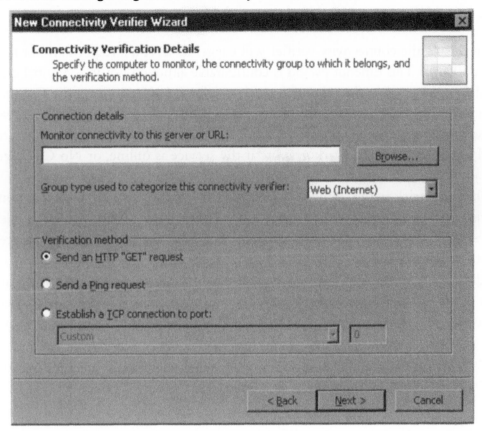

- As with anything related to the network, this will work better if you enter the IP address of the server you are trying to monitor instead of its name. Obviously, you can do this only if it has a static IP address.

- You can also select a group type for the verifier. The possible selections are Active Directory, DHCP, DNS, Others, Published Servers, Web (Internet).

- Lastly, select a verification method from one of the following:

    i. Send an HTTP "GET" request

    ii. Send a Ping request

    iii. Establish a TCP connection to port: (select the port or service you wish to monitor).

4. Click **Next**.

5. Click **Finish**.

By default, the connectivity verifier will trigger an alert if a response is not received within 5000 ms. This timeout period is configurable although not in the initial creation wizard. In order to adjust this value, you need to right-click the verifier in the Connectivity Verifiers tab, and select properties. In addition to triggering an alert, the connectivity verifier will be displayed in the Monitoring–Dashboard screen. There you will see a status of Good with a green checkmark graphic if the service is online, or No Connection with a red X if it is offline.

The main trick with Connectivity Verifiers is knowing exactly what it is you are verifying. Any group selection other than **Active Directory** or **Web (Internet)** defaults to a verification method of pinging the host. This does not verify that the service you wish to monitor is online at all. All it does is check to see that the host itself is online. In order to be sure that your individual services are functioning as intended it is generally better to set the verifier to establish a TCP connection, except in the case of checking on web servers where sending an HTTP GET request would be preferred. However, these verification methods require more overhead for both the ISA Server and the service host, but pinging the host does not accurately determine whether individual services on a Server are responding to requests.

Configuring & Implementing...

Connectivity Verifier Refresh Rate

By default the method for verifying connectivity is attempted every 30 seconds, but this can be configured to a value from 15 to 1,440 seconds. Unfortunately, this cannot be done through the Graphical User Interface. You must set the RefreshRate property of the FPCConnectivityVerifiers Windows Management Instrumentation (WMI) collection. Microsoft does provide a script for doing this at this link on their Web site: www.microsoft.com/technet/isa/2004/plan/settingrefreshrate.mspx. To use the script, type **cscript SetConnectivityRefresh Rate.vbs** *RefreshTime* at a command prompt where SetConnectivityRefresh Rate.vbs is the full path to the script you saved, and RefreshTime is a numeric value in seconds for the refresh rate.

Logging

This tab allows the user to configure the way logs are stored, provides easy access to the logs, and includes capabilities to query the logs, making it incredibly useful for troubleshooting connectivity issues. There are three built-in queries that can be run immediately. You can also add and save new queries by clicking the Edit Filter task from the Task pane on the right. Select the query parameters in the dialog box that is displayed, and click Add to List. When you return to the Logging tab, simply select the new query, and click Start Query in the Task pane on the right. Your results will be displayed in the bottom of the Logging tab under the query list as shown in Figure 11.19.

Figure 11.19 Running Queries against Your Logs

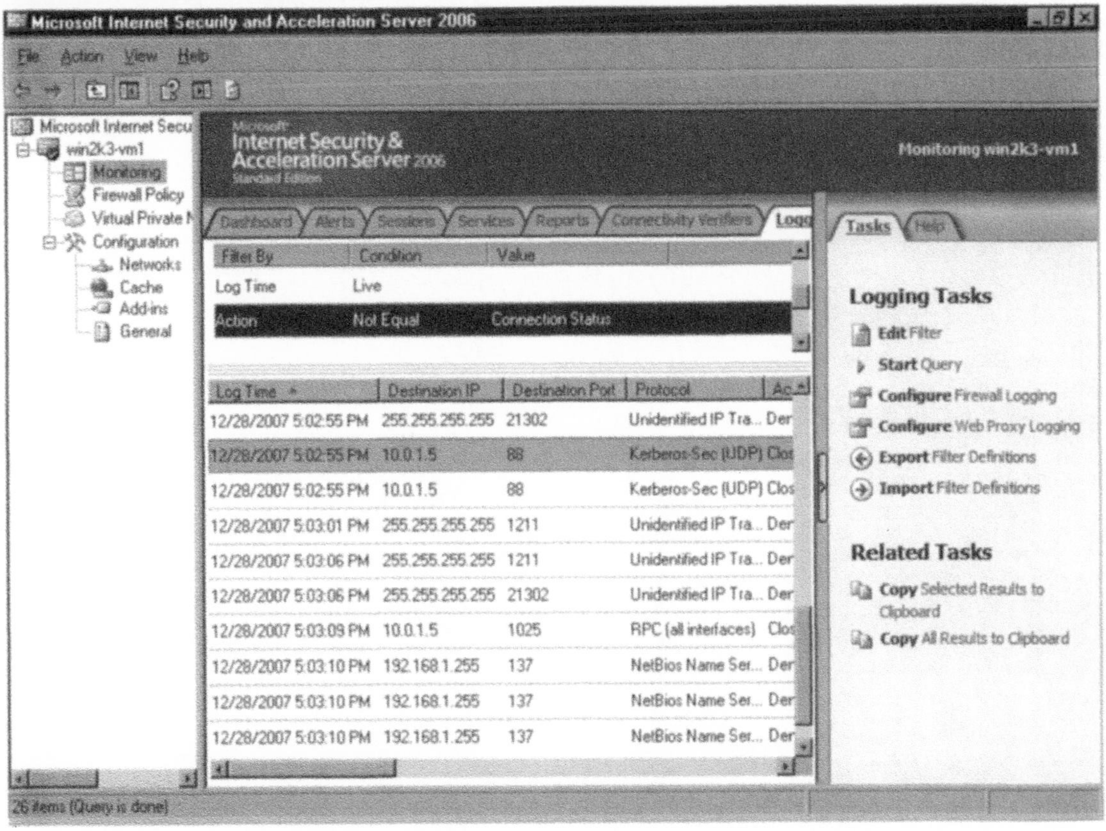

As noted, this tab also does allow you to configure logging options for both the firewall and the web proxy. Both sets of options are basically identical. Logs can be kept in a Microsoft SQL Server Desktop Engine (MSDE) format. A Microsoft SQL Server Desktop Engine is installed on the ISA Server if you selected the Advanced Logging option during install. Logs can also be kept in a separate SQL Server installation or a W3C log file. If you opt to have the ISA Server log to a file, be sure to set some options regarding how large the file can be, and how and when events should be overwritten. Regardless of where the logs are stored, you can also select what fields of data to log from an extensive list.

Summary

ISA Server offers a great deal of functionality, the interface is accessible for experienced Windows administrators, and the software can integrate tightly with a Windows network infrastructure. At the minimum, administrators can effectively deploy a firewall and router using a Windows box, but the following additional network perimeter services can also be deployed with ease:

- A caching web proxy
- A remote client VPN server
- Site-to-site VPN connections
- Simple IDS functionality
- Internal network service monitoring

One of the main drawbacks you will find with ISA Server is the somewhat weak IDS functionality. However, Microsoft does not tout ISA Server as a full-fledged IDS. Also of concern is the fact that there are a myriad of firewall rules installed by default, but which are hidden from view by default.

After a default installation of ISA Server, Nessus scans from both inside and outside of the firewall came up clean, showing no vulnerabilities and no open services or protocols. Although steps should be taken not to unintentionally open unnecessary vulnerabilities in either the firewall or your internal network, ISA Server does come fairly well secured out of the box. The Nessus scan initiated, however, was done on a fully-patched system. In order to ensure that your firewall does not very quickly become a prime target for exploitation, keep the operating system (which ISA sits on top of) up to date with patches, service packs, and hotfixes. Although the ISA Server software itself may not have a history of vulnerabilities, there have been many documented cases of the security vulnerabilities of the underlying Windows OS.

Solutions Fast Track

Installing Microsoft Internet Security and Acceleration Server 2006

☑ Before installing ISA Server you should carefully plan your network topology, map out which services you need to allow in both the inbound and outbound directions, and make sure you have the proper network hardware to make your deployment a success.

☑ The main difference between the Standard and Enterprise Editions of ISA Server is the ability to configure arrays of ISA Servers in Enterprise Edition, and to manage those servers as a group call an array.

Configuring Microsoft Internet Security and Acceleration Server 2006

☑ ISA Server includes templates that will allow you to quickly and easily set your ISA configuration to match your network topology.

☑ Set routing and NAT options in the Networks area of the ISA Server Management console.

☑ Configure firewall rules allowing needed protocols and services in the Firewall Policy area of the ISA Server Management console.

Monitoring Microsoft Internet Security and Acceleration Server 2006

☑ ISA Server provides a robust and flexible log monitoring and analysis utility that should be useful when attempting to troubleshoot network connectivity issues.

☑ The reporting functions in ISA Server can allow administrators to view a periodic summary of information regarding the firewall.

☑ Connectivity Verifiers can allow you to keep an eye on internal network services, and receive alerts when they go offline.

☑ Administrators will find the log querying capabilities in ISA Server to be an extremely useful built-in data mining utility.

Frequently Asked Questions

Q: What are the main differences between ISA Server Standard Edition and Enterprise Edition?

A: There are three categories of differences between ISA Server Standard and Enterprise Editions: hardware support; network architectures supported; and administrative features provided. Table 11.4 summarizes these differences.

Table 11.4 ISA Server Standard Edition versus ISA Server Enterprise Edition

	Standard Edition	Enterprise Edition
Hardware	4 CPUs and 2 GB of RAM	Unlimited by ISA Server although may be limited by OS support
Network architectures	Single-server caching store	Unlimited number of cache servers in an array
	No support for Windows Network Load Balancing (NLB)	Windows NLB support (up to 32 nodes)
Management	Network templates	Network templates
	Single-server management console with Microsoft Operations Manager (MOM) Management Pack	Multiple-server management console with MOM Management Pack
	Local policies	Array-wide policies integrated with Active Directory

Q: What operating systems can I install ISA Server on?

A: ISA Server 2006 is supported on only 32-bit Windows operating systems. Microsoft currently lists only the 32-bit versions of Windows Server 2003 with Service Pack 1 and Windows Server 2003 R2, but when Windows Server 2008 is released the 32-bit version should be supported as well.

Q: I thought my firewall rules were built in the Firewall Policy section of the ISA Server Management interface. What is the Network Rules section for, then?

A: The Firewall Policy section of the management interface allows you to configure firewall rules for blocking and allowing protocols to pass through the ISA Server packet filter. Network rules allow you to configure routing and NAT rules for traffic between various network segments.

Q: I can connect to the web from an internal client, but not from the ISA Server itself. What is wrong?

A: You need to have a rule that allows traffic to and from the local host. You can create the rule yourself, or find the built-in system rule that provides the configuration you need and enable it.

Q: Users on my network have started complaining that web browsing is terribly slow. I quickly checked Task Manager on the firewall, and the CPU and memory are being heavily used. What is the problem?

A: In many cases the problem will be related to caching as part of the web proxy service. Web proxy caching requires lots of RAM, and depending on the number of clients supported and cache settings, can require lots of disk space as well. If these resources start to run out the CPU can become heavily taxed as well. Check your cache settings to determine if you can lighten the load on the box. Also, try to determine which resources are most lacking, and add more if possible.

Q: I am having network problems. How can I fix them?

A: If you are having intermittent connectivity issues your primary troubleshooting tools should be alerts, sessions, and logging. Use these monitoring utilities built into the ISA Server Management interface to try to zero in on the specific issue you are having. I would begin by looking for something obvious in the Alerts tab. Then use the Sessions tab to monitor what is happening as it happens as well as using the query functionality on the Logging tab to mine for evidence.

Q: I have configured Connectivity Verifiers for my main network services such as DNS and AD. However, DNS keeps going down, but ISA Server always reports it as online

A: You have probably set up verifiers that rely on pinging the host to determine if the service is online, but this validates only that the host is running. The service may have locked up or been accidentally stopped. The TCP connect verification option is the only way to reliably ensure that the service is still running on the host. Keep in mind that although both options require minimal resource the TCP connect option is more resource-intensive for both the remote and the ISA Server. On taxed hosts these relatively small additional resource requirements can add up.

Microsoft Internet Security and Acceleration 2006 Server Publishing

Solutions in this chapter:

- Publishing Servers behind a Microsoft Internet Security and Acceleration 2006 Server Firewall

- Troubleshooting Publishing Servers behind a Microsoft Internet Security and Acceleration 2006 Server Firewall

☑ Summary

☑ Solutions Fast Track

☑ Frequently Asked Questions

Introduction

The days of having Web servers directly connected to the Internet should be a thing of the past for any company with even the slightest security concerns. Servers should never be left out on the Internet where they can be attacked in a relentless manner. Companies need to protect Web and other servers by placing them on the internal network behind the firewall.

Microsoft Internet Security and Acceleration 2006 Server, part of the Forefront Suite, allows firewall administrators to publish their servers behind the internal networks. Using publishing, administrators can help to further protect Web, Mail, and other servers by keeping these boxes from being located directly on the Internet. If these boxes were to be directly placed on the Internet without protection mechanisms like a firewall in place, they would be attacked relentlessly and eventually be compromised.

Microsoft Internet Security and Acceleration 2006 Server, which is an integral part of the Forefront Security Suite, makes it easy for firewall administrators to publish their internal servers through the use of wizards. Microsoft Internet Security and Acceleration 2006 Server also allows multiple Web sites and Web server farms on the internal network to be published. By publishing internal servers behind a firewall, such as Microsoft Internet Security and Acceleration 2006 Server, the number of threats and vulnerabilities to that sever is greatly reduced.

Publishing Servers behind a Microsoft Internet Security and Acceleration 2006 Server Firewall

Microsoft Internet Security and Acceleration (ISA) 2006 Server is an integrated security application that help s to protect mission critical applications from internet threats. Microsoft Internet Security and Acceleration 2006 Server also helps to provide secured access of internal resources from the Internet. Publishing is the feature in Microsoft Internet Security and Acceleration Server that allows external users from accessing a published server without knowing the actual name and IP address of the server.

Publishing can be used with many different scenarios. The following are some commonly used scenarios for publishing in Microsoft Internet Security and Acceleration 2006 Server:

- Allow external access to Outlook Web access

- Allow external access to Terminal Services

- Allow external access to Web server

We will discuss different scenarios in later sections. Now, let's talk about basics of Web publishing.

Basics of Publishing

When publishing is used to allow users access to a server within the Internet, all requests arrive at the Microsoft Internet Security and Acceleration 2006 Server machine first. Requests then are forwarded to the published machine. How packets get forwarded is controlled by the conditions defined within the publishing rule in Microsoft Internet Security and Acceleration 2006 Server.

As shown in Figure 12.1, publishing in Microsoft Internet Security and Acceleration 2006 Server works so that separate TCP connections are established to external clients and internal servers.

Figure 12.1 How Publishing Works

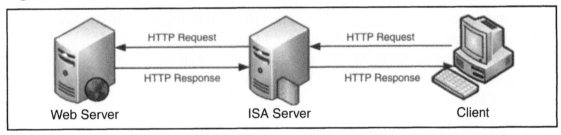

To enable publishing, we need to configure publishing policy in Microsoft Internet Security and Acceleration 2006. There are different types of publishing policy, depending on the situation. Policies include the Web publishing rule, server publishing rule, secure Web publishing rule, and mail server publishing rule. The Web chaining rule also helps in publishing.

Microsoft Internet Security and Acceleration 2006 Server handles publishing for HTTP/HTTPS traffic differently from publishing for other traffic. When HTTP/HTTP traffic arrives, Microsoft Internet Security and Acceleration 2006 Server will check against the Web publishing rule to see if the traffic is allowed, and the Web chaining rule to see where the traffic should be routed. Microsoft Internet Security and Acceleration 2006 Server always processes the Web publishing rule first, and then uses the configuration in the Web chaining rule to determine from where to get the requested object. The following example illustrates how Microsoft Internet Security and Acceleration 2006 Server handles Web publishing.

1. External client requests an object from www.testingdomain.com/page1.

2. Server intercepts the request and checks against the Web publishing rule. The rule determines that the object should be retrieved from server1 in the internal zone.

3. Server then checks against the Web chaining rule to see how to contact server1 to retrieve the object.

For non-HTTP/HTTPS traffic, Microsoft Internet Security and Acceleration 2006 Server checks the network rule to see if the published traffic is allowed and then checks against the server publishing rule to see to which server the traffic should be routed. When traffic arrives at the ISA Server, server publishing rules then define how the server should map the received socket to the internal server. Everything is happening at the socket level, so you can define a server publishing rule to map traffic at external interface port 21 to an internal FTP server. Technically, you can use the server publishing rule to publish the web server to public, but it is not recommended. This is because some functionalities are available only if we use the Web publishing rule. For example, the Web publishing rule allows the publishing of a virtual directory only, but the server publishing rule will publish only the Web server. It is a good practice to use the server publishing rule for all non-Web-based publishing, like publishing terminal service traffic, FTP server. Web publishing rules should be used for all HTTP and HTTPS traffic.

Server Publishing Rule

Microsoft Internet Security and Acceleration Server 2006 support publishing traffic such as SMTP, FTP, and POP3, to Internet users. Using the server publishing rule tells Microsoft Internet Security and Acceleration Server 2006 how to process traffic that arrives at the Microsoft Internet Security and Acceleration Server 2006 and gets redirected to appropriate internal servers. You can use the server publishing rule to publish any type of traffic you want. This is the basic way to get internal resources accessible to users on the Internet. In addition to publishing the traffic, Microsoft Internet Security and Acceleration Server 2006 provide the following key functionalities:

- **Multiple Protocols on Shared Address** Similar to the functionality of the Web publishing rule. Microsoft Internet Security and Acceleration 2006

Server supports sharing IP addresses among different protocols, for example, having one IP address for SMTP and POP3 protocol, but they are actually served by different servers in your internal or private network.

- **Application-level Filter Support** Similar to the same functionalities of the Web publishing rule. This feature enables Microsoft Internet Security and Acceleration 2006 Server to filter the actual content passing through. For example, the SMTP filter allows filtering of unwanted SMTP commands from entering into internal mail systems.

- **Port Redirection** Usually, well-known ports are used for external users to get access to Internet resources. But in some cases, well-known ports may not be used internally. Thus, port mapping is used to redirect traffic between ports. A good example would be if a user requested to connect the external SMTP server at port 25 but the request is actually served by an SMTP server hosted internally at port 2525.

Web Publishing Rule

The Web publishing rule configures how Microsoft Internet Security and Acceleration Server 2006 will handle HTTP and HTTPS traffic it receives. As you know, Microsoft Internet Security and Acceleration Server 2006 works at application level, and this is the key differentiation when compare to other firewall or gateway devices. This means filtering or processing against data transferred over HTTP and HTTPS is possible. For instance, you can perform Path Mapping against HTML content published. This is the reason why we should use the Web publishing rule instead of the server publishing rule for HTTP and HTTPS traffic. Here are the key advantages of using the Web publishing rule when compared with traditional port-based publishing in other firewall or gateway devices:

- **Application-level Filtering Support** Microsoft Internet Security and Acceleration 2006 Server comes with filters to inspect the content transmitted over HTTP and HTTPS protocols, which provide additional security. For example, link translation can be performed within the published HTTP content to replace all internal server names before content gets transferred to external clients.

- **Path Mapping** This feature helps to hide internal details from external users. For example, a user requesting http://www.testingdomain.com/folder1 would actually retrieve content from http://internalserver1/folder2. This also helps to provide a consistent path to external users no matter where the internal folder path is located.

- **User Authentication** This feature enables Microsoft Internet Security and Acceleration 2006 Server to authenticate the user before sending the packet to the internal server. This ensures users can reach the internal server only if they are authenticated.

- **Content Caching** This feature commonly is referred to as Reverse Proxy. Microsoft Internet Security and Acceleration 2006 Server can be configured to cache content provided by an internal server. Thus, it helps to reduce the loading generated against internal servers as content can be provided by the cache.

- **Link Translation** This feature allows administrators to define the internal links that need to be removed before content gets released to public. Usually, for example, SharePoint sites consist of a number of these types of links. Using link translation can help to replace the internal server name to an external accessible link so the broken link will not be displayed.

- **Publishing Multiple Internal Resources Under a Single Web Address** This feature allows users to use a common server name for accessing different internal resources. For instance, user request http://www.testingdomain.com/content1 is actually getting content from http://server1, whereas http://www.testingdomain.com/content2 is getting content from http://server2.

- **Support SSL Bridging** All SSL traffic actually terminates at Microsoft Internet Security and Acceleration 2006 Server. A separate SSL tunnel is established to the internal server, if ISA is configured to use SSL to access internal resources. Microsoft Internet Security and Acceleration 2006 Server can be configured to off-load SSL-related processing from internal servers, which, in turn, helps to improve the performance of the internal server. This feature also enables ISA 2006 to inspect the content because it is unencrypted during processing.

Web–server publishing prerequisites are discussed in following section.

Network Configuration and Name Resolution for Publishing

Publishing in Microsoft Internet Security and Acceleration 2006 Server requires two separate connections between external clients and internal server. That means

Microsoft Internet Security and Acceleration 2006 Server needs to know the way to reach both external and internal resources. In order to do so, the ISA server needs to be able to send packets to external clients and the internal server. In order to do that, make sure that the ISA server and internal and external network cards are properly configured. Also, be aware that the default gateway of the ISA server's external network card should point to the external zone. Otherwise, Microsoft Internet Security and Acceleration Server 2006 would not be able to retrieve data from internal servers.

These two commonly used network configurations for Microsoft Internet Security and Acceleration 2006 Server are multihomed configuration and dedicated demilitarized zone configuration, respectively (see Figures 12.2 and 12.3). There are some other ways to place the Microsoft Internet Security and Acceleration 2006 Server, but they are less common and will not be discussed here. No matter how the network is configured, the ISA server must be able to contact the published host. Otherwise, publishing will not work as expected.

Figure 12.2 Multihomed Scenario

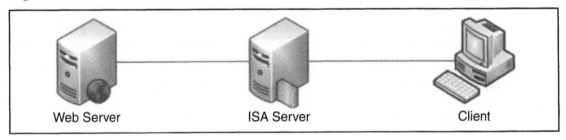

Figure 12.3 Dedicated DMZ Scenario

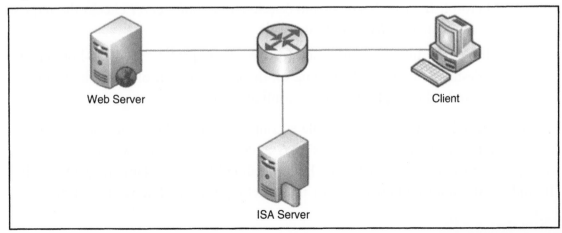

With network configuration, name resolution is a problematic area for many network administrators. Several ways to configure the name resolution in ISA are as follows:

- **Configure ISA to use external DNS** The server is configured to use an external Domain Name Service server. This configuration ensures Microsoft Internet Security and Acceleration 2006 Server is able to resolve external DNS names. However, this will not allow ISA to resolve names on the internal network.

- **Configure ISA to use internal DNS** The server is configured to use an internal Domain Name Service server hosted in the internal zone. Usually, this kind of server is able to resolve both internal and external domain names. Often, the administrator will be configured to override some of the DNS records with internal IPs. For example, users in an internal zone would get internal IPs when trying to resolve www.testingdomain.com, but public users would get the external IP Address of the Web site.

- **Configure to use name resolution in HOSTS file** The server is not configured to use any DNS server, but all host name mapping is performed at the HOSTS file. This gives lots of overhead to the administrator as a HOSTS file needs to be updated whenever there is a change in network. The host file is located in \%systemroot%\system32\drivers\etc.

The following steps describe how an HTTP or HTTPS request is handled in ISA 2006:

1. A HTTP client request arrives.
2. Microsoft Internet Security and Acceleration 2006 Server checks the request for any matching Web publishing rule.
3. The HTTP request would then forward the request to the next-hop server or destination server (depending on the configuration of the Web chaining rule and other application filter configurations).

In step 2, what will happen if a rule is configured using Domain Name but the user request is made using IP address? ISA 2006 would perform a reserve lookup query against the DNS server for the Fully Qualified Domain Name (FQDN) of the IP and use the resolved host name for the matching process. The reserve of this is also true. This means if an IP address is used in the publishing rule, Microsoft Internet Security and Acceleration 2006 Server would perform a forward lookup for IP address if the request is made using the host name but the rule is configured with an IP address. So in general, either the IP address or FQDN would match the rule. If any problem happens during resolution, the rule may not match and the packet would get rejected.

I would suggest the following configuration with your ISA 2006 Server: Configure the server to use an internal Domain Name Service server in your organization that resolves internal and external domain names.

Using the preceding configuration, the IP address or host name contained in the external request is ensured to get resolved properly, but Microsoft Internet Security and Acceleration 2006 Server is still able to locate the correct internal server for the serving user's request.

Also, it's a good idea to have all publishing rules configured to use the host name instead of the IP address for matching an external request. This helps to ease the complexity when troubleshooting issues in publishing on Microsoft Internet Security and Acceleration 2006 Server.

Designing & Planning…

Name Resolution

Ensure Microsoft Internet Security and Acceleration 2006 Server is able to perform forward and reserve lookup against the host name and IP address contained in the external request. Otherwise, some traffic may get rejected because of incorrect name resolution.

Configuring the Web Listener

The Web Listener is an object in ISA 2006 that defines how the server listens to HTTP and HTTPS traffic. The listener defines the IP address and port on which the server will listen. Also, the Web Listener will define how to authenticate external users and the behavior of handling HTTP and HTTPS traffic.

When configuring Web Listener, you need to specify the settings about how clients would get authenticated before they have access to published resources. Figure 12.4 shows a screen of configuring authentication options in a Web Listener. Once the authentication setting is configured to HTML Authentication or HTTP Authentication, the ISA 2006 server would perform a check on all incoming requests and see if they are authenticated. If not authenticated, the ISA server would then prompt the user for authentication.

Figure 12.4 Configuring Authentication in a Web Listener

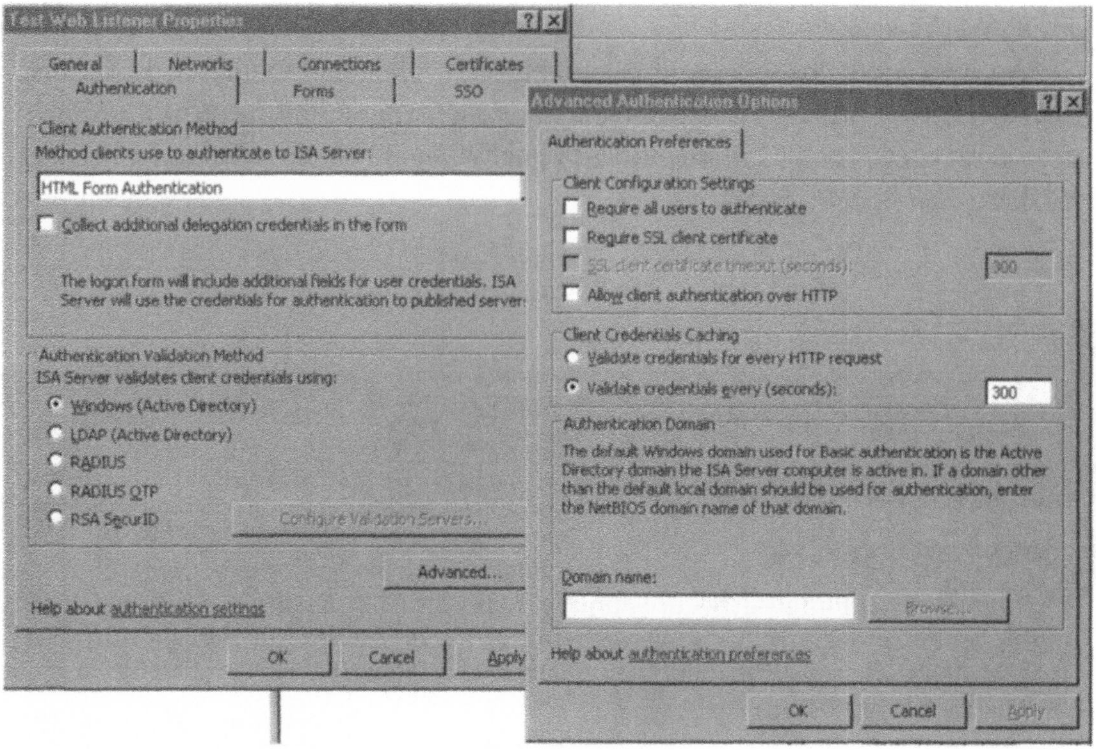

There are three types of authentication that you can configure:

- **No Authentication** Basically, no authentication would take place and all users would access internal resources using anonymous identity. This method is best for public Web sites that cannot enforce authentication.

- **HTML Authentication** This also known as Form-based Authentication. When Microsoft Internet Security and Acceleration 2006 Server detects that a user is not an authenticated user, a HTML form would be presented to the user and asked for credentials.

- **HTTP Authentication** The user is not prompted for credentials; instead, it relies on the client application they use to access the published application. For instance Internet Explorer would need to include the credential and authentication information in the HTTP headers. The ISA server would then extract the information from the HTTP header and authenticate the user.

The authentication process does not actually take place on the Microsoft Internet Security and Acceleration 2006 Server. Instead, an authentication provider does the job. All credentials received by Microsoft Internet Security and Acceleration 2006 Server would then be forwarded to the Authentication Provider for further processing (see Figure 12.5).

Figure 12.5 How ISA Server Handles Authentication Requests

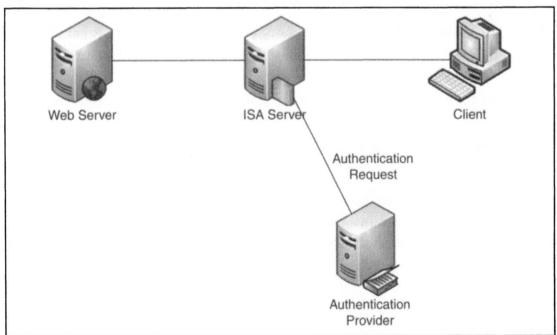

Once a client is authenticated, the request would then be processed by the ISA Server according to what is specified in the publishing rule. Sometimes, the published server also requires authentication in order to identify the user who accesses the application. Microsoft ISA Server supports passing the credential received from the client to the published server. This feature is called delegation. The following describes the delegation methods supported by Microsoft Internet Security and Acceleration 2006 Server.

- **No delegation, but the client may authenticate directly** This is the default setting. This setting means Microsoft Internet Security and Acceleration 2006 Server would not pass credentials to a published server, but allows a published server to ask for credentials from users directly.

- **No delegation, and the client cannot authenticate directly** This setting means Microsoft ISA Server would not pass credentials to a published server or allow published servers to send credentials directly.

- **Basic** This setting means the ISA Server would attach the credential information into the HTTP header and send to the published server in plaintext.

- **NTLM** This setting means NTLM challenge/response protocol is used to authenticate against the published server.

- **Negotiate** This setting means the ISA Server would first try to use Kerberos to authenticate against the published server. If Kerberos authentication fails, it would then use NTLM challenge/response protocol to authenticate.

- **Kerberos constrained delegation** This setting means use Kerberos delegation to send credentials to the published server.

- **SecurID** This setting asks ISA to send the SecurID cookies to the published server for authentication.

As you can see, there are many different types of delegation methods supported in ISA Server. But as you can imagine, some delegation methods will not work with some authentication methods. Table 12.1 summarizes the valid combinations between authentication methods and delegation methods.

Table 12.1 Valid Combinations between Authentication and Delegation Methods

Authentication Method	Delegation Method
HTML Authentication (with Password)	No delegation, but client may authenticate directly
HTTP Authentication (Basic)	No delegation, and client cannot authenticate directly Basic NTLM Negotiate Kerberos constrained delegation
HTML Authentication (with Passcode or one-time password)	No delegation, but client may authenticate directly No delegation, and client cannot authenticate directly SecurID Kerberos constrained delegation
HTTP Authentication (Certificate, Digest, and Integrated)	No delegation, but client may authenticate directly No delegation, and client cannot authenticate directly Kerberos constrained delegation

If HTML Authentication is used, Microsoft ISA 2006 Server can be configured to enable a Single Sign-On among different applications. To do so, enable the Single Sign-On option in the Web listener properties and specify the Single Sign-On domain. One point to note about Single Sign-On domain: it should be the common part of the host name among different host names used by different applications. For example, testingdomain.com should be specified in Single Sign-On domain if www.testingdomain.com and mail.testingdomain.com is used by two applications. One common scenario is to have Single Sign-On enabled with Outlook Web Access. Many organizations also make use of SharePoint to store documents, and usually links would be embedded into a mail message. So if Single Sign-On is enabled, the user would not be prompted to authenticate again when they click the SharePoint link embedded in a mail message. Thus, calls to the help desk would be minimized.

Designing & Planning…

Single Sign-On in Multiple Web Listener

Please note that Single Sign-On is not supported across multiple Web Listeners. To use Single Sign-On, all applications must be configured to use a common Web Listener.

Exercise: Creating a Web Listener

The following is an exercise that demonstrates how to create a Web Listener on your ISA firewall.

You are an administrator of your organization. You are now configuring your Microsoft Internet Security and Acceleration 2006 Server for Web publishing rules that support both HTTP and HTTPS traffic (see Figure 12.6).

Figure 12.6 Scenario for Web Listener Exercise

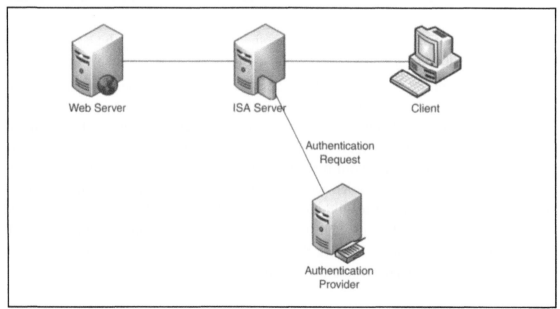

1. Open ISA Server Management console, and navigate to Firewall Policy.
2. Choose **New | Web Listener** in the Network Object Toolbox (see Figure 12.7).

Figure 12.7 Create Web Listener in ISA Server Management Console

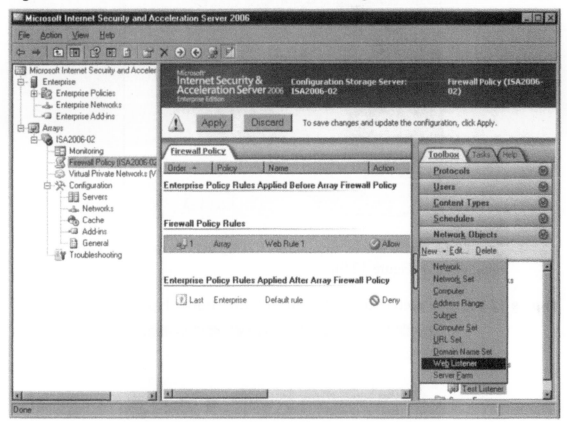

3. Specify **Testing Web Listening** as the name of the Web Listener (see Figure 12.8).

Figure 12.8 Create Web Listener Wizard – Specify Web Listener Name

4. Specify the Web Listener required to handle SSL traffic. Click **Next** to continue (see Figure 12.9).

Figure 12.9 Create Web Listener Wizard – Choose Traffic Type

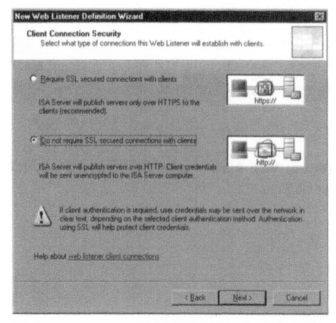

5. Check the checkbox next to **External**. Click **Select Address**. In the dialog box, specify the Web Listener to listen to all IP addresses. Click **OK** to save the configuration (see Figure 12.10).

Figure 12.10 Create Web Listener Wizard – Choose Network Address

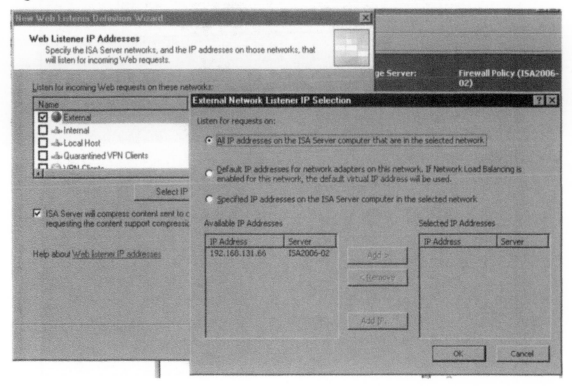

6. Select the certificate for use with this Web Listener. Click **Next** to continue (see Figure 12.11).

Figure 12.11 Create Web Listener Wizard – Select SSL Certificate

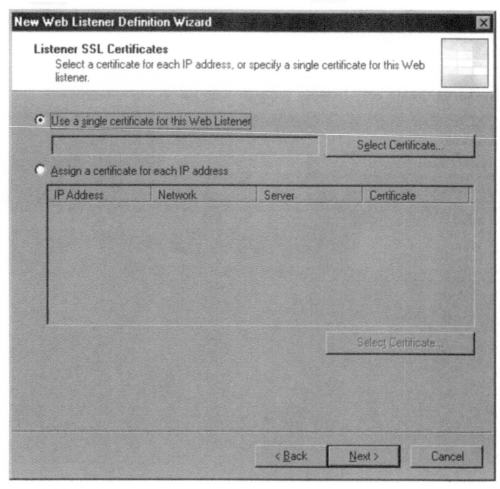

7. Select to use **HTML Authentication** method and choose **Windows (Active Directory)** as Authentication Provider. Click **Next** to continue (see Figure 12.12).

Figure 12.12 Create Web Listener Wizard – Choose Authentication Method

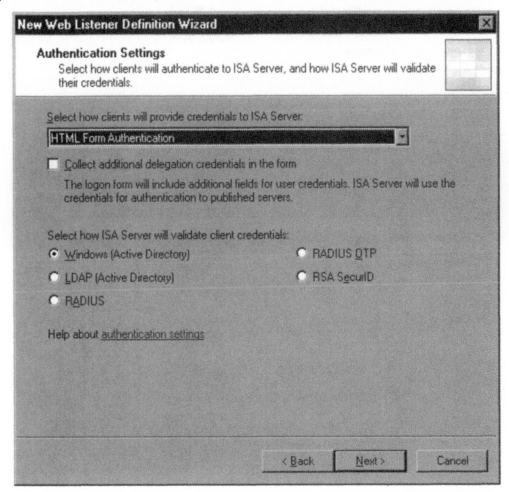

8. Check the checkbox to enable Single Sign-On in this Web Listener. Specify testingdomain.com as the Single Sign-On domain. Click **Next** to continue (see Figure 12.13).

Figure 12.13 Create Web Listener Wizard – Choose Single Sign-On

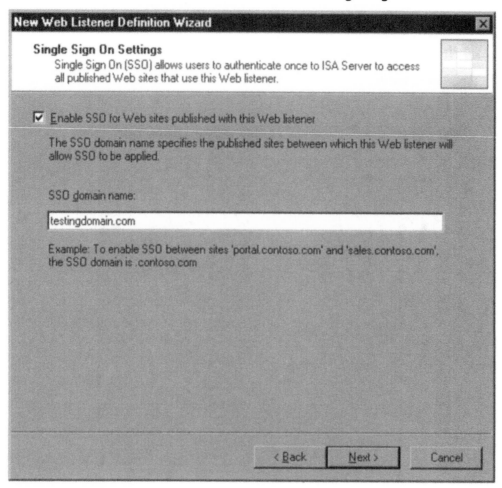

9. Review the configuration selected, click **Finish** to close the wizard and create the Web Listener (see Figure 12.14).

Figure 12.14 Create Web Listener Wizard – Review Configuration

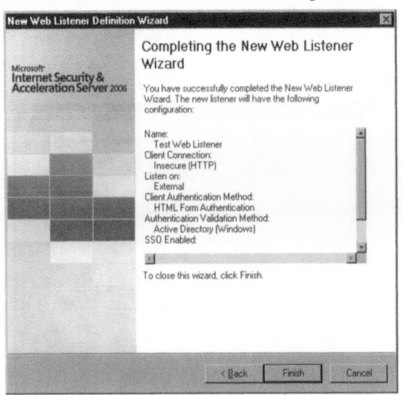

Configuring & Implementing...

SSL Certificate

Make sure all SSL Certificates are imported into the machine certificate store but not the administrator. To do so, you need to use the Certificate Snap-in in Microsoft Management Console.

Configuring Publishing

Once the Web Listener is configured, you can proceed to create and configure the Web publishing rule. When you are creating a Web publishing rule, the following key information is required.

Under the Action tab, determine if the rule is used to Allow or Deny web requests that match the condition specified in the rule (see Figure 12.15).

Figure 12.15 Action Tab of a Web Publishing Rule

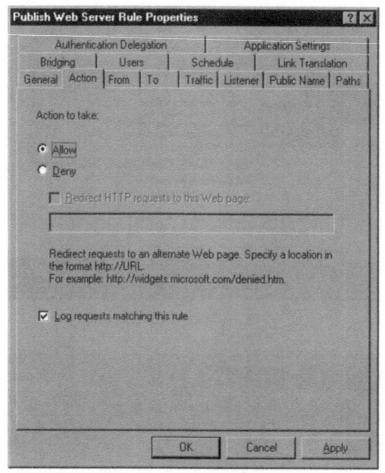

Under the From tab, specify if the rule applies to all networks or a specify network. You can configure the rule to only partner so that the Web publishing is valid only when users are accessing from a partner network (see Figure 12.16).

Under the To tab, specify where the published Web resource is and how Microsoft Internet Security and Acceleration 2006 Server should forward the original headers to the published server (see Figure 12.17).

Figure 12.16 From Tab of a Web Publishing Rule

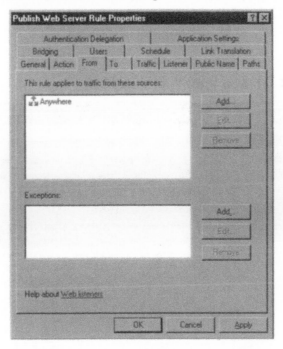

Figure 12.17 To Tab of a Web Publishing Rule

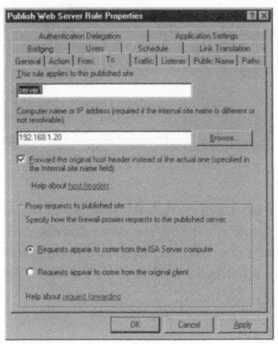

Under the Traffic tab, specify which properties of HTTP and HTTPS are traffic filtering (see Figure 12.18).

Figure 12.18 Traffic Tab of a Web Publishing Rule

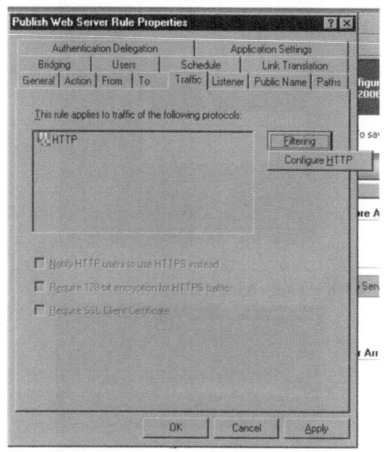

Under the Listener tab, specify which Web listener to use (see Figure 12.19).

Under the Public Name tab, specify the name that external users used to access the published resources. If the user uses http://www.testingdomain.com, the value specified should be www.testingdomain.com (see Figure 12.20).

Figure 12.19 Listener Tab of a Web Publishing Rule

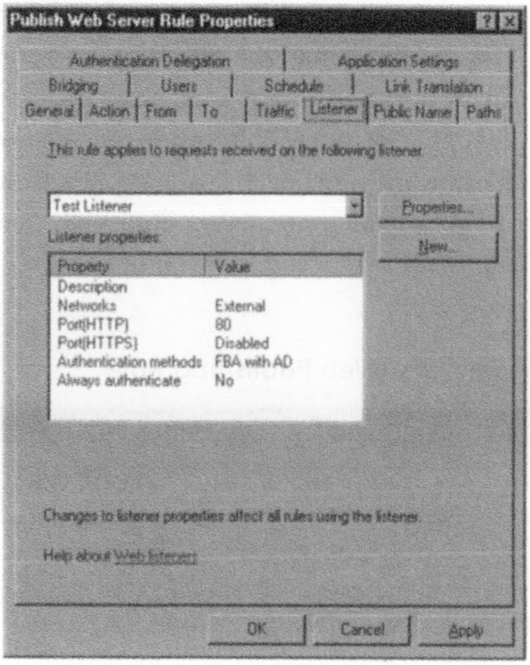

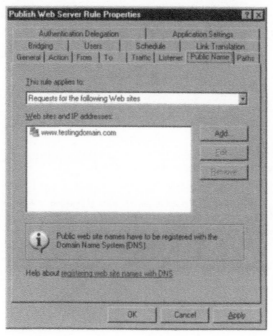

Figure 12.20 Public Name Tab of a Web Publishing Rule

Under the Bridging tab, specify how to connect the internal resources. You can choose to connect the Internet resources by using various protocols, like HTTP or HTTPS, regardless the protocol that external users use for accessing the Web site. Publishing FTP site to in web publishing rule is also supported. Using this option, users would be able to use HTTP or HTTPS to access files stored in an internal FTP server. This is used commonly when a company needs to provide read-only file access to public but require read-write access internally (see Figure 12.21).

Figure 12.21 Bridging Tab of a Web Publishing Rule

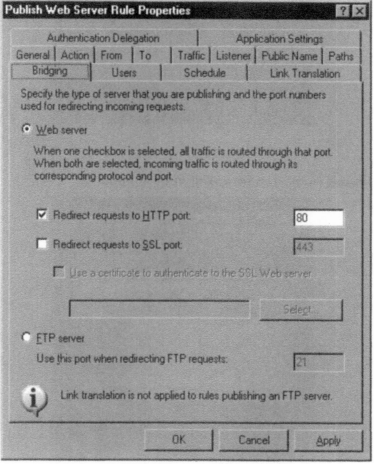

Under the Users tab, specify which user is considered to be a match in this Web publishing rule. By default, a rule includes **All Authenticated Users** only. You can choose **All Users** if you want the rules to apply to unauthenticated users. Otherwise, change the rule to another user group to which the rule wants to be applied (see Figure 12.22).

Figure 12.22 Users Tab of a Web Publishing Rule

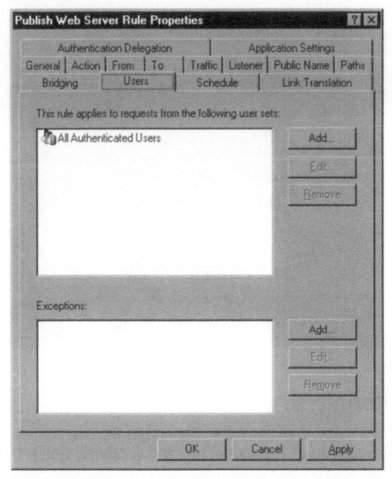

Under the Schedule tab, specify if the rule is effective on all days or specific schedule. A schedule set is used for defining when the effective period for the Web publishing rule is (see Figure 12.23).

Figure 12.23 Schedule Tab of a Web Publishing Rule

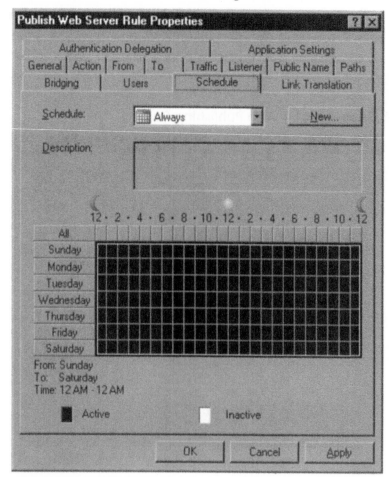

HTTP Filtering

HTTP filtering is a feature of ISA Server that enables filtering unwanted HTTP traffic if an internal resource is published by a Web publishing rule. HTTP filtering supports filtering HTTP traffic by using several HTTP properties. We will now discuss these properties.

Maximum Header Length

All HTTP requests would be rejected if the header length exceeded the value specified. The default value is 32 KB, which is enough for most cases; changing this value if there are problems encountered, which is about a header is longer than 32 KB (see Figure 12.24).

Maximum Payload Length

Specify if the size of the payload section of HTTP requested. You have an option to **Allow Any Payload Length** or specify a value for the maximum allowed payload length (see Figure 12.24).

Maximum URL Length

Specify maximum allowed number of characters of whole URL (see Figure 12.24).

Maximum Query Length

Specify the maximum allowed number of characters in the query of an HTTP request (see Figure 12.24).

Verify Normalization

Specify if HTTP request should be blocked if there are special characters after the URL gets normalized (i.e., converted from escape characters back to actual characters) (see Figure 12.24).

Block High-Bit Characters

Specify if HTTP request should be blocked if there are high bit characters in the HTTP request. High big characters means characters in double byte characters set or Latin 1 characters set (see Figure 12.24).

WARNING

Enable Block high bit characters would affect functionalities of some Web applications that require processing of Double Byte Characters, like Outlook Web Access or SharePoint sites.

Block Request Containing a Windows Executable

Specify if HTTP request should be blocked if Windows executable files exist in the request (see Figure 12.24).

Figure 12.24 General Tab of HTTP Filtering Properties

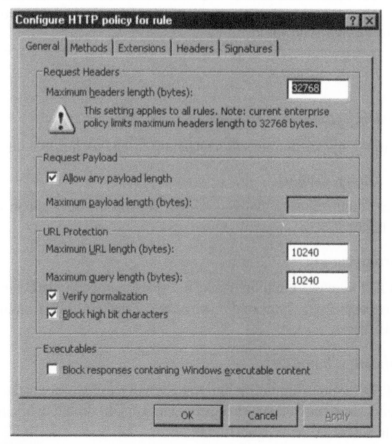

HTTP Method

Specify if a certain HTTP method is allowed or denied (see Figure 12.25).

Figure 12.25 Method Tab of HTTP Filtering Properties

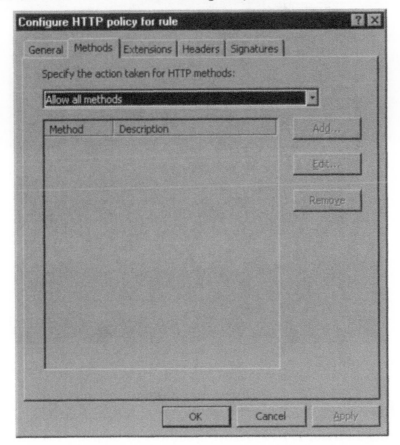

File Extension

Specify whether a HTTP request should be blocked if requesting for a file with the file extension specified (see Figure 12.26).

Block Requests Containing Ambiguous Extensions

Specify whether HTTP request should be blocked if requesting a file with a file extension that cannot be determined (see Figure 12.26).

Figure 12.26 Extension Tab of HTTP Filtering Properties

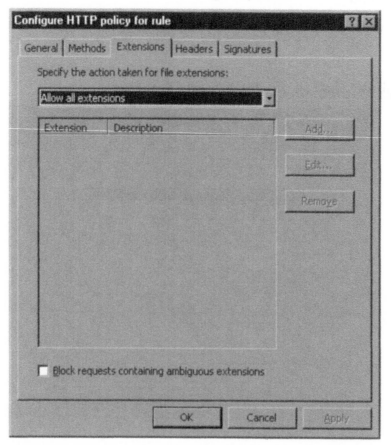

HTTP Header

Specify whether a certain HTTP header is allowed or denied. This setting can be configured to apply to HTTP requests or responses (see Figure 12.27).

Server Header Rewrite

Specify if the Server Header in HTTP response should be removed or the value get replaced with another value. This helps to prevent internal host information getting exposed to public (see Figure 12.27).

Via Header Rewrite

Specify if the VIA header in HTTP response should be removed or the value get replaced with another value. This helps to prevent internal host information getting exposed to public (see Figure 12.27).

Figure 12.27 Header Tab of HTTP Filtering Properties

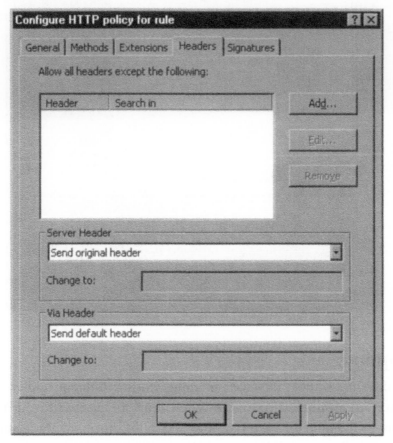

Specific HTTP Header Value in Request or Response

Specify HTTP Request or Response should be blocked if a certain value of a HTTP header exists (see Figure 12.28).

Figure 12.28 Signature Tab of HTTP Filtering Properties

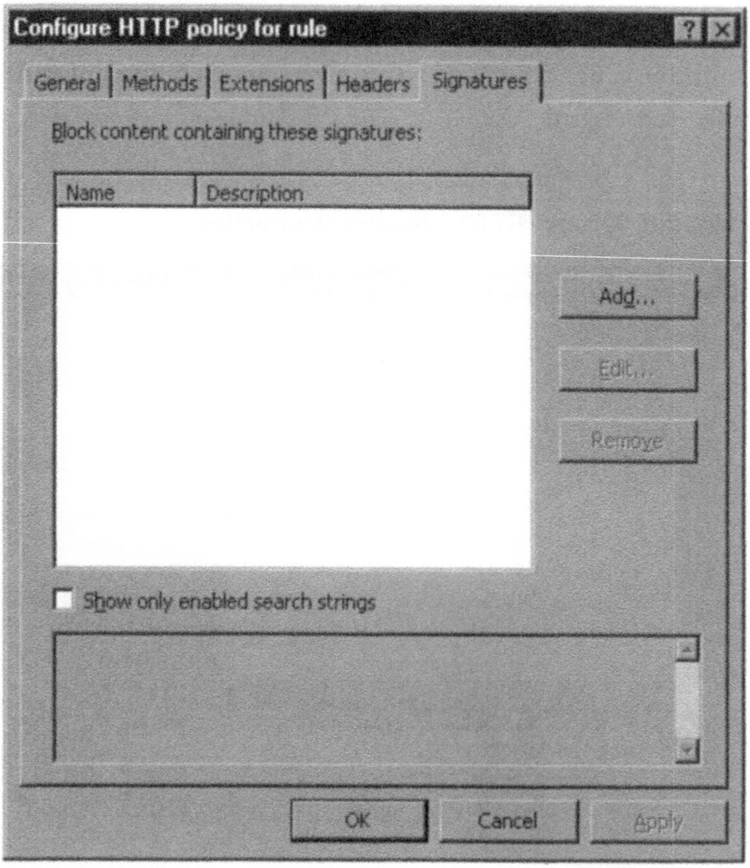

Path Mapping

Web publishing rules in ISA 2006 Server support using different folder names for content hosted in an internal resources when they are accessed from public. For example, content requested by external users via URL http://www.testingdomaind. com/folder1 actually is served by content located at http://server1/FolderA. Using this technique can help to provide external users more user-friendly and easier to remember URLs for accessing resources. Also, this helps to hide the internal structure of published resources. Microsoft ISA 2006 Server also supports using wildcard characters (*) in the path to specify mapping between multiple folders in one path mapping entry (see Figure 12.29).

Microsoft ISA Server will check against a Web publishing rule if any path mapping is defined. If such a rule exists, the path will get replaced before forwarding to a published host (for HTTP request) or sent back to the requesting host (for HTTP response).

Figure 12.29 Path Mapping Tab of a Web Publishing Rule

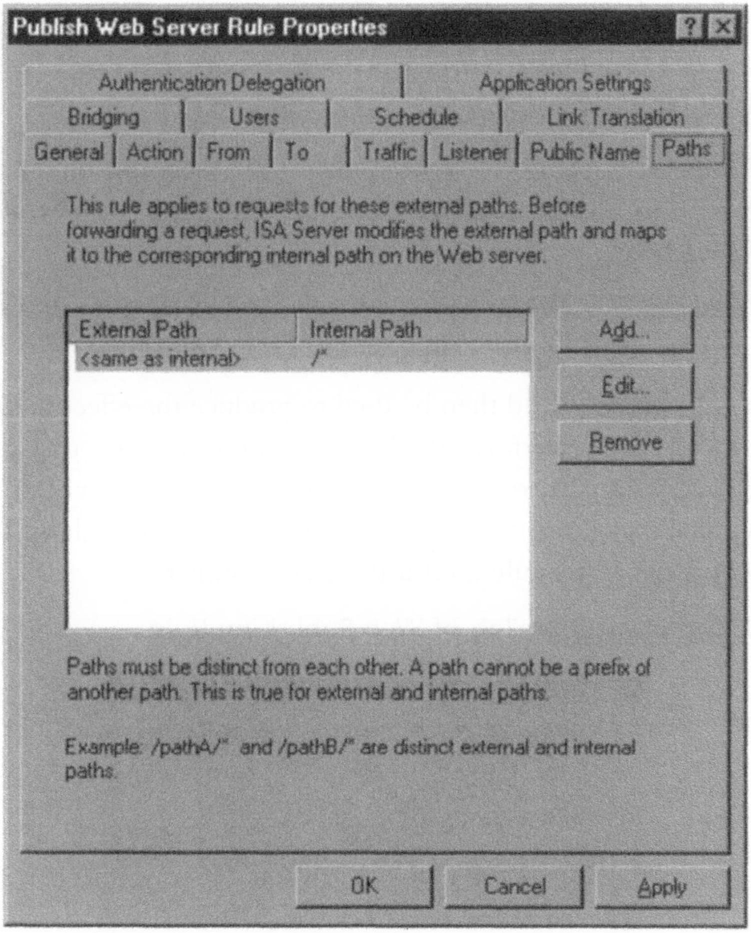

Link Translation

Link Translation is a feature of Web publishing that is designed to replace any internal links contained within the published Web content. For example, a published SharePoint site could contain internal references to another web server http://server2/file1.aspx. This is not a valid link if this content gets published to public Internet users. Thus, Link Translation is used to remove similar content and replace with a publicly accessible URL (see Figure 12.30).

There are different types of link translation supported in Microsoft Internet Security and Acceleration 2006 Server.

- Implicit local mapping – This mapping is not changeable by the administrator and is used to translate between internal and public names defined in a Web publishing rule.

- Local mapping – This is defined at the Web publishing rule level to perform translation for traffic that matches the web publishing rule.

- Implicit global mapping – This mapping is not changeable by the administrator and is used to translate between internal and public names of all Web publishing rules.

- Global mapping – This mapping set is defined by an administrator at server level (for Standard Edition) or array level (for Enterprise Edition).

All entries of mapping would then be used to produce the effective link translation dictionary, which is used to perform the link translation. There is one effective link translation dictionary for each of the Web publishing rules. And when the effective link translation dictionary is generated, mappings defined at the global level would override those defined at the rule level if there is a conflict.

Figure 12.30 Link Translation Tab of Web Publishing Rule

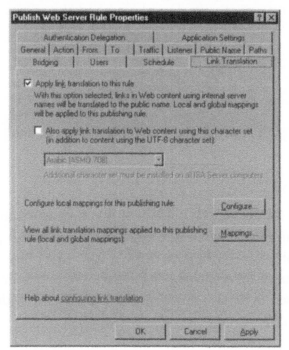

The following are exercises for you to understand the steps to create a Web publishing rule on your Microsoft Internet Security and Acceleration 2006 Server.

Exercise: Configure Web Publishing Rule

In this exercise, we would create a Web publishing rule that is to publish an internal Web server to public and make it accessible via HTTP only. NTLM authentication would be enabled to support the application hosted on the internal Web server.

1. Open ISA Server Management console, navigate to Firewall Policy.
2. Choose the **Tasks** tab, select **Publish Web Sites** (see Figure 12.31).

Figure 12.31 Create Web Publishing Rule – Launch Web Publishing Rule Wizard

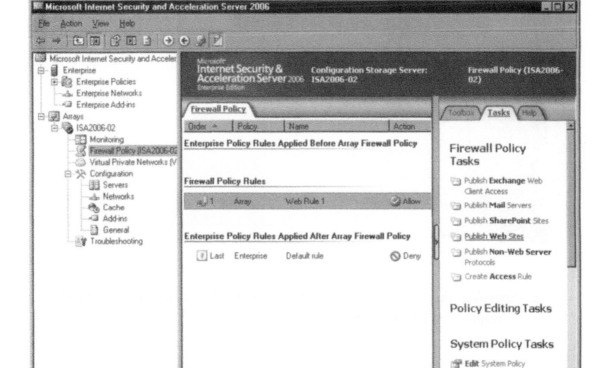

3. Specify **Publish Web Server Rule** when prompted for Web publishing rule name; click **Next** to continue (see Figure 12.32).

Figure 12.32 Create Web Publishing Rule – Specify Web Publishing Rule Name

4. Specify if this rule is to allow traffic to the published server; click **Next** to continue (see Figure 12.33).

Figure 12.33 Create Web Publishing Rule – Specify Rule Action

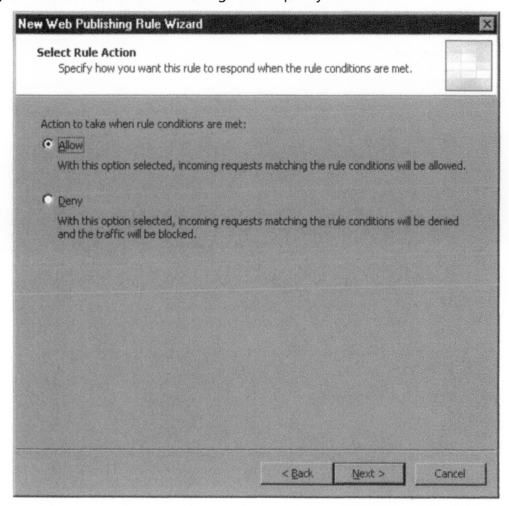

5. Specify this rule to **Publish a Single Web site or load balancer**. Click **Next** to continue (see Figure 12.34).

Figure 12.34 Create Web Publishing Rule – Specify Publishing Type

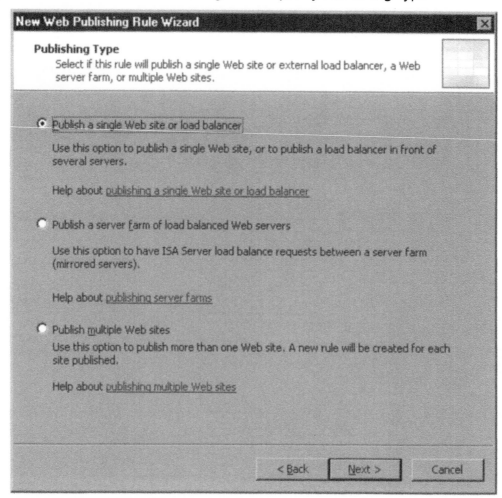

6. Specify this rule to connect published Web site using HTTP. Click **Next** to continue (see Figure 12.35).

Figure 12.35 Create Web Publishing Rule – Specify Server Connection Security

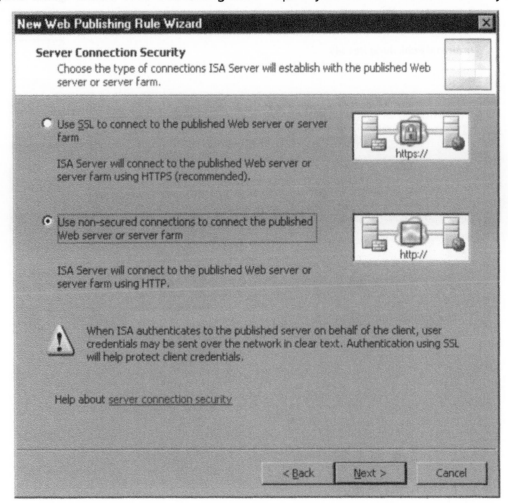

7. Specify **server1** as the internal resources name and use **192.168.1.20** to connect the internal resources. Click **Next** to continue (see Figure 12.36).

Figure 12.36 Create Web Publishing Rule – Specify Internal Publishing Details

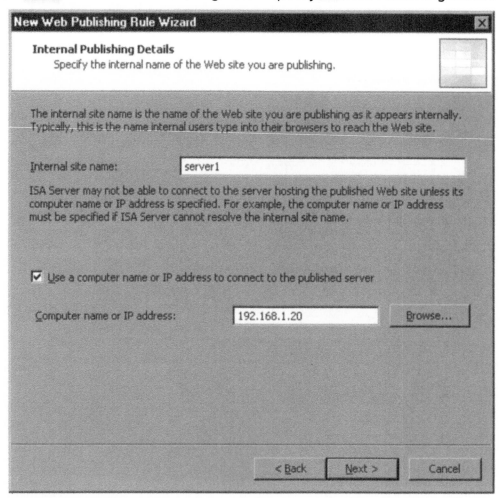

8. Specify to route all paths to same internal published server. Select to forward original host header to the published server. Click **Next** to continue (see Figure 12.37).

Figure 12.37 Create Web Publishing Rule – Specify Internal Path

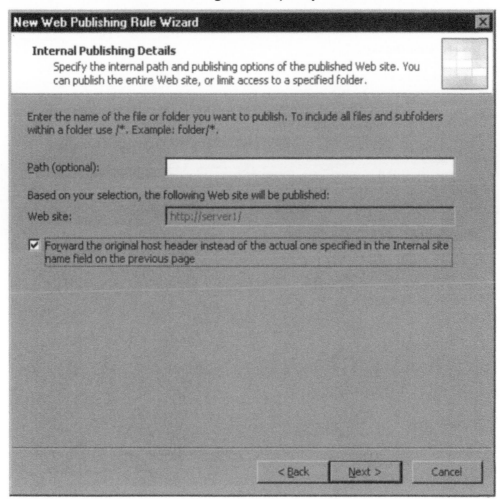

9. Specify that the Web publishing rule should listen to host name **www. testingdomain.com** and forward all paths below this host name. Click **Next** to continue (see Figure 12.38).

Figure 12.38 Create Web Publishing Rule – Specify Public Name Details

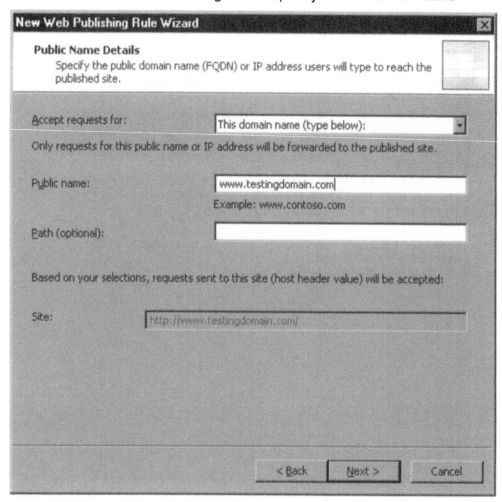

10. Select to use the **Test Listener** created in the previous exercise. Click **Next** to continue (see Figure 12.39).

Figure 12.39 Create Web Publishing Rule – Specify Web Listener

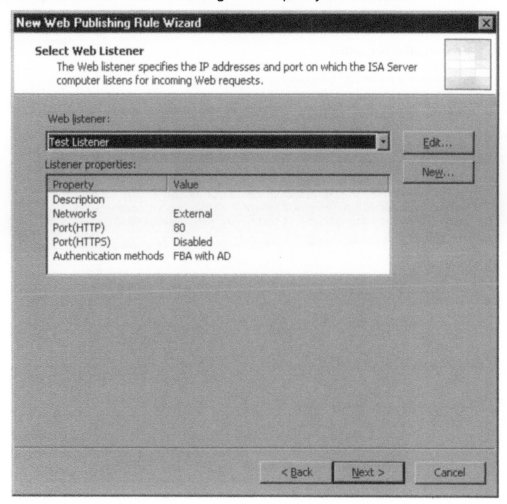

11. Select **NTML Authentication** as the delegation method. Click **Next** to continue (see Figure 12.40).

Figure 12.40 Create Web Publishing Rule – Specify Authentication Delegation

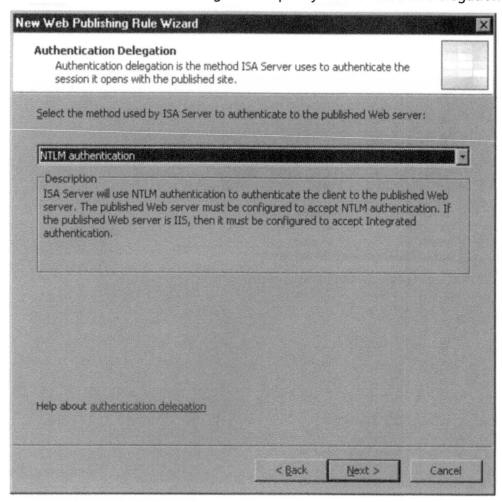

12. Select **All Authenticated Users** as the set of users authorized to access published resources. Click **Next** to continue (see Figure 12.41).

Figure 12.41 Create Web Publishing Rule – Specify User Set

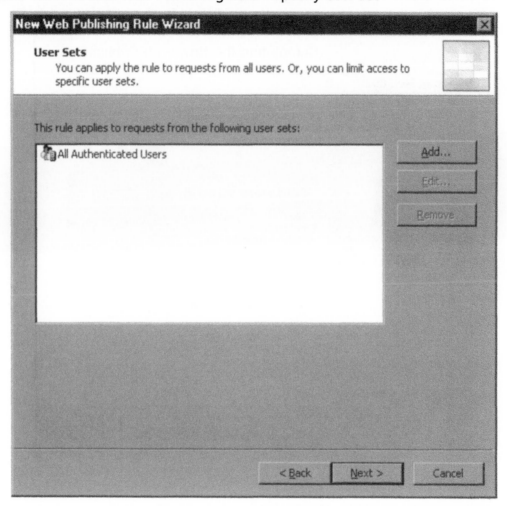

13. Review the configuration and click **Finish** to apply the configuration (see Figure 12.42).

Figure 12.42 Create Web Publishing Rule – Review

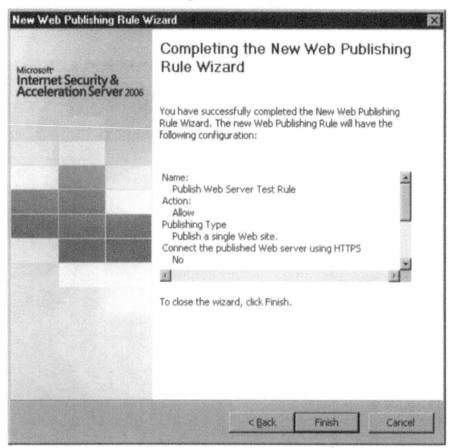

Publishing Exchange Web Client Access

Publishing Web-based client access (i.e., Outlook Web Access, Outlook Anywhere, Exchange ActiveSync) in ISA 2006 is similar to the steps used to publish a Web site. The following are some key points to note when configuring Web publishing rules for Exchange 2007.

When HTML authentication is enabled on the ISA Server, form-based authentication at the Exchange 2007 side should not be enabled. With Exchange 2007, client Web access should be configured to accept Basic or Windows Authentication and corresponding delegation settings needs to be configured at the Web publishing rule so that credentials would be passed to the Exchange 2007.

Basically, Exchange publishing rules are a type of Web publishing rule that has specific folders defined in the rule. As an administrator, you have a choice whether to use the Publish Exchange Web Client Access Wizard. Using the wizard will simplify the administrator's workload by remembering all paths required to enable the publishing. Or, you can create your own Web publishing rule with folder paths listed in Table 12.2. Make sure you do not publish the whole server to public (not recommended by Microsoft).

Table 12.2 Folder Paths Required for Publishing Exchange 2007 Client Access

Client Access Method	Path Required
Outlook Web Access	/owa/*
	/public/*
	/exchange/*
	/Exchweb/*
Outlook Anywhere	/rpc/*
Outlook Anywhere with additional folders for support automatic discovery in Outlook 2007	/unifiedmessaging/*
	/rpc/*
	/OAB/*
	/ews/*
	/AutoDiscover/*
Exchange ActiveSync	/Microsoft-Server-ActiveSync/*

You can put all paths into a single Web publishing rule, if you want to. Using the wizard you are not allowed to do so, but quite a lot of time we need to do that when we have only a single box for all services or roles in Exchange 2007 (see Figure 12.43).

Figure 12.43 Path Mapping Tab of a Web Publishing Rule for Exchange 2007

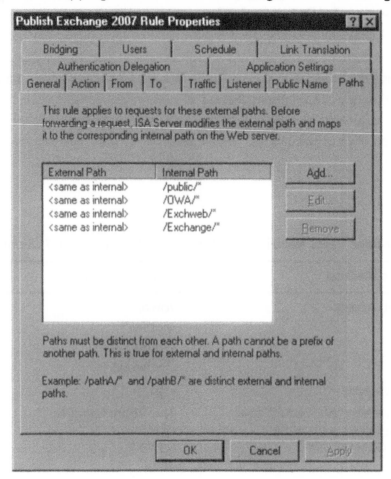

One additional point to note about how link translation works with Outlook Web Access in Microsoft Exchange Server 2007: ISA Server will also detect and replace the links contained within an e-mail message. But, because the way that hyperlinks are handled is different, link translation is a bit different than the other web content. When users click a link in an e-mail message, a HTTP request is sent to the Exchange 2007 server and then the user would be forwarded to the actual content. The actual link user click looks like http://exchange.testingdomain.com/owa/redir.

aspx?URL=http://server1. So the link translation not only needs to translate the server name, it needs to translate the URL attached at the back of the link. Microsoft ISA 2006 Server would not translate the link attached at the back, but adds a new HTTP parameter containing the translated link to the end of the URL, for example, http://exchange.testingdomain.com/owa/redir.aspx?URL=http://server1&Translated Url=http://server1.testingdomain.com/. This helps Exchange 2007 server to determine if link translation is defined by ISA.

Publishing SharePoint Sites

Publishing a Microsoft SharePoint site is the same as publishing a traditional Web resource. The only difference is the need to configure Alternate Access Mapping in SharePoint side. This is because some link fails to get translated by ISA Server.

Also, SharePoint uses Windows Authentication as the authentication method. Thus, delegation settings in ISA Server must be configured to use NTLM to delegate the credentials. Otherwise, the SharePoint Server will not able to get the proper user credentials. It's also a good idea to have the ISA 2006 Server configured to forward original headers to the SharePoint site because some functionalities in SharePoint require this information.

Publishing a Web Farm

Microsoft Internet Security and Acceleration 2006 Server supports publishing Web content hosted in a Web farm environment. To do so, a Server Farm object needs to be created on the ISA server. Server Farm objects also need to define a verifier, which Microsoft ISA Server uses to perform health checks against servers in the farm. Regular health checks against each server in the server farm are performed and traffic will not be forwarded to the server if the server is found to be unavailable.

Microsoft Internet Security and Acceleration Server supports three type of connection monitors that are used to monitor the health of the server. They are **Sending HTTP/HTTPS GET request**, **Send a PING request**, and **Establishing a TCP connection**. For the most case, using HTTP/HTTPS GET is suggested for server farms. Do a check against a GET request just to ensure all aspects of the server are up and running (see Figure 12.44).

Figure 12.44 Connectivity Verification Tab of a Server Farm

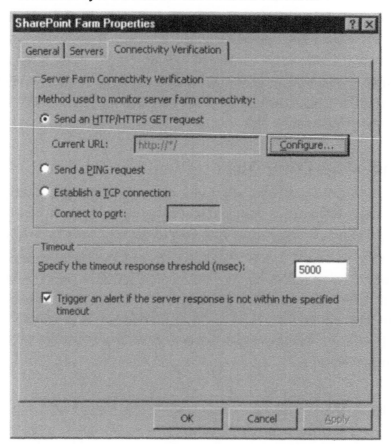

Publishing Non-Web Server Protocols

Web publishing rule is to publish HTTP or HTTPS content to public, whereas server publishing rule is used to publish content other than HTTP and HTTPS. For example, server publishing rule is used to publish FTP, Terminal Services to public.

If a predefined publishing rule does not exist, additional rules can be created, but the protocol definition must exist. If the protocol definition does not exist, it needs to be created prior to creating the server publishing rule. Fortunately, many protocol definitions are included as part of the default ISA installation. If there are some protocols that are not found in the list, a protocol definition can be created.

To create a Protocol, choose **New | Protocol** in the Toolbox tab of ISA Management Console. When creating a protocol, you need to specify only where the connection is initiated and the direction. There is no need to specify both direction for most cases as Microsoft Internet Security and Acceleration Server would help to establish the required tunnel for sending data back. If publishing any server that is not predefined, the administrator will need to create a protocol definition for ports (TCP or UDP) in the inbound direction, not both directions. Both would imply inbound and outbound, and outbound requests are for users on your LAN, not users from the Internet. As a general rule, when you are doing the publishing of servers, you are talking about inbound connections. The outbound connections generally are designated for users on your LAN.

If required, you should select the application filter if it is required to make publishing work. Some protocols will not work if an appropriate application filter is not installed and selected. FTP is a good example of this protocol. Application filters are small add-in programs to ISA that help to handle protocols that require more than opening a port. This might include some additional tuning on the protocol itself. For example, the FTP filter will tell the ISA server to open a required secondary FTP data channel by looking at the FTP command passing through the server.

Once protocol is defined, we can than proceed to create the server publishing rule. The following is an exercise for publishing Terminal Services to public.

Exercise: Publishing Terminal Services

In this exercise, we would create a server publishing rule for publishing terminal services to external users.

1. Open ISA Management Console.

2. Click **Publish Non-Web Server Protocols**.

3. Give **Publish Terminal Services Rule** as the name of the server publishing rule. Click **Next** to continue (see Figure 12.45).

Figure 12.45 Prompt for Name of Rule in New Server Publishing Rule Wizard

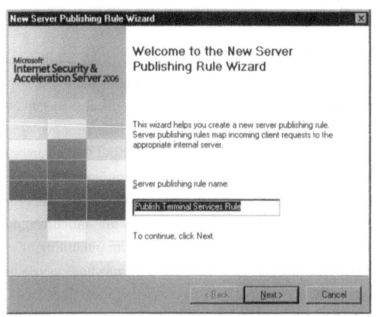

4. Specify the IP address of the published server. Click **Next** to continue (see Figure 12.46).

Figure 12.46 Specify the Published Server in New Server Publishing Rule Wizard

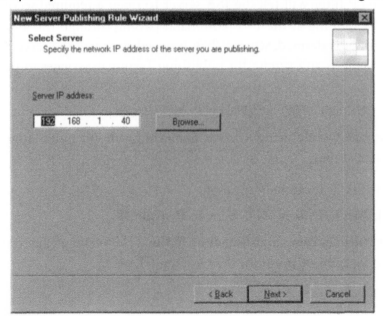

5. Specify **RDP (Terminal Services) Server** the Protocol to be published against the published server. Click **Next** to continue (see Figure 12.47).

Figure 12.47 Specify the Protocol in New Server Publishing Rule Wizard

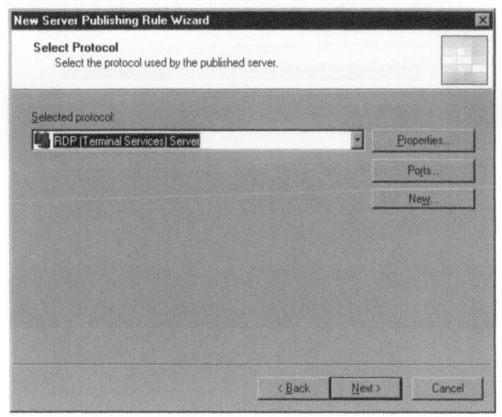

6. Select **External** as the network to publish to. Click **Next** to continue (see Figure 12.48).

Figure 12.48 Select Network in New Server Publishing Rule Wizard

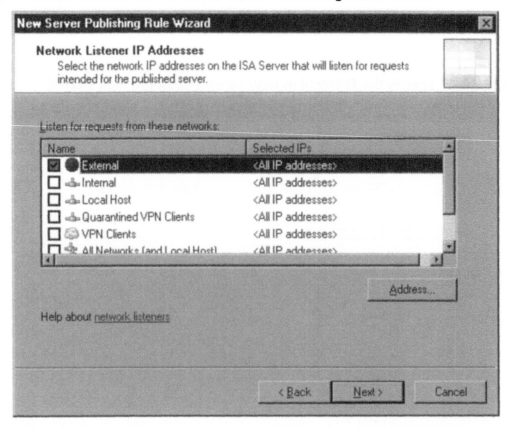

7. Review the configuration selected. If you also want internal users to have access to this resource, check **Internal** also. Click **Finish** to save the changes (see Figure 12.49).

Figure 12.49 Review Configuration in New Server Publishing Rule Wizard

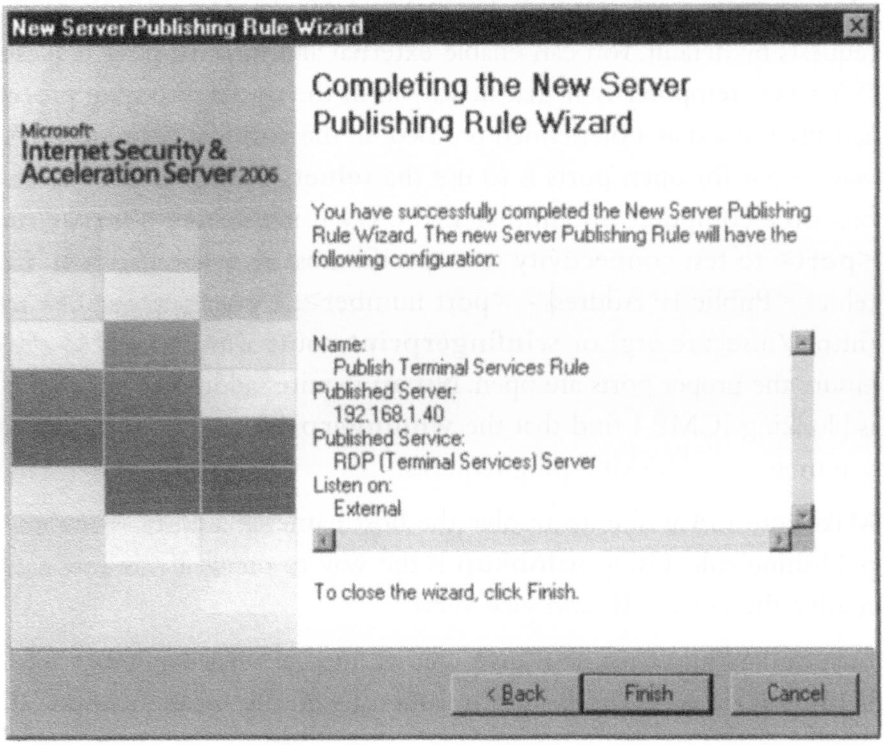

Publishing Mail Servers

Publishing Mail Server is the same as creating a server publishing rule with mail-related protocols, like SMTP, POP3, and IMAP4. It is noteworthy to mention that there is a SMTP application filter that comes with Microsoft ISA 2006 Server. This SMTP filter allows us to perform some blocking against unwanted SMTP command entering the published SMTP server.

Troubleshooting Publishing Servers behind a Microsoft Internet Security and Acceleration 2006 Server Firewall

As a Microsoft Internet Security and Acceleration 2006 Server administrator, it may be difficult to identify the cause of problem when publishing is not working. Here are some suggested ways to identify the cause of the problem.

- Make sure ISA server is able to connect to the publishing host. Using the **ping** command will not help because ISA blocks internal and external ping requests by default. You can enable external and internal ping requests to the ISA server temporarily if that helps you in the troubleshooting process. (Ping actually is listed as a predefined protocol in the protocol definitions.) A simple way to test for open ports is to use the **telnet** command from an external box on a computer on another LAN. Try using **telnet <server name> <port>** to test connectivity to a specific host on a specific port. Example: telnet <Public IP Address> <port number>. A port scanner like **nmap** (http://insecure.org) or **winfingerprint** could also be used to check to ensure the proper ports are open. **Nmap** requires additional switches if a host is blocking ICMP. I find that the **winfingerprint** tool does a great job of scanning hosts blocking ping requests.

- Make sure ISA is able to resolve the host name/IP address specified in the publishing rule. Using **nslookup** is the way to check if the host name can resolve the correct IP and vice versa.

- Turn on logging because it gives you an idea of what happened. The logs can be utilized to get more details on issues specifically related to firewall rules.

- Do not forget to check the Application log of the event viewer. Sometimes configuration problems are indicated here.

Summary

Publishing can be used within Microsoft Internet Security and Acceleration Server to allow public to access server resources in internal network.

There are two types of ISA publishing, Web publishing and server publishing. Web publishing is to handle HTTP and HTTPS traffic, whereas server publishing handles other types of traffic.

Using Web publishing allows internal Web resources to be accessed in a secure manner. Authentication can be performed before reaching the internal server resources. This helps to ensure an unauthenticated or unauthorized user will not able to access published resources. SSL bridging is also a key feature in Microsoft Internet Security and Acceleration 2006 Server. SSL bridging allows SSL traffic to terminate at the ISA server, thus allowing inspection of content but also providing a secure communication channel to external users. Additional features like path mapping and link translation also help to hide structure of internal server resources to public.

Server publishing is a way to allow public access of non-HTTP traffic to get published to public. Application filters enable support of complex protocol, like FTP, if that protocol is getting published to public. Application filters also help to provide an extra layer of security. For instance, SMTP application filters allow filtering of unwanted SMTP command from entering into a published server.

Solutions Fast Track

Publishing Servers behind a Microsoft Internet Security and Acceleration 2006 Server Firewall

☑ For publishing HTTP/HTTPS server, use a Web publishing rule instead of a server publishing rule.

☑ Use SSL bridging for publishing SSL content when possible.

☑ Perform Link Translation for publishing content that may cross-reference other web resources.

☑ Use path mapping if you want to hide internal folder structure from public.

☑ Configure authentication at the ISA Server to enforce authentication before the request reached the internal server.

☑ Use application filter with the server publishing rule when publishing non-HTTP content, like FTP or SMTP traffic.

Troubleshooting Publishing Servers behind a Microsoft Internet Security and Acceleration 2006 Server Firewall

☑ Ensure Internet users are able to access published resources.

☑ Ensure DNS resolution gives both correct host name and IP for reserve and forward query.

☑ Turn on logging in Microsoft Internet Security and Acceleration 2006 Server to see if the correct rule get matched or traffic get rejected.

Frequently Asked Questions

Q: Should we use the Web publishing rule or server publishing rule for HTTP/ HTTPS traffic?

A: The Web publishing rule should be used for HTTP/HTTPS traffic. Web publishing allows inspection of HTTP and HTTPS content, like HTTP header filtering, whereas server publishing does not allow such content inspection.

Q: Should we enable authentication on ISA 2006 Server?

A: It is always a good idea to have authentication enabled at the ISA Server level. This filtering requests using user identity and also ensures only authorized users can have access to published resources.

Q: When configuring a server publishing rule to a nondefault port of a protocol, do we need to create a new protocol definition?

A: You don't have to create a separate protocol definition for nondefault ports. You can use the port mapping feature in server publishing rule to direct traffic to internal servers listening to nondefault ports of a protocol.

Chapter 13

Managing ISA 2006 Server Connections between Sites

Solutions in this chapter:

- **VPN Protocols: Advantages and Disadvantages**

- **Connecting Two ISA 2006 Servers on Different Physical Sites**

- **Troubleshooting Connections between Sites**

☑ Summary

☑ Solutions Fast Track

☑ Frequently Asked Questions

Introduction

If a company has more than one physical connection to the Internet, more than one Microsoft Internet Security and Acceleration Server 2006 will be needed. Microsoft Internet Security and Acceleration Servers are software firewalls that will protect each location's internal network. In the case of a branch office, the employees at the remote location will often need to utilize the internal network resources of the main office.

By creating Firewall Policies, the different offices will be able to securely communicate over the Internet. Secure communication can be ensured via firewall policy and by utilizing other security mechanisms such as certificates. Once a secure connection is established between the internal networks of the branch office and the main office, users on either network can have access to resources, such as databases, network shares, and printers.

If an Active Directory is present in the infrastructure, replication of the Directory Service can also take place over a secure connection. Network administrators need to carefully configure the firewall polices of their ISA Servers to ensure internal servers on both networks can communicate over the secure channel. Microsoft offers several tools, such as replemon, to verify that replication of the Active Directory database is functioning properly. In summary, ISA firewall policies can be used to connect the internal networks of a main and an office branch in a secure manner.

Years back it was tedious and complicated, not to mention expensive, to connect remote sites or satellite offices to a network. However, due to technology enhancements, better means have been developed to connect sites. With Microsoft's ISA Server 2006, this method is a security gateway that acts as a firewall gateway joining two networks over the Internet, protecting an IT environment from Internet-based threats and attacks while providing the environment fast and secure access to applications and data utilizing a VPN site-to-site connection.

A virtual private network (VPN) is an extension of a private network in any large or small business environment where links are shared across a public network such as the Internet connecting two or more networks using a VPN link. The site-to-site configurations work like any LAN router, addressing packets addressed to IP addresses at sites routed through the ISA Server 2006 firewall.

A quicker definition is depicted in Figure 13.1 showing how a VPN works.

Figure 13.1 Visual Representation of VPN Process

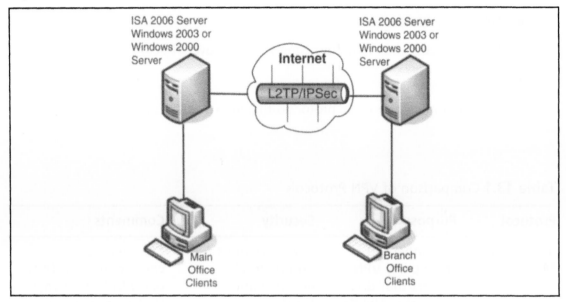

ISA Server 2006 is available in two versions: Microsoft Standard Edition and Microsoft Enterprise Edition. For demonstration purposes, Microsoft ISA Server 2006 Enterprise will be used.

Designing & Planning...

A Simple Rule: Plan Ahead

Configuring ISA Server 2006 as a site-to-site gateway is straightforward and not a complicated procedure, and is made even less complicated by using the wizards that will walk you through the steps. However, planning is an essential part of any configuration plan. Plan ahead; know what VPN protocol best suits your environment and business situation (see Table 13.1). Know if you are going to be requiring a static IP pool for your site(s) or the use of a Dynamic Host Configuration Protocol (DHCP) configuration. Following this simple guideline will lead to less configuration headaches and trouble.

Site-to-site links can be used with one of the following VPN protocols:

- IPSec Tunnel Mode
- L2TP/IPSec (Layer Two Tunneling Protocol over IPSec)
- PPTP

Table 13.1 compares the three protocols that are most common.

Table 13.1 Comparison of VPN Protocols

Protocol	Purpose	Security	Comments
IPSec Tunnel Mode	To connect to third-party VPN servers that do not support L2TP/IPSec or PPTP.	Low—Provides "tunneling" encapsulation for data protection.	Can be used to connect to with third-party VPN gateways that do not support PPTP or L2TP/IPSec.
L2TP/IPSec	To connect to an ISA Server 2000, ISA Server 2004, or Windows VPN server.	High—Requires Public Key Infrastructure (PKI). Server 2003 can be set up with certification authority to issue machine certificates to authenticate both users and computers.	Requires the remote VPN server to be an ISA Server computer or Windows VPN server. Less restricted than IPSec Tunneling solution. Uses Routing and Remote Access.
PPTP	To connect to an ISA Server 2000, ISA Server 2004, or Windows VPN server.	Moderate—Does not require Public Key Infrastructure (PKI), uses CHAP/EAP to authenticate user. Does not authenticate the computer.	Requires the remote VPN server to be an ISA Server computer or Windows VPN server. Less restricted than IPSec Tunneling solution. Uses Routing and Remote Access.

VPN Protocols: Advantages and Disadvantages

IPSec Tunneling Mode is the best suited option when you are using ISA Server 2006 as your VPN server and the site you are connecting to is using a third-party NON-Microsoft VPN gateway that does not support PPTP or L2TP/IPSec as its VPN server, while providing a higher level of security than PPTP.

Advantages of IPSec Tunneling Mode

IPSec Tunneling mode has the following advantages:

- Security: Is IPSec Tunneling mode secure? Somewhat, but not the best. In actuality, it's somewhat vulnerable to some exploits. IPSec Tunneling is secure; in fact IPSec Tunneling mode encrypts the portion of creating a VPN Tunnel and encapsulates the tunnel creation verifying packet integrity.

- Good protection from Denial of Service (DoS), replay, and man-in-the-middle attacks.

- Scalability through IPs, IPSec can be applied in networks of all sizes including LANs to global networks. This is a big plus for medium to large enterprises.

- Not limited to applications, thus guaranteeing they will be routable with IPs, making IPSec compatible.

Disadvantages of IPSec Tunneling Mode

IPSec Tunneling mode has the following disadvantages:

- Encryption of small packets generates a lot of network overhead, thus reducing network performance.

- IPSec is complicated and complex with many features. This complexity increases the probability of loopholes being discovered by hackers.

- The Data Encryption Standard (DES) algorithm is very susceptible to brute-force attacks using readily available software on the Internet.

L2TP/IPSec should be the preferred site-to-site protocol where security and routing is a concern if the infrastructure is in place to support it.

Advantages of L2TP/IPSec

L2TP/IPSec has the following advantages:

- Security: L2TP/IPSec VPN protocol provides a higher level of security due to the fact it uses the IPSec encryption protocol securing the connection and enforcing machine authentication as well as user authentication. For an even higher level of security, computer and user certificates can be provided to the L2TP/IPSec connection. If the infrastructure is not ready to deploy a certificate server, a preshared key can be created to the site-to-site L2TP/IPSec VPN connection.

- Provides data confidentiality and data integrity.

- Routing: Uses routing and remote access on Windows Server 2003 servers.

Disadvantages of L2TP/IPSec

L2TP/IPSec has the following disadvantages:

- More difficult to install when utilizing the security certificates.

- IPSec encryption is processing intensive and on some low-end servers you may see a decrease in performance.

PPTP is a point-to-point Tunneling Protocol that provides secure transfers of data from a client to private enterprise servers via TCP/IP VPN connections. PPTP allows traffic to be encapsulated in an IP header to be sent across a corporate network or public networks such as the Internet.

Advantages of PPTP

PPTP has the following advantages:

- Security: PPTP provides a moderate level of security due to the fact that it is dependent on the complexity of the password used to authenticate the PPTP connection. You can enhance the level of security applied to a PPTP link by using EAP/TLS-based authentication methods.

- Widely supported by many major firewall appliances and enterprise software firewalls such as ISA servers.

- No Public Key Infrastructure (PKI) required, EAP uses the digital signatures for both client and server security.

- Routing: Uses routing and remote access on Windows Server 2003 servers.

- Low overhead on performance.

Disadvantages of PPTP

PPTP has the following disadvantages:

- Moderately secure compared to L2TP/IPSec.

- Limited to Microsoft OS platforms.

- Provides a tunnel, but no encryption.

Connecting Two ISA 2006 Servers on Different Physical Sites

To start off, let's navigate to start the configuration process by configuring the ISA firewall at the corporate Main Office ISA firewall.

Step one of this process is to navigate to the Remote Site Network in the Microsoft Internet Security and Acceleration Server 2006 management console.

1. Open the **Microsoft Internet Security and Acceleration Server 2006** management console and expand the server name.

2. Click the Virtual Private Networks (VPN) node.

3. Click the **Remote Sites** tab in the details pane. Click the **Tasks** tab in the Task pane. Click **Create VPN Site-to-Site Connection**.

4. On the **Welcome to the Create VPN Site-to-site Connection Wizard** page, enter a name for the remote network in the **Site-to-site network name** text box. In this example, enter **Branch**. Click **Next**.

5. On the **VPN Protocol** wizard page (see Figure 13.2), you have the choice of using the different protocols that you deemed as your primary protocol that meets your standards for your organization. Click **Next**.

Figure 13.2 VPN Protocol

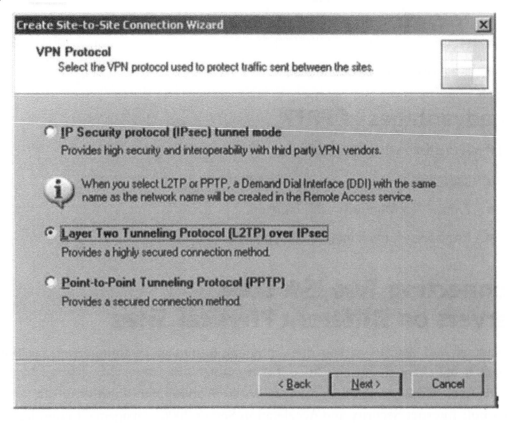

Remember, if your security plan or your infrastructure is not capable to roll out to a PKI standard or does not require security certificates to be installed on your main office server and branch PCs, or you do not plan to deploy keys in the future, it's best to use the PPTP option. However, if you have certificates installed choose the L2TP/IPSec option.

Another method of security is preshared keys. Using preshared keys can be a weak spot in your security and is really recommended only for demonstration purposes or testing where no security issues are of concern. This option works well with L2TP/IPSec.

For demonstration purposes, I will be choosing the use preshared keys for the site-to-site VPN along with Layer Two Tunneling Protocol (L2TP) over IPSec.

A dialog box will prompt requiring you to create a user account matching the network name on the MAIN OFFICE ISA firewall (see Figure 13.3). This user account will be used by the branch's office ISA firewall to authenticate to the MAIN OFFICE ISA firewall. Without this user account, no authentication can be established when the firewall attempts to create its site-to-site VPN connection to the MAINOFFICE ISA firewall.

1. Click **OK**.

Figure 13.3 VPN Protocol Warning Screen

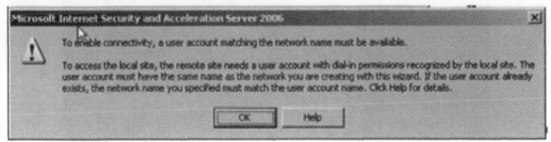

NOTE

It is very important that the user account have the same name as the BRANCH network we're creating, and that it is defined by the name from the first page in the wizard. In this example, we named the site-to-site Network connection BRANCH, so the user account we create on the main office ISA firewall must also have the name BRANCH. Do not forget to grant dial-up access for this account.

---

2. On the **Local Network VPN Settings** page select the **Dynamic Host Configuration Protocol (DHCP)**, button for this demonstration (see Figure 13.4).

If you do not have a DHCP server on the branch side of the network, then the Static address pool would apply. Also if we had multiple-server arrays on our network, DHCP would not be possible.

Figure 13.4 Local Network VPN Settings

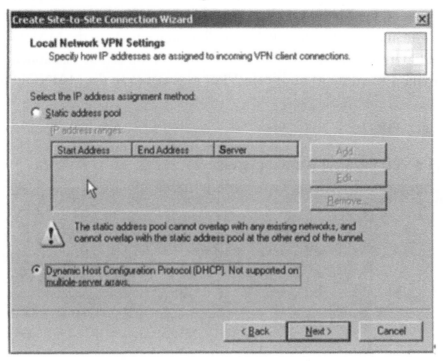

Remember the DHCP Server Location

If your design includes the use of a DHCP server to assign IP addresses to your VPN clients, then you will need to have your DHCP server located on the internal network side of the ISA 2006 server. If your network does not utilize DHCP servers, you can use static IPs configured on each ISA Server 2006 gateway.

Next in the setup steps comes the **Connection Owner** page, where you select which machine in the array should be the connection owner for this site-to-site VPN connection.

NOTE

This option is seen only in the ISA Enterprise Edition and not in Standard Edition. If you have NLB enabled from when you installed ISA Server 2006, then you don't need to manually assign the connection owner; as part of the NLB process it will automatically assign a connection owner when NLB is enabled on the array.

If you are working with the ISA Standard Edition, you can skip the NLB section.

Network Load Balancing, or NLB, provides automatic routing of client requests to the ISA server that is hosting the VPN connection. If a VPN connection fails, the NLB process automatically redistributes the connection to another server array one good example, if you have multiple ISA servers with VPN connections connected to the Internet. NLB will evenly inbound VPN requests, preventing any one server from being over-tasked, allowing VPN clients to connect to the same IP and be automatically sent to the appropriate server array.

In this demonstration, MainOffice, we are not using NLB on the MainOffice array, plus we have only one member of our MAIN OFFICE ISA firewall Enterprise Edition array.

Making things simple then, take the default entry, which is the name of the ISA firewall at the MainOffice.

1. Click **Next**.

2. On the Remote Site Gateway wizard screen, enter the IP address or FQDN representing the external interface of the branch ISA firewall: Branch.Demo.Org.

3. Click **Next**.

4. On the **Remote Authentication** screen you will see the checkbox **Allow the local site to initiate connections to remote site, using This user account:** Checking this box allows the local site to initiate connections to the remote site using the account specified.

5. Enter the account name that you will create on the branch office ISA Server 2006 firewall to allow the MainOffice ISA firewall access. In this demonstration, the user account will be named MainOffice. This is an important step with

authenticating to the branch office ISA firewall when creating the VPN connection.

6. The Domain name is represents the branch office ISA Server 2006 firewall, which in this example is DEMO. Enter a password for the account and confirm the password. Remember this password—you will need it again when you create the account later on the branch office ISA 2006 firewall.

7. Click **Next**.

8. Figure 13.5 shows you the **L2TP/IPSec Outgoing and Incoming Authentication** wizard screen. Remember that planning step I spoke about? Well, it's back. At this point you will have to decide on which authentication method you want to authenticate your machine. In this example, I choose to select the preshared key authentication option, entering a preshared key in the **Pre-shared key** text box.

9. Click **Next**.

Figure 13.5 L2TP/IPSec Authentication Method

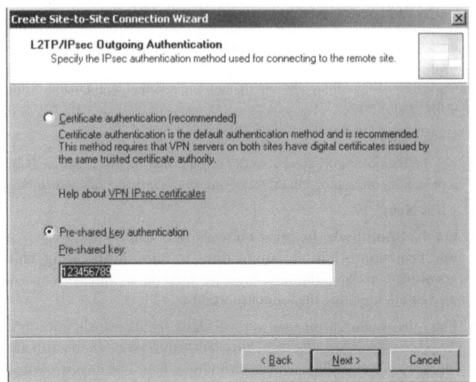

Figure 13.5 Continued. L2TP/IPSec Authentication Method

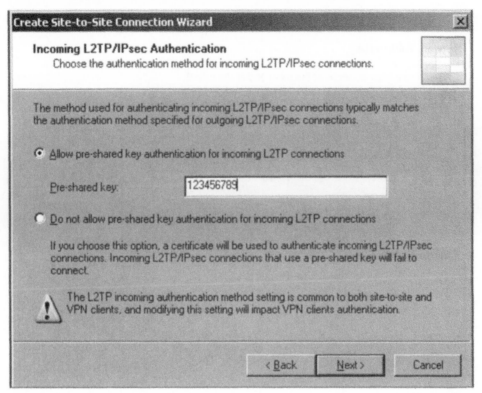

Remember! Jot this key down somewhere for safe keeping; also we'll need this information when configuring the machine authentication settings at the branch office.

10. The **Network Addresses** wizard screen displays IP Ranges properties.

11. Click **Add Range** on the **Network Addresses** page.

12. In the **IP Address Range Properties** dialog box, enter **10.0.1.0** in the **Starting address** text box. Enter **10.0.1.255** in the **Ending address** text box (see Figure 13.6).

13. Click **OK**.

14. Click **Next**. on the **Network addresses** page.

Figure 13.6 Setting Network Addresses

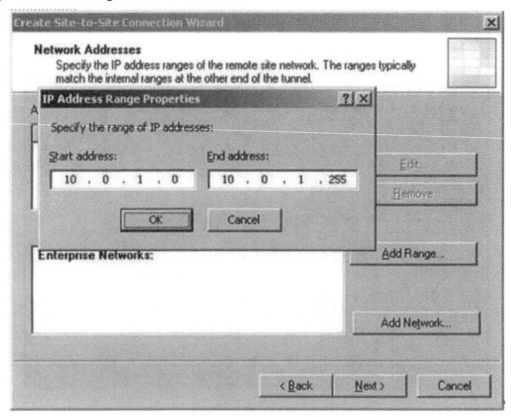

Obviously your network IPs will be different than the ones stated here. If you are not sure, contact your Network Administrator. Again, this falls back to the planning stages of implementing any configuration.

15. The **Remote NLB** wizard page will prompt asking if you want to enable the NLB option. Again in this demonstration, I chose not to enable it, so no checkmark is needed at "**The remote site is enabled for Network Load Balancing**" box.

16. Click **Next**.

Firewall Policy

Now let's discuss the steps for setting up a firewall policy.

Creating an Access Rule

On the **Site-to-site Network Rule** wizard, Figure 13.7, you can configure a Network rule that connects the MainOffice and Branch Office ISA firewall networks.

WARNING

ISA 2006 firewall requires that you always have a Network rule to connect ISA firewall networks to each other for proper security and communications. Do not forget even if you create an Access Rule—the connections will not work until you create a Network Rule.

---

1. Select the Create a network rule specifying a route relationship option along with the default name. Keep in mind that you have the option to manually create the network rule at anytime by clicking the **I'll create a network rule later** option.

2. Click **Next**.

Figure 13.7 Site-to-Site Network Rule

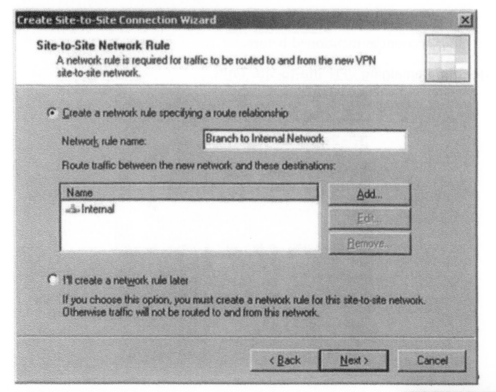

3. On the **Site-to-Site Network Access Rule** screen, select the **Create and Allow Access Rule. This rule will allow traffic between the internal network and the site-to-site network for all users'** option. In the **Apply the rule to these protocols** dropdown box you will have a choice of three selections, as described in Table 13.2.

Table 13.2 Options for Access Rules

All outbound traffic: This option allows all traffic from the main office to the branch office.

Selected protocols: This option allows control in which traffic can move from the main office to the branch office. This option also will allow the option to limit the connections to a selected list of protocols.

All outbound traffic except selected: Selecting this option will allow all traffic with the exception of a few protocols.

If you want to block certain protocols, click **Add** to select which protocols you want to block.

---

4. Select the **All outbound traffic option** and click **Next**.

5. Click **Finish** on the **Completing the New Site-to-Site Network Wizard** page.

Remember: For the Branch Office, Figure 13.8 reminds you to create a user account as mentioned before.

Figure 13.8 Remaining VPN Site-to-Site Tasks

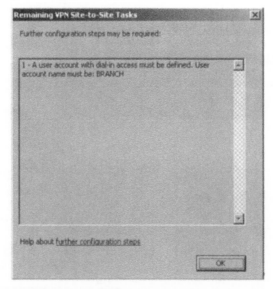

6. Click **OK**.

7. Click **Apply** to save changes and update the configuration (see Figure 13.9).

Figure 13.9 Remaining VPN Site-to Site Tasks

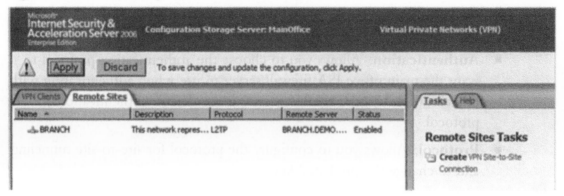

8. Select the **Remote Sites Task** panel and click EDIT Selected Network in the Task Panel (see Figure 13.10).

Figure 13.10 Remote Sites Task

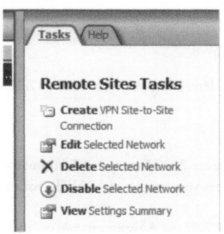

9. Click on the **Branch Properties** box. You will see the following tabs:

   ■ **General**: Information about the Remote Site Network. This is also where you can enable or disable the VPN site-to-site connection.

- **Remote NLB**: Allows you to enter specific IP addresses on the remote site VPN Gateway.

- **Connection**: Allows credential changes.

- **Addresses**: Allows you to change or add addresses to the IP range.

- **Server**: Allows you to change the **Connection Owner** for the site-to-site.

- **Authentication**: Allows you to choose the authentication protocol to want the main office ISA firewall server to use when authenticating with branch offices VPN. CHAP Version 2 is the default authentication protocol.

- **Protocol**: Allows you to configure the protocol for site-to-site tunneling and to change the preshared keys.

Dynamic Host Configuration Protocol (DHCP) Configuration

You are almost done with configuring. Now it is time to verify the DHCP configuration for your site-to-site VPN gateway. Two IP Address options are also part of the planning stages:

- DHCP
- Static address pool

Which to use? In this demonstration, I chose the DHCP option due to the simplicity.

Static Address Pool

If you are running ISA Server 2006 Enterprise Edition and you have an array with two or more array members you cannot use DHCP; you must use Static Pool address assignment.

After you select the IP Address Assignment tab on the Virtual Private Networks (VPN) properties screen in the left pane of the console, your options are there for Static address pool or DHCP (see Figure 13.11).

Figure 13.11 VPN Properties Screen

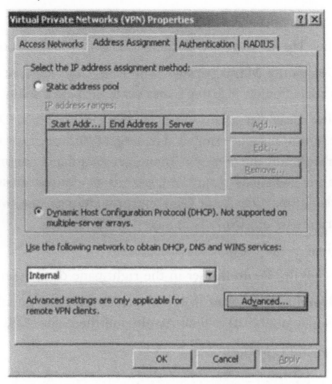

Choose **The Dynamic Host Configuration Protocol (DHCP)** and click **OK**. Again for this demo, DHCP was chosen.

> **NOTE**
>
> The Dynamic Host Configuration Protocol (DHCP) option is available only on ISA Standard Edition or single-member ISA Enterprise Edition arrays.

VPN Dial-in Account at the Main Office

A user account must be created on the Main Office ISA firewall allowing the Branch Office firewall to authenticate when the site-to-site connection is complete. The user account must have the same name as the demand-dial interface on the Main Office computer.

Follow these steps to create the account needed to connect to the Main Office VPN gateway.

1. Right-click **My Computer** on the desktop and click **Manage**.

2. In the **Computer Management** console, expand the **Local Users and Groups** node. Right-click the **Users** node, and click **New User**.

3. In the **New User** dialog box, enter the name of the Main Office demand-dial interface. In our current example, the demand-dial interface is named **Branch**. Enter **Branch** into the text box. Enter a password and confirm the password. Remove the checkmark from the **User must change password at next logon** check box. Check the **User cannot change password** and **Password never expires** check boxes. Click **Create**.

4. Click **Close** in the **New User** dialog box.

5. Double-click the **Branch** user in the right pane of the console.

6. In the **Branch Properties** dialog box, click the **Dial-in** tab. Select **Allow access** (see Figure 13.12). Click **Apply** and then click **OK**.

Figure 13.12 Branch Properties

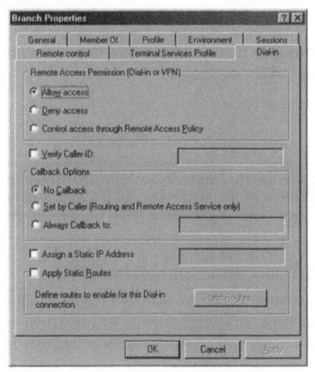

Branch Configuration

We are almost done. The last part is to set up and configure the Branch Office side of this demonstration and set up the Remote Site Network at the Branch Office. You will repeat the steps that we've just completed, with a few minor changes for the Branch configuration.

1. In the **Remote Gateway** Screen wizard, your Remote Site VPN Server box should have MainOffice.Demo.Org.

2. In the **Remaining VPN Site-to-site Tasks** dialog box, it reminds you that you need to create a user account with the name **Branch**. Click **OK**.

3. Make a note of the firewall policy created by the VPN wizard and then click **Apply** to save the changes. Click **OK** in the **Apply New Configuration** dialog box (see Figure 13.13).

Figure 13.13 Firewall Policy

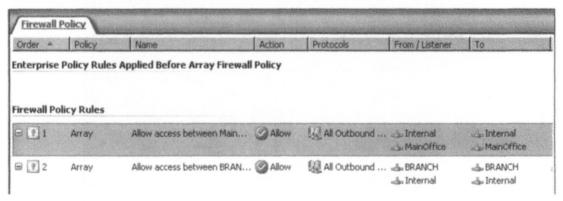

VPN Dial-in Account at the Branch Office

Perform the following steps to create the account the remote ISA Server 2006 firewall will use to connect to the Main Office VPN gateway:

1. Right-click **My Computer** on the desktop, and click **Manage**.

2. In the **Computer Management** console, expand the **Local Users and Groups** node. Right-click the **Users** node, and click **New User**.

3. In the **New User** dialog box, enter the name of the Main Office demand-dial interface. In our current example, the demand-dial interface is named

MainOffice. Enter **MainOffice** into the text box. Enter a password and confirm the password. Write down this password because you'll need to use it when you configure the remote ISA Server 2006 VPN gateway machine. Remove the checkmark from the **User must change password at next logon** check box. Place checkmarks in the **User cannot change password** and **Password never expires** check boxes. Click **Create**.

4. Click **Close** in the **New User** dialog box.

5. Double-click the **MainOffice** user in the right pane of the console.

6. In the **MainOffice Properties** dialog box, click the **Dial-in** tab. Select **Allow access** (see Figure 13.14). Click **Apply**, and then click **OK**.

Figure 13.14 Main Properties Screen

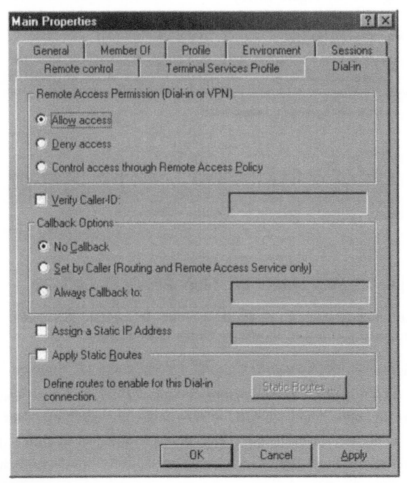

Troubleshooting Connections between Sites

Troubleshooting VPN connections can be the most tedious and difficult tasks you will encounter when it comes to communications between sites. Most common problems that you may expect to see are related to the VPN server or the VPN client configuration due to the fact the ISA server software does very little interaction in regard to VPN connections.

A few common configuration issues to look out for are:

- Name resolution: Verify you have in place and configured all network services such as NetBIOS, WINS, DNS, DHCP, and directory services.

- IP issues: Verify you have installed the DHCP relay agent. The agent will proxy for the VPN clients and allow them to receive DHCP information. Also, keep in mind, if you are using static IP addressing; verify you are not assigning duplicate IPs to your clients.

- VPN client issues: Verify client VPN settings that work with your network.

- VPN gateway: Verify only the remote/branch site is capable of initiating the VPN connection. If both servers initiate a call simultaneously, this will prevent both servers from accepting an incoming connection.

- Authentication issues: Verify that your VPN protocols are the same on both the ISA Server and the VPN Clients. Misconfigurations will cause headaches with troubleshooting connectivity.

Verifying Connectivity

Now that both the MainOffice and Branch site ISA Server 2006 firewalls are configured as VPN routers, let's test the site-to-site connection.

The simplest today is the ping test to verify any connectivity loss between networks and even hardware.

1. From the branch computer, click **Start**, and then click **Run**.

2. In the run dialog box, type **cmd**.

3. In the command window, type **ping** –t 10.0.0.2 and press **Enter**.

4. This ping should return packet ping information verifying the host is the replying.

5. The same test should be performed also on the Main Office, pinging 10.0.1.2 the Branch Office.

Summary

The intent of this chapter is to give you the basic understanding of how to connect two ISA 2006 servers from different site locations. The examples covered demonstrated how to configure two sites to connect via a VPN connection utilizing the Microsoft Internet Security and Acceleration Server software. This was demonstrated by creating the Remote Site Network at the main office ISA firewall and setting up a user account so that both the main office and branch office ISA firewall can connect via VPN.

In the Branch section of the chapter, I demonstrated pretty much the same procedures from the first section of creating the Main Office ISA steps so that the Branch Office ISA firewall can contact the Main Office ISA firewall, again creating a user account so that the Branch Office can communicate.

We discussed the differences between the protocols and chose the most secure one creating an L2TP/IPSec site to site VPN connection between two ISA firewalls. Due to the complexity of certificate authentication process and the scope of the chapter, our discussion was limited to using a preshared key between the ISA firewalls at the Main and Branch Offices. However, in corporate enterprise situations, it is recommended to use certificate authentication in lieu of preshared keys.

Finally, we spoke about troubleshooting connections between sites. This was accomplished by simple means, using the ping command. We pinged the site(s) and verified the log files and session information to verify what the ISA console is seeing when a successful VPN session is communicating properly.

Solutions Fast Track

VPN Protocols: Advantages and Disadvantages

☑ IPSec Tunnel Mode is the best-suited option when you are using ISA Server 2006 as your VPN server and the site you are connecting to is using a third-party NON-Microsoft VPN gateway.

☑ L2TP/IPSec (Layer Two Tunneling Protocol over IPSec) provides secure transfers of data from a client to private enterprise servers preferred site-to-site protocol where security and routing is a concern.

☑ PPTP provides secure transfers of data from a client to private enterprise servers via tunneling.

Connecting Two ISA 2006 Servers on Different Physical Sites

☑ This option is seen only in ISA Enterprise Edition and not in Standard Edition.

☑ If you have NLB enabled from when you installed ISA Server 2006, you do not need to assign the connection owner manually; it will automatically assign a connection owner when NLB is enabled on the array.

Troubleshooting Connections between Sites

☑ All outbound traffic. Remember ISA does not allow traffic to pass unless you create a rule to allow it.

☑ Selected protocols. This option allows control in which traffic can move from the main office to the branch office, also allowing the option to limit the connections to a selected list of protocols.

☑ All outbound traffic except selected. This option will allow all traffic with the exception of a few protocols.

Frequently Asked Questions

Q: What is recommended for the most secure VPN connection protocols?

A: L2TP/IPSec is the most secure for VPN tunneling.

Q: During the setup steps while doing the configuration, the wizard prompts me to select a **Connection Owner** for the array, but the option is already selected automatically. Why?

A: This is a feature within the ISA 2006 Enterprise edition only. When **Networking Load Balance, NLB** is enabled on the array, the NLB process will automatically assign a connection owner.

Q: Which is the most restrictive for **Site-to-Site Access Rules**?

A: Most restrictive is **All outbound traffic except selected.** This option will allow all traffic with the exception of a few protocols.

Chapter 14

Proxy Functions of Microsoft Internet Security and Acceleration Server 2006

Solutions in this chapter:

- Using Microsoft Internet Security and Acceleration 2006 as a Proxy Server

- Configuring Microsoft Internet Security and Acceleration 2006 to Cache BITS Content

- Using the Differentiated Services on Microsoft Internet Security and Acceleration 2006 to Regulate Traffic

☑ Summary

☑ Solutions Fast Track

☑ Frequently Asked Questions

Introduction

A Proxy Server provides a number of useful functions in a company's network infrastructure. Proxy Servers will go out and retrieve Web pages and content and return the Web pages to the internal network users. The fact that the proxy is retrieving the Web pages and not the actual clients adds an extra layer of protection to the clients because their internal IP addresses are hidden from the Internet. The proxy mechanism makes surfing external Web sites safer for internal clients.

If employees are constantly requesting pages from the same Web sites, the proxy server can store those requests locally on the server. When additional requests are made for content that has already been retrieved and stored locally, the proxy server will send the requesting client the copies of the pages from its stored cache. Utilizing this function, a proxy server will not have to go back out again and fetch the requested Web pages.

Proxy can also serve as a valuable tool because it is a single point to the Internet for internal network users. Most companies are concerned with the abuse of the Internet by employees and other internal users. A proxy can track user's statistics by determining which Web sites are most frequently visited and what client IP addresses are generating most of the Web traffic in the company.

Using a proxy server as a single point of entry to the Internet also allows the network administrator to filter which sites can be blocked. Lists of banned sites can be easily updated to prevent employees from visiting Web sites that are outside the scope of their job. There are many benefits to using the proxy functions of Microsoft Internet Security and Acceleration 2006 Server. Implementing a Proxy Server using Microsoft Internet Security and Acceleration 2006 Server in a company's network infrastructure will help reduce security vulnerabilities.

Using Microsoft Internet Security and Acceleration 2006 as a Proxy Server

Microsoft Internet Security and Acceleration Server 2006 can be configured to act as a proxy server in your environment to accelerate the performance of Internet access, as the name implies. Microsoft Internet Security and Acceleration Server 2006 supports two types of caching:

- **Forward Caching** To cache all Internet traffic from external to internal. That's all Internet pages requested by internal users.

- **Reverse Caching** To cache all objects sent from internal to external. This works with publishing to help offloading the published server.

No matter which type of caching you use, they work the same way. The only difference is the source of object being cached. Forward caching caches objects from the Internet, whereas reverse caching caches objects from a published server. The following describes the process by which Microsoft Internet and Acceleration Server 2006 handles a object request.

1. When a request arrives on the Microsoft Internet Security and Acceleration Server 2006, it checks against a list of caching rules and sees if the object is to be cached or not.

2. If rules determine the object needs to be cached, it checks against the pool of objects currently at the cache pool (first check memory cache (RAM) then disk cache).

3. If an object is found and not expired, Microsoft Internet Security and Acceleration Server 2006 will return the object from cache.

4. Otherwise, Microsoft Internet Security and Acceleration Server 2006 requests the destination server (either external server or published server) for the requested object. Before the object is sent to the end user, the retrieved object would be saved to cache.

5. The object is then returned to the user.

A common misconception is that the Microsoft Internet Security and Acceleration Server 2006 solely determines if the object should be cached. But in fact, some HTTP headers in HTTP Response can affect the way Microsoft Internet Security and Acceleration Server 2006 caches an object. Table 14.1 summarizes which HTTP header can affect the way Microsoft Internet Security and Acceleration Server 2006 cache objects.

Table 14.1 HTTP Header That Affects Whether Microsoft Internet Security and Acceleration Server 2006 Would Cache an Object

Header	Value	Description
Cache-Control (HTTP 1.1 response)	No-cache	Indicates the requested object should be cached. Microsoft Internet Security and Acceleration Server 2006 would not cache the requested object.
	Private	Indicates the requested object is for specific user only. Microsoft Internet Security and Acceleration Server 2006 will then ensure the object is available only to the user who originally requests the object but not others.
Cache-Control (HTTP 1.1 request)	No-store	Indicates the request and response should not be cached. Microsoft Internet Security and Acceleration Server 2006 would ensure content in response to this request is not cached.
Pragma (HTTP 1.0 response)	No-cache	Indicates the requested object should not be cached. This header is usually included in response for secured object (i.e., HTTPS). Microsoft Internet Security and Acceleration Server 2006 will ensure the object is not cached.
Www-Authenticate (HTTP 1.0/1.1 response)		Indicates this is a response to a client when the requested object requires authentication. Microsoft Internet Security and Acceleration Server 2006 would not cache this request.
Set-Cookie (HTTP 1.0/1.1 response)		Indicates this is a response to the requesting client when there is a cookie for your requested object. Microsoft Internet Security and Acceleration Server would not cache the response to this request.

Continued

Table 14.1 Continued. HTTP Header That Affects Whether Microsoft Internet Security and Acceleration Server 2006 Would Cache an Object

Header	Value	Description
Authorization (HTTP 1.0/1.1 request)		Indicates this is a request to a where the request contains authorization information. Microsoft Internet Security and Acceleration Server would not cache response of this request. There is an exception to this if the Cache-Control: public header is specified in the response. If Cache-Control: public HTTP header is included in the response, Microsoft Internet Security and Acceleration Server 2006 would cache the content of the response.

As you may notice, the Web application or the Web server has the ability to control how Microsoft ISA Server 2006 caches objects. The configuration of the originating server also plays a role in determining whether an item will be stored in the cache of the ISA Server. It is also important to note that secured content (i.e., HTTPS content) will not be cached.

If your network configuration contains remote office, how should we have Microsoft Internet Security and Acceleration Server 2006 deployed? Usually, we would have a centralized cache array placed in the central office, which acts as the single gateway to the Internet for all users. This benefits all users in the way all data cached is available to all other users, thus chances of needing to access the actual server to retrieve the requested object is lower, thus helping to improve the performance of Internet surfing.

But sometimes, the connection between central office and remote office is slow, or there are a large number of users in the remote site. In this situation, we could put a dedicated Microsoft Internet Security and Acceleration Server 2006 in the remote office and have it configured to use cache chaining. Cache Chaining is a feature to link different ISA 2006 Servers that downstream server request objects that are not found in their cache from the upstream ISA Server. The purpose of having a dedicated ISA Server in the remote office helps to bring the cache closer to end users and helps to increase chances of a hit in cache. This helps to increase performance further.

To configure cache chaining, perform the following.

1. Open ISA Server Management Console.

2. Navigate to **Configuration | General**.

3. Click **Configure Firewall Chaining** and specify the address of upstream server. Click **OK** to apply the settings (see Figure 14.1).

Figure 14.1 The Firewall Chaining Configuration

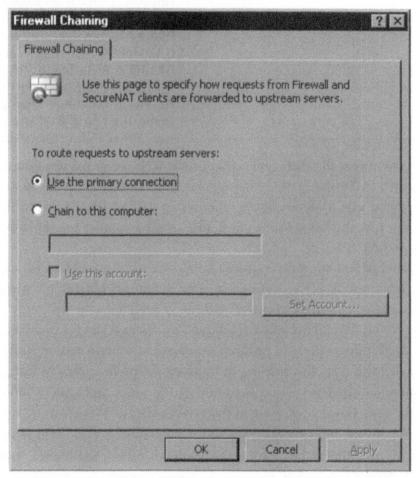

Designing & Planning…

Microsoft Internet Security and Acceleration Server 2006 at Remote Site

Consider having a dedicated Microsoft Internet Security and Acceleration Server 2006 when the remote site has more than 25 users. Standard Edition is always a good start for Microsoft Internet Security and Acceleration 2006 deployed in this case.

One point to note about using compression with caching: compressed content will be saved to cache if HTTP compression is enabled on the ISA Server. That means content cached would be exactly the same as the state that was retrieved from the source server in the case of compression. There is a exception to this: if a web filter is required for compressed content, ISA would save the decompressed version of the content and send the compressed version to user when requested. This could increase the load on Microsoft Internet Security and Acceleration Server.

Configuring Internet Security and Acceleration 2006 as a Proxy Server

Enabling caching in Microsoft Internet Security and Acceleration Server is simple. All you need is to add a cache drive and create some cache rule to define when to cache. The following are steps to add a cache drive.

1. Open ISA Server Management Console.

2. Navigate to **Configuration | Cache**, and double-click the entry for server.

3. Specify the size to be allocated for the disk cache. Click **OK** to apply the settings (see Figure 14.2).

Figure 14.2 The Cache Drive Configuration

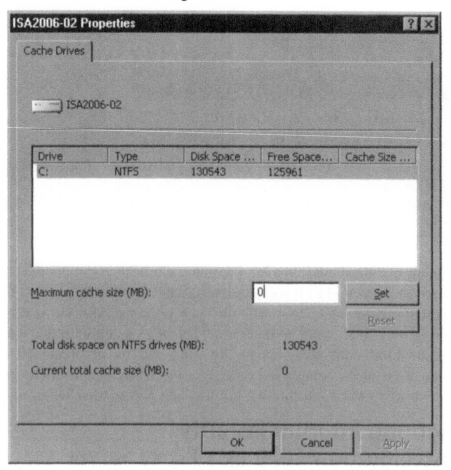

I always got questions about what the most appropriate size allocated to Microsoft Internet Security and Acceleration Server 2006 for storing cache is. Well, I always say, more is better. You should allocate as much disk space to Microsoft Internet Security and Acceleration Server 2006 in order to reduce the chances to hit the cached item that needs to be removed from the cache because it is full. This definitely will reduce the cache hit ratio (i.e., the percentage of requested object retrieved from cache) of Microsoft Internet Security and Acceleration Server 2006. This also minimizes the performance improvement brought to the network by placing a Microsoft Internet Security and Acceleration Server 2006 as a proxy server. But of course, there is a recommended formula to calculate the recommended minimum size for disk cache:

Total size of web cache = 100 MB + 0.5 MB × Number of Web Proxy Client

There are some more advanced tuning tips listed in an article on Microsoft's Web site, "Best Practices for Performance in ISA Server 2006" (http://www.microsoft.com/technet/isa/2006/perf_bp.mspx). It's always a good idea to review the cache size according to the steps listed in this guide. This helps to make sure your Microsoft Internet Security and Acceleration Server 2006 is running in optimal state.

Once the cache drive is configured, there is a .cdat file created on the drive; all .cdat files are located in the folder \urlcache of the configured cache drive. Microsoft Internet Security and Acceleration Server 2006 would remove a cached object from a cache file if the cache file is full. You may wonder why there are no options to clear the cache file if you want to remove all cached content for some reason. There is no way to clear content of a .cdat file, but disabling the cache on the cache drive would serve the same purpose. Microsoft created a script to programmatically create content of a cache drive without disabling it. You can get the script from http://go.microsoft.com/fwlink/?LinkID=51685.

Microsoft Internet Security and Acceleration Server 2006 supports cache files only up to 64 GB. If you configure the size of the cache on a drive larger than 64 GB, Microsoft Internet Security and Acceleration Server 2006 will split into multiple cache files.

Configuring & Implementing...

Cache Drive

Make sure you have a drive formatted with NTFS, because cache drives support only partitions formatted as NTFS. Also, it is always a good idea to have a cache drive put in a dedicated RAID 5 volume to further improve performance and minimize the impact to an operating system. Also, Microsoft suggests keeping the cache drive and paging file in separate drives.

There are some settings to control caching in a Microsoft Internet Security and Acceleration 2006 Server. The following are configuration options that control how caching behaves for some exceptional situations:

- **Cache objects that have an unspecified last modification time** This option allows you to specify if content should be cached if there are no last modification times specified in the object (see Figure 14.3).

- **Cache objects even if they do not have HTTP status code of 200** This option allows you to specify if objects should be cached if they return a status code other than 200 (see Figure 14.3).

- **Maximum size of URL cached in memory** This option allows you to specify if content should be cached when the length of the URL exceeds the value specified (see Figure 14.3).

- **If Web site of expired object cannot be reached** This option allows you to specify if an object should be returned to the user if the Web site hosting the expired object is not reachable (see Figure 14.3).

Figure 14.3 Advanced Cache Properties

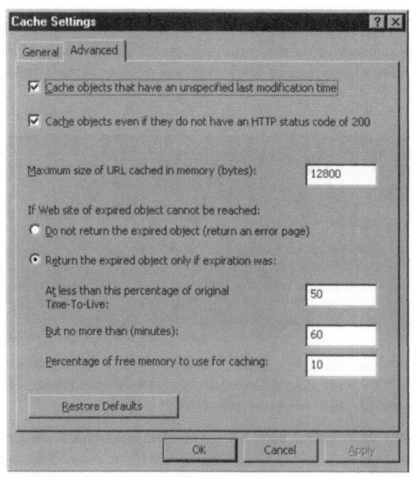

Configuring & Implementing...

Cache Objects Even If They Do Not Have HTTP Status Code of 200

Enabling this option may cause an error page to be cached and returned to the user even if the server resumed the service. Use this option with caution.

A cache rule is required to enable caching on Microsoft Internet Security and Acceleration Server 2006. If there are multiple cache rules, rules are evaluated according to the order they are listed in the cache rule list. And, whether you enable caching or not is determined by the setting at each rule. Thus, you are given the flexibility to control if you want caching enabled for a particular site or not. Also, you can control if caching is enabled for a particular group of users in your environment. For example, you can specify a rule to enable caching for WiFi users but not other users.

The Cache Rule contains various settings to control how content should be cached. We'll now describe various settings in a cache rule.

Under the To tab, you are able to specify if the rule applies to where the content is requested from (see Figure 14.4).

Figure 14.4 The To Tab of Cache Rule Properties

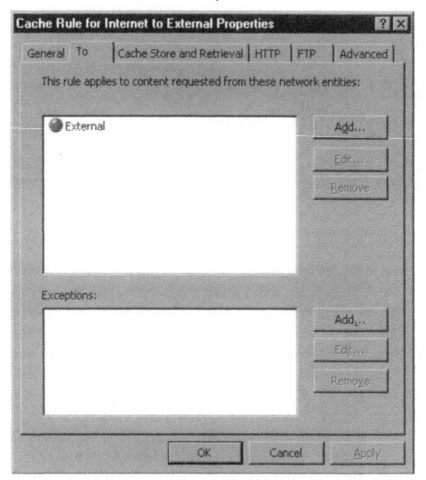

Under the Cache Store and Retrieval tab, you have two options:

- **Retrieve from Cache** This option allows you to specify whether content will be retrieved from the cache or from the server directly (see Figure 14.5).

- **Store in Cache** This option allows you to specify if the retrieved content should be cached (see Figure 14.5).

Figure 14.5 The Cache Store and Retrieval Tab of Cache Rule Properties

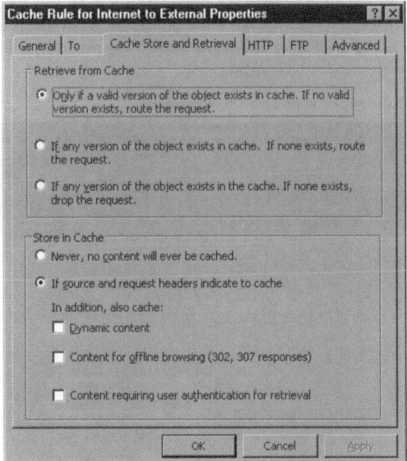

Under the HTTP tab, you have the following options:

- **Enable HTTP Caching** This option allows you to specify if the HTTP cache should be enabled (see Figure 14.6).

- **Set TTL of objects (% of the content age)** This option allows you to specify the amount of time an object is considered to be valid when in cache. Usually this is about 20 to 30% of the TTL of object (i.e., the expiry time of the object) (see Figure 14.6).

- **TTL Time Boundaries** This option allows you to specify the TTL value range. This also means specifying the expiry time of objects in cache (i.e., maximum amount of time an object would remain in cache) (see Figure 14.6).

- **Also apply these TTL boundaries to sources that specify expiration** If TTL is specified in the content source, Microsoft Internet Security and Acceleration Server 2006 will follow that setting. If this setting is enabled, the settings specified in **TTL Time Boundaries** would override the one given by the server (see Figure 14.6).

Figure 14.6 The HTTP Tab of Cache Rule Properties

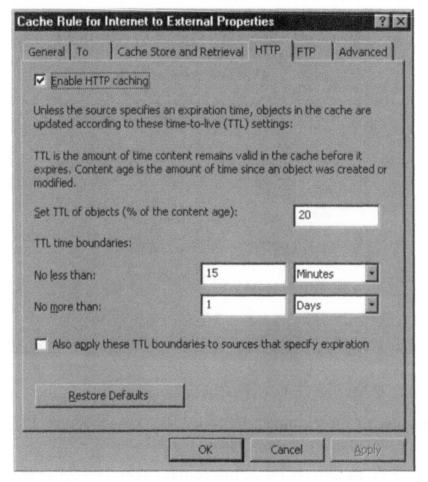

Under the FTP tab, you have the following options:

- **Enable FTP Caching** This option allows you to specify if FTP caching is enabled (see Figure 14.7).

- **Time-To-Live for FTP objects** This option allows you to specify when FTP objects are considered to be expired (see Figure 14.7).

Figure 14.7 The FTP Tab of Cache Rule Properties

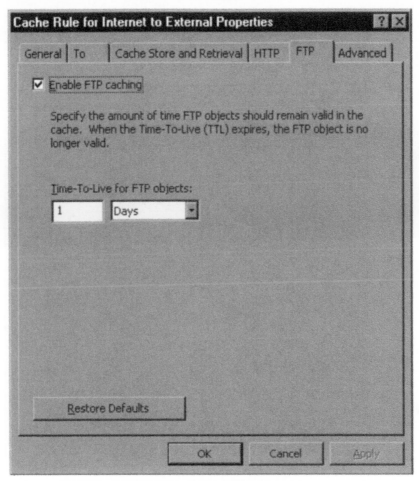

Under the Advanced tab, you have the following options:

- **Do not cache objects larger than** This option allows you to specify size restriction on object to be cached (see Figure 14.8).

- **Cache SSL responses** This option allows you to specify if content retrieved by SSL should be cached (see Figure 14.8).

- **Enable caching of content received through the Background Intelligent Transfer Service (BITS)** This option allows you to specify if content received via BITS should be cached. This option is always disabled for user-defined cache rules and enabled only in Microsoft Update cache rules (see Figure 14.8).

Figure 14.8 The Advanced Tab of Cache Rule Properties

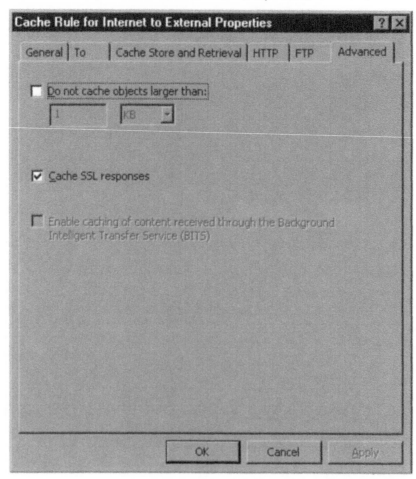

Exercise: Creating a Cache Rule

This exercise will create a cache rule to enable caching for content retrieved from all external hosts.

1. Open ISA Server Management Console.

2. Navigate to **Configuration | Cache**.

3. witch to the **Cache Rule** tab and click **Create Cache Rule** in the taskpad at right-hand side.

4. Specify the **Cache Rule for Internet to External** and click **Next** to continue (see Figure 14.9).

Figure 14.9 Specifying the Cache Rule Name in the Create Cache Rule Wizard

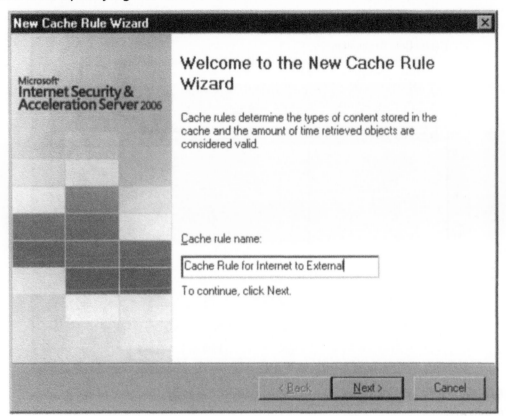

5. Select **Internal** as the destination of the cache rule. Click **Next** to continue (see Figure 14.10).

6. Specify how the rule controls content retrieval. Select the first option and click **Next** to continue (see Figure 14.11).

Figure 14.10 Specifying the Destination in the Create Cache Rule Wizard

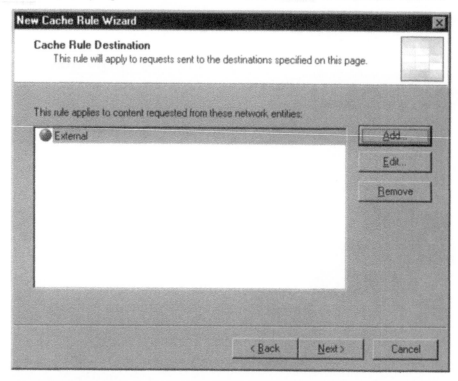

Figure 14.11 Specifying the Content Retrieval Setting in the Create Cache Rule Wizard

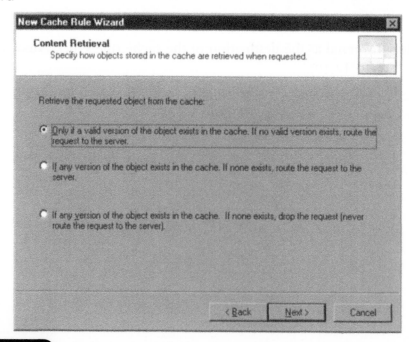

7. Specify if the content should be cached. Accept the default and click **Next** to continue (see Figure 14.12).

Figure 14.12 Specifying the Cache Content Setting in the Create Cache Rule Wizard

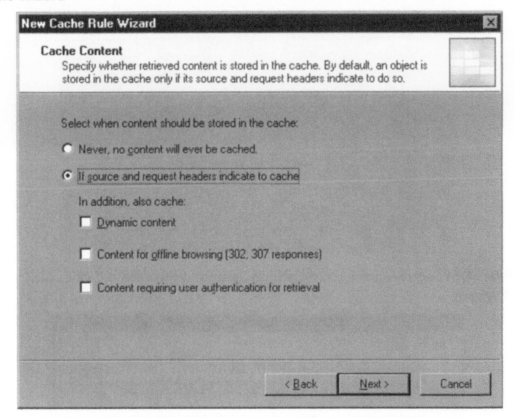

8. Specify **Cache SSL responses** but not a restriction on the size of the object to be cached. Click **Next** to continue (see Figure 14.13).

9. Specify if HTTP Caching should be enabled. Accept the default to enable HTTP caching and click **Next** to continue (see Figure 14.14).

Figure 14.13 Specifying the Advanced Cache Setting in the Create Cache Rule Wizard

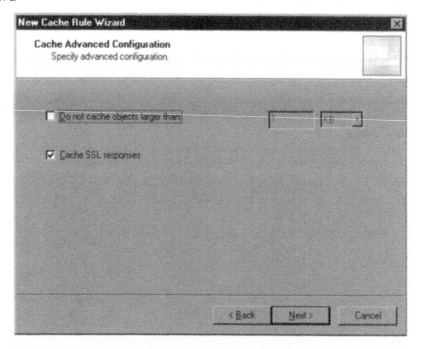

Figure 14.14 Specifying the HTTP Caching Setting in the Create Cache Rule Wizard

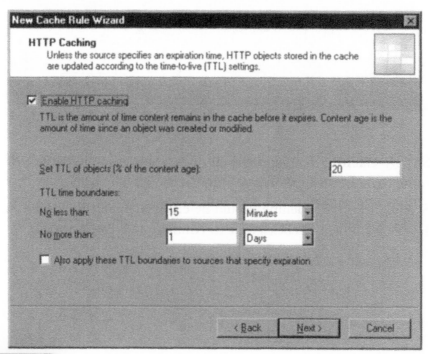

10. Specify if FTP caching should be enabled. Accept the default to enable FTP caching and click **Next** to continue (see Figure 14.15).

Figure 14.15 Specifying the FTP Caching Setting in the Create Cache Rule Wizard

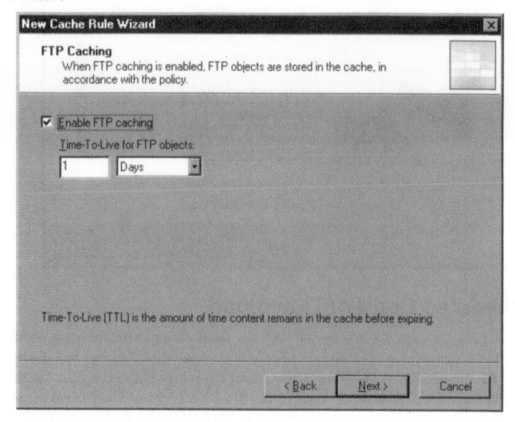

11. Review the configuration and click **Finish** to create the rule (see Figure 14.16).

Figure 14.16 Reviewing the Configuration in the Create Cache Rule Wizard

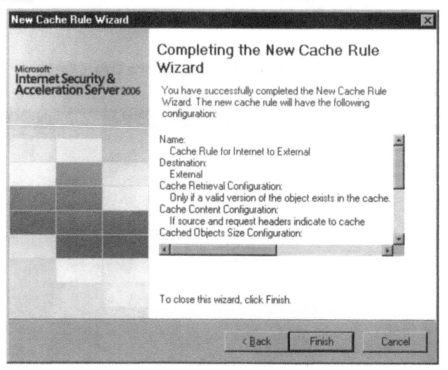

Scheduled Content Download

When I was younger, the dog would fetch the paper for us in the morning. Similarly, ISA Server can also be scheduled to download content from Web sites before anyone arrives at the office in the morning. The Content Download Rule configures Microsoft ISA 2006 to download Web site content at a defined schedule. Downloaded content would then be placed into the cache of the ISA Server. Usually, the Content Download Rule is used for preloading the cache with content before the first user request content from a frequently used site.

To use the content download rule, make sure the following is configured:

- Web Proxy Filter is configured to listen on the local network
- Scheduled download job configuration group in System Policy is enabled

Content download is performed at the schedule specified in the content download rule. Microsoft Internet Security and Acceleration Server 2006 maintains its work scheduler for content download. It does not rely on scheduler in Windows.

The following exercise lists the steps to create a content download rule.

Exercise: Create Content Download Rule

These steps show how to create a content download rule for Microsoft.com to avoid additional bandwidth consumed when a user tries to access Microsoft.com.

1. Open ISA Server Management Console.

2. Navigate to **Configuration | Cache**.

3. witch to the **Content Download Rule** tab and click **Create Content Download Rule** in the taskpad at the right-hand side.

4. Specify **Microsoft.com** as the name of the rule, and click **Next** to continue (see Figure 14.17).

Figure 14.17 Specifying the Rule Name in the Create Content Download Rule Wizard

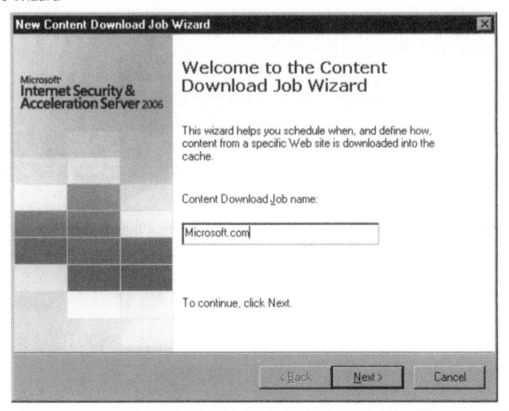

5. Specify the download frequency to download content, select **Daily**, and click **Next** to continue (see Figure 14.18).

Figure 14.18 Specifying the Download Frequency in the Create Content Download Rule Wizard

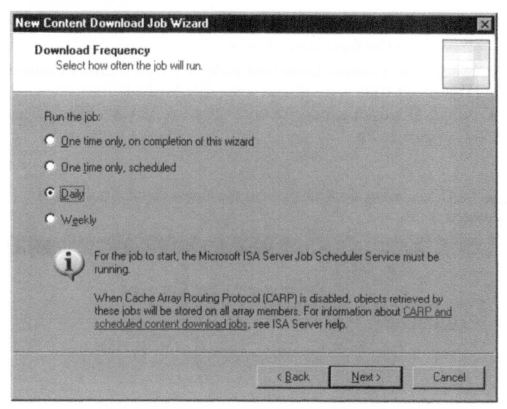

6. Specify the detail schedule of rule. Accept the default and click **Next** to continue (see Figure 14.19).

Figure 14.19 Specifying the Detailed Frequency in the Create Content Download Rule Wizard

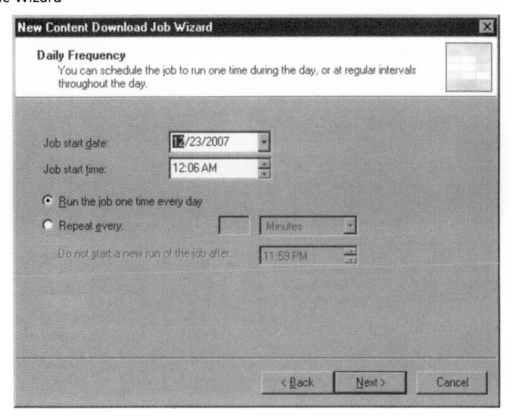

7. Specify the URL to download content. Specify **http://www.microsoft.com** and check **Do not follow link outside the specified URL domain name** to avoid content not in www.microsoft.com from getting downloaded. Also check **Maximum depth of links per page** to restrict the link depth of download to avoid the whole Web site, which can be huge. Another option is to restrict the maximum number of objects to be downloaded in this job by specifying value in **Limit number of objects retrieved to maximum of**. You can also limit the number of concurrent TCP connections by specifying a value in **Maximum number of concurrent TCP connection to create for this job**. For the purpose of this exercise, accept the default. Click **Next** to continue (see Figure 14.20).

Figure 14.20 Specifying the Content Download in the Create Content Download Rule Wizard

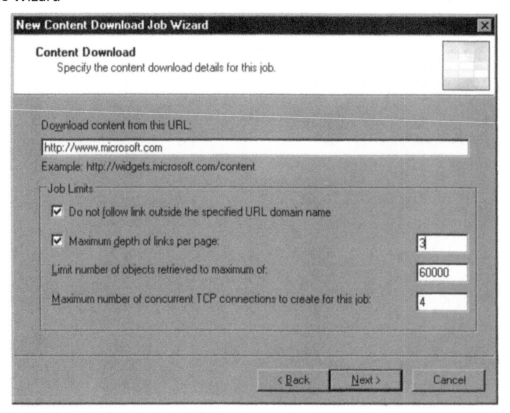

8. Specify which object to be cached and the time-to-live value of the downloaded object. Accept the default and click **Next** to continue (see Figure 14.21).

9. Review the configuration and click **Finish** to close the wizard (see Figure 14.22).

Figure 14.21 Specifying Content Caching in the Create Content Download Rule Wizard

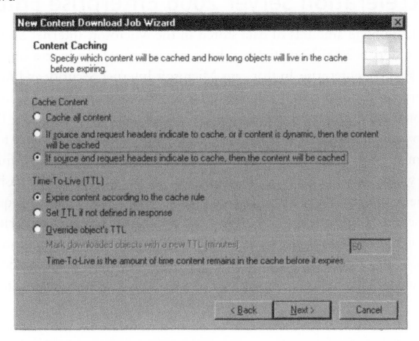

Figure 14.22 Reviewing the Configuration in the Create Content Download Rule Wizard

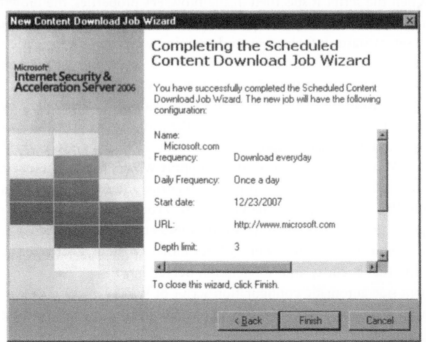

Caching in Microsoft Internet Security and Acceleration Server 2006 Enterprise Edition

There could be huge amounts of data stored in the Microsoft Internet Security and Acceleration Server 2006. Sometimes, it becomes impossible to have a single server to support a whole enterprise. In that case, Microsoft Internet Security and Acceleration 2006 Enterprise Edition comes into the picture. Microsoft Internet Security and Acceleration 2006 Enterprise Edition supports using Cache Array Routing Protocol (CARP) to group multiple servers into a single logical cache farm in order to balance the load among different servers. CARP works in a way that uses a hash function to determine which server in the farm should handle the client request. The hash function takes in the requested server name and gets the hashed value. Thus, all requests for the same server would always go to the same Microsoft Internet Security and Acceleration Server 2006 in the farm. CARP also ensures that no duplicated object is being cached in a different server within the array. Also, CARP automatically adjusts the way it works when there are changes to a cache array. This makes the administrator's life easier.

CARP could work at the server side or client side. Microsoft Internet Security and Acceleration Server 2006 provides an automatic configuration script for the client to determine which server in the CARP cache farm it goes to for the object it wants to retrieve. When the script is specified in the browser's properties, the browser would send information to the script and the script would use the information provided as well as the server status information to determine which member of the CARP cache farm the request should forward to. The URL of the automatic configuration script is http://yourisaserver:port/Array.dll?Get.Routing.Script.

Apart from using the script, the Web Proxy Automatic Discovery (WPAD) mechanism can be used instead of specifying the script in the client browser. Either you can create a DHCP scope option (option code 252) or a DNS entry WPAD in your domain. Your client browser needs to support WPAD before these settings can help to determine which Microsoft Internet Security and Acceleration Server 2006 should go to. You need to specify the URL http://yourisaserver:port/wpad.dat in the DHCP option or the server name in WPAD DNS entry. If automatic configuration is enabled in your browser, they will look for either of these records to locate the Microsoft Internet Security and Acceleration Server 2006.

If a client side automatic configuration script or WPAD is not used but CARP is enabled in the array, server side CARP would be used. The client PC can be configured to any member in the array. When a request arrives at the server, CARP then is used to determine which member of the array is responsible for handling the requested object. If the responsible server is not the same as the current server, the request will then be forwarded to the corresponding server.

Configuring Microsoft Internet Security and Acceleration 2006 to Cache BITS Content

Microsoft Internet Security and Acceleration Server 2006 includes support for Background Intelligent Transfer Service (BITS) content. A default rule is included in every deployment of Microsoft Internet Security and Acceleration Server 2006 to cache data transferred by BITS. BITS is the underlying protocol used by the Windows Update client to download security updates and hot fixes from the Windows Update site. With BITS caching enabled, it helps to conserve bandwidth that is used by Windows Update.

Microsoft Update Cache Rule

The Microsoft Update Cache Rule caches content transferred via BITS from the Windows Update site. This is the only rule that can be enabled for BITS caching. If you have other applications that leverage BITS as the underlying transport protocol, the only thing you can do is to modify the network set in the Microsoft Update Cache Rule to cover an additional site.

You can click the **Create Microsoft Update Cache Rule** in the taskpad of the ISA Server Management Console to create the Microsoft Update Cache Rule if it is missing in your list of cache rules.

Using the Differentiated Services on Microsoft Internet Security and Acceleration 2006 to Regulate Traffic

When networks get complex, there are always challenges in ensuring mission critical traffic gets enough bandwidth to avoid a delay in processing. Microsoft ISA 2006 Server includes support of Differentiated Services (DiffServ). Microsoft Internet Security and Acceleration Server 2006 can be configured to add a Differentiated

Services field (DS field) into the packet. This gives ISA Server the ability to work with other Quality of Service (QoS) devices to prioritize packets in the required manner. But why use DiffServ in Microsoft Internet Security and Acceleration Server 2006? Microsoft Internet Security and Acceleration Server 2006 supports application level inspection, which gives an administrator more leverage to control priorities. Microsoft ISA 2006 supports applying DS field values by means of IP, Network, URL, or Domains.

Configuring & Implementing...

DiffServe for QoS

One point to note about using DiffServe for QoS is that Microsoft Internet Security and Acceleration Server 2006 adds a DS field only to HTTP/HTTPS packets.

To enable DiffServe support:

1. Open ISA Server Management Console.

2. Navigate to **Configuration | General**. Click **Specify DiffServ Preference**.

3. Check the checkbox **Enable network traffic prioritization according to DiffServ bits** (see Figure 14.23).

4. In the Priorities tab, specify a list of priorities values to be used in Microsoft Internet Security and Acceleration Server 2006. This list usually is made to be consistent with the value specified in other QoS devices (see Figure 14.24).

Figure 14.23 The General Tab of DiffServe Properties

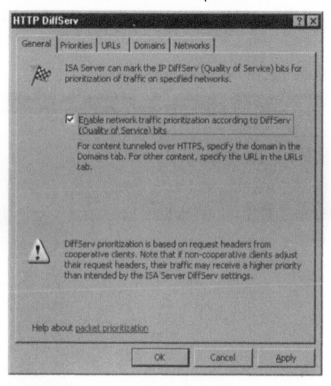

Figure 14.24 The Priority Tab of DiffServe Properties

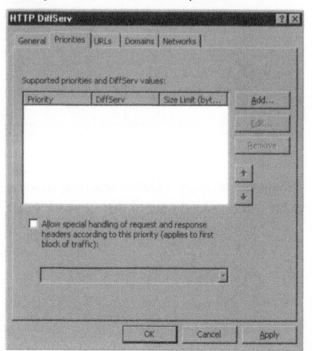

5. Specify when to apply the DiffServe bit according to the URL or domain listed in the URL and Domain tabs (see Figure 14.25 and 14.26).

Figure 14.25 The URL Tab of DiffServe Properties

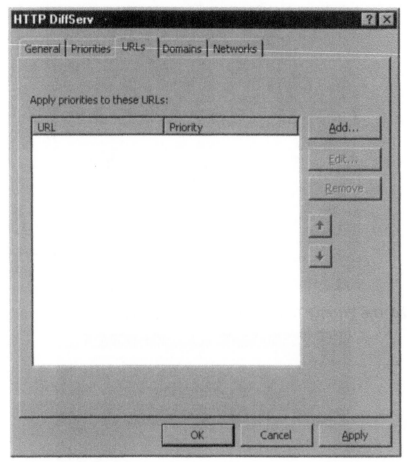

6. Specify which network to apply a DiffServe setting to. By selecting the network, the DiffServe bit will be added only to that network (see Figure 14.27).

Figure 14.26 The Domain Tab of DiffServe Properties

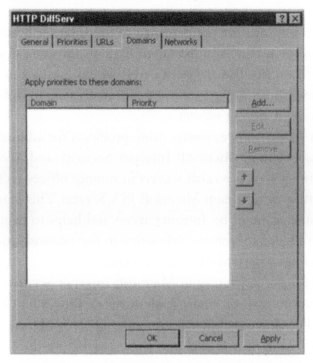

Figure 14.27 The Network Tab of DiffServe Properties

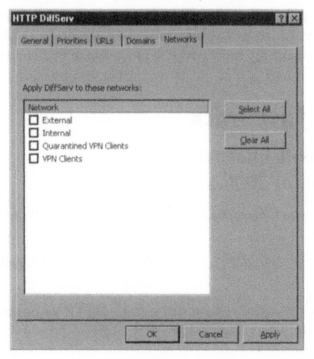

Summary

Caching is a way to improve the performance of the Internet by saving a copy of the requested object on the server. All subsequent requests for same object can be served by the version saved on the ISA Server. CARP would be used to group multiple servers into a cache farm in order to avoid duplicated cache in different servers, and to balance the workload among servers.

Remote site or branch offices always cause problems for administrators, especially with implementing caching. Microsoft Internet Security and Acceleration Server 2006 supports chaining servers so that servers in remote offices will request objects from the central office or upstream Microsoft ISA Servers. This configuration ensures better centralized management on Internet access and helps to bring the cache closer to the end user. This helps to improve efficiency in the network and creates an overall better browsing experience for the end user.

The Cache rule is the key entity in Microsoft Internet Security and Acceleration Server 2006 to control when or where to perform caching. The Content Download rule helps to schedule download of site content and loads objects into ISA's cache. This helps to ensure content is loaded into the cache before the first user requests the content.

DiffServ support also is included in ISA 2006, which helps to flag different packets with a DS field so that QoS devices know how to prioritize the packet.

Utilizing theses features of ISA appropriately will help to provide a more reliable and secure environment for end users. The proxy function is a critical part of ISA, which in turn is a critical part of the Microsoft Forefront Security Suite.

Solutions Fast Track

Using Microsoft Internet Security and Acceleration 2006 as a Proxy Server

☑ Create Content Download Rules to preload frequently used content into the cache.

☑ Override the default TTL value only if you want to refresh content at your schedule.

☑ Specify not to cache content that returns HTTP status code 200 if you do not want to cache error pages.

☑ Create a cache rule to specify exceptions on cache configuration, for example, disabling HTTP on specific site.

☑ Make sure to consider the impact of compression settings.

Configuring Microsoft Internet Security and Acceleration 2006 to Cache BITS Content

☑ Keep the Microsoft Update Cache Rule enabled to cache BITS for caching hot fix and security update files downloaded through the Windows Update site and Automatic Updates.

Using the Differentiated Services on Microsoft Internet Security and Acceleration 2006 to Regulate Traffic

☑ Define a list of DiffServe bits in Microsoft Internet Security and Acceleration Server 2006.

☑ Assign a DiffServe bit according to URL and Domain.

Frequently Asked Questions

Q: Does DiffServe support non–HTTP content?

A: No, DiffServe in Microsoft Internet Security and Acceleration Server 2006 supports only HTTP/HTTP content.

Q: Should we enable the Content Download rule to download a whole Web site?

A: Always avoid downloading entire Web sites from the destination server as that could be a huge amount of data downloaded.

Q: Should we allow caching of all objects in the Cache rule?

A: It is always is a good idea to apply restrictions on caching. For example, apply size restrictions on cached objects to avoid cache sizes that increase a lot on the ISA Server.

Q: How can you increase the Internet performance of a remote site?

A: Adding a dedicated Microsoft Internet Security and Acceleration 2006 Server and setting up proxy chaining. This helps to bring the cache closer to the end user, which gives better performance and reduces bandwidth consumption between sites.

Conducting Penetration Testing on an Enterprise Using the Microsoft Forefront Security Suite

Solutions in this chapter:

- Understanding Penetration Testing Methodologies

- Penetration Testing Techniques

- Identifying Test Types For Forefront System

☑ Summary

☑ Solutions Fast Track

☑ Frequently Asked Questions

Introduction

After you learn how to implement and configure Microsoft Forefront Security in an enterprise environment, it is important to test and ensure that the configurations are working correctly and are properly configured to handle the various threats and ensure that your Forefront infrastructure can stand up to malicious attacks. Extensive knowledge of the systems being tested is important for successful penetration testing. The goal is to effectively determine any weaknesses in Forefront and exploit those weaknesses in an attempt to gain access or disrupt normal activity. Gathering information on simulated attacks against Forefront will allow administrators to more securely control and configure Forefront in the enterprise

While penetration testing can give you a better look at your security landscape, you must also be aware that conducting penetration tests on any systems should be planned and executed after careful consideration. The possibility of slow network performance and the potential for unstable systems should be taken into consideration prior to the start of any penetration test. For this reason, penetration tests are often scheduled when usage of the services are minimal or in a controlled environment like a lab or test network. Penetration tests should never compromise a production Forefront implementation that will leave clients exposed to malicious threats.

Since penetration testing is simulating an attack on a system, it is important to get permission from the system owner prior to conducting any tests or attacks. This is done in the form of the rules of engagement document provided by the penetration tester and agreed upon and signed by the owner of the system. The rules of engagement form is typically specific about the types of tests and how they will be performed.

Understanding Penetrating Testing Methodologies

There are two commonly accepted methods of conducting penetration tests. Overt testing (Blue Team) is conducted when the tests are performed with the knowledge and consent of the Information Technology (IT) staff. Blue Team testing is most common because it is the least expensive and easier to coordinate. Covert testing (Red Team) is conducted without the knowledge of the IT staff but with the consent of management. Red Team testing is often done by an independent group in the organization or a third-party vendor to ensure that prior knowledge of the tests does not affect the outcome. Because of their covert nature, Red Team testing can take a lot longer to perform. For example, a Red Team tester may slow down the network discovery scans to ensure extra traffic is not generated, which may be noticed by intrusion detection systems (IDSes). Conducting a penetration test this way will better represent and test the controls in place when determining whether you're infrastructure is secure.

Penetration tests can also be conducted as authenticated or non-authenticated users. Testing as an authenticated user more closely simulates what can be done with someone who has regular, user-level access to the system. An authenticated user will have a mailbox on the system and access to an ISA server to login and view their mailbox and SharePoint portal sites. This will allow for uploading files without being further challenged if access is granted. An unauthenticated user represents someone who plugs into the network with no user ID or password, and tries to authenticate to any of the infrastructure systems. The unauthenticated user will not have a login ID or password and will not be able to access the systems without gaining them by exploiting vulnerabilities. Testing these two different methods of access will provide a better picture of how the Forefront suite for the enterprise is performing.

Phases of Penetration Testing

When conducting penetration testing in a corporate environment, it is important to follow industry best practices. There are two common penetration testing methodologies available. One is the Open Source Security Testing Methodology Manual (OSSTMM) and the other is from the National Institute of Standards and Technology (NIST). Familiarizing yourself with the testing methodologies detailed in these standards will ensure that you prepare and conduct penetration testing successfully.

The OSSTMM is more technically focused and details what needs to be accomplished before, during, and after a security test, and how to assess the results. The OSSTMM is well known for its emphasis on having defined Rules of Engagement both for the penetration tester and the client. The Rules of Engagement details how the test will be run and what the client can expect to receive in the final report. Information on international best practices, laws, regulations, and ethics are regularly added.

The NIST released Special Publication 800-42, Guideline on Network Security Testing, which provides NIST's methodology for security testing. Following these guidelines, especially when conducting penetration tests within government agencies or government contracts, will be more readily accepted. While the NIST document provides accepted methodologies, it references the OSSTMM because it is less comprehensive.

In the subsequent sections, we will use the OSSTMM and NIST guidelines as a reference to go over common phases of penetration testing. The planning, information gathering, attack, elevation of privilege, and reporting phases go through the lifecycle of a successful penetration test and will provide an understanding of how to approach each phase. Successful completion of each of these phases will increase and improve your penetration test results and allow for the most value added from the testing process.

Planning

Microsoft Forefront secures a wide range of applications, which can make for a challenging planning phase. It is imperative to properly plan for each of the penetration tests that will be done, defining the purpose of each test and the expected results. Detailed planning of the penetration tests will minimize the risk to the systems being tested and ensure that the data collected will assist in strengthening the security configuration of the Forefront implementation.

During the planning stages of penetration testing, you will need to determine whether you will be testing the ability of Forefront to detect and contain viruses, the ability of Forefront to filter phishing and malicious code from e-mail on the exchange server, the ability to detect malicious code uploaded to SharePoint servers, or if the ISA edge device is protecting and encrypting data properly. When testing on an enterprise that is using the complete Forefront suite, break down the test that will be conducted to various categories and determine which ones will be tested. Maintaining flexibility is important, as the results received from one test may provide additional information that can be used for further tests. What also needs to be determined is whether the penetration testing will be testing the Incident Response capabilities, responding to alerts generated by the test.

NOTE

It is important to remember that during the planning phase, no applications testing should occur. At this time, we are strictly determining what test will be run during the following phases (attack and elevation of privileges) and preparing the application and scripts that will be used to test the Forefront infrastructure.

Information Gathering

In this appendix, we are going to go over penetration testing techniques as well as the methodology used and how we can implement them on an enterprise using the Microsoft Forefront suite. The applications that are used for the information gathering process are constantly changing. Understanding the information gathering concepts will allow you to gather the necessary information using whatever applications are currently available.

One of the best ways to determine whether or not the infrastructure is secure is by conducting a penetration test as an external or unauthorized hacker with no prior knowledge of the infrastructure. Conducting a penetration test this way will better test the controls in place when determining whether you're infrastructure is secure. Conduct tests as authenticated or normal users to determine if there are any security concerns that may arise from an internal threat.

Information gathering is one of the most important parts of penetration testing. Without the ability to gather as much information as possible prior to launching any attacks on the system, you may be missing potential exploit vectors that could compromise the system. Information gathering can include determining the system name, IP address, operating system, open ports, installed application, and so forth. With the information gathered during this phase of the penetration tests, we will be able to conduct targeted attacks on weak controls.

During the information-gathering stage we're also looking to see if all the latest security patches have been applied. Earlier you read about the importance of deploying the WSUS server on the infrastructure and allowing for the download of approved patches to client and server systems. If a patch that needs to be on the system is detected missing, this is a perfect opportunity for an attacker to potentially gain unauthorized access to a system.

Note

There are many open source utilities available that do a wonderful job automating many test procedures, making it possible for people with little security experience to conduct penetration tests. This can be quite dangerous, as often there is no difference between the test and the actual exploit that is in use by attackers. If you do not have experience conducting penetration tests, you may want to research commercial applications that are designed to test corporate information systems. These exploits are designed to maintain the integrity of the assets, ensuring that your server or client is not permanently damaged as a result of a penetration test.

Attack

Launching attacks against vulnerabilities is what many people think of when discussing penetration testing. Using the information gathered, we are now going to execute attacks to determine whether or not we can gain unauthorized access to a system. We can also determine whether or not proper procedures are in place to deter attacks that are occurring.

If you're able to gain unauthorized access into the system, you may now be able to escalate privileges and harvest information from the system that will provide additional information on the infrastructure or the configuration of Microsoft Forefront security. The goal of any successful exploit is to escalate privileges to that of root or administrator. This level of access is needed to change configurations and ultimately do anything on the server or client that the attacker wants.

Once the penetration tester has administrative access to the system, the system has been fully compromised and is no longer secure. With administrative access, configuration settings can be viewed and changed as well as access to information stored on the system such as Personally Identifiable Information (PII). It is important to remember to stay within the scope of the penetration test. Document all steps taken to obtain access for analysis by system administrators and management.

Penetration Testing Techniques

There are many different tools that can be used to conduct penetration tests on a network. It is important to know the full impact of running any tool against a system, especially if it is a production system, as it may cause instability or a Denial-of-Service (DoS) condition. Many penetration testers have customized scripts or written applications to take advantage of specific vulnerabilities. The purpose of this Appendix is to provide you with the concepts needed to successfully conduct a penetration test. While the tools change, the concept behind the testing remains the same.

TIP

BackTrack (www.remote-exploit.org/backtrack.html) is a popular Linux live distribution focused on penetration testing. With no installation whatsoever, the analysis platform is started directly from the CD-ROM and is fully accessible within minutes.

A great resource for the latest security tools used for penetration testing can be found at www.sectools.org/.

Network Scanning

Network scanning is the process of using an application to scan the network and determine information about hosts. This can be done using a broad sweep to get information on all hosts on the network, or to a specific machine, determining all open ports and protocols. Determining what protocols are open on the host will help to identify the services running, and which ports to target for further testing. For example, Microsoft MOM uses Transmission Control Protocol (TCP)/User Datagram Protocol (UDP) on port 1270 to communicate with the agents. Scanning for machines with this port open will help identify which machines have a Forefront agent installed, and also determine if there are any machines that are not being protected by the enterprise implementation of Microsoft Forefront.

Most applications use standard ports for communication, which can be mapped to specific applications. This will allow for quicker identification of installed applications. Remember to scan for TCP and UDP ports, as some applications will not find them. A list of ports used by Microsoft server products can be found at http://go.microsoft.com/fwlink/?LinkId=86643. Associating a port with an application helps to get a better picture of the enterprise landscape.

Some network scanners like Nmap allow for the identification of open ports by grabbing banners and other identifying information from the system. When a network scanner queries a port, the system will typically respond as it would to any traffic connecting at the port. The response is cross-referenced with standard responses and the application can determine the version, application, and system that are running the open port. This process is often called *fingerprinting*.

These techniques will allow us to determine which machines are running exchange, Internet Information Server (IIS), and MOM services. With this information, we can target attacks against these systems to ensure that they are configured securely.

It is important to note that network scanning applications such as Nmap detect open and active ports, not vulnerabilities. Vulnerabilities may be identified as a result of a known open Trojan port, but that is dependent on the penetration tester during the analysis of the results. Our goal during the network scanning phase of the penetration test is to gather as much information as possible for analysis and planning subsequent phases of the penetration test.

Virus Detection

The propagation of viruses throughout an enterprise can quickly bring down the entire network. Malicious code is often the primary cause of problems and is one of the hardest problems to resolve because of the ever-changing threats that are released daily. These viruses are designed to exploit known vulnerabilities to gain unauthorized access to systems. Often, the most successful viruses exploit vulnerabilities that are new and that administrators have not had a chance to update the definitions to detect.

Viruses have multiple ways of entering an enterprise, and Forefront will need to be tested to see if it is correctly detecting and eradicating the threat. Each of the following points may be a potential pathway for a virus to enter a system, and therefore, needs to be tested.

- **Exchange Server** Forefront protects the Exchange server by using filters and multiple antivirus engines to detect malicious files.

- **SharePoint Server** Forefront protects SharePoint server by scanning files uploaded and accessed in real time.

- **Client** Forefront protects clients by conducting real time and scheduled scans.

- **ISA** Forefront protects ISA by securing communication with encryption and providing end users with secure portal access to resources.

One of the tests that will be conducted is whether Forefront is configured to release definition files quickly to detect new exploits. Depending on the environment, you can upload the code with the latest virus signatures and see if it is detected by Forefront. While this may be a good test to determine if virus patterns are getting updated, be sure to verify that the rules of engagement agreed upon by the administrators and penetration testers to ensure no production systems are actually compromised. A lab environment that duplicates the production environment is the ideal place to conduct more aggressive testing.

TIP

Eicar and Spycar files can be used to test the detection of spyware and malicious code. An eicar file will help to determine if Forefront security is configured properly and providing protection from real-time threats.

The eicar file was developed by the European Institute for Computer Antivirus Research. It was designed to test the response of a computer's antivirus program like Microsoft Forefront. The file consists of a string of characters that most modern virus scanners will detect as a test virus. The eicar file can be found at http://www.eicar.org/anti_virus_test_file.htm.

Spycar is a set of tools designed to imitate spyware behavior. Spycar was created by Intelgardians to test the ability of anti-spyware application to detect the activity of spyware in a benign way. The Spycar file can be found at http://www.spycar.org.

Identifying Test Types For Forefront Systems

As we have discovered from reading the previous chapters, Forefront Security has multiple components. There are many different tools available on the Internet to assist in penetration testing. The ability for anyone to download security tools has made it more important that security suites like Forefront be tested and configured for optimum performance and functionality. Depending on the information gathered during the information gathering stages and what the scope of the penetration tests are, you will want to ensure you have access to the proper applications or have written the scripts needed to conduct the test.

Microsoft Forefront essentially breaks down to a security agent and central management server. Forefront uses Structured Query Language (SQL) as a backend to store agent data, which brings to light that any dependent systems used by Forefront may lead to vulnerabilities in the implementation. If vulnerabilities in dependent systems can be detected and exploited, you may be able to compromise the Forefront Suite.

During the information gathering stage, it is important to research existing vulnerabilities and use that information during the penetration test. An enterprise that does not quickly patch their systems is a vulnerable enterprise, which may be a perfect opportunity for the penetration tester to gain unauthorized access to a client by utilizing Forefront vulnerabilities. There are many places online where you can find the latest vulnerability information such as the Common Vulnerability and Exposure list by Mitre, the National Vulnerability Database by NIST, and Security Focus. Attackers will use the sites to determine if exploits or public code is available to gain access to a system.

TIP

Researching past exploits and using them during the penetration test will display an enterprises patching methodology and may lead to the exploit of a known vulnerability. For example, in February 2007, Microsoft released Security Bulletin MS07-010, which detailed a vulnerability in the Microsoft malware protection engine that could allow remote code execution (http://www.microsoft.com/technet/security/Bulletin/MS07-010.mspx). This vulnerability existed because of the way that the malware engine parsed Portable Document Format (PDF) files. An attacker could exploit the vulnerability by constructing a specially crafted PDF file that could potentially allow remote code execution when the target computer system receives, and the Microsoft Malware Protection Engine scans the PDF file.

It is also important to understand how these attacks will be detected by the system. Reviewing logs generated by the Forefront security application and systems during the attacks will provide information as to the state of the system and if Forefront took the proper corrective action. While log review is not often considered a penetration test, it can provide a dynamic view of the security activities on the system. Be sure to check the IIS, Exchange, ISA, OWA, SharePoint, Event Log, and Forefront Security logs to determine what actions were recorded by the system. This will also provide insight into detecting actual attacks on the systems.

Client Security

The goal of client security is to protect against malicious code and attacks. During a penetration test, it is important to look for configuration issues and ways that the user can receive and execute malicious code so that unauthorized access to the client can be obtained. With security implementations and protections being so closely scrutinized, most attackers feel that the best success will be by attacking the end users. Often, awareness training and good practices are not followed, such as knowing when not to click on links in e-mails to external Web sites, which may contain malicious code from unknown sources. If the systems are patched fairly quickly and the proper security software has been installed, it is very difficult to gain unauthorized access to the system. Most attacks will attempt to trick users into unknowingly executing malicious code. This is where a defense in depth strategy combining Exchange, SharePoint, and ISA Forefront Security is important.

Forefront uses WSUS to deploy Forefront definitions. These definition updates are digitally signed to protect the client from false definition from attackers. On the server side, most implementations will harden the Forefront servers by minimizing the attack surface by stopping unnecessary services and opening required ports. As a penetration tester, scan the clients for open ports and determine if services are not configured for secure communication.

Exchange

As a penetration tester, it is important to understand the features of the systems that you will be testing. Forefront for Exchange Server is designed to protect e-mail from threats using multiples virus scanning engines to determine if a malicious code is passing through the exchange system. Forefront can be configured to use up to five virus scanning engines at once, which are constantly being updated to the latest definitions. This is done because vendors have different strengths and Forefront for Exchange leverages the strengths of the multiple antivirus vendors to detect and eliminate viruses.

Since the definitions are updated frequently, attempting to send a malicious code through the system will require bypassing Forefronts heuristics technologies. Heuristics scanning looks for attachments that show similarities to malicious code to detect and remove threats.

Phishing e-mails are often targeted towards the end users, to get them to click links and download malicious code through the Web. Depending on the scope of the penetration testing being conducted, social engineering attempts can be attempted by sending e-mails similar to those received by phishing schemes, to determine if subject or sender filtering is enabled. Forefront will also filter based on body content. If a user clicks on the link, he or she will be able to also test Forefront's perimeter defenses at the ISA server.

NOTE

Forefront for Exchange receives filter lists from Microsoft's Web site. If possible, take a look at these filter lists and determine if e-mails that you are sending through the Exchange system do not use the same words in the body or subject of the e-mail.

If an e-mail sender is on the allowed sender list, Forefront for Exchange will bypass all filtering that has been enabled for the list. During the information gathering phase, the penetration tester should attempt to determine companies or groups that would likely be members of the approved senders list. If you send an e-mail with a spoofed sender address from one of those companies, you may be able to get phishing e-mails past the spam filters.

SharePoint

One of the biggest issues with collaboration environments is that many people can upload files, allowing for viruses to proliferate rapidly throughout an organization. Microsoft Forefront for SharePoint is designed to scan files in real time as they are uploaded and accessed, to ensure that viruses are eradicated without affecting the performance and usability of the system.

SharePoint can detect inappropriate content even if the extension has been changed. This is important to note when testing SharePoint sites, as it will limit some of the attacks that can be accomplished.

SharePoint Forefront monitors for true file types, which will not allow a certain file type to be uploaded, even if the file has been renamed. While this is a little limiting, the user may be able to take advantage of additional security vulnerabilities.

ISA

ISA Server 2006 protects the perimeter of the network by the implementation of secure Virtual Private Network (VPN), firewall, portal, and encryption services. As organizations have more users working remotely, the importance of a secure edge device becomes much more important. This is the public-facing device for many companies and will most likely be hit the hardest from external attacks. Implementing the proper hardening techniques to reduce the system's attack area and the proper configuration is crucial for a secure infrastructure. Forefront Security for ISA Server provides protection in the following three areas: *remote access, branch office security*, and *Internet access security*. As a penetration tester, it will be important to test each area of security to determine if the controls that are in place are adequate and functioning properly.

Remote access provides access to the internal network for remote users through Secure Sockets Layer (SSL) implementations. During our penetration testing, determining if the server is configured correctly for the SSL protocol and that it is authenticating users correctly will be a focus. The access provided to the end user is done through a Web portal. Using penetration testing applications to determine if the Forefront implementation of the Web site is configured correctly, may produce information that can be used to do further testing.

Branch office connectivity allows for remote locations to be brought up quickly, connecting to the main network through the public Internet. With the use of BITS technology and automated deployment and configuration tools, the security of this type of connection must be tested thoroughly. The connectivity between the sites should be encrypted with Internet Protocol Security (IPSec), which will be verified as part of the penetration test.

Internet Access Protection provides security for ISA servers with a proxy-firewall architecture that inspects network traffic and has comprehensive alerting and monitoring capabilities. As a penetration tester, we will be attempting to bypass the controls put in place by Forefront and ISA server to gain unauthorized access to the network. With enhanced remediation techniques, it will not be easy to bypass these controls. Researching current vulnerabilities in the application and using the latest penetration testing tools will provide the testing framework to determine if Forefront for ISA server is working correctly.

ISA Server 2006 and Forefront Security have a lot of security layers that make it difficult for a penetration tester to exploit the system. For example, SSL traffic can be decrypted as it passes through the device, so the data can be examined for malicious code. Then the data is re-encrypted before being sent to the destination. This is something that should be kept in mind when trying to send data through the ISA server. If a client is compromised, ISA should be able to detect malicious code and eradicate. This information is available to the system administrator through the management console.

Forefront also monitors network traffic at the application level, and determines if the traffic is consistent with the protocol it is using. Sending data that is different than the protocol that was designed is a technique that is used to send exploits through an approved port to a target system and generate buffer overflows or execute arbitrary code. While Forefront is designed to detect and mitigate these techniques, and depending on whether you are conducting a Red Team or Blue Team penetration test, the tester may consider using this type of an attack to determine if Forefront and ISA are configured correctly.

Summary

Ultimately, the goal of the penetration tester will be to circumvent the security features of Microsoft Forefront Security based on information gathered about the system design and implementation. Using information-gathering techniques, the penetration tester will identify potential vulnerabilities and weaknesses in the Forefront security suite, and design tests to attack these weaknesses. Once it has been decided which tests will be conducted, the tester will attempt to gain access to the system. This can be done by exploiting vulnerabilities, targeting configuration inconsistencies, or discovering methods to take advantage of insecure design decisions.

Penetration testing provides valuable information to the system administrators and security analysts that will allow them to determine ways to optimize the security of their systems. It is a time-intensive process that requires a high level of expertise to ensure that the risk to existing systems is minimized by targeting attacks to specific vulnerabilities. During testing, systems may become slow and unresponsive due to network scanning and vulnerability assessment efforts. There is also the possibility that an exploit or scan may cause damage to the system, rendering it inoperable. The goals of many tests are to cause a DoS situation or terminate running processes to generate an insecure state. Working with the system administrator and ensuring proper precautions such as backups of systems being tested are conducted prior to any testing, will ensure that the risk is minimized.

Solutions Fast Track

Understanding Penetration Testing Methodologies

☑ The Planning phase is used to prepare what tests will be run against the target systems and establish testing parameters for the overall penetration test being conducted against the Forefront infrastructure.

☑ The Information Gathering phase is used to determine the detailed information about the Forefront infrastructure and determine what specific tests will be run. At this stage, vulnerabilities and configuration issues will attempt to be determined for exploitation.

☑ The Attack phase is when the actual exploitation of vulnerabilities is attempted and the tester tries to gain unauthorized access to the Forefront infrastructure. The tester will also attempt to use vulnerabilities and configuration issues in Forefront to gain unauthorized access to Client, Exchange, SharePoint, and ISA resources.

☑ The Elevation of Privilege phase is conducted if the Attack phase is successful in exploiting a Forefront vulnerability to gain unauthorized access to a system. Ultimately, the goal of the penetration test is to gain system-level or administrative access.

☑ The Reporting phase is conducted at the end of the penetration test to provide results to the system administrators and management. These reports will likely present data differently, but should be focused on providing actionable information that can be taken to improve the security landscape of the Forefront infrastructure.

Penetration Testing Techniques

☑ Network scanning is done in conjunction with vulnerability scanning to determine what systems have Forefront installed, and to identify the different components. This is done by scanning for open and active ports on the target systems and mapping them to known Forefront default port configurations.

☑ Virus detection engines need to be tested, as they are an integral part of the Forefront Security Suite. Determining that each Forefront product (Forefront for Exchange, SharePoint, ISA, and Client Security) properly handles virus files, is an important test of functionality and vulnerability.

☑ Phishing is becoming a more common occurrence, as technical controls tighten on products like MS Forefront Client Security. Attackers have moved from technology to users as their access point to secure systems. Ensuring that Forefront handles phishing e-mails by filtering correctly will minimize the threat to the network.

☑ Encryption is an important part of the ISA model. Verifying that traffic being sent is encrypted and secure will allow for a more secure environment. Utilizing test techniques to analyze network traffic is an important verification of this configuration.

Identifying Test Types for Forefront systems

☑ Forefront for Client Security tests should be conducted against machines to determine if the installation has opened any ports that can be exploited by DoS or buffer overrun conditions. Assessing the security of the client/server communication between the Forefront components and how the scan engines interact with malicious files, should be targeted.

☑ Forefront for Exchange testing should include assessing the content filter and analyzing if a bypass can be exploited. Tests should be included to determine if Forefront for Exchange is correctly identifying and eradicating spam, phishing, and virus activity.

☑ Forefront for SharePoint virus testing is important due to the collaborative nature of the application. The fast distribution of viruses in a shared workspace can cause serious problems for any enterprise and should be tested. The testing of how Forefront handles cross-site scripting vulnerabilities may also be included.

☑ Forefront for ISA testing needs to incorporate testing for Internet access protection and secure remote access. These tests should focus on whether the attack surface of ISA has been reduced significantly by implementing sufficient hardening and that firewall and VPN functionality is operating properly.

Frequently Asked Questions

Q: Why should I do a penetration test?

A: Penetration testing can give you a better look at your security landscape. The results from the test provide detailed information that the enterprise can use when making security decisions. Having a well-documented penetration testing plan that is routinely performed also provides metrics detailing improvements or the need for improvements with infrastructure security.

Q: What is the difference between automated/scripted penetration testing and manual penetration testing?

A: Over the past few years, more and more applications are available for downloading on the Internet. While this allows for administrators to perform penetration tests on their systems, they may not know the full impact of the tools that is being run. Professional penetration testers often customize applications and write detailed scripts to attack vulnerabilities. For an automated attack, an automated penetration application will be fine. However, to utilize the experience and expertise of a dedicated penetration tester, manual penetration testing may be preferred.

Q: Should I run a penetration test on a specific Forefront component when I know that it will fail?

A: Yes. Remember that the goal of penetration testing is not exclusively to gain unauthorized access to the server, but to test the controls in place to ensure they are working properly. Even if a penetration test fails, it may provide valuable information about the reaction of the system that will aid the administrators for the server. The test may also provide additional information that can be used in subsequent tests.

Q: Should I complete an external or internal penetration test of the Forefront Security Suite?

A: Successful penetration testing will provide an overview of the entire implementation of security. If the environment contains an ISA server that is acting as an edge device, conducting an external test will provide necessary information toward the security of the device. If the server has exchange or client components, conduct tests that will provide a sense of the configuration. If you have to choose, decide on the test that most likely provides information that may be more applicable to your environment.

Q: Should I use Social Engineering techniques during the penetration testing process?

A: Many of the attacks that an Exchange server or ISA server will receive will be a result of exploits or attempts that can accurately be simulated with penetration tests. Many companies are uneasy about conducting social engineering attacks, but they are one of the best indicators of vulnerabilities. Security awareness training can provide users with training that can deter clicking on links in spam and phishing attempts.

Index

Syngress: *The Definition of a Serious Security Library*

Syn·gress (sin–gres): *noun, sing.* Freedom from risk or danger; safety. See *security*.

Syngress: *The Definition of a Serious Security Library*

Syn·gress (sin-gres): *noun, sing.* Freedom from risk or danger; safety. See *security*.

Cyber Spying: Tracking Your Family's (Sometimes) Secret Online Lives

Dr. Eric Cole, Michael Nordfelt,
Sandra Ring, and Ted Fair

Have you ever wondered about that friend your spouse e-mails, or who they spend hours chatting online with? Are you curious about what your children are doing online, whom they meet, and what they talk about? Do you worry about them finding drugs and other illegal items online, and wonder what they look at? This book shows you how to monitor and analyze your family's online behavior.

ISBN: 1-93183-641-8

Price: $39.95 US $57.95 CAN

Stealing the Network: How to Own an Identity

Timothy Mullen, Ryan Russell, Riley (Caezar) Eller,
Jeff Moss, Jay Beale, Johnny Long, Chris Hurley, Tom Parker, Brian Hatch

The first two books in this series "Stealing the Network: How to Own the Box" and "Stealing the Network: How to Own a Continent" have become classics in the Hacker and Infosec communities because of their chillingly realistic depictions of criminal hacking techniques. In this third installment, the all-star cast of authors tackle one of the fastest-growing crimes in the world: Identity Theft. Now, the criminal hackers readers have grown to both love and hate try to cover their tracks and vanish into thin air...

ISBN: 1-59749-006-7

Price: $39.95 US $55.95 CAN

Software Piracy Exposed

Paul Craig, Ron Honick

For every $2 worth of software purchased legally, $1 worth of software is pirated illegally. For the first time ever, the dark underground of how software is stolen and traded over the Internet is revealed. The technical detail provided will open the eyes of software users and manufacturers worldwide! This book is a tell-it-like-it-is exposé of how tens of billions of dollars worth of software is stolen every year.

ISBN: 1-93226-698-4

Price: $39.95 U.S. $55.95 CAN

Syngress: *The Definition of a Serious Security Library*

Syn·gress (sin-gres): *noun, sing.* Freedom from risk or danger; safety. See *security*.

Syngress: *The Definition of a Serious Security Library*

Syn·gress (sin–gres): *noun, sing.* Freedom from risk or danger; safety. See *security*.

Syngress: *The Definition of a Serious Security Library*

Syn·gress (sin-gres): *noun, sing.* Freedom from risk or danger; safety. See *security*.

Winternals Defragmentation, Recovery, and Administration Field Guide

Dave Kleiman, Laura E. Hunter, Tony Bradley, Brian Barber, Nancy Altholz, Lawrence Abrams, Mahesh Satyanarayana, Darren Windham, Craig Schiller

As a system administrator for a Microsoft network, you know doubt spend too much of your life backing up data and restoring data, hunting down and removing malware and spyware, defragmenting disks, and improving the overall performance and reliability of your network. The Winternals® Defragmentation, Recovery, and Administration Field Guide and companion Web site provide you with all the information necessary to take full advantage of Winternals comprehensive and reliable tools suite for system administrators.

ISBN: 1-59749-079-2

Price: $49.95 US $64.95 CAN

Video Conferencing over IP: Configure, Secure, and Troubleshoot

Michael Gough

Until recently, the reality of videoconferencing didn't live up to the marketing hype. That's all changed. The network infrastructure and broadband capacity are now in place to deliver clear, real-time video and voice feeds between multiple points of contacts, with market leaders such as Cisco and Microsoft continuing to invest heavily in development. In addition, newcomers Skype and Google are poised to launch services and products targeting this market. *Video Conferencing over IP* is the perfect guide to getting up and running with video teleconferencing for small to medium-sized enterprises.

ISBN: 1-59749-063-6

Price: $49.95 U.S. $64.95 CAN

Syngress: *The Definition of a Serious Security Library*

Syn·gress (sin-gres): *noun, sing.* Freedom from risk or danger; safety. See *security*.

How to Cheat at Designing Security for a Windows Server 2003 Network

Neil Ruston, Chris Peiris

While considering the security needs of your organiztion, you need to balance the human and the technical in order to create the best security design for your organization. Securing a Windows Server 2003 enterprise network is hardly a small undertaking, but it becomes quite manageable if you approach it in an organized and systematic way. This includes configuring software, services, and protocols to meet an organization's security needs.

ISBN: 1-59749-243-4

Price: $39.95 US $55.95 CAN

How to Cheat at Designing a Windows Server 2003 Active Directory Infrastructure

Melissa Craft, Michael Cross, Hal Kurz, Brian Barber

The book will start off by teaching readers to create the conceptual design of their Active Directory infrastructure by gathering and analyzing business and technical requirements. Next, readers will create the logical design for an Active Directory infrastructure. Here the book starts to drill deeper and focus on aspects such as group policy design. Finally, readers will learn to create the physical design for an active directory and network Infrastructure including DNS server placement; DC and GC placements and Flexible Single Master Operations (FSMO) role placement.

ISBN: 1-59749-058-X

Price: $39.95 US $55.95 CAN

How to Cheat at Configuring ISA Server 2004

Dr. Thomas W. Shinder, Debra Littlejohn Shinder

If deploying and managing ISA Server 2004 is just one of a hundred responsibilities you have as a System Administrator, "How to Cheat at Configuring ISA Server 2004" is the perfect book for you. Written by Microsoft MVP Dr. Tom Shinder, this is a concise, accurate, enterprise tested method for the successful deployment of ISA Server.

ISBN: 1-59749-057-1

Price: $34.95 U.S. $55.95 CAN

SYNGRESS®

Printed and bound by CPI Group (UK) Ltd, Croydon, CR0 4YY

03/10/2024

01040340-0015